WAYNE ASPINALL
AND THE SHAPING OF THE AMERICAN WEST

WAYNE ASPINALL

AND THE SHAPING OF THE AMERICAN WEST

STEVEN C. SCHULTE

UNIVERSITY PRESS OF COLORADO

© 2002 by the University Press of Colorado

Published by the University Press of Colorado
5589 Arapahoe Avenue, Suite 206C
Boulder, Colorado 80303

All rights reserved
First paperback edition 2017
Printed in the United States of America

The University Press of Colorado is a cooperative publishing enterprise supported, in part, by Adams State University, Colorado State University, Fort Lewis College, Metropolitan State University of Denver, Regis University, University of Colorado, University of Northern Colorado, Utah State University, and Western State Colorado University

The paper used in this publication meets the minimum requirements of the American National Standard for Information Sciences—Permanence of Paper for Printed Library Materials. ANSI Z39.48-1984

Library of Congress Cataloging-in-Publication Data

Schulte, Steven C., 1955–
  Wayne Aspinall and the shaping of the American West / Steven C. Schulte.
    p. cm.
  Includes bibliographical references and index.
  ISBN 0-87081-665-9 (hardcover : alk. paper) — ISBN 978-1-60732-628-1 (pbk. : alk. paper)
  1. Aspinall, Wayne N. 2. Legislators—United States—Biography. 3. United States. Congress. House—Biography. 4. West (U.S.)—Environmental conditions. 5. Environmental policy— West (U.S.)—History—20th century. 6. Conservation of natural resources—Government pol- icy—West (U.S.)—History—20th century. 7. Land use—Government policy—West (U.S.)— History—20th century. 8. Water rights—West (U.S.)—History—20th century. I. Title.
  E748.A249 S38 2002
  328.73'092—dc21

                                                            2002001555

Cover design by Laura Furney
Text design by Daniel Pratt

To my family—Tracy, Anders, Inge, and Kirstin.
Thanks for your love and encouragement.

CONTENTS

PREFACE

To newcomers, western Colorado's Grand Valley looks strange—fertile stretches of verdant land surrounded by the tans and browns of the western desert—a shocking color contrast produced by the magic of irrigation. Exploring the chain of towns that have sprung up along the banks of the Colorado River, the new arrivals begin to see and hear the name "Aspinall." Local citizens refer to "Aspinall's town" or "Aspinall's river." Streets are named for Wayne Aspinall; so is the federal court building, and a series of dams on the Gunnison River. An Aspinall Foundation supports the academic programs at the local state college. And this list of honors is by no means complete.

Colorado and the American West's lively contemporary civilization owe a debt of gratitude to Wayne N. Aspinall and other visionary politicians who came to power in the early to mid-twentieth century. These individuals addressed the region's critical lack of water. Aspinall and other leaders devoted their careers to obtaining and protecting an adequate supply of this precious resource. As writer John Gunther said in the book *Inside U.S.A.*, "Water is blood in Colorado"; "touch water in the West and you touch everything."

Congressman Wayne Norviel Aspinall (D-CO) served in the U.S. Congress from 1949 to 1973 after a long and distinguished career in state politics. As chair of the House Interior and Insular Affairs Committee from 1959 to 1973, Aspinall left his imprint on almost every significant piece of legislation affecting the American West during that era. Major reclamation projects, wilderness legislation, mining laws, and bills pertaining to national parks and monuments all came under his scrutiny. Raised in the immediate post-frontier West, he subscribed to a value system emphasizing economic growth based upon utilizing the region's natural resources. From his viewpoint, nature and its bounty were placed by the Creator to be used wisely by humanity. In the 1960s, the United States underwent what many scholars have called an environmental or ecological revolution. Wayne Aspinall, however, continued to champion the interests of economic development at the expense of environmental protection. Because of this, he suffered an avalanche of criticism from national journalists, conservation and environmental organizations, other members of Congress, and ultimately the citizens of his own state. By the early 1970s, Aspinall seemed like a relic from an earlier era in western American history. After a hostile redistricting that added a new, young, and urban population element to his congressional territory, Aspinall was defeated in the 1972 primary election. But the concerns of Aspinall's long congressional career anticipated the Sagebrush Rebellion, a western political backlash in which he proudly took a leadership role during retirement.

Aspinall's life story is vital to an understanding of the shifting currents that have conditioned the development of the modern West. Although his influence has been largely ignored outside Colorado, those writers who have considered him either unabashedly admire or roundly condemn him. Aspinall, however, was neither a saint nor a sinner. The admirable product of an earlier time, he championed policies of economic development that he judged to be in his region's best interests. Rising from humble origins to dizzying heights of power and influence, he failed to understand the groundswell of change affecting all sectors of U.S. society during the 1960s and 1970s. Like many other U.S. leaders of this era, he lost touch with crucial elements in his constituency during this confusing time. Comprehending Wayne Aspinall's rise and fall brings us closer to understanding the forces that have shaped the modern American West.

ACKNOWLEDGMENTS

No book writes itself. In this more than six-year process, I have accumulated a large ledger of debts. My family has been supportive from the start. My wife, Tracy, and three children, Anders, Inge, and Kirstin, have all wondered what I was doing in my office all that time. I've tried to interest them in the magic of Wayne Aspinall; I may not have succeeded, but I'm all the better for trying. Thanks for your love and the many pleasant diversions that you—and family cats Zachary, Clio, Annie, and Olaf—have offered along the way. My father, Robert P. Schulte, has always offered unqualified love and support to his historian son.

Financial backing arrived at crucial stages from the Mesa State College Foundation and the travel funds of Mesa State College's Department of Social and Behavioral Sciences. Additional support was forthcoming from the offices of the vice president for academic affairs and the dean of humanities and social sciences—thank you, Samuel Gingerich and Janine Rider. A sabbatical in the fall of 2000 enabled me to finish the manuscript. To longtime departmental secretary Theresia Holman, who helped me with my word-processing problems, all I can say is thanks for your assistance and good humor. Gail Thompson's word-processing assistance was helpful in the final stages. I have also benefited from the collective expertise of the wonderful interdisciplinary Department of Social and Behavioral Sciences at Mesa State College and from the technical expertise of some of its members, including Chris Buys, Michael Gizzi, and Gene Starbuck. Other deserving thank-yous go out to Shane Henry and Tim Gasperini for providing me with useful research materials. Gordon and Stephanie Martin offered both lodging and great hospitality during a research trip to the JFK Presidential Library.

Finally, I want to thank the many wonderful archivists and librarians who take joy in helping others find crucial source materials. They seldom receive the recognition they deserve. At a small state college, interlibrary loans are vital, and no one facilitates them better than Jane Heitman at Mesa State College. Kathy Tower, the Mesa State College archivist (and my neighbor), pointed me toward some key collections in the college's archival holdings. Judy Prosser Armstrong of the Museum of Western Colorado not only helped me discover important source material but also offered me encouragement. Archivist Steve Fisher of the University of Denver went out of his way to make me comfortable in the course of many research trips to Wayne Aspinall's alma mater. David Hays was always helpful and willing to assist me at the University of Colorado Archives in Boulder. Thanks also to the archival staffs of the John F. Kennedy Presidential Library (Boston), Lyndon B. Johnson Presidential Library (Austin, Texas), Arizona State University Library (Tempe), and the University of Arizona (Tucson). I'd like to offer a special thank-you to all the people who sat down and allowed me to interview them about Wayne Aspinall, especially Mary White and Vivian Passer. Final thanks go out to the pleasant and thorough staff at the University Press of Colorado. Editor Darrin Pratt and copy editor Deborah Korte were especially helpful. You have all contributed to this book, though you are in no way responsible for the interpretations and errors. I hope you find the work to be honest, fair, and interesting.

LIST OF ABBREVIATIONS IN ENDNOTES

CSHS	Colorado State Historical Society, Denver, CO
DPL	Denver Public Library, Denver, CO
fd	folder
JFKPL	John F. Kennedy Presidential Library, Boston, MA
LBJPL	Lyndon B. Johnson Presidential Library, Austin, TX
LC	Library of Congress, Washington, DC
MSC	Archives and Special Collections, Mesa State College, Grand Junction, CO
MWC	Research Center and Special Library, Museum of Western Colorado, Grand Junction, CO
NA	National Archives, Washington, DC
SCASUL	Special Collections, Arizona State University Library, Tempe, AZ
SCUAL	Special Collections, University of Arizona Library, Tucson, AZ
TWS	(Papers of) The Wilderness Society, Denver Public Library, Denver, CO
UCAUCB	University of Colorado Archives, University of Colorado at Boulder, Boulder, CO
UDA	University of Denver Archives, Denver, CO

UPPER COLORADO RIVER BASIN

UPPER COLORADO RIVER
COMMISSION

SCALE OF MILES

CHAPTER ONE

THE EDUCATION OF A WESTERN POLITICIAN

VIEW FROM THE COLORADO RIVER

In his final years, Wayne Aspinall often sat in his home on Aspinall Drive in Palisade, Colorado, gazing down upon the Colorado River. The river meant life to the aging former congressman, and to many others in the arid West. His family had arrived in Colorado's Western Slope more than seventy years earlier, when young Wayne was eight years old. Some of his earliest memories concerned diverting precious river water into his family's peach orchard. By the late 1970s, near the end of his life, the Colorado fed Aspinall's memories while still giving sustenance to the parched American West.

Though the waters still flowed, the Colorado and its major tributaries had changed almost beyond recognition in Aspinall's lifetime, altered to the degree that some modern observers hesitate to call it a river at all. These days, it more closely resembles a machine or a sophisticated plumbing system.[1] Diversions, siphons, ditches, dams, and reservoirs have remade the river to do the work of man. The transformation of the Colorado from Wayne Aspinall's free-flowing boyhood waterway into the most litigated and overworked river in North America is intertwined with his life and political career. No twentieth-century politician from the American West achieved more success in hoarding and manipulating water for human benefit. Historian Donald Worster termed Aspinall the modern West's "consummate water politician." Aspinall liked to boast that he was responsible for nearly $1 billion in reclamation projects for his congressional district alone. According to one commentator, "Aspinall never met a dam he didn't like."[2]

During his retirement, Aspinall wrote an autobiography for his family. In it, he remembered, with special fondness, his early work with water: "Getting water in the right place on the land was always a challenge . . . whether as a boy with a hoe or an adult with a shovel. To learn the value of controlled water to the agricultural and horticultural products we raised was always a most satisfying labor.[3] Later in his autobiography, Aspinall refers to himself as a "Teddy Roosevelt Conservationist" who believed that natural resources were "to be used wisely" and "for the good of the people of today with a view to the fact that others will follow who may or may not need such natural resource values in the days ahead." A "non-harvesting philosophy" such as those embraced by many extreme environmentalists was "not part of my thinking," Aspinall asserted.[4]

It is hardly surprising that Wayne N. Aspinall, who grew up on one of the American West's last remaining frontiers, the irrigation frontier, maintained a distinctive early American attitude toward the use of water, timber, minerals, and grazing resources. Above all, it was water—its capture, use, and politics—that inspired Aspinall and, along with the shaping of the Wilderness Act of 1964, led to his most significant political achievements.

The reasons for Aspinall's political infatuation with water are not difficult to discern. More than 50 percent of the seven-state Colorado River Basin's water originates within Colorado; water is therefore the state's "most valuable natural resource." Aspinall himself said, "In this semi-arid and arid state water is to be wisely husbanded with all of the ingenuity and dedication that is possessed by man. On this resource as on no other resource, the life and progress of the people of Colorado succeed or fail. It is truly our life's blood—the most precious of all of nature's blessings."[5]

At the height of the controversy over the Colorado River Storage Project in 1955, Aspinall wrote to a constituent that reclamation "makes the desert bloom." Stand next to an irrigation canal, he challenged. On the uphill side, "you have virtually a barren desert with nothing but scrub growth and little green." On the downhill side, "you have green and growing crops, houses, cities, and life." Aspinall concluded, "This is the choice in the West, irrigation or desolation, abundance or scarcity."[6]

After ascending to the chairship of the House Interior and Insular Affairs Committee in 1959, Aspinall made himself into the federal reclamation program's staunchest defender. "Reclamation pays," Aspinall liked to say. It was a sound investment for the nation's tax dollars because reclamation projects almost pay for themselves while providing clean hydroelectric power, irrigation water, and recreational facilities for an active nation. To those critics who charged that reclamation lands merely added to the agricultural surplus, Aspinall pointed out that the many specialized fruits and vegetables grown in these fields were in "high demand." Finally, he justified hefty reclamation budgets as a Cold War necessity. The nation's ability to produce ample foodstuffs was but one way to meet the Soviet challenge. Aspinall deftly linked the American West's thirst for water with the region's ability to add to the nation's Cold War strength.[7] This argument would be his coup de grâce during the fight to authorize the Collbran Project in the early 1950s.

Later, when federal reclamation projects became prime targets for congressional budget cutters and environmentalists, Aspinall willingly answered the critics. After a 1963 *Life* article equated reclamation with pork-barrel spending, Aspinall responded with a hearty rejoinder of "Hogwash!," then proceeded to attack the literary and scholarly credentials of the article's five authors. None of the writers, Aspinall asserted, had ever published anything on a subject as technical as reclamation. By the 1970s, when reclamation projects were being routinely slowed down or halted by conservation organizations, Aspinall railed against the environmental movements as "over-indulged zealots" to whom "balance means nothing."[8] By the early 1970s, he had become the focal point of attacks by a strengthening national environmental movement. The chairman's opposition to early drafts of Wilderness legislation, his pro-development perspective toward public-land policy, and his entrenched position in Congress made him a tempting target not only for the environmental movement, but for members of Congress who favored political and social reforms.

This, then, is Wayne Aspinall's story.

COMING OF AGE ON COLORADO'S WESTERN SLOPE

Wayne Norviel Aspinall was born on April 3, 1896, on a farm between Bellefountain and Maryville, Ohio. The nearest town of appreciable size was Columbus, the state capital, about forty-five miles southeast. Aspinall's first home was a tenant farm, which father Mack Aspinall leased from his father-in-law. Young Wayne's favorite grandparent was his mother's father, a local politician who helped inspire his eldest grandson's interest in public service.

When Wayne was four, the family moved a mile and a half to another farm, owned by Mack's parents. On its 160 acres, the Aspinalls raised corn, wheat, and hay and maintained a small orchard with peaches, apples, and pears. When he was old enough, Wayne walked three-quarters of a mile to Whitehall, the local one-room schoolhouse, where life's important lessons were imparted in the pages of *McGuffey's Reader*. As Aspinall recalled late in life, the *McGuffey* books "were dedicated to the furtherance of the private enterprise system of economics. Undoubtedly, the lessons from those books . . . made a great (and to me good) imprint on my life."[9] *McGuffey's Reader* also taught the discipline of hard work, Christian ethics, and obedience to authority, values Aspinall would come to embody in his later political career.[10]

Restless after years of tenant farming and depending upon the goodwill of his in-laws and parents, Mack Aspinall desperately sought greater economic independence for his family. The allergies and asthma he had developed while working in local woolen mills may have helped argue for a change. In 1902, Mack traveled to Oklahoma Territory on a reconnaissance trip. Upon his return, he resolved to move—not to Oklahoma but to Wray, Colorado. Issues other than land availability figured into the decision. Mack had a cousin who now lived there, but, more importantly, following the birth of her second son, Ralph, in 1897, Wayne's mother, Jessie Aspinall, began suffering from what was commonly called "consumption," or tuberculosis. Wet climates like Ohio's were considered either the cause of the dreaded illness or a roadblock to health for those who suffered from it. By 1900, the arid West—Colorado in particular—had acquired a reputation as, in the words of pioneer journalist Samuel Bowles, "a fountain of health." Tens of thousands of people like Jessie Aspinall, afflicted by pulmonary diseases, migrated to the Centennial State for the purported health benefits of its dry, sunny climate.[11]

Following the public sale of their small Ohio estate in February 1904, the Aspinalls set out for Wray, high on the plains of eastern Colorado, near the Nebraska border. Mack found work in a flour mill, but after only a short time, he decided to move the family to the booming town of Palisade on Colorado's Western Slope, that region of the state west of the Continental Divide.[12] The Western Slope had been opened to general settlement only after a series of wars, treaties, and agreements with Native American tribes in the 1870s and early 1880s.

By 1904, Palisade was enjoying tremendous growth. A booster pamphlet published by the *Palisade Tribune*, the town's one-year-old newspaper, touted the region's "balmy weather," making it the "ideal place for invalids to regain their health." The pamphlet, typical of many publications from the region, touted land prices from $100 to $300 per acre, claiming that those same acres, through the miracle of irrigation, would be worth $1,000 each once fruit trees began producing four years later. "It will net the owner from 30 to 40 percent on his investment each year," the pamphlet confidently predicted. Moreover, land prices were "steadily advancing." Under the sway of such a sales pitch, Mack Aspinall and others found it difficult to resist the Western Slope's allure.[13]

Mack booked rail passage to Palisade on an emigrant car, traveling with the family's furniture and livestock. Wayne and the rest of the family followed their father west at the end of the school year, heading first to Denver, then to Palisade on the Colorado Midland Railroad. Wayne had just finished second grade when he first set eyes on the Grand Valley.[14]

The Aspinalls stayed in a small house in Palisade while Mack finished the family's first dwelling, a tiny tarpaper shack one mile west of Palisade on First Street. This ten-acre site would remain the base of the family's fruit-growing enterprise until Mack's death in 1948. In 1905, a lean-to kitchen was added to the tarpaper structure, and a more permanent, two-story dwelling was constructed in 1906.[15] The Aspinalls' lives were focused around the orchard, nearby Mount Lincoln school, and the Palisade Methodist Church. Ironically, it was while attending a Sunday school picnic on the banks of the Colorado River that

Wayne Aspinall's first home near Palisade, Colorado (ca. 1904), beside a tent that the family had occupied while building the small dwelling. The surrounding arid land begged for the application of irrigation water. Courtesy, Mary White.

young Wayne fell in and was swept downstream by its swift current. A local boy, Boss Reynolds, risked his life by diving in and pulling the Colorado River's future shaper and guardian to safety.[16]

Wayne, Ralph, and, later, younger sister Mary walked a mile to the rural school, from which Aspinall would graduate in 1914. But the epicenter of the family's life was the ten-acre peach orchard. With the application of irrigation water from the nearby Grand River, Mack's orchard became a lucrative enterprise. By 1909, he was serving as secretary for the Palisade Peach Growers' Association. By 1912, eight years after planting his orchard, Mack Aspinall's property was assessed at $3,000. Of the 130 Palisade property owners listed in the 1912–1913 *Mesa County Directory*, only nine had land with a higher valuation. Mack was already one of the area's wealthiest growers. In 1915, Mack constructed a solid two-story house that would remain the Aspinall family home for the rest of Mack's life. The barnlike structure that had replaced the tarpaper shack would become the Aspinalls' peach-packing shed.[17]

The peach business. Wayne Aspinall (standing), *sister Mary, and brother Ralph with a load of peaches in front of the Aspinall peach-packing shed, ca. 1915. Courtesy, Mary White.*

By 1910, Aspinall's Mount Lincoln teachers had gently guided him toward his ultimate vocations: teaching and law. Wayne knew already that he did not aspire to the life of a peach grower like his father. Aspinall's world had revolved around the peach business from the time he moved to the Grand Valley. As the eldest son, Wayne not only helped his father in the orchard but was expected to assist his frequently ailing mother with domestic chores. It was Ralph who enjoyed the orchard work and would end up following in his father's footsteps. According to Wayne, Ralph became "more successful at making money [through fruit growing] than I ever was." Still, the future congressman worked long hours in the orchard, becoming a fast box maker and boss of the packing shed.

In a typical harvest season, after a sufficient number of peaches had been picked, sorted, and boxed, the fruit was loaded onto a wagon and carted one mile to the Palisade Peach Growers' Association loading platform near the town's railroad station. From there, the fruit underwent inspection and was packed into refrigerated railroad cars and shipped to markets. In winter, Wayne and Ralph would assist Mack with tree pruning and orchard maintenance.[18]

Wayne Aspinall's first home in the Grand Valley was this tent on the Aspinall property, approximately one mile west of Palisade, Colorado. Wayne (left), father Mack (center), and brother Ralph (right). Courtesy, Mary White.

Mack believed his sons would follow him into the peach-growing business, yet he also expected all three of his children, including Mary, born near Palisade in 1907, to take education seriously and finish high school. This posed no problem for Wayne, an avid learner.

High school not only helped prepare him for the political future that awaited him, it also introduced him to two women who would play crucial roles in his life. In ninth grade, he began dating Essie Jeffers, daughter of a retired Methodist minister. The following year, her family moved out of the school district, ending Wayne and Essie's short association. They remained close friends, however, and would ultimately marry in 1970, following the death of Aspinall's first wife, Julia Kuns. During Wayne's sophomore year, the Kuns family moved into the Mount Lincoln school district and enrolled their daughter in the Mount Lincoln school. "I can remember seeing for the first time their daughter standing on the stairwell of the school . . . from that time on my mind was made up as to the woman with whom I wished to share my life," Aspinall recalled. Over the next few years, Wayne and Julia spent time together at church and school until her family moved to Lincoln, Nebraska. Still, from 1913 to 1920, the two kept in contact through the mail. They would renew their relationship at the end of Wayne's undergraduate years.[19]

During his senior year of high school, Wayne informed his father that he planned to attend college at Denver University. To Mack, a college education seemed not only unnecessary but well beyond the family's limited financial resources. Wayne's dream of becoming a lawyer was "reaching a little too far," in the elder Aspinall's eyes. Mack ultimately relented, but only after Wayne assured his father that his college education would be strictly self-financed.[20] Graduating second in a class of five, Wayne gave the salutatory address at his Mount Lincoln graduation ceremony, discoursing on the history of Colorado. His sister, a first-grader in 1914, nervously walked across the stage and presented her big brother with a gold watch, the family's graduation present.[21]

College education for rural or small-town Americans in the early twentieth century was not the norm. The cost was prohibitive for many young men and women, and most families did not understand the need for higher education. Undeterred, Wayne Aspinall began assembling a plan to finance his educational dreams. First, he negotiated with his father, securing $100 for orchard work during the summer. He would successfully renew this proposition after each academic year in Denver. Wayne also managed to win a small scholarship from the Methodist Church, which covered the first semester of his freshman year. Perhaps most importantly, the Stewarts, some influential friends of the Aspinall family, saw the young man's promise. The Aspinalls would stay at the Stewarts' ranch on their way to nearby 11,000-foot-high Grand Mesa to camp, fish, and picnic. At the end of the summer, Mr. Stewart would drive his cattle out of the high country to pass the winter in the desert lands surrounding

Wayne N. Aspinall upon graduating from Mount Lincoln School, 1914. Courtesy, Mary White.

Palisade and the Grand Valley. Stewart would stay with the Aspinalls when he passed through to check on his cattle. During long evenings at the Aspinall home, Stewart, a well-educated gentleman rancher, became aware of Wayne's lofty ambitions. As Wayne's sister Mary later recalled, "Mr. and Mrs. Stewart were scholarly people and well educated. They were interested in Wayne and wanted him to be able to afford college." Wayne was able to borrow money from the Stewarts for college and embark on the educational journey that would change his life.[22]

In the fall of 1914, Wayne Aspinall boarded the Colorado Midland Railroad car that would carry him to his first term at the University of Denver.[23] In 1914, Denver was alive with the progressive reforms of Mayor Robert Walter Speer. "Boss" Speer was in the process of transforming the Rocky Mountain mining boomtown into a modern city. The University of Denver, a college with historic ties to the Methodist Church, was growing right along with it. Henry Augustus Buchtel, in the midst of his twenty-year presidency, was leading the university out from under a threatening shadow of debt while expanding its physical plant with a new library, gymnasium, science hall, and chapel.[24]

Aspinall loved college life. In his words, he studied "arduously," worked to make educational support money "continually," and played "strenuously." With a strong constitution requiring little sleep, the Palisade "peach," as he became known, was a whirling dervish of activity, rarely sleeping more than six hours a night. Rising at 5:30 A.M., a habit formed as a boy doing chores with his father, he attended classes and worked various jobs all day and studied until nearly midnight. Trying out for the football team his first fall, Wayne quickly discovered that his 155-pound frame could not take the pummeling from much larger players, no matter how fast and determined he was. He had better success in basketball, making the team as a substitute. Aspinall lived near the campus, first with a friend from Palisade and later, after his freshman year, in the home of Dr. Herbert Russell, a University of Denver mathematics professor.[25]

Aspinall was active in numerous college organizations, including the Debating Club, English Club, German Club, Biological Society, and a social fraternity, Beta Theta Pi, for which he served as house manager during his junior year. He was also a member of the Scroll and Torch Society, a club devoted to "the study of historical factors in their definite relations to modern problems." President of the campus chapter of the YMCA in 1918, he was also the business manager for the university newspaper, the *Clarion*. The 1918 yearbook describes him as a good friend and "hard worker."[26]

Aspinall was scheduled to graduate in the spring of 1918, but President Woodrow Wilson interrupted Wayne's plans by declaring war against Germany on April 2, 1917. Aroused by the president's idealistic pronouncements, Aspinall and several of his fraternity brothers left college several days later to join the army. Already a strong Wilson supporter, Aspinall was ready when the president charged the nation to "make the world safe for democracy."[27] Wayne's driving ambition for his thirteen-month army stint was to be a flyer. Hoping to attend ground school in Austin, Texas, he placed first among the ten candidates who took the entrance exams. The Armistice, however, signed in November 1918, dashed Aspinall's hopes. On the threshold of becoming a commissioned officer and an army flyer, he chose to accept a discharge and return to Denver to finish his undergraduate education.

Though his World War I service did not yield actual combat experience, Aspinall remained proud of his military accomplishments, especially being admitted to candidacy for flying school. He was scheduled to go overseas three times, but his commanding officers chose to keep him stateside because of his unusual competence and educational achievements.[28] Aspinall returned to the University of Denver in March 1919. Fortunately, the college gave him credit for many of the courses he had taken during ground school in Austin, Texas. After only three additional months of course work, the University of Denver granted him an A.B. in June 1919 with majors in history, economics, and sociology and minors in biology and public speaking.[29]

Returning to the Grand Valley, Aspinall worked for his father while leasing a twenty-acre peach orchard. He also rekindled his relationship with Julia Kuns, courting her and then marrying her on January 27, 1920, in Lincoln, Nebraska. After living briefly with Mack Aspinall in the fall of 1920, Wayne and Julia obtained teaching jobs, Wayne at the high school in Palisade, Julia in the nearby Mount Lincoln school district. At this time, Aspinall purchased the orchard he had been leasing.

In 1921, he enjoyed his first taste of politics as president of the Mount Lincoln District No. 35 school board. In this capacity, Aspinall supported a plan to consolidate Mount Lincoln with the larger Palisade school district. In a 1922 election, Aspinall's first public proposal met with a resounding defeat (85–16). The proposal's only real proponents were the families of other board members. He learned an important lesson about listening to constituents and would not lose another election until 1972, when voters failed to return him to Congress.[30]

Aspinall enjoyed the classroom and would always pride himself on being a teacher, but his first taste of politics, however disappointing, had whetted his appetite for more. He was anxious to get to law school. But, as in 1914, tuition and living costs posed a problem. This time Aspinall's greater experience in the world paid dividends. Speculation in orchard land was a fact of life in the Grand Valley. In the spring of 1922, Aspinall sold his peach orchard at a good profit (the land, on East Orchard Mesa, had been irrigated via the federal reclamation program). With his earnings, he was able to finance his legal education.

In the fall of 1922, Wayne and Julia moved to Denver. The University of Denver's law school, founded in 1892 and located several miles from the main campus, offered courses in most traditional legal subjects, as well as specialized topics pertinent to life in the West, among them mining law, water rights, and irrigation law.[31] Aspinall found himself in classes with a who's who of future Colorado politicians. Several classmates would soon find themselves in the state legislature, including Aspinall and Byron Rogers. Rogers and Aspinall would both enjoy long and successful careers in Congress. Another classmate, John Gorsuch, became one of Colorado's most successful attorneys.

In June 1923, Wayne and Julia welcomed their first child, Wayne, Jr., who would later be joined by three siblings—Owen Stewart in 1928, Richard Daniel in 1929, and Ruth JoAnne in 1931. A second daughter, born some time later, survived only a day.

Aspinall's law-school education provided a solid foundation for his later activities. He studied irrigation and water law with L. Ward Bannister, "one of the great water lawyers of Colorado." Bannister, as legal spokesman for the Denver Civic and Commercial Association, voiced Denver's position during hearings leading up to the Colorado River Compact of 1922. Aspinall also made the acquaintance of Delph Carpenter, the great Colorado water lawyer who was instrumental in framing the Colorado River Compact and vigorously defended Colorado's prerogatives at the Santa Fe meetings that preceded it.[32]

During his law-school years, Aspinall secured an internship at the well-respected law firm of Gunter and Lindsey in Denver. Wayne would make valuable political contacts here; the firm's leader was Julius C. Gunter, Democratic governor of Colorado from 1917 to 1919, one of the state's most prominent politicians. Aspinall was offered a position with the firm upon his graduation from law school in 1925. In addition, he received a job offer from the Denver Chamber of Commerce to serve as its water consultant. Though tempted, Aspinall turned down both offers to return to the Western Slope to pursue a career as a small-town lawyer and politician. Except for his years in Congress, Aspinall would reside in Palisade for the rest of his life.[33]

WATER AND THE GRAND VALLEY'S GROWTH

The Grand Valley in the 1920s was growing rapidly, exuding prosperity. For an enterprising individual like Wayne Aspinall, it was the perfect time to begin a career in politics. The chain of small towns that stretched from Palisade to Grand Junction to Fruita had become stable communities with the arrival of federal reclamation initiatives. Whereas most early irrigation projects had been private ventures, by the early twentieth century the region was thriving as a fruit-growing mecca due to the arrival and construction of large-scale federal irrigation projects. After the National Reclamation Act of 1902, the federal government became a major force in promoting irrigation development.

The Federal Reclamation Service had arrived in the Grand Valley, consolidating existing systems and servicing deteriorating and failing projects while breathing life into the economic backbone of the region—all at taxpayer expense and, most remarkably, without expecting a profit. An added benefit of federal involvement was that communities could now "avoid the difficulty of pleasing outside investors" who had often financed early irrigation ventures. Examinations of Mesa County land values indicate a sharp rise after each project's completion. As one early twentieth-century Palisade booster publication remarked, raw land, valued at $100 an acre, "under irrigation can easily be made worth over $1,000 in four years."

With the arrival of reliable irrigation water, the Aspinall family experienced a surge in prosperity. From 1912 to 1925, Mack Aspinall's ten acres of land, planted mostly in peach trees, was assigned a value that fluctuated between $3,000 and $4,000. Most irrigated fruit-tree acreage in the Palisade region was valued at $200-$300 per acre. By comparison, high, dry, non-irrigated land in the region near the Mesa County town of Collbran was valued at between $3 and $5 per acre. The foundation of the Grand Valley's early prosperity was the fruit industry, but that agricultural prosperity assumed an air of permanence only after the arrival of the federal reclamation program.[34]

Wayne Aspinall's interest in the future of federal reclamation was piqued in 1922 when the seven Colorado River Basin states gathered at the behest of Secretary of Commerce Herbert Hoover to divide the waters of the Colorado River. Under western water law, rights accrued to those who used the water first in time. Every year, California was putting more irrigation water to use. If irrigation structures to the Colorado River could be built, few observers doubted that California would use an ever larger share of the river's water. If this became the case, under western water law, California would have a strong legal claim to the Colorado's waters. In addition, California contributed the least amount of runoff to the great river system. Delph Carpenter, the astute Greeley, Colorado, water attorney, had proposed to Hoover that the seven states negotiate a compact to determine each state's share of the river water, thus saving considerable time and money in inevitable protracted legal proceedings. After a series of frustrating talks between representatives of the Colorado River Commission, Hoover scheduled public hearings throughout the West, in Phoenix, Los Angeles, Salt Lake City, Denver, Cheyenne, and Grand Junction. The Grand Junction hearing, held on March 29, 1922, was the only session held on the Colorado River itself.[35]

In the spring of 1922, when Wayne Aspinall was teaching in Palisade and preparing to enter law school in the fall, he attended the Grand Junction sessions of the Colorado River Commission, meeting future president Herbert Hoover. Observing the proceedings, Aspinall learned several stark lessons about Colorado River politics. On the eve of the commission meeting, Grand Junction *Daily Sentinel* editor Walter Walker expressed the feelings of many Grand Valley residents when he bluntly stated in his newspaper column that the Upper

Colorado River states needed to devise "some way to keep water from running down hill" to California and the lower Colorado River states. This fundamental principle and its political ramifications were not lost on Wayne Aspinall and would later form the basis of his reclamation philosophy.

Walker, Aspinall, and others in attendance in the crowded Grand Junction federal courtroom the following day told Hoover and other commissioners that the water rights of Colorado's Western Slope should not be abridged merely because California was moving more quickly to develop its resources.[36] The Western Slope, the *Daily Sentinel* wrote, was a "land of promise," and the Grand Valley's lands were "as productive per acre-foot of water used as any lands to be found further down the stream." Colorado's commissioner, Delph Carpenter, then pointed out another trouble spot, one that would occupy Aspinall in the years ahead. Carpenter predicted trouble for the Grand Junction hearings unless "every . . . objection by Grand Junction people against possible future tunnel diversions by Denver can be eliminated." Colorado's growing Eastern Slope would always covet the population-sparse Western Slope's abundant supply of water.[37]

The public and private wrangling over the future of the Colorado River continued until November 1922–long after Wayne had departed for law school in Denver–when Hoover called the commission delegates to Bishop's Lodge outside Santa Fe, New Mexico. There, the Colorado River Compact was drafted, apportioning the river between two groups of states–the Upper Basin, comprising Wyoming, Colorado, Utah, and New Mexico, and the Lower Basin, comprising Arizona, Nevada, and California. Each basin was to receive 7.5 million of the river's estimated annual flow of 17.5 million acre-feet. An additional 1.5 million acre-feet was reserved for Mexico's water claims. The final 1.0 million was given to the lower basin states when they threatened to leave the negotiations. The compact was taken back to the seven states to be ratified by their respective state legislatures.

The compact's legacy is a mixed one for the future of water resources in the modern American West. As historian Norris Hundley has pointed out, the Colorado River Compact relied on imprecise stream-flow data, overestimating the annual flow by several million acre-feet. Much of the excessive interstate litigation and vituperative political discourse in later years can be explained by fears over water supply. Interstate rivalries were actually exacerbated by the compact, especially the spirited and contentious legal battle between Arizona and California, which would not be resolved until 1963. Finally, the compact failed to address issues such as the increasing salinity of Colorado River water or the well-founded water claims of Native American tribes. Yet the Colorado River Compact remains an important precedent for large-scale federal planning of natural resources. The West had become a laboratory for the enlargement of federal power, and the management of water resources was crucial to this experiment.[38] During his long and influential career in Congress, Wayne Aspinall would work to enhance federal regulation of the region's natural resources; the lessons he learned during the 1920s and 1930s would bear fruit when he went to Washington, D.C.

GRAND JUNCTION IN THE 1920S

By the 1920s, Grand Junction was the largest and most prosperous town on the Western Slope. Though he would always reside in the nearby small town of Palisade, Wayne Aspinall's political, financial, and vocational orientation would be, for the most part, toward the larger town, the seat of Mesa County. In 1920, its population had grown to 8,665, making it the largest population center between Denver and Salt Lake City.[39] Already the region's unofficial capital, Grand Junction was on the rise due to the healthy fruit industry, a reliable water supply, good railroad service, and the leadership of a series of farsighted local entrepreneurs and politicians, including William J. Moyer and Walter Walker. The careers of these two men were brilliantly chronicled and satirized by notable American writer Dalton Trumbo in his 1935 novel *Eclipse*.

Trumbo, who grew up in Grand Junction, was a contemporary of Aspinall's. While Aspinall toiled in Palisade as a schoolteacher and attorney, young Trumbo attended Grand Junction High School, worked for the Grand Junction *Daily Sentinel*, and attended the University of Colorado courtesy of local businessman and philanthropist William J. Moyer.[40] In 1924, Trumbo's father lost his position in a local shoe store, and an embittered Trumbo family moved to California to begin a new life. Trumbo never forgot or forgave his hometown for the way it had treated his father. Based closely upon real people and events in Grand Junction, *Eclipse* satirizes the petty, vituperative small-town citizens who quickly turn against John Abbott (a character based upon William Moyer) after his financial empire collapses during the Great Depression.[41]

Trumbo's fictional Grand Junction, lightly disguised as "Shale City," is a bustling town reclaimed from the desert by the genius of irrigation. As Trumbo set the scene, Shale City "encroached bravely upon the natural domain of sagebrush and desert . . . the very fact of its existence was almost an impertinence," due only to its ability to command water. "Without it the town would wither, burn up, return to dust within a single season." Residents of Shale City obsessed over their gardens and lawns; to them, the color green symbolized the "civilization they had wrested with such toil from the desert."[42] Trumbo's fictional city was dominated by a powerful clique of businessmen who imposed their social and economic standards upon the region. Foremost among this group was Abbott (Moyer) and Stanley Brown, editor of the local paper, a character based on Walter Walker, Grand Junction's most powerful citizen. Walker heavily influenced the life and careers of both Trumbo and Aspinall.

Walker moved to Grand Junction from Kentucky in 1903, joining the staff

Wayne Aspinall as a young man, before he launched his political career as the West's foremost reclamation advocate. Courtesy, MWC.

of publisher I. N. Bunting's ten-year-old Grand Junction *Daily Sentinel*. In 1910, Walker left the *Sentinel* to own and operate *The Plain Dealer* in Ouray, Colorado. Following Bunting's death in 1911, Walker returned to edit the *Daily Sentinel*, which he purchased from the Bunting estate in 1917. Walker used the newspaper to advocate a vision of growth and progress for Grand Junction and the Western Slope. He would later serve several years as Colorado's state Democratic chair. In 1932, Colorado governor Billy Adams appointed Walker to U.S. senator Charles W. Waterman's seat after Waterman's sudden death in 1932. Walker served little more than two months before failing to win the 1932 election against Republican senator Karl C. Schuyler. Walker's political influence as the leading Democrat in western Colorado would both create and destroy political careers for almost five decades.[43] His support and counsel were sought after not only locally but by Democratic politicians at the state and national levels. Wayne Aspinall's political aspirations would only be realized with Walker's support.

ASPINALL ENTERS THE POLITICAL ARENA

After graduating from the University of Denver's law school in 1925, Wayne Aspinall returned to Palisade. Six weeks after passing the Colorado bar exam, he was busy setting up a law practice with DU classmate Howard Roepnack, who would remain his partner until 1929. Aspinall also had political aspirations that he did little to hide. In addition to soliciting business, Wayne asked the Palisade Town Board to let him fill the office of town attorney, which he understood was likely to become vacant.[44]

A social individual who joined almost every fraternal organization imaginable, Aspinall decided against membership in the revitalized Ku Klux Klan, which had gained a large following in Colorado's Grand Valley and the nation during the 1920s. Aspinall realized that any public position he took could affect his political aspirations. The Colorado and national Democratic Party had fallen on hard times in the Republican ascendancy of the mid-1920s, and Aspinall, a Democrat for as long as he could remember, hoped his party might position itself to capitalize on the Klan issue. In the fall of 1925, Aspinall told prominent Denver Democrat Paul Prosser that the best strategy for Democrats was not to wage war on the Klan. Far better, Aspinall reasoned, to avoid extremism on either side of the issue; if it could be "left alone for a few months," the issue would soon wither and die. Aspinall, insightful into the minds of his future constituents, understood the fears that influenced many rural and small-town Americans to cling tenaciously to doctrines of tradition by joining the Ku Klux Klan. The Klan seemed to uphold time-honored values in a world buffeted by the forces of modernization. Prosser heartily agreed with Aspinall's assessment, calling the Klan issue "a Republican baby" that could easily tear the Republicans apart. If Democrats said little or nothing about the Ku Klux Klan, "thousands of disgruntled Klansmen [could] aid in the election of a . . . Democratic ticket."[45]

Aspinall's estimation proved correct. By late 1925, the local Klan was in sharp decline. Influential members like newspaper editor Walter Walker had quit, and the public no longer seemed interested in risking membership in an organization that embraced such extreme positions. Several Grand Junction police officers had been accused of corrupt and brutal behavior; as well-known Klan members they had tarnished the reputation of the entire organization. By 1927, Klan membership in Mesa County was clearly a liability: all Klan-endorsed candidates for the Grand Junction City Council were defeated. In 1927, both the Mesa County Democratic and Republican Parties passed resolutions "denouncing the hooded order."[46]

In this charged political atmosphere, Aspinall worked to build a local political base. Teaching school, serving as attorney for the Town of Palisade, and working as a small-town lawyer brought the ambitious future politician into contact with many Grand Valley citizens. In 1926, at age thirty, Aspinall was ready for his first great political leap, eyeing a position in the Colorado General Assembly. The local Democratic power broker was, of course, Walter Walker. Any potential Democratic candidate from the Western Slope had to secure Walker's—and by extension the *Daily Sentinel*'s—blessing. Aspinall desperately needed to court Walker's favor.

The ethos of 1920s America and the small-town West fueled Wayne Aspinall's political ambitions. Raised in a simpler time that prized clean living, public virtue, duty, and sacrifice, Aspinall brought these core values to his political career.[47] Doris Kearns wrote that Lyndon Johnson's small-town roots recognized "success [as] a reward for virtuous effort." Ambition was "an admired good," and there was "little room for cynicism."[48] Aspinall, like Lyndon Johnson and other early twentieth-century politicians, conformed to the social expectations of their era. In this happy and secure world where each town was "self-dependent for its society and amusements," each person lived in a world that was clear in its outlines and comprehensible, "where people saw . . . the people they knew."[49]

Aspinall believed he had been preparing for a career in politics since childhood, when he began discussing political theory with his grandfather in Ohio. His entire education directed him toward this vocation, which he saw as most honorable.

Early 1926 found Aspinall still trying to broker the tension between Klan and anti-Klan Democrats. If stories about this internal division could be hushed, all would be well for the party, Aspinall predicted.[50] By May, Aspinall had written to Walter Walker, offering his name as a candidate for either state senator or state representative if the incumbent Democrats chose not to run for reelection. "I do this at the earnest solicitation of several friends . . . especially the ex–service men." More tellingly, Aspinall admitted he desired state office "because I love the game."[51]

Editor Walker did not take long to consider Aspinall's offer. His quick but polite reply indicated that the incumbent senator, Ollie Bannister, planned on running again, and incumbent state representative C. J. McCormick had not made his political plans public. Walker made it crystal clear that although there was no reason Aspinall "should not aspire" to a seat in either house of Colorado's General Assembly, no endorsement would be forthcoming in the 1926 election year. In short, Walker considered Aspinall's bid ill-timed and premature.[52]

Aspinall was learning that in politics, timing accounts for a great deal—a lesson he would ultimately adopt as a personal creed. After all, as he would later remember, Walker had not been opposed to him personally in 1926. "He faulted me because Wayne Aspinall, a young man, wasn't ready to be accepted for these jobs."[53] Still, Aspinall had attracted the attention of some important local people; he was placed on the campaign committee of the Mesa County Democratic Committee, and Walter Walker solicited Aspinall's state Democratic convention proxy vote. Aspinall had successfully made an impression on the newspaperman.

Aspinall settled down to a routine of teaching at Palisade High School, establishing his law practice, and working with his father as a peach grower. At one point, he even drove a school bus. He joined numerous clubs and service organizations, becoming particularly active in the Masonic Order and the American Legion, while maintaining strong ties with the armed services as a second lieutenant in the infantry reserves. Aspinall and his father bought forty acres of land on East Orchard Mesa, just south of Palisade, in advance of the arrival of irrigation water. Wayne, Ralph, and Mack had to clear the rocky land before planting their peach trees. For over a year, they hauled water in tanks from the Colorado River, more than a mile away. It was backbreaking work, but the arrival of precious irrigation water made it all worthwhile. Aspinall promoted East Orchard Mesa land to anyone who would listen. "It looks now as if in five or six years the district will be the fruit country of the Upper Valley," he predicted to a friend. "I hardly believe that one could make a mistake in obtaining such land."[54]

In 1928, Aspinall again approached Walker in hopes of securing the editor's blessing for a run at the state legislature. As in 1926, Walker rejected the young man's appeal, favoring incumbent C. J. McCormick. McCormick, a Democratic state representative, lost the 1928 election in a year of strong Republican sweeps.

After the 1929 stock-market crash, the Great Depression slowly took hold of the Grand Valley and the nation. Local institutions like the Grand Valley National Bank went into receivership, and William Moyer's Fair Store was forced to close. The Colorado Democratic Party, which had struggled for survival in the Republican-dominated 1920s, enjoyed a resurgence beginning in about 1930 as voters sought to blame President Hoover and his party for the nation's economic woes. As in 1926 and 1928, Wayne Aspinall stood ready to make his political debut.[55]

After dissolving his legal partnership with Roepnack in 1929,[56] Aspinall focused on teaching, fruit growing, and building local support for his political ambitions. Still a relative unknown, he found once again that support in Grand Junction was difficult to come by. This time, however, Aspinall gained the backing of some of Palisade's most powerful citizens, including former state senator Herman W. Kluge. In the Democratic county assembly meeting on July 24, 1930, Aspinall polled 42 votes, finishing second to former state representative C. J. McCormick's 46 and ahead of Ralph W. Lockard's 41. Fortunately for Aspinall, McCormick stepped aside after the meeting, saying to Aspinall, "Well, you got out of the way for me last time . . . I'll get out of the way this time and help you."[57] In what the *Daily Sentinel* described as an "unusually light" primary vote on September 9, 1930, Aspinall, the "popular Palisade candidate" for state representative, defeated Ralph W. Lockard by a decisive margin (520-279). The town of Palisade stood firm with Aspinall, giving him 146 of 152 primary votes cast. Lockard immediately offered his support to Aspinall in the general election.[58]

By early fall 1930, it became clear that the Colorado Democratic Party, long out of voter favor, had the opportunity to gain great ground. Walter Walker, recently installed as the Democratic state chair, predicted imminent success for the state ticket. Both nationally and locally, the electorate had started to question President Hoover's economic recovery program. Aspinall's Republican opponent in the 1930 election was a woman, Bess Billings, the wife of a Grand Junction dentist. Billings made a strong appeal to local women and attempted to distance herself from the voters' wrath popularly heaped on the Republican Party.[59]

In fall campaign speeches, Aspinall confessed to his great political ambitions. Ever since boyhood, he had aspired to a legislative seat. In a speech at the rural ranching town of Collbran, Aspinall explained how he had "shaped his school and college study to fit him for the opportunity that [was] now his." Less than two weeks before the election, the *Daily Sentinel* awarded Aspinall a ringing endorsement. "A resident of Mesa County since a small boy, in close touch with the agricultural and fruit growing industries, well-educated, splendidly equipped through his educational and legal work, a veteran of the World war, Wayne Aspinall," the *Sentinel* concluded, "surely offers a set of qualifications that would be hard to discount."[60]

Evidently the voters of Mesa County agreed. On November 4, 1930, Aspinall defeated Bess Billings by a decisive margin (4,432-3,543), carrying twenty of twenty-six precincts. Palisade voters were particularly supportive of his candidacy: East Palisade voters favored him 243-66, West Palisade voters 339-111. Students at Palisade High School celebrated the victory of "our beloved Wayne N." with "a very enthusiastic pep meeting."[61] Four years of county-level Democratic Party work and a high public profile as a citizen, lawyer, prominent fruit grower, and popular high-school teacher, coupled with the Democratic Party's rising fortunes, had made Aspinall's election a near certainty. The "Palisade Peach," as his college classmates called him, had won the first of twenty straight state- and national-level elections that would return him to office until 1972.

STATE POLITICIAN

Aspinall had a highly successful career as a state representative and state senator in the 1930s and 1940s, serving as Speaker of the State House, and as senate majority and minority leader. It would prove the perfect tutelage for his future congressional career. From 1931 to 1948, Aspinall served in the Colorado Legislature every year but two. After two years in the Colorado House of Representatives, Aspinall took an additional post as district counsel for the Roosevelt administration's Home Owner's Loan Corporation. In this capacity, Aspinall helped provide people with emergency loans so they could avoid mortgage foreclosures. An admirer of Franklin Roosevelt, Aspinall believed in the positive social role that government could play in people's lives, an attitude he retained until the 1960s, when social and political upheavals caused him to rethink his positions.[62] His job with the administration allowed Aspinall to travel widely in western Colorado and afforded him the opportunity to make a valuable network of political contacts.

As late as 1933, Aspinall still taught school, drove a school bus, and served both in the state legislature and on the Palisade Town Board—all this while working with the Roosevelt administration. As one Palisade citizen told Aspinall's wife, Julia, "the trouble with Wayne is he's trying to hog it all." Near the end of Wayne's first term as a state representative, the Home Owner's Loan Corporation ruled that district counsels could not hold elected political office. Family finances were tight, so Aspinall decided to retain his counsel post and not seek re-election to the Colorado House in 1934. This seemed like a good economic decision for a young man with a growing family in hard economic times, but Aspinall soon came to regret it. Three days after the 1934 primary, Aspinall received word that the Home Owner's Loan Corporation had discontinued the office of district counsel. His major source of income was gone.[63]

From 1934 to 1936, Aspinall worked hard at bolstering his law practice. To this end, he relocated his office from Palisade to the larger and more politically connected Grand Junction, though he continued to reside in Palisade. He also became a lobbyist for the Continental Oil Company, putting his state political ties to good use.[64]

Through the mid-1930s, the Great Depression's grip worsened in Colorado. Lorena Hickok, an investigative journalist working for key Franklin Roosevelt advisor Harry Hopkins, found Colorado smarting from a combination of economic and natural disasters. Farmers, plagued by their fifth straight year of drought in 1934, had been unable to show a profit for years. Reduced to despair by the prolonged drought and dust storms, they even woke one morning, Hickok reported, to find all their cattle dead, drowned in a flash flood. Overall, Hickok found Colorado's economic situation almost hopeless. Exploitation of children and Mexican immigrant labor in the sugar-beet fields, corruption in state relief agencies, abandoned coal camps—all came to the crusading journalist's attention.[65]

Still, the Roosevelt administration poured federal money into Colorado and the Western Slope. Grand Junction became a major state center for New Deal relief agencies. Aspinall's Home Owner's Loan Corporation office was located there, as were regional Civilian Conservation Corps offices, Federal Emergency Relief Administration projects, and Resettlement Administration home tracts. The Grand Valley's steady supply of irrigation water seemed especially attractive to Eastern Slope Dust Bowl refugees who settled on federal project lands near Grand Junction.[66]

While Aspinall had been toiling away for the Grand Valley in the state legislature, Democratic congressman Edward T. Taylor of Glenwood Springs was reaching the apex of his power and influence in the U.S. House of Representatives, funneling federal influence and funds to his Western Slope congressional district. Serving from 1909 until his death in 1941, Taylor established an almost legendary reputation among both his congressional colleagues and his Fourth Congressional District constituents. Other than Walter Walker, Taylor played the most important role in shaping Aspinall's political ideals, serving as his model and inspiration.

As Aspinall later admitted, his political career followed "in the footsteps of Taylor.[67] In the raucous days of the silver boom, Taylor had taught school in the high-mountain mining town of Leadville, Colorado. After serving as Leadville's school principal and superintendent, Taylor studied law at the University of Michigan, graduating in 1884. In 1885 he moved first to Aspen and two years later to Glenwood Springs, where he set up a law practice specializing in water litigation. In 1897, Taylor was elected to the Colorado State Senate, moving on to the U.S. House of Representatives in 1908. One of the most powerful men in Congress and chair of the House Appropriations Committee after 1937, Taylor is best known for sponsoring one of the most important pieces of western New Deal legislation, the Taylor Grazing Act. As Taylor told his congressional colleagues in 1934, the public-land states of the American West were suffering from both drought and severe overgrazing. "We are rapidly permitting creations of small Sahara Deserts in every one of the Western states today," Taylor warned.[68]

Taylor's solution to the problem was to extend federal control and management to those lands in the name of fair access and conservation of threatened resources. The Taylor Grazing Act passed Congress in 1934, ending the era of free and open access to the public domain. Homesteading would no longer be permitted. More than 80 million acres would be managed by a new federal agency, the U.S. Grazing Service, a division of the Department of the Interior. Local grazing districts were established, their management policies to be set by the rancher-users. Though more than a few ranchers objected to this extension of federal control, the fact that a western congressman of Taylor's reputation had sponsored the bill deflated all but the most extreme critics. Taylor made it clear that the bill would not revolutionize historic land-use patterns, but only manage the lands more wisely. Preference for grazing permits would go to "land-owners engaged in the livestock business."[69] Aspinall admired Taylor's commanding approach to this and other western resource issues and would draw political inspiration from him numerous times over the coming years.

Taylor's unimpeachable political reputation was rooted in his ability to promote the economic growth of the huge, lonely, rural, and mountainous Fourth Congressional District. The inhabitants of its small mountain and valley towns, surrounded by rural ranchers, sheepherders, and irrigation farmers, took special pride in Taylor's personal approach to campaigning. Almost every adult could say that he or she had met the legendary congressman. His vigorous defense of his district's resources placed him beyond the reproach of voters of either political party. By the mid-1930s, Taylor had become one of the most senior members in House history. Though Taylor enjoyed the respect of his congressional colleagues, he understood it was promoting the development of his congressional district's resources that won him election after election. Always foremost in Taylor's mind were the defense and aggrandizement of its water resources—a lesson that would not be lost on Wayne Aspinall.[70]

By 1937, Aspinall had begun playing a major role in Colorado's water deliberations. After successfully running for his old state legislative seat in November 1936, he adopted a higher political profile. Immediately after the election, he began writing letters to influential Colorado Democrats asking for their support in his bid for the House speakership. Now that his good law-school friend Byron Rogers had been elected Colorado's attorney general, and the Western Slope's Ed Johnson was headed to Washington as a U.S. senator, Aspinall's voice would be heard more frequently in Democratic political councils.[71]

In January 1937, Aspinall was elected Speaker of the House for the Thirty-first Colorado General Assembly. In July, Democratic governor Teller Ammons appointed Aspinall to the recently created Colorado Water Conservation Board. Because he had needed Eastern Slope legislators' votes to win the speakership, Aspinall viewed his election as a portent of close cooperation from all sections of the state. Aspinall's election was termed "unusual" by one newspaper because he had not served in the preceding General Assembly. Denver's *Rocky Mountain News* described the forty-year-old Palisade legislator as "stocky," with "horn-rimmed glasses" and a "pleasant, modest manner."[72]

Serving in the state legislature and on the state water board acquainted Aspinall with both the hydraulic needs of the growing Eastern Slope and the state's fear of California's designs on the Upper Colorado River Basin water supply. For Aspinall, the strong stance Edward Taylor had championed in defense of Western Slope water was only reinforced by local political mentor Walter Walker's equally aggressive position. In his political and editorial capacities, Walker told Aspinall that he would continue "to uphold the position of the Western Slope against any program that will jeopardize the losing of any of our water resources." However, as the Colorado House Speaker and as a member of the state water board, Aspinall believed he had a mandate not only to protect Western Slope water supplies, but to promote broader intrastate cooperation on water issues.[73]

In this pursuit, Aspinall and other Western Slope members of the Colorado Water Conservation Board were subjected to outbursts of public anger as various state interests negotiated an acceptable settlement that would result in passage of the controversial Colorado-Big Thompson Project (C-BT). As a state water board member, Aspinall traveled widely throughout the Western Slope, discussing the proposed C-BT Project—and future reclamation projects—with the county commissioners of Mesa, San Miguel, Delta, Montrose, Garfield, and Pitkin Counties during the summer of 1937. He reported to water board director Clifford Stone that most of the people he encountered believed that intrastate cooperation was necessary on the C-BT Project and in any future reclamation plans. To Aspinall's pleasure and surprise, water problems were being viewed as a state problem rather than a "sectional" problem. The exceptions to this generalization were the strong Western Slope–water–protectionist statements emanating from Walter Walker's *Daily Sentinel.*[74]

A complex system of dams, reservoirs, and tunnels, the Colorado–Big Thompson Project was signed into law by President Franklin D. Roosevelt on December 28, 1937. Western Slope politicians, led by Edward Taylor, demanded compensatory storage capacity for waters lost through transmontane diversion to the Front Range. In its simplest outlines, the project built two dams to store water in Granby and Shadow Mountain Reservoirs. From there, the water flowed by gravity to Grand Lake, exiting via a thirteen-mile tunnel under Rocky Mountain National Park and the Continental Divide, passing through a power plant at Estes Park, and flowing into the Big Thompson River. From there, water was fed through a system of Eastern Slope siphons, canals, and reservoirs into the farm ditches of northeastern Colorado. Denver newspaperman Alva Swain credited a "new" political element for making Colorado–Big Thompson a reality. These new leaders realized that as long as the Eastern and Western Slopes fought over water, the entire state "would suffer for all time to come." Swain credited Aspinall, Clifford Stone, Byron Rogers, Glenwood Springs Democratic water attorney Frank Delaney, Governor Teller Ammons, and northern Colorado water planners Charles E. Hansen and Thomas Nixon with forging the compromise leading to the C-BT agreement. In particular Swain commended the Eastern and Western Slope "friendships formed during the last three sessions" of the state legislature for bringing "order out of chaos."[75]

While the Front Range received an augmented water supply with Colorado–Big Thompson, the Western Slope also received valuable considerations.

Congressman Edward Taylor had long insisted the Western Slope be compensated acre-foot for acre-foot for water diverted to the Front Range. In other words, reservoirs needed to be included in the project's final form. C-BT construction began in 1938, thanks to a large congressional appropriation that Taylor carried through. The first elements to be built were the Green Mountain dam, reservoir, and power plant. In Colorado-Big Thompson historian Daniel Tyler's words, these features were "the West Slope's *sine qua non* for participation in the C-BT." With another war looming, project funding would be difficult to obtain in the years ahead. It would be 1947 before the first water flowed through the Alva B. Adams Tunnel to farms on Colorado's Eastern Slope. Even then, the massive project was still seven years from completion.[76]

On September 4, 1941, Taylor's storied legislative career came to an end when he died at the age of eighty-three. Western Slope Democrats immediately began scrambling to find a replacement for the legendary congressman, whom *Sentinel* editor Walter Walker called the "father of Reclamation" and "western Colorado's greatest asset." Press reports in the days following Taylor's death identified Aspinall, Colorado Supreme Court justice William Lee Knous, and Glenwood Springs attorney Frank Delaney as leading candidates. Colorado law did not require a special election in the event of a vacated congressional seat, leaving it to the discretion of the governor to appoint a replacement or call for an election. Republican governor Ralph Carr waited several days before deciding on an election, arguing that the unique character of the large Western Slope district demanded the selection of an individual familiar with irrigation issues, the Colorado River, grazing rights, mining, and other natural-resource issues. The special election was set for early December 1941.[77]

State and Western Slope newspapers soon buzzed with rumors of Walter Walker's possible candidacy. After Walker refused to enter the race, preferring to play his familiar role of kingmaker, Aspinall, Delaney, and other prominent Democrats[78] had either announced or were seriously considering joining the race. Delaney's official announcement came on September 19, only two days after he had told a friend that he needed to talk to Walter Walker before mounting a serious campaign.[79] Several Republican candidates also announced their intentions, most notably close Taylor friend Charles J. Moynihan of Montrose, and state senator and former lieutenant governor Robert F. Rockwell of Paonia. Rockwell officially announced his candidacy on September 22 and would go on to easily capture the Republican nomination in October.[80]

Despite Aspinall's best efforts, Delaney took an early lead in organizing support. On October 18 in Grand Junction, Frank Delaney defeated Aspinall and other challengers for the Democratic nomination, securing it on the fourth ballot. Aspinall had mounted his first bid for Congress and been stymied once again by Walker, who threw his support behind Delaney. Aspinall had wanted to run for Congress in 1941 "even more than I did later on in '48," but he would have to continue biding his time in the state legislature.[81]

Robert Rockwell defeated Delaney by a 3,000-vote margin on December 9, 1941. Rockwell and the Republicans played to the Fourth District voters' natural conservatism and Republican leanings. To stay in office, a Republican advertisement noted days before the election, Congressman Taylor, a Democrat, had found it necessary to vote against the efforts of the Roosevelt administration "to hamstring the progress and development of the Western Slope." Fourth District Democratic candidates would always suffer from that district's small number of core Democrats; any aspiring Democratic candidate would need to follow Taylor's lead and cultivate a bipartisan appeal—something Wayne Aspinall well realized.[82]

Rockwell managed to overcome Walter Walker and the Daily Sentinel's overwhelming support of Delaney by playing up voter disgust with the Roosevelt administration, fear over Pearl Harbor, and Democratic apathy after holding the Taylor seat for more than thirty years. Rockwell's deep campaign war chest certainly hadn't hurt. Walker believed Rockwell had spent at least $15,000 and camouflaged many other personal expenses—a huge sum for a Fourth District congressional election. Republican rancher and businessman Robert F. Rockwell would represent the Fourth Congressional District for the next seven years.[83]

THE WAR YEARS—AND AFTER

World War II revived prosperity in Colorado and the West. The Front Range corridor became host to a massive military presence. Lowry Field and Buckley Field near Denver, and Fort Carson and Peterson Field near Colorado Springs were only the most visible signs. The Denver Arms Plant employed more than 20,000 workers at its height. The Rocky Mountain Arsenal, north of Aurora, constructed chemical weapons. Fitzsimons Army Hospital, built near Denver during the First World War, was modernized for another major war. Camp Hale, near Leadville, was constructed as a high-altitude training site for the ski troops of the Tenth Mountain Division. The war also made immediate demands on Colorado's natural resources, particularly minerals. War production requirements and the subsidies they paid brought prosperity to molybdenum, tungsten, and vanadium miners. As one well-known Colorado history book put it, no single event in the state's history "transformed Colorado to the extent that World War II did."[84]

The roots of Grand Junction's and western Colorado's rise to dominance in the uranium industry date back to 1910. Western Colorado mines had long been a source of radium and vanadium. The large piles of tailings near western Colorado's vanadium mines contained low concentrations of uranium. In December 1941, the federal government formed the Metals Reserve Company to stockpile key war production minerals.[85] Just days after the bombing of Pearl

Harbor, the *Daily Sentinel* reported that federal funds were en route to build better access roads to the vanadium-mining region south of Grand Junction. Ninety-five percent of the nation's supply of vanadium, a component vital to steel production, was mined on Colorado's Western Slope. Soon the government was interested in the area as a source of uranium as well.[86]

The war impacted the lives of every citizen of the Grand Valley. Plagued by a labor shortage, the local fruit industry would cry out for help numerous times during the conflict. Prisoners of war would be located in the Grand Valley to assist with the fruit harvests.[87] National transportation needs would inspire plans to modernize air travel to Grand Junction and the Western Slope.[88] The Grand Valley would emerge from the war as the uranium capital of the American West. As such, the Western Slope's uranium mines would produce raw materials for the weapons that would defeat Japan in 1945 and in the long Cold War that followed. Large movements of people would begin arriving in the region, seeking jobs in the extractive industries. Soon, political leaders would be demanding new, reliable sources of water to meet this growing population's needs.

Citizens all faced choices of how best to use their time and talents in the war effort. For state senator Wayne Aspinall, now in his mid-forties and no longer a young man, the war's arrival presented a serious dilemma: should he continue to serve his state and community in the Colorado Legislature, or should he attempt to serve his nation in the armed forces? The decision would prove an important one. For Aspinall's generation of U.S. politicians, the choice to serve the military in some capacity during the war would provide the patriotic gloss necessary to be taken seriously by America's Cold War electorate.

Aspinall's political ambitions were clearly established by 1941. He believed that an additional stint in the armed forces would do his political dreams no harm; indeed, not joining might allow an opponent to label him unpatriotic or cowardly. Aspinall had always regretted not seeing military action in Europe during World War I. However, in that conflict, Aspinall had been an unmarried college junior. In 1942, he was well into middle age, married with four children, and caring for an aged father who was his business partner. In addition, his career as a well-regarded lawyer and state politician had established him as a community leader in Palisade, Grand Junction, and, indeed, the entire Western Slope.[89]

As U.S. forces entered the conflict, Aspinall felt called to serve again. His wife, Julia, understood her husband's ambition; father Mack Aspinall told his son that he was "crazy" to abandon a wife, four kids, and a good career to chase patriotic glory again. Hoping to enter the Judge Advocate Corps (the legal branch of the army) but finding no openings, Aspinall next applied for a captain's commission in the Allied military government and was accepted for service as a legal officer. In early August, Aspinall advised Colorado governor John Vivian that he would likely be taking a leave from his post in the state senate. By late

August 1943, Aspinall was in Denver purchasing his officer's uniforms and signing correspondence "Captain Wayne Aspinall."[90]

As he later admitted, his World War II service provided little in the way of opportunities to help his country.[91] Still, Aspinall's World War II career provided a reservoir of experience and valuable contacts that he would draw upon during his years in Congress. Spending most of 1944 in Europe, Aspinall traveled extensively, participating in the reassembly of the civilian governments of Belgium and France. By the fall of 1944, Aspinall had received word that his request to resign his commission had been accepted. He had contributed what he could to the war effort and was anxious to return to the political arena.[92] By early 1945, he was back in the Grand Valley, resuming his law practice, fully reimmersed in state politics.

Aspinall had chosen a good time to take a sabbatical. Politically, 1944 had been a quiet year in the state as Colorado's citizens focused their energies on concluding the war effort. Locally, both the Republicans and Democrats "had no active local organization." Fourth District congressman Robert F. Rockwell had no trouble winning re-election, brooking little more than token opposition from the Democratic Party.[93]

After several long conversations with Walter Walker in December 1944 about local and state politics, Aspinall was ready to resume his job as minority leader of the Colorado State Senate.[94]

Aspinall conducted his Senate program in accordance with Walter Walker's December briefings. "I have remembered our talks together . . . and have tried to conduct the program here in the Senate accordingly," Aspinall wrote to his mentor. Colorado was being asked to ratify the Mexican Water Treaty, negotiated in 1944, which recognized Mexico's rights to 1.5 million acre-feet of water from the Colorado River. California took the lead in opposing treaty ratification, arguing that Mexico should receive no more than 0.75 million acre-feet. The Roosevelt administration pressured western politicians to accept the pact out of diplomatic concerns inspired by the Second World War. Ratification would also advance Roosevelt's "good neighbor" policy toward Latin America. Walker counseled Aspinall to "stand pat" on treaty ratification because "our interests, as Coloradans, usually are entirely opposite to the interests of California." This advice—underscoring the fundamental rule of Upper Colorado River Basin water politics—was another piece of wisdom Aspinall would never forget.[95]

While Aspinall was away in Europe, Walter Walker had protected the future congressman's political interests. Now, the Western Slope editor seemed interested in promoting Aspinall's political future. In November 1945, Walker told the divisional news editor of the Associated Press office in Denver that "we are particularly interested in the activities and leadership work of Senator Wayne N. Aspinall from Mesa County." Aspinall, according to Walker, had been "one of the most influential men" in the Colorado Assembly for many years. The evidence suggests that Aspinall was now considering a campaign for governor. As early as 1940, the position had been on his mind, and it would remain there for years to come.[96]

Clearly, he was now being viewed as a viable candidate by other Colorado Democrats. The governorship was no doubt appealing because the Fourth Congressional District appeared to be firmly locked up; Rockwell had won by larger margins in every election since 1941. Yet by 1948, events conspired to vault Aspinall into the limelight as the Democratic Party's next hopeful against strong Republican incumbent Robert Rockwell.

ENDNOTES

1. This is Philip L. Fradkin's argument in his study, *A River No More: The Colorado River and the West* (Berkeley: University of California Press, 1996). See also High Country News, *Western Water Made Simple* (Washington, DC: Island Press, 1987), 153–216.

2. Donald Worster, *Rivers of Empire: Water, Aridity, and the Growth of the American West* (New York: Pantheon Books, 1985), 277; the "never met a dam" quote is only a slight corruption of Russell Martin's description of Aspinall as a politician "who never met a water project he didn't like." See Russell Martin, *A Story That Stands Like a Dam: Glen Canyon and the Struggle for the Soul of the West* (New York: Henry Holt, 1989), 325.

3. Wayne Aspinall Autobiographical Mss., 64, Vivian Passer Collection, Grand Junction, CO.

4. Ibid., 46–47.

5. Wayne N. Aspinall, "Irrigation and Federal Participation in Colorado," July 18–20, 1977, Western State College, Gunnison, CO, speech transcript, Vivian Passer Collection.

6. Carol Edmunds, *Wayne Aspinall: Mr. Chairman* (Lakewood, CO: Crown Point, 1980), 31.

7. "Reclamation Pays," from *Congressional Record*, June 27, 1961, Box 88, fd: 50, Wayne Aspinall Papers, University of Denver Archives, Denver, CO (hereafter cited as UDA); Wayne Aspinall, "Capital Comments," reprinted in Grand Junction (CO) *Daily Sentinel*, February 15, 1962.

8. Wayne Aspinall, "Capital Comments," August 17, 1963, Box 147, fd: "Pub 4," Wayne Aspinall Papers, UDA.

9. Aspinall Autobiographical Mss., 9–10; Mary White interview with author, Grand Junction, CO, February 14, 1996.

10. James West Davidson, Mark H. Lytle et al., *Nation of Nations: A Narrative History of the American Republic*, 3d ed. (Boston: McGraw Hill, 1998), 655.

11. Mary White interview, February 14, 1996; Carol Abbott, Stephen J. Leonard, and David McComb, *Colorado: A History of the Centennial State*, 3d ed. (Niwot: University Press of Colorado, 1994), 229–233.

12. Aspinall Autobiographical Mss., 11.

13. No author, "Palisade, Colorado: Its Advantages, Resources, Possibilities" (*Palisade Tribune*, ca. 1904), Research Center and Special Library, Museum of Western Colorado, Grand Junction, CO (hereafter cited as MWC). In its first issue, on June 6, 1903, the

Palisade Tribune boasted that "no town in Colorado has a better outlook, or a more promising future before it, nor has one improved more . . . in the past three or four years than Palisade." See *History of Palisade, Colorado*, vol. 1 (Palisade, CO: *Palisade Tribune*, 1963), copy in Research Center and Special Library, MWC.

14. Aspinall Autobiographical Mss., 11.

15. Aspinall Autobiographical Mss., 12; Wayne Aspinall interview with Al Look, Mesa County Oral History Project (OH-120, Part 1), Research Center and Special Library, MWC, January 10, 1978. Aspinall recalled the joys of living in a tarpaper shack: "we came home from church one Sunday morning and Mother stepped into the kitchen and there was a rattlesnake underneath the stove. So we were very careful after that."

16. The near-drowning story is from Ben Cole, *Arizona Republic*, July 28, 1963.

17. Mary White interview, February 14, 1996; R. L. Polk, *Grand Junction City and Mesa County Directory, 1909*; R. L. Polk, *Grand Junction City and Mesa County Directory, 1912–13*, vol. 6, Research Center and Special Library, MWC. Statistical information compiled from the section called "Land Owners of Mesa County."

18. Mary White interview, February 14, 1996; Aspinall Autobiographical Mss., 12–13.

19. Aspinall Autobiographical Mss., 15–16.

20. Mary White interview, February 14, 1996; Aspinall Autobiographical Mss., 12–13; Wayne Aspinall interview, January 10, 1978.

21. Ibid.

22. Ibid.

23. Aspinall traveled to the University of Denver with Frank Best, an old school friend who would be the first husband of Essie Jeffers. Aspinall's association with Frank would help maintain his friendship with Essie. Both Wayne and Essie's first marriages, to Julia and Frank respectively, lasted just shy of fifty years.

24. Stephen J. Leonard and Thomas J. Noel, *Denver: From Mining Camp to Metropolis* (Niwot: University Press of Colorado, 1990), 128–150, detail the Speer years in Denver's history. Jim Norland, *The Summit of a Century: A Pictorial History of the University of Denver* (Denver: University of Denver, 1963), 43–46. Buchtel's reputation for integrity caught the attention of Colorado's Republican Party, which nominated him for governor in 1907. When the Democratic ranks split, Buchtel was able to win the governorship. He held simultaneous posts as state governor and Denver University president for two years, from 1907 to 1909. See Carl Ubbelohde, Maxine Benson, and Duane Smith, *A Colorado History*, 7th ed. (Boulder, CO: Pruett Publishing, 1995), 268–269.

25. The "peach from Palisade" nickname appears in the University of Denver yearbook *Kynewisbok* (1918), 50, UDA. Also see Aspinall Autobiographical Mss., 17–18; Wayne Aspinall interview, January 10, 1978.

26. *Kynewisbok* (1918), 50; Wayne Aspinall interview, January 10, 1978; Carol Edmunds, "Young Wayne Aspinall Had a Good Head for Wrangling, a Good Hand for Gavels," in "Westworld" (Sunday magazine supplement), Grand Junction (CO) *Daily Sentinel*, April 30, 1978, 5.

27. Aspinall Autobiographical Mss., 28; Wayne N. Aspinall to Greg [last name unknown], June 21, 1971, Box 34, Wayne Aspinall Papers, UDA.

28. Aspinall Autobiographical Mss., 28–30; Wayne Aspinall interview, January 10, 1978.

29. Aspinall Autobiographical Mss., 31–32; *Kynewisbok* (1920), 19.

30. Carol Edmunds, "Wayne N. Aspinall Biographic Sketch," Box 1, fd: 1, Wayne N. Aspinall Papers, University of Colorado Archives, University of Colorado at Boulder, Boulder, CO (hereafter cited as UCAUCB); Wayne Aspinall, "A Family Message to My Family," Vivian Passer Collection.

31. Wayne Aspinall interview, January 10, 1978; *University of Denver Catalogue* (1925), 238, UDA.

32. Wayne Aspinall interview, January 10, 1978; Aspinall Autobiographical Mss., 23; for background on Gunter's administration, see Ubbelohde, Benson, and Smith, *A Colorado History*, 279, 284.

33. Wayne Aspinall interview with Al Look, Mesa County Oral History Project (OH-120, Part 2), Research Center and Special Library, MWC, January 1978, is the source of the quotation about L. Ward Bannister; Aspinall, Speech to Upper Colorado River Commission, n.d., ca. 1980, Box 38, fd: 3, Wayne N. Aspinall Papers, UCAUCB; Norris Hundley, Jr., *Water and the West: The Colorado River Compact and the Politics of Water in the American West* (Berkeley: University of California Press, 1975), 156. Hundley includes numerous statements about Carpenter's key role in the 1922 Colorado River Compact negotiations.

34. This information is based upon an examination of the *Grand Junction City and Mesa County Directory* in the years 1912–1925. See also Bradley F. Raley's discussion of the link between irrigation and land speculation in "Irrigation, Land Speculation, and the History of Grand Junction, Colorado," 6–8 (paper presented at the Western History Association Meeting, October 17, 1996). Raley discusses the link between outside investors and the speculative atmosphere in the Grand Valley. An example of the booster literature is "Palisade, Colorado: Its Advantages, Resources, Possibilities," MWC.

35. Hundley, *Water and the West*, 152–159; Worster, *Rivers of Empire*, 209.

36. Wayne Aspinall interview with Nancy Whistler, Association of Former Members of Congress Project, Manuscript Division, Library of Congress, Washington, DC, February 15, 1979; Richard Allan Baker, *Conservation Politics: The Senate Career of Clinton P. Anderson* (Albuquerque: University of New Mexico Press, 1985), 192–193. Baker asserts that Aspinall was present at the 1922 meetings in Santa Fe, where the Colorado River Compact was signed. This is highly unlikely, as Aspinall would have been at the University of Denver law school at that time. Baker took his information from the previously cited Aspinall interview with Whistler in which Aspinall remarked that he had met "President-to-be [Herbert] Hoover in 1922, during the Colorado River Compact hearings." It is likely that this reference is to the Grand Junction hearings held in late March.

37. *Daily Sentinel*, March 29, 1922; Hundley, *Water and the West*, 158.

38. Marc Reisner, *Cadillac Desert: The American West and Its Disappearing Water*, rev. ed. (New York: Penguin Books, 1993), 124–125; "Law of the River: Colorado River Compact," Box 52, no file, Wayne Aspinall Papers, UDA; Norris Hundley, "Water and the West in Historical Imagination," *Western Historical Quarterly* 27 (Spring 1996): 13–14; Carl Abbott, "The Federal Presence," in *The Oxford History of the American West*, ed. Clyde A. Milner II, Carol A. O'Connor, and Martha A. Sandweiss (New York: Oxford University Press, 1994), 475.

39. Richard E. Tope, "Objective History of Grand Junction, Colorado, Part Two," *Journal of the Western Slope* 10, no. 2 (1995): 28.

40. This is not officially documented but is sound historical supposition. Apparently, most local people who knew Moyer and Trumbo believed Moyer financed Trumbo's one year of college at the University of Colorado at Boulder. In addition, there were several strong ties between Moyer and the Trumbo family, including the fact that both families were active in the Grand Junction Christian Science Church. See Dave Sundal interview with Al Look, Mesa County Oral History Project (OH-444), Research Center and Special Library, MWC, May 14, 1981, and Dave Sundal interview with Evelyn Kyle and Alberta Francis, Mesa County Oral History Project (OH-493), Research Center and Special Library, MWC, March 1, 1982.

41. Dalton Trumbo, *Eclipse* (London: Lovat Dickson and Thompson, 1935), 286; Bruce Cook, *Dalton Trumbo* (New York: Charles Scribner, 1977), 79–84; David Golden, "William J. Moyer: The Rise and Fall of a Small-Town Progressive in Western Colorado," *Journal of the Western Slope* 10, no. 3 (1995): 13.

42. Trumbo, *Eclipse*, 15–17.

43. Walter Walker begs for more historical attention. This short sketch was culled from several sources, including a number of articles published in the Grand Junction *Daily Sentinel* after his death, which came on October 9, 1956. See also Emma McCreanor, *Mesa County, Colorado: A 100 Year History, 1883–1983* (Grand Junction, CO: Museum of Western Colorado Press, 1983), 47.

44. Wayne Aspinall interview, January 10, 1978.

45. Wayne Aspinall to Town Board, Palisade, Colorado, October 26, 1925, and Wayne Aspinall to Paul Prosser, November 7, 1925, Box 1, fd: "Aspinall and Aspinall," Wayne Aspinall Papers, UDA; Aspinall to Prosser, November 7, 1925; Paul Prosser to Wayne N. Aspinall, November 18, 1925, Box 1, fd: "Aspinall and Aspinall," Wayne Aspinall Papers, UDA.

46. Robert Alan Goldberg, *Hooded Empire: The Ku Klux Klan in Colorado* (Urbana: University of Illinois Press, 1981), 161; Kenneth Baird, "The Ku Klux Klan in Grand Junction," *Journal of the Western Slope* 4, no. 1 (1989): 40–51.

47. This is how Robert Dallek describes the ethos of 1920s small-town America. See Robert M. Dallek, *Lone Star Rising: Lyndon Johnson and His Times, 1908–1960* (New York: Oxford University Press, 1991), 68–69.

48. Dallek, *Lone Star Rising*, 68–69, quotes Doris Kearns, *Lyndon Johnson and the American Dream* (New York: Harper and Row, 1976), 56.

49. William E. Leuchtenburg, *The Perils of Prosperity: 1914–1932* (Chicago: University of Chicago Press, 1958), 6.

50. Wayne N. Aspinall to Paul Prosser, February 10, 1926, Box 1, fd: "Aspinall and Aspinall," Wayne Aspinall Papers, UDA.

51. Wayne N. Aspinall to Walter Walker, May 19, 1926, Box 1, fd: "Aspinall and Aspinall," Wayne Aspinall Papers, UDA.

52. Walter Walker to Wayne Aspinall, May 11, 1926, Box 1, fd: "Aspinall and Aspinall," Wayne Aspinall Papers, UDA.

53. Edmunds, "Young Wayne Aspinall," 6.

54. Mary White interview, February 14, 1996; Wayne N. Aspinall to James B. Stone, March 26, 1926, Box 1, fd: "Aspinall and Aspinall," Wayne Aspinall Papers, UDA.

55. Wayne Aspinall interview, January 10, 1978; Stephen J. Leonard, *Trials and Triumphs: A Colorado Portrait of the Great Depression, with FSA Photographs* (Niwot: University Press of Colorado, 1993), ix–x; Golden, "William J. Moyer," 12.

56. In 1929, Roepnack and Aspinall dissolved their partnership when they became involved on opposing sides of a case. Dr. Weidlein, a country practitioner, became embroiled in a legal dispute over his professional reputation, a conflict that split the Palisade community. Aspinall sided with Weidlein, who ended up losing his physician's license for six months. Aspinall's loyalty to Weidlein, a beloved local doctor, paid political dividends in his bid for political office in 1930. "It helped me a great deal . . . because Dr. Weidlein's friends were all over this county and I had stayed with Dr. Weidlein" through the controversy. See Wayne Aspinall interview, January 10, 1978.

57. *Daily Sentinel,* September 6, 1930; Wayne Aspinall interview, January 10, 1978.

58. *Daily Sentinel,* July 15 and 30, 1930, and September 11 and 18, 1930.

59. *Daily Sentinel,* September 19, 1930; Wayne Aspinall interview, January 10, 1978.

60. *Daily Sentinel,* October 24 and 29, 1930.

61. *Daily Sentinel,* November 5, 1930; Leonard, *Trials and Triumphs,* 22.

62. William E. Leuchtenburg, *Franklin D. Roosevelt and the New Deal* (New York: Harper and Row, 1963), 53.

63. Wayne Aspinall interview, January 10, 1978.

64. Alta Noland interview with author, January 24, 1996; Wayne Aspinall interview, January 10, 1978.

65. Richard Lowitt and Maurine Beasley, eds., *One Third of a Nation: Lorena Hickok Reports on the Great Depression* (Urbana: University of Illinois Press, 1981), 280–297; Richard Lowitt, *The New Deal and the West* (Norman: University of Oklahoma Press, 1984), 21–24.

66. Leonard, *Trials and Triumphs,* 50–53, 125; James F. Wickens, *Colorado in the Great Depression* (New York: Garland Publishing, 1979), 146–147.

67. Wayne Aspinall interview, February 15, 1979.

68. Wayne Aspinall interview, February 15, 1979; Wayne Aspinall interview, January 10, 1978; *Denver Post* obituary fragment, undated, ca. 1941, Edward T. Taylor Papers, Mss. 618, Box 1, fd: 55, Colorado State Historical Society, Denver, CO (hereafter cited as CSHS).

69. Robert G. Athearn, *The Mythic West in Twentieth-Century America* (Lawrence: University Press of Kansas, 1986), 97, 201; R. McGreggor Cawley, *Federal Land, Western Anger: The Sagebrush Rebellion and Environmental Politics* (Lawrence: University of Kansas Press, 1993), 72–73. The quotation is from Cawley, 73. One of the first public hearings on setting up a grazing district was held in Grand Junction in September 1934. More than 1,000 sheep ranchers and cattlemen attended the hearing, including Taylor and F. R. Carpenter of Hayden, Colorado, who was chosen by Secretary of the Interior Harold Ickes to administer the new law. Oscar Chapman, assistant secretary of the interior, also attended. It is not known whether Aspinall was present, but it is likely he would have attended.

70. *Denver Post*, May 19, 1935; *Daily Sentinel*, November 22, 1934; *Denver Post* obituary fragment, undated, ca. 1941, Edward T. Taylor Papers, CSHS.

71. Less than two weeks after the November 1936 election, Aspinall was sending dozens of letters to prominent Colorado Democrats, fellow state legislators, and people of influence in a bid to capture the House speakership. See numerous letters in Box 10, fd: "Grand Junction District, Mesa County," Wayne Aspinall Papers, UDA.

72. Wayne N. Aspinall to Sterling Lacy, November 12, 1936, Box 10, fd: "L," Wayne Aspinall Papers, UDA; Teller Ammons to Wayne Aspinall, July 8, 1936, and Wayne Aspinall to Teller Ammons, July 10, 1937, Box 10, fd: "Correspondence, 1937," Wayne Aspinall Papers, UDA; *Rocky Mountain News*, January 6, 1937.

73. Wayne Aspinall to Clifford Stone, January 31, 1938.

74. Wayne Aspinall to Colorado Water Conservation Board, August 7, 1956; Wayne Aspinall to Clifford Stone, August 5, 1937; Clifford Stone to Wayne Aspinall et al., August 3, 1937; and Porter [no last name indicated] to Clifford Stone, July 31, 1937, all in Box 56, no file, Wayne Aspinall Papers, UDA.

75. Ubbelohde, Benson, and Smith, *A Colorado History*, 306–309; Alva A. Swain, "Under the Capitol Dome," column printed in Grand Junction *Daily Sentinel*, n.d., ca. 1937, Box 56, fd: "Waterboard," Wayne Aspinall Papers, UDA. For several decades, Swain reported on Colorado political issues for Colorado newspapers.

76. Daniel Tyler, *The Last Water Hole in the West: The Colorado–Big Thompson Project and the Northern Colorado Water Conservancy District* (Niwot: University Press of Colorado, 1992), 37–80, details Congressman Taylor's opposition to C-BT without Western Slope compensation; Ubbelohde, Benson, and Smith, *A Colorado History*, 306–309; Abbott, Leonard, and McComb, *Colorado: A History of the Centennial State*, 183.

77. *Daily Sentinel*, September 4–8, 1941.

78. One newspaper article listed Judge John B. O'Rourke (Durango), Aspinall, Delaney, former state senator Ollie Bannister (Grand Junction), Hugh V. High (longtime secretary to Congressman Taylor), Dr. W. H. Twining (Aspen), Charles H. Leckenby (Steamboat Springs), and Eugene Bond (Leadville) as possible candidates after Walker's refusal to run. See *Daily Sentinel*, September 18, 1941.

79. Frank Delaney to Ralph White, September 17, 1941, Box 196, fd: 24, Frank Delaney Papers, UCAUCB.

80. *Daily Sentinel*, September 22, 1941.

81. *Daily Sentinel*, October 19, 1941; Wayne Aspinall interview, January 10, 1978.

82. *Daily Sentinel*, November 27, 1941, and December 4 and 10, 1941.

83. Walter Walker to Frank Delaney, December 29, 1941, Box 38, fd: "1306–1941 Campaign," Frank Delaney Papers, UCAUCB; Frank Delaney to Byron Rogers, December 11, 1941, Box 196, fd: "Politics, 1941 Congressional Campaign, R," Frank Delaney Papers, UCAUCB; Frank Delaney to Walter Walker, December 13, 1941, Box 38, fd: "1306–1941 Campaign," Frank Delaney Papers, UCAUCB; Walter Walker to James A. Marsh, December 11, 1941, Box 38, fd: "1306–1941 Campaign," Frank Delaney Papers, UCAUCB; "Statement of Election Expenses," Box 49, fd: "1599, Delaney, Frank, Campaign File," Frank Delaney Papers, UCAUCB. This document revealed that the Delaney campaign spent a total of $3,614.29 during the 1941 special-election campaign.

84. Abbott, Leonard, and McComb, *Colorado: A History of the Centennial State*, 301–303; Ubbelohde, Benson, and Smith, *A Colorado History*, 321–327.

85. For overviews of western Colorado and the uranium industry, see William L. Chenoweth, "Raw Materials Activities of the Manhattan Project on the Colorado Plateau," *Nonrenewable Resources* 6, no. 1 (1997): 33–41; Robert Sullenberger, "100 Years of Uranium Activity in the Four Corners Region," *Journal of the Western Slope* 7, no. 4 (1992): 1–82.

86. *Daily Sentinel*, December 17 and 19, 1941.

87. Kristi Mease, "The Labor Shortage and Its Solution During World War II in the Grand Valley of Western Colorado," *Journal of the Western Slope* 7, no. 3 (1992): 1–5.

88. Hugh High to Walter Walker, June 21, 1941, Box "Aviation II," fd: "Walker Field," Walter Walker Papers, Archives and Special Collections, Mesa State College (hereafter cited as MSC); E. C. Johnson to Charles Donaldson, January 27, 1942, Box "Aviation II," fd: "Walker Field," Walter Walker Papers, MSC. See other letters in this box and file in Walter Walker Papers.

89. Wayne Aspinall interview, January 1978; Wayne Aspinall Autobiographical Mss., 32.

90. Ibid. See miscellaneous correspondence from this period in Box 15, Wayne Aspinall Papers, UDA; Wayne Aspinall to John C. Vivian, n.d., Box 15, no file, Wayne Aspinall Papers, UDA. Mack Aspinall would die in July 1947.

91. At least one Mesa County resident resented Aspinall's enlistment as a captain. Preston Walker, son of Walter Walker and future editor of the *Daily Sentinel*, wrote from his military post in Italy that Aspinall's commission "makes me boil." "Sacrifices, hell, they [Aspinall's type of soldier] don't know the meaning of war. Political gain in time of nation's peril would fit [him] better." See Preston Walker to Walter Walker, June 10, 1944, no box or file number, Al Look Collection, Research Center and Special Library, MWC.

92. Wayne Aspinall Autobiographical Mss., 32–44; Wayne Aspinall interview, January 1978; Wayne Aspinall to Clarence G. Kendeigh, January 22, 1945, Box 16, no file, Wayne Aspinall Papers, UDA.

93. Walter Walker to Preston Walker, August 8, 1944, no box or file number, Al Look Collection, MWC. Rockwell, according to Walker, had no chance of losing the 1944 election, "no matter how strong the man running against him" might be. In 1941, Rockwell beat Delaney by 3,000 votes. In 1942, he increased that margin to 7,000 votes over Betty Pellet. In 1944, Rockwell prevailed by more than 10,000 votes over Garfield County's John Heuschkel despite Walker's strong endorsement of the latter.

94. Wayne Aspinall to Walter Walker, February 1, 1945, Box 16, no file, Wayne Aspinall Papers, UDA.

95. Wayne Aspinall to Walter Walker, February 1, 1945; Walter Walker to Wayne Aspinall, February 27, 1945, Box 11, fd: "W," Wayne Aspinall Papers, UDA; Norris Hundley, Jr., "The West Against Itself: The Colorado River—An Institutional History," in *New Courses for the Colorado River: Major Issues for the Next Century*, ed. Gary D. Weatherford and F. Lee Brown (Albuquerque: University of New Mexico Press, 1986), 25–28.

96. See several letters from 1945 that either hint at or openly discuss Aspinall in connection with the governorship. Edwin Rogers to Wayne Aspinall, August 8, 1945, Box 16, fd: "R," Wayne Aspinall Papers, UDA; Wayne Aspinall to J. K. Groves, March 13, 1945, Box 16, no file, Wayne Aspinall Papers, UDA; Neil Bishop to Wayne Aspinall, August 17, 1945, Box 16, fd: "B," Wayne Aspinall Papers, UDA. Edmunds, *Wayne Aspinall,* contains an entire chapter outlining Aspinall's statehouse ambitions. See pp. 33–38. Even after election to Congress in 1948, Aspinall continued to "cast backward glances at the governor's mansion."

CHAPTER TWO

MR. ASPINALL GOES to WASHINGTON

A RELUCTANT CONGRESSMAN

In 1946, election to Congress seemed a distant possibility for Wayne Aspinall. Instead, the middle-aged state senator seemed content to dream about a run for the governor's mansion, expand his law practice to make it more profitable, and enjoy returning to civilian life after his stint in the armed forces.

It is impossible to imagine a better connected, more experienced local politician than Wayne Aspinall as he prepared for election year 1948. Rumors of Aspinall's gubernatorial ambitions continued to circulate. In 1947, Clifford Houston, former president of Grand Junction's Mesa Junior College and the University of Colorado's dean of students, thanked Aspinall for being a "good and loyal friend of education," to whom all Colorado educators were "indebted deeply" for his work in the legislature. Houston, obviously well acquainted with Aspinall's political aspirations, invited Wayne to visit him in Boulder, adding, "If you are elected Governor, you will have many opportunities to visit . . . I sincerely hope that you will be given that responsibility 'some of these days'."[1]

But Colorado already had a Democratic governor. In 1946, another national Republican tide had engulfed the nation. In unpredictable Colorado, two Democrats pulled major upsets: John A. Carroll unseated Republican Dean Gillespie as Denver-area congressman. In the gubernatorial race, Colorado Supreme Court chief justice Lee Knous became the first Democratic governor since Teller Ammons's 1936 victory, .defeating Leon Lavington (the Republicans had repudiated two-term governor John Vivian).[2]

In 1948, the state chair of the Democratic Party, Denver publisher Gene Cervi, announced his intention to challenge longtime senator "Big Ed" Johnson for his U.S. Senate seat. To make the campaign, Cervi resigned as state chair in March 1948. The Colorado Democratic Party immediately selected Wayne Aspinall to succeed Cervi.[3]

In November 1947, Cervi had written Mesa County Democrats, asking which local Western Slope party members would be the strongest candidates for state and national offices. Former Mesa County chairman Eugene Mast replied that both Senator Johnson and Governor Knous could count on strong Western Slope support. "I would also expect . . . that Wayne Aspinall can go to the State Senate for as long as he desires." Venturing into the realm of speculation, Mast confirmed what many local Democrats thought: "Wayne is the one man in my district who could defeat [Robert F.] Rockwell for Congressman." Mast quickly added that unfortunately Aspinall had no such ambition, but if he did, he would be a "natural" candidate for Congress in 1948.[4]

At the end of 1947, party chair Cervi spoke of a "genuine boom" pushing Aspinall to challenge for the congressional seat. By early 1948, Aspinall's was the name mentioned as the only Western Slope Democrat capable of a serious challenge to the incumbent Rockwell. This time, Aspinall appeared to have full party backing, though he was far from certain that he wanted to challenge a strong, well-funded candidate like Rockwell. Aspinall continued to dream of the governor's mansion and probably would have been satisfied with the lieutenant governor's post. World War II and Aspinall's deep involvement in state and local affairs had altered his aspirations. As he admitted in a letter to Ed Johnson, "my personal ambitions have subsided somewhat during the past few years."[5]

By late February 1948, Aspinall and first-term congressman John Carroll exchanged correspondence discussing angles from which Rockwell might be vulnerable, including the incumbent's reputation for not working hard on routine constituent issues.[6] Carroll encouraged Aspinall's possible House bid but also cautioned him because Truman's 1948 election prospects and the "national scene look very dark at this time." The president's problems, Carroll lectured, would have an effect on any Democratic candidate for Congress.[7]

The Democratic Senate seat battle between Big Ed Johnson and Gene Cervi also threatened to disrupt any Colorado Democrat's 1948 chances. Cervi represented the party's new liberal element, whereas Johnson continued to champion the more moderate and independent temperament of many Coloradans. When Cervi announced his challenge to the two-term senator, Aspinall flew to Big Ed's defense, offering his assistance. Johnson had always had an independent voice, almost a prerequisite for aspiring Colorado Democrats in a largely Republican state. Johnson, in turn, appreciated Aspinall's support and endorsed his yet unannounced bid for Congress. "I know you would make a great Congressman and become a leader overnight," Johnson told Aspinall. Still, Johnson, like Carroll, sounded a note of caution to the prospective candidate. Rockwell

would be tough to defeat. But, echoing Eugene Mast's November 1947 assessment of Aspinall's chances, he added, "you are the only man in Colorado who
can come close." Never one to mince words, Big Ed estimated Aspinall's chances
at less than 50 percent, largely because of the Western Slope's traditional Republican orientation.[8]

As late as March 1948, Aspinall denied any interest in the congressional
seat, sounding a now familiar refrain: "I have always had my eyes on the Governorship," he told Johnson. Yet his colleagues—among them Governor Lee Knous—
continued urging him to join the House race. Political encouragement also
arrived from more unexpected sources. Former Republican governor John C.
Vivian congratulated Aspinall on being named chair of the state Democratic
Party but expressed his bewilderment at how Aspinall could act as such and
consider a run for Congress at the same time. Vivian reflected the thinking of
many Republicans in saying that Aspinall's selection as party chair would give
the Republicans "honest opposition." Aspinall had earned a reputation among
the state's Republican leadership for his forthright manner.[9]

Despite overwhelming encouragement, Aspinall continued to straddle the
fence. Colorado's Democratic national committeewoman, Marguerite Peyton
Thompson, expressed fear that because he had taken the state party chairship,
Aspinall would refuse to run for Congress. Thompson reported that Fourth
Congressional District labor interests were lining up behind the only announced
candidate, railroad conductor Tom Matthews, the party's unsuccessful 1946 congressional candidate. In an almost blasé manner, Aspinall declared to Thompson that as long as labor seemed to favor Matthews, "I feel I can serve the
[Democratic Party's] program in other capacities." Clearly playing coy, Aspinall
waited, sifting through his many options. Despite professions of reluctance,
Aspinall clearly was enjoying himself. His political stock had never been higher,
and being courted by the party for several possible political positions was an
exhilarating experience. As he told a former World War I associate in April
1948, "I grow peaches and practice law and have one hell of a big time playing
politics."[10]

Following July's Democratic National Convention, Aspinall's political whirlwind gained momentum. On July 17, neighboring Delta County's Democratic
assembly resolved to ask Aspinall to make the race against Rockwell. Meeting
just prior to the state Democratic convention over which Aspinall would pre-
side, the Fourth Congressional Assembly awarded him its nomination to challenge Rockwell, who had announced his intention to seek another term on July
10. The Fourth Congressional Assembly had had to choose between Aspinall,
who had overwhelming support, and Tom Matthews. A loyal party man, Matthews
had motioned that Aspinall's nomination be made unanimous.

With no primary-election opposition, Aspinall immediately started, in the
Daily Sentinel's words, to "turn his guns" on Rockwell.[11] Both Aspinall and Presi-

dent Truman faced uphill battles during the fall of 1948. In many ways, Aspinall's and Truman's fates would be tied together. Yet both candidates had more resources at their disposal than were readily apparent. Aspinall had been studying Rockwell's record for months, rehearsing possible campaign themes to close associates. What he had discovered was that Rockwell was vulnerable on several issues important to Western Slope voters.

A veteran Colorado politician, Robert F. Rockwell was finishing his third full term as a member of Congress in the fall of 1948. He had, of course, won the special election in 1941 to succeed Edward Taylor. Prior to that, Rockwell had served in both houses of the Colorado state legislature and as lieutenant governor from 1923 to 1924. Twice the Paonia, Colorado, rancher had failed in bids for the governorship. Rockwell sought and failed to obtain his party's nomination in 1924; in 1930 he became the Republicans' last-minute nominee, only to be trounced by popular Democratic governor "Billy" Adams. Returning to politics with the Republican resurgence of the late 1930s, Rockwell won election to the state senate in 1938 and 1940. Rockwell and Aspinall served together on the Senate Committee on Education and Educational Institutions.[12]

As a U.S. Representative from 1941 to 1948, Rockwell chose committees linked closely to the economic activities of the Fourth Congressional District: Public Lands, Mines and Mining, and Irrigation and Reclamation. Still, Rockwell maintained close business ties with his family's New York roots, serving as board chair of the Tuttle and Rockwell Company until his death in 1950.[13] A wealthy man, Rockwell had the financial resources to run a long and expensive campaign, a possibility Aspinall both anticipated and feared. "I am of the opinion that Rockwell and his group will use five times as much money as I possibly can get together," Aspinall confided to an associate.[14]

To curtail campaign expenses, Aspinall ran the campaign from his law offices in the First National Bank building in downtown Grand Junction. In fact, he ran it himself, electing not to hire a formal campaign manager. Aspinall and his former legal secretary, Alta Leach, oversaw the campaign, with Leach as its only paid employee. With a campaign war chest of between $3,000 and $4,000 ($2,500 of it contributed by the candidate himself), Aspinall began his run for Congress.[15]

Wayne Aspinall's campaign strategy was one he would follow for most of his elections until the late 1960s—mount a short, intensive, personal campaign entailing appearances in all twenty-four of the huge rural counties in his district. In 1948, Aspinall visited the small towns of western Colorado, where he would walk the streets, shake hands, and distribute literature. The day's campaigning usually ended with Aspinall giving an address to a gathering of local Democrats. Meanwhile, from the Grand Junction office, secretary Leach would arrange campaign advertisements and answer correspondence.[16]

Two events shed light on Aspinall's campaign methods while also illustrating his integrity. Purchasing several hundred signs with the Kilroy character proclaiming "Aspinall was here," Aspinall tacked them up everywhere he traveled during the fall of 1948. Near the end of the campaign, Aspinall was in Artiseia (now Dinosaur), a small hamlet in the northwest corner of the state. After being introduced around town by a local Democrat, Aspinall noticed one of his "Kilroy" signs on the screened porch of a small bungalow. Aspinall asked his guide for the name of the "good Democrat" who lived there. The surprising answer: a young lady who practiced "the oldest of professions." Aspinall let the sign stand and later recalled that he never lost the Artiseia precinct.[17] While campaigning in the high-mountain mining town of Leadville, Aspinall was escorted by a former Democratic state senator. After spending the afternoon among the town's merchants, church officials, and local elite, they spent the evening on the lower side of town, a much different environment that included Leadville's red-light district. The former state senator offered Aspinall a lesson in practical politics: "Wayne, get acquainted with these voters—their vote counts just as much as anyone else's." Not judging society's downtrodden would pay rich political dividends. As Aspinall remembered, he "learned quickly and well" during his first congressional campaign.[18]

Though he faced an uphill battle against an incumbent blessed with unlimited financial resources, Aspinall discovered that his strong name recognition and energetic personal approach to campaigning gave him a chance to unseat Rockwell. More importantly, Aspinall had uncovered several issues that resonated with Fourth Congressional District voters in 1948.

As a member of the House Interior Committee's Subcommittee on Public Lands, Rockwell had participated in a series of controversial hearings on grazing in the national forests. The 1947 hearings, chaired by Congressman Frank Barrett (R-WY), developed into a forum for criticizing federal control of the West's natural resource–based economy. Western-born journalist and historian Bernard DeVoto argued that national forests, contrary to Barrett and Rockwell's findings, "have been dangerously overgrazed."[19] DeVoto charged that Barrett and Rockwell arranged for witnesses hostile to the National Forest Service to appear at a hearing in Grand Junction.[20]

The subcommittee's merciless pummeling of National Forest Service bureaucrats did not escape notice by members of Colorado's press corps. The *Denver Post* termed the subcommittee hearings Barrett's "Wild West show." Grand Junction's *Daily Sentinel* took a dim view of Barrett and Rockwell's antics by arguing that Grand Junction's long-term interest in a reliable water supply would be better served by a well-managed federal watershed. In both his "Easy Chair" column and other writings, DeVoto called Barrett's "Wild West show" an old-fashioned western landgrab, a move by western economic interests in the cattle and mining industries to transfer federal lands to state and private interests.

Ironically, in his later life, Aspinall would participate in another movement by western states to gain more control over the federal landlord: the Sagebrush Rebellion of the late 1970s and 1980s.

Aspinall and the Democratic Party also benefited from the Eightieth Congress's parsimonious reputation. Aspinall consistently exploited the Republican-driven budget cuts, especially those affecting the operations of the Bureau of Reclamation. By 1948, plans for Upper Colorado River development were being generated by local politicians, representatives of the regional business community, and Bureau of Reclamation planners. Water development was, in one historian's words, "perhaps the most important" campaign issue for western politicians seeking national offices in 1948.[21]

It was in 1948 that the Upper Colorado River Commission finally agreed to a state-by-state division of the Upper Basin states' 7.5 million-acre-foot share of the Colorado River's annual flow. Under the final terms of the Upper Colorado River Basin Compact, Colorado, which contributed 70 percent of the Upper Basin's total water supply, received 51.75 percent, Utah 23 percent, Wyoming 14 percent, and New Mexico 11.25 percent.[22] For several decades, the thinly populated Upper Basin states had not felt compelled to organize and divide their share of the river. But the events of the 1940s changed everything. The complacent frame of mind that had gripped the Upper Basin states disappeared with the economic boom inspired by World War II. Upper Basin states, now certain that they needed to put the river to work for them, feared both California's explosive growth and its earlier success at laying claim to Colorado River water.[23]

Ratified in 1949, the Upper Colorado River Basin Compact demonstrated that the growing intermountain states were finally ready to proceed with large-scale reclamation planning. During the 1948 election, the Republican-controlled Eightieth Congress suffered under a steady barrage of criticism from the West for trimming the Bureau of Reclamation's budget. Aspinall reaped the political benefits of Republican fiscal stinginess, blaming both Rockwell and the congressman's party for policies that Aspinall believed compromised the future of the West.

The controversial budget cuts were implemented in 1947 when the House of Representatives slashed many Interior Department programs, including those of the Bureau of Reclamation. *The New Republic* reported that congressional budget cuts would destroy key water projects or critically prolong the completion of projects currently under way, including Colorado–Big Thompson, already delayed by World War II. The budget cuts were linked by *The New Republic* with Republican plans to privatize western land, power, and resources.[24] Republican attacks against the U.S. Grazing Service and National Forest Service were "all part of this campaign" against federal administration of the nation's natural resources.

Aspinall and other Democrats quickly seized upon Republican privatization efforts as an exploitable issue. As *The New Republic* concluded, "development of the West depends on government capital. Private capital has not been, and will not be able to finance such colossal projects" as the Bureau of Reclamation was planning. Aspinall, Truman, and the Democrats, with strong New Deal credentials supporting federal control and management of western resources, emerged as champions of an enlarged federal presence in the regional economy during the 1948 campaign.[25]

The Aspinall and Truman campaigns joined forces briefly in September 1948 during the president's now legendary Whistle Stop journey across the country. With Dewey favored to capture the White House, Truman ran a spirited and energetic campaign, traveling 22,000 miles, delivering more than 275 prepared speeches, and offering up countless more "off the record" comments along the railroad lines wherever the presidential railroad car, the Ferdinand Magellan, took him.[26] Ignoring dire predictions of impending political doom from both pundits and pollsters, Truman took the case for his election directly to the American people. Throughout Colorado and the West, President Truman charged the Republican Party with being the instrument to "skim the cream from our own natural resources to satisfy their own greed."[27] Taking a cue from his party leader, Wayne Aspinall also conducted a vigorous campaign, long on speeches and handshakes and short on the generalizations and feel-good bromides of Dewey and Rockwell.[28]

Truman arrived in Colorado on September 20, relentlessly attacking Dewey and the Republican Eightieth Congress. Aspinall traveled east to Denver, joining Truman's campaign train after the president spoke to a large crowd near the state capitol. Soon, the Ferdinand Magellan headed west from Denver and over the Continental Divide.[29]

The following morning, Truman and Aspinall rolled into Grand Junction at 9:05. Speaking from the back of the Ferdinand Magellan, stopped near Grand Junction's Denver and Rio Grande railroad station, Truman was introduced by old acquaintance Walter Walker to a roaring crowd estimated at 8,000 people. Truman gave a rousing speech, leaving little doubt that he and the Democrats were closely attuned to western issues. The federal government, Truman promised, could cause the development of the West to proceed much faster. Warming to his audience's concerns, Truman noted that "reclamation, irrigation and power . . . these are the life blood of the West," claiming that the Eightieth Congress had attempted to sabotage the region's future by cutting or delaying reclamation projects. "You got your reclamation projects cut down," Truman thundered. "You got your power projects . . . wiped out. Every appropriation that affects the West was slashed, and it was slashed with malice!"[30] As the Ferdinand Magellan rolled west toward Utah, Aspinall later remembered thinking, "Old boy, you've got a chance, but that poor devil [Truman] doesn't have a chance in the world."[31]

Truman's visit energized the Democratic campaign in western Colorado. Aspinall began a month of vigorous campaigning, quickly gathering the endorsement of Walter Walker's *Daily Sentinel,* which claimed that the people of the Fourth Congressional District, "Colorado and all the West," had been searching for a "worthy successor" to Edward T. Taylor since his death in 1941. Wayne Aspinall, proclaimed the *Sentinel,* "possesses the qualifications demanded in a real successor to Ed Taylor." Without castigating Rockwell by name, the newspaper nevertheless indicted him by predicting that Aspinall's loyalties "would not be divided between outside interests and his constituency." The newspaper was alluding to the wealthy Rockwell's far-flung business interests.[32]

Both Aspinall and Rockwell campaigned throughout the mountainous Fourth Congressional District in October. Rockwell told an incredulous group of Grand Junction Rotarians that Colorado and the Upper Colorado River Basin had nothing to fear from California's many well-publicized attempts to grab additional Colorado River water.[33] About a week later, the *Daily Sentinel* printed an article proclaiming that California's "fight to secure more Colorado River water" had not been stymied by cool assurances to the contrary from either Rockwell or Republican vice presidential candidate Earl Warren, who had recently appeared in Grand Junction. The *Daily Sentinel* blamed Rockwell for allowing the Bureau of Reclamation's development fund to be slashed.[34]

In the week prior to the election, the Rockwell campaign suffered several additional blows, including allegations of hypocrisy for hiring additional campaign staff at federal expense while touting governmental economy on the campaign trail. Noted national columnist Drew Pearson first broke the news of Rockwell's action, but the *Daily Sentinel* wasted little time in recording local citizens' dismay that Rockwell would add to his payrolls while favoring elimination of some 800 Bureau of Reclamation jobs."[35] On October 26, Pearson labeled Rockwell "one of the wealthiest" men in Colorado and someone "who has voted consistently against all progressive measures," listing him second on a list of western members of Congress "who don't deserve to be re-elected."[36]

Editor Walker reminded his readers that Rockwell's meager accomplishments paled when measured against the legendary record of former Democratic congressman Edward Taylor. Wayne Aspinall, Walker predicted, would place "Western Colorado interests above partisan politics or the decisions of party caucuses." Wayne Aspinall, Walker claimed, was a worthy successor to Taylor's lofty mantle.[37] Aspinall had made a strong effort to associate himself with his political idol, calling himself in a late October 1948 advertisement "a second Edward Taylor."[38] Two days before the election, both political parties predicted a close race, but the *Daily Sentinel* noted that "Democrats are hopefully happy over the vigorous campaign Aspinall is making. Many Republicans are worried about Rockwell."[39]

On November 2, 1948, Colorado and Western Slope voters went to the polls and stunned the nation by helping to elect Harry S. Truman to his first full presidential term. Fourth Congressional District voters not only opted for Truman, they also desired a change in congressional representation. At the age of fifty-two, Wayne N. Aspinall won the election, unseating Robert F. Rockwell. The official tally gave Aspinall 34,695 votes to Rockwell's 32,206.[40] In the ultimate insult to Rockwell, Aspinall even managed to defeat the incumbent in his home territory of Delta County. A proud Aspinall wrote to an old World War I buddy several days later that he was now busy preparing to move to Washington after Christmas. "It was a great campaign," Aspinall crowed, "and I had the pleasure of ousting an old reactionary who apparently thought he was in for good."[41]

There was some truth in Aspinall's boastful remark. Rockwell had seemed increasingly out of touch with the average person in the Fourth Congressional District. His aristocratic social background made it easy for Aspinall, Walker, and others to style the congressman as unable to relate to the needs of his constituents. A tireless campaigner, Aspinall had visited every county in the huge Fourth Congressional District, articulating a clear message to potential voters. In speech after speech, Aspinall hammered Rockwell over cuts to the federal reclamation budget, Rockwell's advocacy of private power, and the congressman's supporting role in Wyoming representative Frank Barrett's controversial 1947 "Wild West" show.

Aspinall also benefited from Truman's energetic campaign. Voters enthusiastically responded to the president's incessant attacks on the "do-nothing" Eightieth Congress. The deep Republican tax cuts, which catered to the interests of the wealthy, also seemed to pose a threat to continued federal management of natural resources in the American West. It was the Republicans of the Eightieth Congress who were holding back reclamation progress in the West, Truman had told large whistle-stop crowds. "At heart," the president had exclaimed, the Republicans "had no real interest in the West—not in water, not in public power."[42]

Aspinall always credited Truman for his election to Congress: "I was elected largely because Truman ran for the Presidency." Truman decisively carried the Fourth Congressional District and polled a thousand more votes than Aspinall.[43] More than fifty Republican House members met Rockwell's fate on election day; the Democrats also regained control of the U.S. Senate. The national election was, in one Truman biographer's words, "an affirmation of Roosevelt's New Deal, plus whatever additions Truman had brought to it."[44]

"In politics, timing is everything." This tired maxim would be repeated by Aspinall at many different points during his long career. Aspinall had learned political timing through his own hardening experiences. Wanting to run for the Colorado General Assembly in 1926, he was counseled by Western Slope Democratic power broker Walter Walker to wait. Desperately seeking the seat formerly held by his political idol Edward Taylor in 1941, he failed to obtain the backing of key Democratic supporters. Desiring to run for Colorado's governorship, he lost opportunities through a Republican resurgence during World War II and the sterling performance of a strong candidate (Lee Knous) in 1946 and 1948. Finally, in 1948, when he appeared to seek higher office least, it sought him. At age fifty-two, when most men had already realized their career ambitions, the country lawyer from Palisade was embarking on a new career in Washington, D.C.

ENTERING CONGRESS IN THE RAYBURN ERA

With the long-distance move to Washington, D.C., rapidly approaching, Wayne Aspinall had little time to reflect on his victory, though he later admitted to not believing he had had a good shot at unseating Rockwell.[45] The new congressman, wife Julia, and longtime secretary Alta Leach began frenzied preparations. After the Christmas holiday, Julia and Wayne left by automobile for the nation's capital. Taking the oath of office on January 3, 1949, Aspinall moved into his new quarters on the third floor of the Old House Office Building. Nearby offices were occupied by future president Gerald Ford and Texas Democrat Lloyd Bentsen. Across from Aspinall was the office of second-term Democratic congressman John F. Kennedy of Massachusetts.[46] Aspinall and Kennedy became friends, often walking to the House of Representatives together. Aspinall recalled that he immediately liked young Kennedy, though they had little in common legislatively. Still, both had served their nation in World War II, and as members of the same party with proximate offices, they always seemed comfortable in each other's presence, despite vast differences in age and social background.[47]

Despite the fresh voices that had joined it in 1946 (among them Kennedy and Richard Nixon), the Congress that Wayne Aspinall joined in 1949 was an archaic institution little resembling what the American public knows today. It was a place of extraordinary decorum, with strict rules, strongly influenced by an institutional commitment to tradition. With the Democrats back in control of both houses, Aspinall's early congressional tutelage would be at the hands of one of the most notable and long-serving Speakers in the history of the House of Representatives, Sam Rayburn of Texas.

First elected Speaker in 1940, Rayburn was famous for his grave, poker-faced expression, which hid an absolute devotion to the traditions of the lower house, traditions he relied upon in guiding House business and the behavior of its members. Representatives always dressed in suits; Aspinall remembered that one elderly senator even retained the custom of wearing a frock coat.[48] A lonely bachelor, "Mr. Sam," as he was affectionately called by those closest to him, controlled Congress down to its most minute details. Brief and direct even in conversations with the many presidents he served under, Rayburn usually con-

Wayne Norviel Aspinall (D-CO), member of Congress, 1949–1973. Courtesy, UCAUCB.

cluded any conversation or phone call in two or three minutes. Impatient with those less efficient than he, he would scold political associates who were late for scheduled meetings.[49]

House members routinely sought Rayburn's advice, and the Speaker eagerly mentored the newcomers. Rayburn urged freshman members to carry their weight, do their committee work, and strive to get along with their colleagues. Most found Rayburn's stock advice useful and illuminating, but a few found it "condescending and stifling." One House member later remarked that Rayburn merely sought blind obedience from new members and hoped to convince congressional neophytes to support his leadership. As an uncompromising advocate of party loyalty, Mr. Sam gave a famous piece of advice to members of Congress: "To get along, you go along."[50] In other words, earn your colleagues' respect, work hard, honor House traditions, and bide your time. Rayburn was a firm believer in all aspects of the congressional seniority system. His career, spanning almost fifty years (1913-1961), embodied order, tradition, and seniority, leadership qualities Wayne Aspinall would take to heart. As Aspinall later remembered, under Rayburn everything "fit into position. There was no waste of time." Mr. Sam would always epitomize effective congressional leadership in Aspinall's eyes.[51]

Few members of the Eighty-first Congress absorbed Rayburn's teachings more thoroughly. Already schooled in the art of political timing, Aspinall understood the importance of tradition and seniority. Many years of service as minority and majority leader in both houses of the Colorado General Assembly had prepared him to be patient with his early assignments. His first few years were spent studying Congress, learning its rules and procedures, and developing a reputation as a thorough and conscientious legislator. Unlike modern members of Congress, Aspinall rarely returned to his district after the start of a congressional session. "Legislators who come back home every week or so [cannot] keep up with their responsibilities," Aspinall later recalled.[52] Associating quickly with other Colorado Democrats like Big Ed Johnson and John Carroll, Aspinall also respected the knowledge of veteran Colorado Republican senator Eugene Milliken.[53]

Aspinall wasted little time in placing himself advantageously, both personally and on behalf of his Fourth District constituents. Believing he had been sent to Washington in part to advocate for Western Slope water rights, he quickly sought a position on the House Interior and Insular Affairs Committee, hoping one day to chair it. The committee's oversight of western issues such as reclamation, mining, Native American affairs, and national parks made it especially attractive to the first-term congressman. Though not as prestigious as an assignment to Appropriations, Rules, or Ways and Means, a position here allowed western representatives to serve "a high proportion" of their districts' special interests from a single committee. Where many congressional committees sought balance in their geographical composition, the Interior and Insular Affairs Committee was a traditional bastion for western members. In the Eighty-sixth Congress, for example, seventeen of nineteen Democratic members were from states west of the Mississippi River, as were six of twelve Republicans.[54] Despite being offered a position on the powerful Ways and Means Committee at the start of the Eighty-second Congress in 1951, Aspinall elected to remain on Interior and Insular Affairs. From this position, he would be well placed to influence legislation vital to Colorado and the West.[55]

Though he was new to Congress, Aspinall's first terms were not devoid of accomplishment. He immediately joined with other western representatives to ratify the Upper Colorado River Basin Compact, negotiated between 1946 and 1948. The compact's ratification by the Eighty-first Congress signified the Upper Basin's readiness to commence large-scale federal reclamation projects. Legislation that would come to be known as the Colorado River Storage Project (or CRSP) would soon be introduced.[56]

During the compact ratification hearings, Aspinall, a member of the House Subcommittee on Public Lands, maintained a low profile but at one point argued that the point of the Upper Colorado River Compact was to ensure orderly development of Upper Basin water, thereby increasing chances of delivering a reliable water supply to the Lower Basin states. Aspinall also gave his colleagues a taste of his strong proprietary interest in Colorado's Western Slope water supply by reminding his colleagues that he represented the congressional district where "sixty-five percent of the water of the Colorado River arises."[57]

When some of his water-user constituents expressed concern over impending reclamation payments owed to the federal government, Aspinall introduced and shepherded a bill through the Eighty-first Congress to amend the repayment contract, extending the deadline for the Uncompahgre Project in western Colorado. Western Slope residents, who had criticized Rockwell and the Republicans for inaction and favoring private-sector interests on reclamation issues, knew from the start that Aspinall heard their voices loud and clear.[58]

ASPINALL AND THE WEST'S POSTWAR POLITICAL CULTURE

By the early 1950s, Aspinall had established a reputation as an effective national legislator. In 1950, Aspinall easily defeated his Republican opponent to win reelection by more than 9,000 votes, beating him in all but two of the Fourth Congressional District's twenty-four counties. Already climbing the seniority ladder, Aspinall was moving into a position on the House Interior and Insular Affairs Committee to be of real service in promoting the interests of his constituents.

World War II had altered the face of the American West, inaugurating a series of revolutionary changes in Colorado while setting in motion a set of issues that would define the state's politics for the next generation. As recently as 1934, writer and westerner Bernard DeVoto had referred to the region as a "plundered province," a place controlled by eastern capital to the detriment of its still sparse population.[59] By 1946, the enhanced presence of the federal government, a legacy of the Great Depression and World War II eras, set the agenda for the generation ahead.

In the early 1940s, "an incredible burst of wartime economic activity" transformed the West.[60] Nearly eight million people migrated across the Mississippi in the 1940s alone, more than half of them heading to the Pacific Coast states. Three of the nine fastest-growing states between 1940 and 1943 lay in the West.[61] Colorado mirrored these demographic trends; its population doubled between 1940 and 1970, and the percentage of Coloradans living in cities rose from 53 to 79. The beginnings of the Front Range urban corridor, extending south from Fort Collins through Boulder and Denver to Colorado Springs, may be traced to this World War II–inspired population boom. Although much of the rural Western Slope lost population in the 1940s, the Grand Junction area began an era of steady growth. Federal activity, including the frenzied search for uranium, brought 2,000 additional people to Grand Junction, swelling its population to more than 14,000 in 1950.[62]

The abundance of federal land, the region's huge open spaces, and the arid climate made the West an ideal setting for defense installations and military posts. Close cooperation between the federal government and the defense industries would continue during the Cold War era ahead; government-sponsored scientific research focused on atomic energy, weapons testing, and electronics.[63] The West's vast empty spaces and desolation had been transformed into assets for a federal government seeking safe locations for its military operations. As historian Gerald D. Nash noted, the West's undeveloped prewar economy proved an advantage during wartime, allowing "unlimited opportunities for experimentation" in both the nuclear-energy and aerospace industries. Aluminum production, plane construction, shipbuilding, and construction-company expansion provided the framework for the region's Cold War economy.[64]

Increasingly, the postwar West would be a metropolitan region, dominated by the incessant demands of a burgeoning urban population.[65] But as the region's economy boomed, political leaders began asking a nervous question: did the region have enough water to meet the population's urban, industrial, and agricultural needs? A finite—and dwindling—water supply cast a pall over the World War II era's boom-born optimism. Increased water storage would emerge as the top priority for political action. Only with additional water control and storage would the growing population's domestic and industrial demands be met.

The war proved, in historian Mark Harvey's words, to be "the catalyst for the Bureau of Reclamation's planning," especially for the Upper Colorado River Basin states. Long neglected, these states had claimed half of the river's annual flow through the 1922 Colorado River Compact. Prior to the war years, however, there was little regional need to proceed with large-scale reclamation projects.[66]

The war and its accompanying frenzy changed that perception quickly. Working closely with Bureau of Reclamation planners, politicians from Colorado, New Mexico, Utah, and Wyoming began agitating for the construction of reclamation projects that would benefit the Upper Colorado River Basin. This was necessary, they argued, to ensure the region's economic future.[67] Almost every western politician and citizen in 1946 strongly supported the Bureau of Reclamation's dreams to harness as much water as possible. Ironically, the apparent political unanimity supporting this vision of progress began eroding in the 1950s and would be challenged in the 1960s by a new conservation and environmental movement that stressed the necessity of taking into account environmental quality before making decisions about public lands. However, these battles remained in the future. In the dizzying atmosphere of the postwar West, Wayne Aspinall hoped to continue helping the Western Slope realize a vision of unending economic growth. In many ways, the issues generated by the 1930s and 1940s set a legislative agenda for Aspinall's long career in Congress.

In the post–World War II era, the federal government became the new engine for development. The West became, in Michael Malone and Richard Etulain's words, "the most citified of American regions" and, with its fast-growing population, a cultural and population trendsetter in the postwar years.[68] In 1947, one in nine Americans lived in the seventeen westernmost states; by 1980, near the end of Wayne Aspinall's life, that number was one in five. As writer Carey McWilliams told his *Harper's Magazine* readers in 1949, the wartime decade had shifted America's center of gravity west. The decade's great population gains, the frenzied level of federal activity relating to World War II and the Cold War, and the urban booms were but some of the most obvious indicators "that the nation's interest and wealth" had tipped west.[69]

So it was only natural that Aspinall, the offspring of western pioneers, would choose the path that promised to lead his state and region toward a vibrant economic future, away from domination by forces beholden to eastern capital. Reliance on the federal government as the engine of development seemed a far safer course, though in time the federal landlord would also engender the wrath of Aspinall and many other westerners.

Aspinall's Fourth Congressional District had a history of voting for the man, not the party. Nevertheless, one political trend in Colorado and the West was clear: the Republican Party was gaining dominance. In 1952, Aspinall only narrowly won re-election; Eisenhower's strong coattails almost swept the congressman's Republican opponent, Howard Schults, into office. Any Democrat hoping to remain in office in conservative western Colorado had to portray himself or herself as largely independent of national party expectations. Aspinall learned this lesson early in his career. Although he usually paid allegiance to Democratic Party standards on most issues, where his district, state, and region were concerned, he voted to take care "of the best interests of . . . my own area." Aspinall recalled that he was at least as friendly to the new Republican president as "many of those Republicans who were elected with him." After the close call of 1952 (a twenty-eight-vote victory), Aspinall deliberately courted the

Republicans of his district during the general election. "I was considered by the majority of my constituents as first a public servant and then a partisan." Aspinall's willingness to maintain an independent stance that reflected the interests of his district provides one explanation for his political longevity.[70]

Staying elected became an Aspinall tradition after 1952. He made Grand Junction, the largest city in western Colorado, the base of his Fourth Congressional District operations. In the post–World War II era, Grand Junction emerged as a major federal outpost for management of key defense-related raw materials. From 1943 to 1946, the federal government's top-secret Manhattan Project acquired land south of the city's downtown to build a uranium refinery. The materials mined on the Colorado Plateau and refined in the Grand Junction and other area mills provided fuel for the first atomic bombs. In the tense Cold War atmosphere of the late 1940s and 1950s, uranium again provided the impetus for a major population boom in the Grand Junction region. In 1951, the Climax Uranium Company began milling operations in Grand Junction and would continue production until 1970.[71] In 1950, Grand Junction proudly embraced the title of "America's Atomic City." By the late 1960s, when *Look* magazine labeled it "America's Most Radioactive City," many citizens and politicians on the Western Slope were forced to rethink their warm and unthinking embrace of the nuclear industry. But in the 1950s, mining and economic progress continued to go hand in hand.

Grand Junction also grew into the regional transportation center in part because it was the largest city between Denver and Salt Lake City. Like much of the American West, the city boomed in the 1940s, growing from a population of 12,479 in 1940 to 14,454 in 1950.[72] By 1960, the city's population had reached more than 18,000—almost a 30 percent increase in ten years.

Walter Walker's newspaper, the *Daily Sentinel*, was a strong friend and supporter of Wayne Aspinall. In his final years now (he would die in 1956),[73] "Senator" Walker could gaze proudly upon his political protégé as Aspinall climbed the congressional ladder to become one of the West's leading voices for economic growth and progress.

Like much of small-town America in the 1950s, Grand Junction and surrounding towns were insular, with unreliable air service, few media options, and no interstate highways, isolated by some of the most dangerous roads and highest mountain passes in North America. A tranquil place, the Western Slope was hospitable to Wayne Aspinall's political philosophy; he closely reflected the opinions and political concerns of most of his constituents at the time. While the anti-communist witch hunt of Joseph McCarthy grabbed the lion's share of national media attention, most small-town Americans remained concerned about issues rooted in their communities—their jobs, quality of life, and economic prospects. The Great Depression and World War II were the formative experiences for Americans coming of age in the 1950s. Both events taught them austerity, self-reliance, and discipline; most believed in finding economic security and conforming to social norms.[74] Despite undercurrents of discontent in the nation, including increasing concerns about poverty, civil rights agitation, and worry over impending environmental doom, most 1950s Americans voiced great confidence in our political system's ability to solve the problems of the age. Eighty-five percent of all Americans in the late 1950s viewed government positively, and almost the same percentage believed government was a positive force in their daily lives. It was a wonderful time to be a politician; a strong consensus ruled U.S. politics, one that the congressional leadership of Sam Rayburn and the political style of Wayne Aspinall accurately reflected.[75]

Aspinall represented an enormous district. But for most of his congressional career, he could easily discern what his constituents believed: the land and water that dissected it existed to be utilized for human benefit.[76] Though Aspinall admired the mountain vistas that defined the skylines of his district, he never doubted that the land's natural resources should serve the needs of the people. The American West, to Aspinall, was a vast storehouse of raw materials. During his years in Congress, he would repeatedly attempt to open up the region's public lands to use—for the benefit of the nation, and, of course, the individuals who lived and worked in the region. To Aspinall, conservation meant careful husbandry, not protection of resources. He regarded himself as a mainstream conservationist, espousing the wise use of those resources as articulated by the Progressive Era exponent of utilitarian conservation, Gifford Pinchot.[77]

This pre-ecological worldview embraced by Aspinall and other western politicians of the era was only natural to a generation that had struggled to build a productive civilization in the stingy, arid West. Aspinall's father had moved west to seek the American Dream—opportunity and economic security. He had found it in Palisade, Colorado. Wayne Aspinall and others who grew up in the late frontier era envisioned a vibrant future for their region if they continued to explore its resources with an eye to continuing economic development. Aspinall and others of his generation would have great faith in scientific and technological solutions to the nation's problems. In terms of the postwar American West, this translated into a belief that the region's chronic water shortages could be solved by an ever growing number of dams, or what journalist Philip Fradkin termed "structural solutions for the region's aridity." Any politician of the era who failed to consistently advocate economic growth by any means could look forward to a short career.[78]

The pre-ecological worldview of the era seemed, at the time, unassailable. Who could have predicated that it would come under such vigorous attack by the environmental revolution of the 1960s? Unfortunately, it is that environmental paradigm's very success that has caused Americans to forget how dominant the pre-ecological worldview was. To Aspinall and his generation, it was a politician's sacred duty to embrace a vision of progress. Growth seemed absolutely necessary to the political leaders of the young western states. Because Aspinall regarded himself as a mainstream conservationist, he regarded the new breed of environmentalists as dangerous radicals who directly threatened the quality of life in his congressional district. Only by advocating economic growth could the newer western states achieve a "more equitable status with older, more established" states of the East. As Peter Iverson analyzed Arizonan Barry Goldwater's worldview, Goldwater and other politicians "cherished growth for its own sake, for it appeared to nourish the kind of fledgling urbanism necessary for a state to be taken at least somewhat seriously."[79]

Not only did Aspinall embrace a philosophy that glorified continuous economic growth, he also believed that scientific knowledge could only improve life in the West. Whether that meant constructing new dams or using new technological findings to better access uranium or oil shale, Aspinall's generation took scientific and engineering expertise as articles of faith. A firm believer in social progress, Aspinall had watched the Grand Valley grow from a small, distant, sagebrush-strewn outpost of Anglo-American civilization to a bustling, modern chain of towns with a collective population of more than 60,000. He knew, based upon personal experience, that the lessons learned in his *McGuffey's Reader* were true: progress was possible. Hard labor, long hours of study, and backbreaking work not only made for a better person, but when undertaken by society as a whole, a better world. This Protestant creed was the key to Aspinall's steady rise in the politics of the American West, but it would also offer insights into his ultimate political demise and marginalization by a new generation of Americans coming of age in the 1960s and 1970s.

WATER POLITICS, 1950s STYLE

The Grand Valley, with an average annual precipitation of only eight inches, is one of the nation's largest desert-climate agricultural and urban settlements. Wayne Aspinall understood the Colorado River's importance; his family had derived an agricultural livelihood from its waters. Aspinall viewed water users as his primary constituents, people like his father whose lives were transformed by the ability to command precious irrigation waters. It should therefore come as no surprise that as a member of Congress, Wayne Aspinall's most notable impact would be in the field of federal reclamation. Aspinall always maintained he was sent to Congress in part to ensure a reliable and enduring water supply for his congressional district, state, and region. Aspinall would become, arguably, the most significant water politician in the immediate postwar American West.

Historian Donald Worster considers Aspinall part of the "water establishment," the small group of influential politicians, government bureaucrats, and private entrepreneurs who helped transform the West into the "hydraulic society" it has become. To Worster, the water establishment included city water departments like the Denver Water Board and southern California's Metropolitan Water District. Working in concert with the Bureau of Reclamation, the Army Corps of Engineers, and other federal agencies, influential politicians like Aspinall smoothed the political path for an elite few who dominated the region and benefited most from the control and manipulation of water. To Worster, it was this water elite that committed the region to "endless economic development," with little concern for the region's fragile environmental limits.[80]

Aspinall's first major reclamation success came during his second term in office when he convinced Congress to authorize the Collbran Project. Achieving authorization while the nation was preoccupied with the Korean War demonstrated astonishing political skill for a second-term member of the House and presaged an active career in congressional water politics.

The project was named for the small Colorado town of Collbran, located near the 11,000-foot-high Grand Mesa. Local farmers and ranchers had long desired a large reservoir to supply irrigation water to the region's high mountain valleys. But the prohibitive costs and the area's relatively sparse population meant the project would never be authorized unless additional beneficiaries could be pinpointed. As plans for the project unfolded, the Grand Valley, home to the growing "Atomic Capital" of Grand Junction, was targeted as a potential recipient. "The normal growth of [the] Grand Valley will soon increase the demand for water beyond the physical capacity of existing works," a Bureau of Reclamation report pointed out in 1949. Local farmers and ranchers needed more reliable and potable sources of water. As late as the 1940s, rural residents of Mesa County were hauling often badly contaminated water from irrigation ditches for home consumption. In addition, the Collbran Project might supply needed power and help develop deposits of uranium, coal, and oil-bearing shales. The Grand Junction *Daily Sentinel*, ever the watchdog of Western Slope interests, argued that gaining approval for the Collbran Project "serves notice that we are preparing to use more and more Western Slope water," an imperative move "if we are to secure our water rights" against actions by the Lower Colorado River states or the growing Colorado Front Range corridor.[81]

The Bureau of Reclamation had been studying the Collbran Project since 1937; by the mid-1940s, the City of Grand Junction had asked the Bureau of Reclamation to include its projected water needs as part of the project. The Bureau was pleased to expand Collbran's scope to include municipal as well as more traditional irrigation needs.[82] When the Bureau of Reclamation finalized its plans for the Collbran Project in 1949, it was also at work on a larger Colorado River Basin project, soon to be known as the CRSP (Colorado River Storage Project). The question soon became, should Collbran be enacted as a stand-alone project, or should it be included as part of the larger, basinwide CRSP development plan?

At the start of his second congressional term in 1951, Aspinall addressed a letter to Bureau of Reclamation commissioner Michael Straus asking his assistance in drafting a bill proposing Collbran as a self-contained project. Aspinall reminded Strauss that Collbran was perhaps "the only project remaining on the Colorado River that will be able to stand on its own feet." Anticipated hydroelectric sales, payments from agricultural users, and revenues from Grand Junction, which would need Collbran water for its municipal water supply, made the project a financially sound one. Aspinall predicted a dire future for Grand Junction if no additional sources of domestic water were found. Aspinall noted that Grand Junction's growth was not a temporary phenomenon, nor was it tied directly to the Korean War effort. Consequently, the project would be needed for both domestic and industrial purposes "in the very near future." Because of Grand Junction's immediate water needs, Aspinall and Senators Ed Johnson and Eugene Milliken did not want the bill linked with the larger, more cumbersome, and ultimately more controversial CRSP.[83]

Aspinall introduced H.R. 2813 on February 22, 1951. That fall, the House Interior and Insular Affairs Committee reported the bill favorably. In a March 1952 letter to Adolph Sabath, chair of the House Rules Committee, Aspinall argued that the project's primary purpose was to furnish water for Grand Junction, "the hub of the uranium and vanadium producing area of the nation." If Grand Junction was unable to enlarge its domestic water facilities, Aspinall warned, it would "cause a serious handicap in the production of these most critical minerals." Speaking on the House floor in May 1952, Aspinall linked Grand Junction clearly to the nation's atomic future. "In effect," he argued, "the Grand Valley is an oasis in the desert supplying the badly needed living facilities for the surrounding uranium mining industry." Though he mentioned the importance of the project to farmers and ranchers near the town of Collbran, the Cold War needs of Korean War America provided the clinching argument for Aspinall's presentation. A short time later, Aspinall had achieved his first major legislative success in the field that he would soon dominate—federal reclamation policy. Congress approved the Collbran Project on July 3, 1952.[84]

The Collbran experience helped familiarize Aspinall with the maze of reclamation politics; it also taught him the importance of presenting a united front and understanding the goals of all parties involved when advocating a water project before Congress. This lesson became dramatically clear when the City of Grand Junction suddenly opted out of the Collbran Project in 1954, two years after its approval by Congress, when a better solution to its municipal water problems presented itself. Grand Junction's decision could have threatened the entire project and damaged Aspinall's credibility as a water legislator. However, Aspinall acted quickly to modify and scale back the project so that it still met with the approval of both the commissioner of the Bureau of Reclamation and the secretary of the interior.[85]

ECHO PARK and CRSP

If gaining authorization for the Collbran Project during a wartime economy demonstrated Aspinall's budding skill as a water politician, his role in the authorization of the controversial Colorado River Storage Project announced his arrival as a major player.

During the heat of battle over Collbran, Aspinall, perhaps inadvertently, revealed his developing philosophy of western American reclamation politics. Colorado, he told Assistant Secretary of the Interior Fred Aandahl, had adhered "as closely to the private enterprise theory of development as . . . any part of the Union." However, because of its unique historical and natural circumstances, the state and region needed and would continue to need "further help in the future." Colorado had given its abundance of furs, grazing lands, minerals, and other natural resources without "receiving a commensurate value in return." The Collbran Project and other reclamation enterprises would not only balance the ledger between the western states and the federal government but enable the West to contribute more economic activity "to the national welfare."[86] Of course, the gigantic Colorado River Storage Project would bring the West into an even stronger economic relationship with the rest of the nation.

World War II and the Cold War ushered in a new era of prosperity and population growth in the American West. The Colorado River Storage Project was the Bureau of Reclamation's safeguard to ensure ample water and economic development. The huge river development program had been in the planning stages for more than a decade but had been delayed by both World War II and the Upper River Basin's hesitancy to divide its half of the river. By 1950, the Bureau of Reclamation's development blueprint was ready. *The Colorado River Storage Project: Project Planning Report* presented an expensive $1.5 billion price tag for a network of six high dams and seventeen subsidiary or participating projects. The CRSP would help ensure the sparsely populated Upper River Basin's economic future while guaranteeing ample irrigation water, flood control, and recreational development.[87] Already controversial, the project was threatened by two potential roadblocks: outrage over its enormous cost and, more ominously, a developing alliance of conservationists who feared the project would damage the integrity of the national park system.[88]

The project, however, had little to fear from the residents of Colorado's Western Slope and the Upper River Basin region. Deeming it "vital," George Sanford Holmes, the Grand Junction *Daily Sentinel*'s Washington correspondent, claimed the project would enable western Colorado to finally achieve industrial and agricultural expansion "despite efforts by California and eastern Colorado to snatch our water." Without the plan, Holmes speculated, the sparsely populated Upper Basin would remain "largely an exploited colonial wilderness." In 1952, that same reporter pronounced Congressman

Wayne Aspinall's work on early drafts of the Colorado River Project legislation "considerable."[89]

The first great conservation battle of the post–World War II era (and there would be many) began brewing in 1949 when the National Park Service and the Bureau of Reclamation clashed over two CRSP dams planned for Dinosaur National Monument in northwestern Colorado and northeastern Utah. Wayne Aspinall would play a central role as the controversy escalated, and not only because the proposed Echo Park Dam was located in his congressional district. Initially, Aspinall strongly advocated the construction of two dams. As the conflict progressed and Aspinall's influence grew, he would become a voice for compromise. The Echo Park struggle hastened Aspinall's transformation into one of the West's most influential reclamation politicians.

The story of the Echo Park controversy and its role in the developing environmental movement has been well told elsewhere. However, Wayne Aspinall and Colorado's Western Slope perspective receive little emphasis in most of these studies.[90] In 1950, residents of the Upper Basin were pleased when Secretary of the Interior Oscar Chapman, a Coloradan, approved dams at Echo Park and Split Mountain in Dinosaur National Monument. Chapman gave the go-ahead only a few days after President Truman had ordered troops into Korea.[91] Before an actual CRSP bill could be drafted, however, supporters and critics of the Dinosaur dams began mobilizing. Prominent conservationists like Horace Albright, Bernard DeVoto, and Arthur Carhart condemned the secretary of the interior's decision, while newspapers like Walter Walker's Grand Junction *Daily Sentinel* applauded it as "wise." By approving the dams, the *Sentinel* argued, Chapman had prevented the "radical conservationist wing" from hindering the development of natural resources that would benefit humankind.[92]

Early on, opponents of the Echo Park Dam discovered their most cogent and persuasive argument: constructing a dam in a national monument would repeat the early twentieth-century Hetch Hetchy controversy, wherein John Muir and the Sierra Club failed to prevent construction of a dam in Yosemite National Park. The sanctity of national park lands remained a key argument by dam opponents throughout the controversy. Beginning in late 1950, 78 national and 236 state conservation organizations began the fight to save Dinosaur from a fate like the Hetch Hetchy Valley's. Led by the Sierra Club's David Brower and The Wilderness Society's Howard Zahniser, conservation organizations pooled their resources, authorizing money for direct mailings and a massive propaganda campaign. Well-known writer and historian Bernard DeVoto, a Utah native, helped bring the campaign to a national audience through his *Harper's Magazine* columns and other publications. His article "Shall We Let Them Ruin Our National Parks?," published in a July 1950 issue of the *Saturday Evening Post*, connected the magnificent natural scenery and the monument's mission. The steep canyons that provided the "pulse-stirring" wild river ride for

John Wesley Powell's historic journey "would become a mere millpond." If the dam were built, "Dinosaur National Monument as a scenic spectacle would cease to exist."[93] There is little doubt that DeVoto's articles transformed the Echo Park controversy into a national issue.

With the Korean War finally over, the nation could turn toward pressing domestic issues, including western reclamation. After almost a year in office, the Eisenhower administration, through its mouthpiece, Secretary of the Interior Douglas McKay, recommended a $1 billion CRSP. However, few people on either side of the issue were pleased by McKay's recommendations. Many in Colorado, including Senator Ed Johnson, reacted with outrage to McKay's plan because it eviscerated the works planned for Colorado and the Upper Basin. Left out of the interior secretary's proposal were Split Mountain Dam and many of the smaller participating projects, including the Curecanti Reservoir near Gunnison, Colorado, in the heart of Wayne Aspinall's congressional district. Aspinall later agreed with Johnson that more local participating projects were needed to complement the large reservoirs—among them, Echo Park and Glen Canyon—still retained in the plan. In particular, Aspinall worried that Denver's proposed Blue River Diversion Project would come at the expense of Western Slope projects such as Curecanti. In 1953, Aspinall concluded that the immediate picture did not look "too propitious for Western Slope development."[94]

The Sierra Club and its vigorous leader, David Brower, saw McKay's plan, which still included Echo Park Dam, as posing the "gravest threat to the national park system since its creation in 1916." A Sierra Club press release noted that a summer 1953 raft trip through Echo Park had only strengthened the club's resolve to fight against the dam. By the end of 1953, the CRSP plan had become a lightning rod for competing visions of the West.[95]

In early 1954, controversy over CRSP erupted as committees in both houses of Congress held hearings over several legislative versions, including one introduced by Wayne Aspinall, that would have authorized the construction of dams in Dinosaur National Monument. The first major House hearing took place before the Subcommittee on Irrigation and Reclamation of the House Interior Committee. Chaired by William Henry Harrison (R-WY), the subcommittee held explosive hearings throughout January 1954. Although the Upper Colorado River Basin project supporters hoped for quick and positive action, few expected a smooth path to legislative success. In 1953, Aspinall had confided to prominent water attorney Frank Delaney of Glenwood Springs, Colorado, that he did not expect any favorable consideration of the CRSP program during the Eighty-third Congress, which still had more than a year to run before the 1954 elections.[96]

Dam supporters and opponents each had a chance to testify before the House Irrigation and Reclamation Subcommittee. Aspinall, William Dawson (R-UT), and Senator Frank Barrett (R-WY) all made cases that the Upper Basin states had contributed heavily to the Bureau of Reclamation's funding over the years through public-land sales. Aspinall challenged California Democratic congressman Clair Engle's assertion that building huge dams for Upper Basin irrigation water was an ill-advised measure as the nation faced huge agricultural surpluses. This would become a constant refrain for dam opponents throughout the controversy. Aspinall argued that under the Colorado River Compact of 1922, the water of the Colorado could be put to whatever use the affected states decided. If it were not, "most of the water that is now being used consumptively would be allowed to flow down to southern California and Arizona and be put to consumptive use down there."[97]

Aspinall also did battle with attorney Glen Saunders of the Denver Board of Water Commissioners. Denver, too, had high expectations for the CRSP, hoping to divert more Western Slope water from the Blue River to the Front Range. In his testimony, Saunders observed that Denver's rapid growth needs could only be met with additional water supplies. The city, he asserted, "would be totally unable to continue to exist without transmountain water." In words that must have chilled Aspinall and others from the Western Slope, Saunders observed that "approximately half of our water just has to come from the Western Slope of Colorado . . . without it we could not live."[98]

Aspinall made it clear that he would not support any Denver or Front Range water aspirations unless his political mentor Edward Taylor's position was honored: acre-foot for acre-foot compensatory storage for the Western Slope. Aspinall maintained this stance during his questioning of Saunders. Saunders argued that Colorado–Big Thompson's compensatory storage provision was not a binding contract. Aspinall countered that the 1937 agreement was meant to serve as the future "criterion for the determination of transmountain diversion in Colorado." From this exchange, it seemed clear that Aspinall's goal of increasing Western Slope water storage capacity might be threatened not only by Lower Basin states but by other Colorado interests as well.[99]

The climax to the 1954 House subcommittee hearings occurred when a series of Echo Park Dam opponents took the stand. David Brower, executive director of the Sierra Club, challenged the Bureau of Reclamation's estimates on evaporation rates. Echo Park's theoretically low rate of evaporation had been one of the proposed dam's strongest features. Historian Mark Harvey calls Brower's appearance before the House subcommittee "a famous episode in the annals of American environmental history, taking on almost legendary proportions." After all, how could Brower, a man with no technical background, take on the Bureau's technical experts and discredit them? During the second day of Brower's testimony, Aspinall challenged his credentials on complicated engineering and mathematical matters, implying that Brower, a layman, was not qualified to dispute Bureau of Reclamation experts. Brower's ready response was the modest claim that he was "just a man who has gone through ninth grade and learned his arithmetic." Brower proceeded to rework the Bureau of Reclamation's own figures and expose a serious miscalculation in evaporation rates. Brower not only demonstrated the fallibility of the Bureau of Reclamation's professional engineers, he also argued that other possible dam sites were preferable to Echo Park in terms of water loss through evaporation.[100]

In the question-and-answer period following Brower's testimony, Aspinall revealed as much about his own wilderness philosophy as Brower. First, Aspinall chided Brower and other environmentalists for their recent "discovery" of Dinosaur National Monument. Aspinall called it a "very beautiful" place but added that it had "no corner on" spectacular scenery. Aspinall proceeded to fire off a list of places in his congressional district that, by implication, he believed were equal to Dinosaur in beauty. Had Mr. Brower, Aspinall wondered, been to Black Canyon, Gore Canyon, Glenwood Canyon, Maroon Bells, Crystal Canyon, Hells Gate, or Hesperus Canyon? Under such direct questioning, Brower could admit to only having seen a small portion of Colorado. He had visited Gore and Glenwood Canyons and the Maroon Bells. Aspinall seized upon this point to argue that local citizens, familiar with the economic potential of the region, should have the principal say in land-use decisions. Out-of-state visitors such as Brower or the occasional river runner did not know "the desires and longings of the people of the area" and merely wanted to use the area as a place "to go . . . play."[101]

Aspinall and other Echo Park Dam supporters remained unmoved throughout the testimony of Brower, Wilderness Society executive secretary Howard Zahniser, Joseph Penfold of the Izaak Walton League, and Charles Callison of the National Wildlife Federation. Aspinall's hopes had been bolstered by the relative absence of constituent mail against the Echo Park Dam, though most members of Congress reported that constituent mail was running 80–1 against the dam. The towns and cities of the Upper Colorado River Basin continued to support the CRSP proposal and Echo Park Dam.[102]

The strong presentations by Brower and others began eroding the public's perception that the Bureau of Reclamation was somehow infallible. Even Interior Secretary Douglas McKay, a great friend of western economic development, scolded the Bureau of Reclamation's commissioner for his "inexcusable negligence." Still, in June the House Interior Committee approved the CRSP, with Echo Park, by a one-vote margin. A short series of Senate hearings ended with its own Interior Committee endorsing the bill 11–1. The conservationists, however, had gained some ground after the hearings, and with off-year congressional elections looming in November 1954, the CRSP proposal remained stalemated until the end of the year.[103] The bill had become entangled in the House Rules Committee, and there was no time to consider it in the waning days of the Eighty-third Congress.[104] The struggle would resume with the swearing-in of a new Congress in 1955.

Both sides were busy courting public opinion while pursuing their legislative goals. The conservationists in particular threw their publicity mechanisms into high gear. Countless articles and pamphlets were written both for and against the Echo Park Dam. Notable publisher Alfred A. Knopf commissioned a handsomely illustrated book, *This Is Dinosaur,* edited by influential western author Wallace Stegner, and sent a copy to every member of Congress in the spring of 1955. Stegner had also written a brilliant analysis of the Echo Park–Dinosaur situation for *The New Republic* in 1954. In "Battle for the Wilderness," Stegner argued that the destruction of Echo Park could lead to further incursions into the national park system—a bad precedent. Similarly, the Sierra Club compared the impending flooding of Dinosaur National Monument with the earlier inundation of Yosemite's Hetch Hetchy Valley. In the pamphlet "Hetch Hetchy—Once Is Too Often," the Sierra Club compared the two valleys and underscored the need to learn a lesson from the earlier, disastrous destruction of wilderness.[105]

With the Democrats back in power after the 1954 elections, Wayne Aspinall's meteoric rise continued. Clair Engle (D-CA) assumed the chair of the House Interior and Insular Affairs Committee, and Aspinall took the leadership of the House Subcommittee on Irrigation and Reclamation, the body that would consider any House drafts of CRSP legislation.[106]

By February 1955, several CRSP bills had been introduced in both houses of Congress, all of them retaining the Echo Park Dam. In March and April, Aspinall's subcommittee held its hearings on the CRSP bills, but with less rancor than in 1954. The same major conservation-group witnesses testified, as did a stronger contingent of Lower Basin CRSP foes. Most of these witnesses hailed from California and feared that Upper Basin reclamation development would impair delivery of water to the Lower Basin states, either in quantity or quality. Howard Zahniser of The Wilderness Society foreshadowed the conservation coalition's new tactics by professing support for the CRSP as long as it dropped the Echo Park Dam, protected Rainbow Bridge National Monument from a reservoir behind any dam at Glen Canyon, and ensured that no part of the CRSP would negatively impact any existing parcel of the national park system. In laying out these conditions while still professing support for the overall CRSP idea, Zahniser offered to CRSP supporters an olive branch containing the seeds of compromise.[107]

Aspinall's support for the Echo Park Dam seemed to soften after the 1955 House hearings. Horace M. Albright, a former director of the National Park Service and one of the nation's leading conservationists, had sent Aspinall a copy of Stegner's *This Is Dinosaur.* Aspinall wrote to thank Albright and noted that the witnesses who had appeared before his subcommittee that year on behalf of the integrity of Dinosaur National Monument "did a magnificent job." However, he did not have similar praise for the southern California interests who, in his opinion, seemed to be "using" a number of the conservationists who were sincerely opposed to Echo Park. In another letter, Aspinall served notice that he intended to continue to "press for the development of the latent riches of the Upper Colorado River Basin" rather than see it become little more than a "playground for people from our crowded cities." In other words, Aspinall still hoped that in its executive sessions, the House Interior Committee would report a CRSP that would facilitate Upper Colorado River Basin development, regardless of the status of Echo Park.[108]

Echo Park remained a thorny problem for Aspinall and other dam support-ers. The nation's conservationists had successfully mobilized national opinion against the dam as an intrusion into the sanctity of the national park system. Aspinall was beginning to realize that he and other CRSP supporters might need to cede some ground in the political struggle ahead. But if Aspinall had to surrender Echo Park, he would do so only reluctantly. In a letter to Congress-man John Dingell (D-MI), who had asked for information on the CRSP, Aspinall took the opportunity to summarize his philosophy of reclamation. "The West-ern part of the nation is arid and semi-arid and only a few spots receive enough rainfall during the growing season to support crops," he lectured. It was recla-mation that "makes the desert bloom." As for Echo Park, Aspinall argued that the CRSP would enhance, not detract from, wilderness values and would "do more to open up this wilderness area for recreation and enjoyment" than if the land were left in its natural state. Candidly, Aspinall told the Michigan con-gressman that Echo Park might well have to be "sacrificed on the altar of oppo-sition" in order to get the remainder of the CRSP.[109]

CRSP supporters from western Colorado continued urging Aspinall to fight on. The Craig, Colorado, Chamber of Commerce urged him to hold out for a CRSP that included Echo Park. Making a veiled political threat, a Craig con-stituent asked Aspinall to do a better job of being "our voice," adding, "It does seem a shame that tax-payers must keep reminding representatives of their du-ties and moral obligations." Aspinall's exasperated response shows that he was learning a valuable political lesson. The power "arrayed against the Colorado project" was tremendous. In the House, Aspinall wrote, "we have nine votes from the Upper Basin; California has 30 votes and of these some 23 are in complete opposition." By late July 1955, Aspinall had to admit that the CRSP bill with Echo Park included had no chance of passing the House that year, something he had been hinting at to constituents since May.[110]

Several key House Committee votes confirmed Aspinall's prognosis for the Echo Park Dam. Though the Senate had passed the bill with the Echo Park Dam included in April 1955, the dam faced a much tougher road in the House, which became the focus of an intense anti-dam publicity barrage by conserva-tion organizations.[111] In early June, anti-dam congressman John Saylor (R-PA) introduced an amendment to eliminate the Echo Park Dam, which the subcommittee voted down. Meanwhile, Aspinall and other Upper Basin reclamation supporters admitted the time had arrived to reassess their support of Echo Park Dam; salvaging most of the CRSP would be preferable to losing the entire project. Working behind the scenes, they revealed their first attempt at a compromise on June 8, 1955. Meeting just two days after Saylor's original amendment had been rejected, the committee voted 15-9 to delete the controversial dam from the bill. To appease infuriated Upper Basin constituents, Aspinall's price for striking the dam was to introduce an amendment calling for a board of engineers to re-examine all alternative dam sites and compare their quality to that of Echo Park. The engineers would report to the president by the end of 1958.[112]

With Aspinall's legislation propelling matters, the House Subcommittee on Irrigation and Reclamation approved the bill, sending it to the full House Interior Committee. On June 14, the Interior Committee approved a CRSP that included a number of major dams: Glen Canyon, Flaming Gorge, Curecanti, and Navajo on the San Juan River. Eleven participating projects, far fewer than in the Senate's version, were proposed, pending feasibility studies. Echo Park, of course, was left out, but Aspinall's amendment for the engineering study remained.[113]

The network of conservationists who had opposed the Echo Park Dam continued to criticize House Interior Committee drafts of the CRSP, fearing that the hated dam's removal was only temporary and committee or conference committee machinations could easily reinstate it. On June 28, the House Interior Committee deleted Aspinall's dam-reconnaissance amendment by a vote of 20-6, removing the Echo Park Dam completely from CRSP legislation. When rumors flew that Echo Park Dam might again be resurrected, House Interior chairman Clair Engle (D-CA) and Aspinall publicly pledged to work against any attempt to bring it back to legislative life. This announcement, on July 20, undermined any remaining hopes for an Echo Park Dam. Engle's support of CRSP was significant because California generally opposed the Upper Colorado River Basin project. Engle had aspirations for other California water projects and hoped to avoid the specter of a politically divided West every time a California water project came before Congress for authorization. Aspinall and Engle knew that a CRSP without Echo Park stood a better chance of passage.[114]

Anti-CRSP mail continued pouring into congressional offices. The American public and, indeed, many members of Congress had failed to differentiate between a bill that included the Echo Park Dam and one that did not. CRSP supporters took polls tracking potential votes in the House of Representatives. The results revealed that in July 1955 the bill did not have a reasonable chance of passage. In this atmosphere, House Speaker Sam Rayburn decided to pull the CRSP legislation and reconsider it in 1956, hopefully in a less emotionally charged atmosphere.[115]

The decision to delay CRSP consideration led to widespread Upper Basin criticism and the search for political scapegoats. Many CRSP supporters blamed some sinister combination of California and conservationist interests; others laid the blame much closer to home. Placed on the defensive by committing to a CRSP without Echo Park and acquiescing to the bill's delay, Aspinall found himself in the position of having to reaffirm his Upper Basin political credentials. Even before the bill's delay, Aspinall had expressed doubts about the decisions his subcommittee and the House had been forced to make with regard to the CRSP. Writing to Frank Delaney, Aspinall confessed that he felt the way "a midwife would feel if she knew that she was about to help with the birth of a being with questioned intelligence. In other words, I can't stop the birth and I doubt if I can add materially to the value of what is to be born."[116]

The most stinging rebukes came from Western Slope reclamation supporters. As Aspinall explained to a concerned James Cinnamon of the *Delta* (Colorado) *Independent*, he had always supported the Echo Park unit. Only when the CRSP with Echo Park included stood no chance of being reported out of committee did he forsake it. Still, Aspinall maintained that a storage and power reservoir at Echo Park "would bring more values to the Upper Basin than the retention of the area in its present condition." In an article reporting the "no Echo Park" pledge made by Aspinall and Engle before the House Rules Committee, Maury Teague, editor of the *Montrose* (Colorado) *Daily Press*, attacked the Palisade congressman with the headline "Aspinall on Record—Congressmen Blast Echo Park in Upper Colorado Project." A worried Aspinall attempted to explain his anti–Echo Park pledge. Echo Park Dam, Aspinall stated in a letter to Teague, would not be approved by the current House membership. Lest he appear to waver from Upper Basin reclamation orthodoxy, however, Aspinall reiterated his remark to Delta's James Cinnamon that the Upper Basin would still benefit more from a dam at Echo Park than otherwise. Clearly, his attempts at salvaging some sort of CRSP bill showed Aspinall the potential for political trouble in his reflexively pro-reclamation district.[117]

After Congress recessed at the end of 1955, Wayne Aspinall went home to prepare his constituents for a pared-down version of the CRSP—one without the Echo Park unit. In several public meetings, Aspinall defended himself from criticisms that he had abandoned the Echo Park Dam. Speaking before the Upper Colorado River Commission, which had lobbied incessantly for a large-scale version of the CRSP, Aspinall urged that body to take a more realistic stance. If a fully inclusive CRSP bill were to be brought before Congress, Aspinall predicted disaster because conservationists had the votes to defeat it. In that case, the Upper Basin's reclamation dreams would be "set back ten years." The Senate version, which still retained Echo Park, had "no more chance of passing in the House than we have [of] taking a trip by rocket this afternoon to the moon," Aspinall predicted. Though he favored the House bill, he still believed it needed reshaping to make it more equitable for all the Upper Basin states and easier on the wallets of the nation's taxpayers.[118]

Aspinall's plea for a scaled-down CRSP met with approval among most Fourth Congressional District audiences. Somewhat surprised by the sudden deletion of Echo Park from the House bill in the summer of 1955, by late fall, most CRSP supporters favored some version of the bill over no bill at all—essentially the stark political options Aspinall presented to his constituents during his fall district tour.[119]

Still, further compromise was needed if the bill was to be salvaged. The conservationists hoped to reverse the verdict of Hetch Hetchy, elevate their cause to a principle, and hopefully prove to critics that they were not mere tools of southern California's water interests. At the same time, the politicians of the Upper Basin needed to pass a water project to satisfy increasingly nervous constituents who were beginning to blame Aspinall and others for failing to pass a bill. In late 1955 and early 1956, Howard Zahniser of The Wilderness Society worked unceasingly at trying to insert a proviso into the CRSP that would protect the sanctity of the park system from future reclamation projects. Conservationists also insisted upon a second provision protecting Rainbow Bridge National Monument from the huge reservoir that would be created by the proposed Glen Canyon Dam. After another round of negotiations on Capitol Hill, Zahniser gained assurances from Upper Basin leaders like Aspinall and William Dawson of Utah that they would support the provisos in return for the cessation of conservation-organization opposition to the CRSP. At long last, the way seemed clear to passage.

Against his better judgment, even David Brower and the Sierra Club acceded to the agreements. Brower's consent was crucial to continuing CRSP negotiations because he had been slowly changing his mind about the entire Upper Basin reclamation program, especially the environmental implications of the Glen Canyon Dam. By late 1955, Brower had expressed an interest in broadening the conservation coalition's opposition from Echo Park to the entire storage project. However, the Sierra Club's board of directors instructed him to withdraw his opposition to the overall project after the two conservation provisos were agreed to.[120] The Sierra Club's board of directors and many other conservation leaders believed that the guarantee of "national park sanctity" represented the campaign's original goal. As historian Mark Harvey assessed the situation, "wilderness and park protection could be made compatible with the growth of the American West."[121]

On January 26, 1956, in his capacity as chair of the House Irrigation and Reclamation Subcommittee, Wayne Aspinall and Utah congressman William Dawson reported to Howard Zahniser that Echo Park had been officially eliminated from the CRSP and the new draft of the bill included the two conservation provisions. Aspinall and Dawson concluded their letter by asking conservation leaders to withdraw their opposition to the CRSP as a whole. Zahniser responded that "you most certainly do have this assurance" and reiterated his personal support of CRSP without Echo Park and with the two provisos. Zahniser thanked Aspinall for the "statesmanlike way in which you have dealt with our representations," noting that as chairman of the subcommittee, the Coloradan held a position requiring him to see both the national and regional interests involved in the CRSP.[122]

The insertion of the conservation provisos prompted a wave of congressional support. On March 2, 1956, the House voted 256-136 in favor of the Colorado River Storage Project. A week later, a House-Senate conference committee ironed out differences between the House and Senate versions of the bill, paving the way for its final passage on March 28. On April 11, 1956, President Eisenhower signed the Colorado River Storage Project into law, ending five years of legislative wrangling.[123]

What had this experience meant to Wayne Aspinall? Perhaps most importantly, he learned that the Upper Colorado River Basin lacked political strength. Future reclamation legislation would need to be carefully constructed with supporting alliances in mind. One way to partially address this situation was to secure influential committee chairships. In future committee assignments, Aspinall would view his role as a defender of not only Western Slope interests, but those of the entire Upper Colorado River Basin. Aspinall also learned that controversial legislation sometimes took years to craft into palatable and therefore successful form. The protracted CRSP controversy reinforced for Aspinall, already a patient man, the importance of persistence and compromise. Finally, he came to realize that not everyone in the American West shared his utilitarian perspective on land use. The CRSP battles announced the arrival of a new political force in natural resource legislation—the conservation movement, "reborn as environmentalism."[124]

The Colorado River Storage Project proved a galvanizing episode for both conservationists and advocates of western reclamation and development. Upper Basin political and economic leaders emerged from the fray with a renewed determination to claim their share of the river's water. Future battles over reclamation and public-land use would be fought with a rancor reminiscent of the most tense moments in the Echo Park struggle. For conservationists, the Echo Park affair proved that realistic and unified organizations with the strength to mobilize public opinion could fight and win major political struggles.[125] However, more hard-line environmental advocates like David Brower felt that the CRSP controversy revealed the inadequacies of compromise solutions to the environmental problems facing the nation. Brower later came to believe that his failure to continue his opposition to CRSP represented one of the great mistakes of his long career: "I should have flown home immediately" after receiving the Sierra Club's orders to withdraw objections to the CRSP, in hopes of persuading the board of directors to lean the other way. With the construction of the Glen Canyon Dam, one of the four major structures authorized by the Colorado River Storage Project, "some of the finest scenic resources on earth" were inundated and destroyed.[126]

For Wayne Aspinall, the entire Colorado River Storage Project provided practical lessons in committee politics, lessons he would soon apply, first as de facto and then as permanent chair of the House Interior and Insular Affairs Committee. His work on the CRSP earned him high marks for fairness from both Echo Park Dam friends and foes. By the end of 1956, he had been elected to Congress for the fifth time, and his influence over the nation's water and natural-resource policies appeared stronger than ever. But Wayne Aspinall's political star had only started to rise.

BECOMING MR. CHAIR

In 1957, Congressman Clair Engle (D-CA), chair of the House Interior and Insular Affairs Committee, decided to seek the Senate seat being vacated by Republican William Knowland. With the start of the Eighty-fifth Congress in January 1957, Wayne Aspinall had become the majority member second highest in seniority on the House Interior Committee. From the start of the congressional session, Chairman Engle was either in California tending to his political future or attending meetings of the prestigious House Appropriations Committee. Engle trusted Aspinall implicitly, and the two men worked closely with each other.[127] When Engle was absent, Aspinall assumed the acting chairship of the House Interior Committee and helped lead the committee through an eventful session.

During the Eighty-fourth Congress (1955–1956), the Interior Committee had dealt with some of the most controversial reclamation issues of the post–World War II era, but passing the Colorado River Storage Project would rank as its greatest accomplishment. Other significant matters, however, remained to be dealt with: establishment of the Outdoor Recreation Resources Review Commission, statehood for Alaska and Hawaii, and, closer to Aspinall's home, evaluation of the Fryingpan-Arkansas Reclamation Project. In addition, large sums of money needed to be allocated for CRSP projects; the Interior Committee would need to make a strong case for every hard-won appropriation.

Aspinall was a sponsor and floor manager for legislation creating the Outdoor Recreation Resources Review Commission (ORRRC), which would assess the nation's recreational needs and set the stage for many additional pieces of Interior Committee legislation, most notably the Wilderness Act of 1964. The ORRRC, signed into law on June 28, 1958, had a September 1961 deadline for completion of its investigation and final report. The ORRRC could conceivably impact the form every important piece of natural-resource legislation might take.[128]

A consistent supporter of statehood for Alaska and Hawaii, Aspinall spoke out both in committee and from the House floor in favor of measures that would soon bear fruit. In 1958, Interior Committee chair Clair Engle appointed Aspinall to handle H.R. 7999, instructing him "to provide for the admission of the State of Alaska" to the Union. Aspinall successfully engineered the bill's passage through the House.[129]

When the Eighty-sixth Congress was seated in January 1959, the Interior and Insular Affairs Committee, with Aspinall as its official chair, faced its first important item of business: Hawaii's admission into the Union. Hopes for Hawaiian statehood had languished in Congress for several years, stifled by southern members' fears of admitting a state with a nonwhite majority. On February 12, Aspinall requested a rule for the Hawaii statehood bill from Howard Smith (D-VA), chair of the House Rules Committee, noting that "this is probably the most important piece of legislation that will be considered by the Committee on Interior and Insular Affairs this Congress." On March 11, 1959, Aspinall urged his committee to attend that afternoon's scheduled floor consideration of the Hawaii statehood bill. The bill passed Congress the next day. Several months later, John Burns, the congressional delegate from Hawaii, told Aspinall's Interior Committee that its members, more than anyone else, were "responsible for the very expeditious passage of statehood legislation."[130]

During his tenure as acting chair of the House Interior Committee, Aspinall sounded themes that would later become his trademark. Appearing before the House Appropriations Committee on May 12, 1958, Aspinall proposed a long-range reclamation program designed, in part, to fund many features of the Colorado River Storage Project. Aspinall asked for a commitment of $300 million annually over an eight-year period, believing that amount was required to "meet a real need . . . for a consistent rate of construction of reclamation projects if we are to obtain maximum benefit from our expenditures." In his testimony, Aspinall called for eight new reclamation starts, a significant request in light of the Eisenhower administration's well-known policy against new starts. The Appropriations Committee responded favorably to Aspinall's appeal, approving money for seven chosen by Aspinall, plus two additional projects. Aspinall's belief in the timely construction of CRSP-authorized projects led to accusations within Colorado that he was a less-than-fervent supporter of the Fryingpan-Arkansas Reclamation Project, which would transfer Western Slope water to southwestern Colorado. Fryingpan-Arkansas, the hydraulic cornerstone of southern Colorado's economic future, would challenge Aspinall's skill as a reclamation coalition builder in the years to come.[131]

The November 1958 elections saw Aspinall's by-now-routine re-election to Congress. His electoral triumph, coupled with Clair Engle's successful bid for the California Senate, opened the way for Aspinall's official election as chair of the House Interior and Insular Affairs Committee in January 1959.[132] Aspinall's excitement at the prospect was palpable. "This will be the first time that anyone from Colorado has ever been Chairman on the Interior and Insular Affairs Committee," Aspinall informed a friend. Aspinall's sense of anticipation emerges most clearly in response to a questionnaire sent by *U.S. News and World Report's* Carson F. Lyman, who asked 1958 election winners to assess why they had been elected. "My victory," Aspinall responded by telegram, "is due to the fact that I have established a reputation for hard work," both in the Fourth Congressional District and around the nation. Tellingly, Aspinall also credited his re-election in part to the "fact that I shall [chair] one of the most important committees as far as the interests of the West are concerned."[133] Aspinall later remembered that he "had always had the ambition" to someday chair the Interior Committee. Aspinall recalled that after his first election in 1948, he had wondered whether he could ever climb the thirteen steps up the seniority ladder to reach the chairship. Amazingly, by 1959, through the retirements and defeats of those ahead of him, coupled with changing political goals and plain good fortune, Aspinall had realized his ambition.[134]

Under Aspinall, the House Interior and Insular Affairs Committee would dominate congressional natural-resource policy, reclamation, and environmental policy over the next fourteen years. Aspinall instantly recognized the importance of his new position to the future of his congressional district and his state, viewing the chairship as the West's most important political position. No new federal policy would take effect until it had passed through Wayne Aspinall's Interior Committee. Aspinall would, in essence, need to be satisfied that any new law would be a law the West—or western Colorado—could benefit from.

An examination of the Interior Committee and Aspinall's methods of operation reveals how thoroughly the Colorado lawmaker came to dominate federal natural-resource policy for the remainder of his congressional career. Aspinall had known as early as 1948 that by seeking membership on the Interior Committee, he could best serve his constituents. According to political scientist Richard Fenno's *Congressmen in Committees*, a classic study of the House of Representatives in the 1950s and 1960s, members of Congress who sought positions on the Interior Committee were interested primarily in "helping their constituents and thereby insuring their re-election." Few initially sought power, prestige, or national recognition. Instead, serving their districts' economic interests and gaining approval for locally important projects occupied their energies. The Interior Committee and its subcommittees handled all legislation concerning irrigation, reclamation, minerals and mining, livestock grazing, public-land law, Native American affairs, and national parks. "The close correspondence between the Interior Committee's jurisdiction and the most pressing constituency problems of Western congressmen makes the Committee uniquely attractive to them," according to Fenno. Thus, many western members of Congress sought to serve on the Interior Committee, at least until their tenure in office was secure.[135] At that point, many transferred to more prestigious or influential committees, such as Ways and Means or Appropriations.[136]

During Aspinall's tenure as chair, the Interior Committee handled about one-fifth of all the House bills introduced, many backed by discrete and powerful constituency groups who demanded action.[137] Early on, Aspinall sought to systematize his committee and its subcommittees and demanded a heavy workload from all members. Aspinall knew his committee, with its small support staff (approximately twelve people in 1959), could only be effective if it functioned efficiently. The chairman went to great lengths to reduce partisan squabbling among committee members. A reliable if conservative Democrat on most issues, Aspinall abhorred partisan bickering when he took up his Interior Committee gavel. "When he gets over here in Committee, politics is adjourned and he thinks in terms of what's good for the West—for miners, for cattlemen, for sheep raisers, and farmers," one former Interior Committee member recalled. Of course, a nonpartisan posture played well with the typical Colorado Fourth Congressional District constituent, who tended to be conservative if a Democrat, but was more likely either an Independent or a Republican.[138]

The benefits of Aspinall's system soon seemed clear. Because the House Interior Committee rapidly gained a reputation for doing thorough work, once a bill cleared the committee, it stood a great chance of passage in the House. As one Interior Committee member described it, "The Committee has a reputation in the House for doing a good job. They know that everything we report has been gone over thoroughly. This isn't true of all committees. The House is suspicious of some." Aspinall later bragged that his committee, despite its tremendous workload, never "lost" a bill once it was favorably reported and brought to the House floor. "Its record," he proudly remembered, "was 100 percent."[139]

Aspinall's systematic approach to committee work contrasted sharply with that of the Senate Interior Committee. By the late 1950s and 1960s, the Senate Interior Committee had become a bastion for western interests. Aside from California and Texas, no western state in Aspinall's era had the population—and hence the representation in the House—of states in other regions. Western senators therefore banded together, creating a more powerful bloc than their House Interior counterparts, making it easier to command the attention of the Senate at large. Interior Committee bills tended to sail through the Senate as compared with bills in the House. The House Interior Committee, though dominated by westerners in the Aspinall years, still represented only a small proportion of the national population. Aspinall's deliberate approach was sometimes mistaken by his critics for rigidity. However, the Colorado congressman justified it as necessary to secure passage of legislation that often made little difference to most House members. Aspinall's 100 percent success record thus is all the more remarkable.[140]

Aspinall established strict committee rules and procedures. Regular meetings were scheduled for Wednesdays at 9:45 A.M., with a timely adjournment fifteen minutes before the commencement of regular House business. Aspinall, like Rayburn, believed in House traditions that emphasized seniority. All subcommittee chairs were selected based on length of tenure, beginning with the ranking member of Aspinall's party immediately below him. Aspinall assigned new Interior Committee members to subcommittees, fixed dates for subcommittee meetings, and exercised strong control over agendas, issues, and deliberations. Though few chairs attended most subcommittee meetings, Aspinall showed up at as many as possible. In his first years as committee leader, it was common for Aspinall to chair subcommittees in the chair's absence. Over time, Aspinall's emphasis on rules and procedures became a source of consternation and criticism for some of his members, notably the younger representatives.[141]

In fact, it is fair to say that those who sat on the Interior Committee found the Aspinall system to be both demanding and rather trying at times. Aspinall was known to dress down members who had the temerity to ask about the policy the Interior Department had adopted on a certain issue. The chairman would invariably explode into a dissertation on how it was Congress and its committees that shaped policy, not the executive branch or the Interior Department. "We make the policy, we are the policy makers," Aspinall would thunder. Committee members criticized him behind his back as an "old maid," a "schoolteacher," a "stickler," and a "perfectionist" who combed through every line of potential legislation, searching for correct word meaning. In addition, like a schoolmaster, he kept attendance records of his committee meetings. As a result, Aspinall knew more than anyone about each bill that emerged from his committee and subcommittees. Because he took his role as ex-officio member of all Interior subcommittees seriously, subcommittee chairs would not make a move without first consulting Aspinall.[142]

In the late 1960s, one member of the Interior Committee remarked that Aspinall had "total control of the Committee, and I mean total." Still others believed that Aspinall's obsession with thorough consideration of every detail resulted in a slowdown of the legislative process. His total immersion in committee and subcommittee agendas made Aspinall the heart and soul of the committee and, by implication, lessened the importance of other members considerably. Congressman Phillip Burton (D-CA), who served under Aspinall from the mid-1960s, disapproved of Aspinall's dictatorial ways. "He ran that committee like it was his personal fiefdom," Burton remembered. "After five years of it, he still treated me like a rank kindergartner. He completely dominated the committee."[143]

Other House members and observers of the congressional process gave the Aspinall system higher marks than Burton. Because the Interior Committee received the most bills in any given session of Congress, a strict and orderly

Wayne Aspinall leaving the House Interior Committee hearing room, where he spent so many hours handling legislation vital to the American West. Courtesy, UCAUCB.

procedure was necessary. The alternative might be chaos and legislative gridlock. Another member who served on both the orderly Interior Committee and the less efficient House Post Office Committee drew some sharp contrasts. Although Aspinall dominated subcommittee chairs, he still was the "best chairman anyone could have." Aspinall let every member talk, but proceeded with questioning according to rules of seniority. "Aspinall," the member recalled, "is fairness personified." He ran his committee "by the numbers, according to good parliamentary procedure." By contrast, the Post Office Committee "was a miserable mess. Everyone yelling and screaming, 'Who's got the floor? . . . Is there a quorum?' It was utter chaos." When the Post Office Committee instituted some badly needed rules and procedures, it knew where to go for inspiration—the House Interior Committee.[144]

By 1959, Aspinall was already known as a hardworking congressman. Soon, his reputation for diligent, exhausting work would elevate him to almost legendary status. One admiring colleague shook his head in awe at Aspinall's work habits, noting his 7:00 A.M. daily arrival, far ahead of other House members, committee staff members, clerks, and secretaries. A former Aspinall aide recalls arriving at the office at 8:00 A.M. to find Aspinall seated at one of the outer office desks, going through the office mail, jotting replies, and signing letters.[145]

Aspinall worked hard all day and cared little for Washington's social life. The Interior Committee, it was said of him, constituted "his whole life" after 1959. He rarely missed a roll-call vote. Aspinall had developed the personal habit of promptness early in his career, when he juggled a busy schedule as a small-town lawyer, schoolteacher, and peach grower. Later, his work as a leader in the Colorado General Assembly left little free time. Aspinall found chairing the busy Interior Committee a perfect match for his methodical approach to life. Constituent mail never lingered long in Aspinall's office; it was usually answered the day it arrived.[146]

Aspinall's promptness became the stuff of Colorado legend and congressional lore. A Grand Junction businessman recalled an irate Aspinall greeting a local delegation with "Where the hell have you been?" when they arrived fifteen minutes late for an 8:30 A.M. appointment because of a Washington, D.C., snowstorm that had paralyzed public transportation, bringing the city temporarily to a halt. To Aspinall, every day was strictly planned, with little time scheduled between hearings or appointments. If people were late, Aspinall either would not meet with them or would cut the interview short by pointing to his watch or a wall clock. If Aspinall was scheduled to arrive somewhere at 3:25, he would arrive at 3:24, not 3:30. A former staff member credits Aspinall's obsession with strict day-to-day planning for his ability to complete a tremendous amount of office and committee work.[147]

Aspinall's rise to the chairship of the House Interior and Insular Affairs Committee marked his emergence into the inner circle of congressional leaders. More importantly, he became the key to every "national park proposal, every wilderness proposal, every one of the giant reclamation projects that generate power and irrigate the West," according to a *Wall Street Journal* article from the early 1970s. Political scientist Richard Fenno, who interviewed many members of Aspinall's House Interior Committee for his study *Congressmen in Committees,* noted that Aspinall and Wilbur Mills (D-AR), chair of the House Rules Committee, dominated the internal life of their committees "with the approval of the majority of the membership."[148]

By the mid-1960s, Aspinall would be called the "unofficial chairman of a bloc of Western congressmen" who met periodically to decide positions on regional issues.[149] To be powerful in Congress is to have the ability to accomplish tasks or influence others to do them for you. By this measure, in the early 1960s, Congressman Wayne Aspinall had arrived at the pinnacle of his influence. Over the next few years, he would shape western history in dramatic ways.

ENDNOTES

1. Clifford Houston to Wayne N. Aspinall, May 5, 1947, Box 18, fd: "Aspinall Personal 1947," Wayne Aspinall Papers, University of Denver Archives, Denver, CO (hereafter cited as UDA).

2. Patrick Fargo McCarty, "Big Ed Johnson of Colorado: A Political Portrait" (M.A. thesis, University of Colorado at Boulder, 1958), 191–194.

3. Ibid., 199.

4. Eugene H. Mast to Eugene Cervi, November 3, 1947, Box 19, fd: "1948, Democratic Mesa County Central," Wayne Aspinall Papers, UDA.

5. Wayne N. Aspinall to Ed Johnson, March 17, 1948, Box 18, no file, Wayne Aspinall Papers, UDA.

6. Wayne N. Aspinall to John A. Carroll, February 26, 1948, Box 63, no file, Wayne Aspinall Papers, UDA; John A. Carroll to Wayne N. Aspinall, March 12, 1948, Box 18, fd: "Aspinall Personal, 1947," Wayne Aspinall Papers, UDA.

7. Carroll to Aspinall, March 12, 1948.

8. Wayne N. Aspinall to Edward Johnson, March 17, 1948, and Edward Johnson to Wayne N. Aspinall, March 25, 1948, Box 19, fd: "Democratic State Central," Wayne Aspinall Papers, UDA.

9. Aspinall to Johnson, March 17, 1948; John C. Vivian to Wayne N. Aspinall, March 29, 1948, Box 19, fd: "Democratic State Central," Wayne Aspinall Papers, UDA.

10. Wayne N. Aspinall to Marguerite Peyton Thompson, April 6, 1948, Box 19, fd: "Democratic State Central," Wayne Aspinall Papers, UDA; Wayne N. Aspinall to William E. Beigel, April 21, 1948, Box 63, fd: "First War—150th Aero Squadron," Wayne Aspinall Papers, UDA.

11. Grand Junction (CO) *Daily Sentinel,* July 24, 1948.

12. "Robert Fay Rockwell Biography," in *Guide to Robert Fay Rockwell Papers,* Robert Fay Rockwell Papers, University of Colorado Archives, University of Colorado at Boulder, Boulder, CO (hereafter cited as UCAUCB).

13. Ibid.

14. Wayne N. Aspinall to Eugene H. Mast, August 3, 1948, Box 19, fd: "Aspinall County Chairman," Wayne Aspinall Papers, UDA; Wayne N. Aspinall to Frank Delaney, August 19, 1948, Box 162, fd: 24, Frank Delaney Papers, UCAUCB.

15. Wayne N. Aspinall interview with Nancy Whistler, Association of Former Members of Congress Project, Manuscript Division, Library of Congress, Washington, DC, February 15, 1979; Alta Leach Noland presentation, Mesa County Oral History Program (OH-1050), Research Center and Special Library, Museum of Western Colorado, Grand Junction, CO (hereafter cited as MWC), March 31, 1989; Alta Noland to Larry Brown, May 4, 1996, Steven C. Schulte Collection, Grand Junction, CO; Alta Noland, untitled memoir, n.d., 1–4, Steven C. Schulte Collection.

16. Wayne N. Aspinall Autobiographical Mss., Vivian Passer Collection, 55, Grand Junction, CO; Wayne N. Aspinall interview, February 15, 1979; Noland, untitled memoir, 4–5.

17. Aspinall Autobiographical Mss., 56.

18. Ibid., 57.

19. Bernard DeVoto, "Sacred Cows and Public Lands," *Harper's Magazine* (July 1948): 45, 51. Mark W.T. Harvey's *A Symbol of Wilderness: Echo Park and the American Conservation Movement* (Albuquerque: University of New Mexico Press, 1994), 93–106, provides an informative discussion of DeVoto's early involvement in conservation issues.

20. DeVoto, "Sacred Cows," 51–52.

21. Jon M. Cosco, *Echo Park: Struggle for Preservation* (Boulder: Johnson Books, 1995), 25.

22. Harvey, *Symbol of Wilderness*, 44–45.

23. *Daily Sentinel*, July 8, 1948.

24. California's huge and expensive Central Valley Project also suffered from the Eightieth Congress's budget cuts. Though vast sums of money had already been appropriated and spent on it, congressional budget reductions would delay the project's completion more than twenty years, according to Angus McDonald in *The New Republic*. During the 1948 presidential campaign, Republican candidate Thomas Dewey toured the Central Valley region. When the candidate was pressed by local media for specific information on his reclamation views, Dewey referred them to a stock speech given weeks earlier in Oklahoma. Outraged Central Valley voters favored Truman by more than 200,000 votes. Dewey lost California by a mere 18,000 votes. Failure to take the western reclamation states more seriously undermined the Republicans and Dewey in 1948. See Angus McDonald, "Turning Off the Tap," *The New Republic* 116 (May 19, 1947): 35–36. Also see Harold I. Gullan, *The Upset That Wasn't: Harry S. Truman and the Crucial Election of 1948* (Chicago: Ivan R. Dee, 1998), 160–161.

25. McDonald, "Turning Off the Tap," 36.

26. Gary W. Reichard, *Politics as Usual: The Age of Truman and Eisenhower* (Arlington Heights, IL: Harlan Davidson, 1988), 38; Robert H. Ferrell, *Harry S. Truman and the Modern Presidency* (Boston: Little, Brown, 1983), 101.

27. Quoted in David McCulloch, *Truman* (New York: Simon and Schuster, 1992), 661.

28. McCulloch, *Truman*, 654–655; Gullan, *Upset That Wasn't*, 167.

29. Wayne N. Aspinall to Barney Whatley, September 13, 1948, Box 19, fd: "1948 Democratic State Central," Wayne Aspinall Papers, UDA; *Daily Sentinel*, September 20, 1948.

30. *Daily Sentinel*, September 20, 1948.

31. Wayne N. Aspinall interview with Helen Hansen, Mesa County Oral History Project (OH-473), MWC, August 10, 1981; Wayne Aspinall interview with Al Look, Mesa County Oral History Project (OH-120, Part 1), MWC, January 10, 1978.

32. *Daily Sentinel*, October 10, 1948.

33. *Daily Sentinel*, October 14, 1948.

34. *Daily Sentinel*, October 22 and 28, 1948.

35. *Daily Sentinel*, October 26 and 27, 1948.

36. *Daily Sentinel*, October 26, 1948. Another strong rumor circulating through western Colorado during the 1948 campaign undoubtedly undermined Rockwell's re-election effort. Aspinall's campaign assistant Alta Leach Noland recalls that Drew Pearson mentioned in his "Washington Merry-Go-Round" column that Rockwell was romantically linked with a young woman, whom he ended up marrying. Noland believes that stories of the Rockwell romance helped damage Rockwell's 1948 campaign. See Alta Noland interview with author, Grand Junction, CO, January 24, 1996. Also see Alta Noland to Steven C. Schulte, January 24, 1996, Steven C. Schulte Collection.

37. *Daily Sentinel*, October 31 and November 1, 1948.

38. *Daily Sentinel*, October 26, 1948.

39. *Daily Sentinel*, October 31, 1948.

40. *Daily Sentinel*, November 3, 1948; "Colorado—Congress Election Results," Box 928, fd: "Colorado Key Factors," John F. Kennedy Pre-presidential Papers, John F. Kennedy Presidential Library, Boston, MA (hereafter cited as JFKPL).

41. Wayne N. Aspinall to William E. Beigel, November 4, 1948, Box 63, fd: "First War—150th Aerosquadron," Wayne Aspinall Papers, UDA.

42. Quoted in McCulloch, *Truman*, 663.

43. Wayne Aspinall interview, January 10, 1978.

44. *Daily Sentinel*, November 3, 1948; Ferrell, *Harry S. Truman*, 103–104.

45. Later, Aspinall also believed that he had violated good governmental practice by running for one office (U.S. Representative) while holding another (Colorado state senator). Wayne Aspinall interview, January 10, 1978; Carol Edmunds, *Wayne Aspinall: Mr. Chairman* (Lakewood, CO: Crown Point, 1980), 38.

46. Noland, untitled memoir, 7; Alta Noland interview, January 24, 1996.

47. For discussions on the early Kennedy-Aspinall relationship, see Noland, untitled memoir, 6–7; Claude DeSautels interview with Louis Oberdorfer, May 16, 1964, JFKPL (DeSautels would later be appointed to President Kennedy's staff in congressional liaison Lawrence O'Brien's office); Joseph F. Dolan interview with Charles T. Morrisey, December 1, 1964, JFKPL; Wayne N. Aspinall interview with Charles T. Morrisey, November 10, 1965, JFKPL.

48. Wayne Aspinall interview, November 10, 1965; Wayne Aspinall interview, January 10, 1978.

49. Robert M. Dallek, *Lone Star Rising: Lyndon Johnson and His Times, 1908–1960* (New York: Oxford University Press, 1991), 164–166; Alfred Steinberg, *Sam Rayburn: A Biography* (New York: Hawthorn Books, 1975), 173–177.

50. Steinberg, *Rayburn*, 179.

51. Morris Udall (D-AZ), who came to Congress in 1961, recalled making the mistake, during his first years in the House, of trying to gain Speaker Rayburn's attention by asking him to appoint a special committee to review the House of Representatives' seniority system. Udall never received a reply. See Morris K. Udall, *Too Funny to Be President* (New York: Henry Holt, 1988), 106.

52. Wayne N. Aspinall interview, February 15, 1979.

53. Alta Noland interview, January 24, 1996; Alta Leach Noland presentation, March 31, 1989.

54. Nicholas A. Masters, "Committee Assignments," in *Congressional Behavior*, ed. Nelson W. Polsby (New York: Random House, 1971), 166–168; Richard F. Fenno, Jr., *Congressmen in Committees* (Boston: Little, Brown, 1973), 5; Wayne Aspinall interview, January 10, 1978.

55. "Biographical Sketch of Wayne Aspinall," Box 4, fd: 2, Wayne N. Aspinall Papers, UCAUCB.

56. "Legislative Accomplishments of Wayne N. Aspinall, Representative from Colorado's Fourth District," Box 8, fd: 35, Wayne N. Aspinall Papers, UCAUCB; no author, "Aspinall, Wayne (Norviel)," *Current Biography Yearbook* (1968): 32–33.

57. Upper Colorado River Basin Compact, Hearings, Subcommittee on Irrigation and Reclamation, House Interior and Insular Affairs Committee, 81st Cong., 1st Sess., on H.R. 2325 et al., 1949, 67.

58. Ibid.

59. Bernard DeVoto, "The West: A Plundered Province," *Harper's Magazine* 169 (August 1934): 355–364.

60. Peter Wiley and Robert Gottlieb, *Empires in the Sun: The Rise of the American West* (New York: Putnam, 1982), 28.

61. Richard White, *It's Your Misfortune and None of My Own: A New History of the American West* (Norman: University of Oklahoma Press, 1991), 503–504.

62. Colorado population statistics are from Carl Abbott, Stephen J. Leonard, and David McComb, *Colorado: A History of the Centennial State*, 3d ed. (Niwot: University Press of Colorado, 1994), 301; Richard E. Tope, "Objective History of Grand Junction, Colorado, Part Two," *Journal of the Western Slope* 10, no. 2 (1995): 28.

63. White, *It's Your Misfortune*, 502–503.

64. Gerald Nash, *The American West Transformed: The Impact of the Second World War* (Lincoln: University of Nebraska Press, 1985), 36.

65. Ibid., 541.

66. Harvey, *Symbol of Wilderness*, 35.

67. In *A Symbol of Wilderness*, Harvey explains each state's World War II–era reclamation dreams but focuses on Utah. See chapter 2, pp. 23–49.

68. Michael P. Malone and Richard W. Etulain, *The American West: A Twentieth-Century History* (Lincoln: University of Nebraska Press, 1989), 121.

69. Carey McWilliams quoted in Carl Abbott, *The Metropolitan Frontier: Cities in the Modern American West* (Tucson: University of Arizona Press, 1993), 26. Richard White also uses the "westward tilt" analogy to describe the region's World War II–induced changes in his *It's Your Misfortune and None of My Own*, 496. Neil Morgan popularized the same notion in his book *Westward Tilt: The American West Today* (New York: Random House, 1963).

70. Wayne N. Aspinall interview, February 15, 1979; Aspinall Autobiographical Mss., 58.

71. William L. Chenoweth, "Raw Materials Activities of the Manhattan Project on the Colorado Plateau," *Nonrenewable Resources* 6, no. 1 (1997): 34; Emma McCreanor, *Mesa County, Colorado: A 100 Year History, 1883–1983* (Grand Junction: Museum of Western Colorado Press, 1983), 28.

72. Tope, "Objective History of Grand Junction," 28.

73. His son Preston took control of the paper and continued its Democratic political direction, but demonstrated more political independence than his father. On the question of Wayne Aspinall, however, Preston Walker never wavered in his support. Walker, a notable sportsman and pioneering white-water enthusiast, died of a heart attack while negotiating the waters of the Dolores River in 1970.

74. Roderick Nash and Gregory Graves, *From These Beginnings: A Biographical Approach to American History*, 5th ed. (New York: HarperCollins, 1995), 260.

75. For studies of U.S. political culture in the 1950s, see Angus Campbell, Philip E. Converse et al., *The American Voter* (New York: John Wiley and Sons, 1960); Samuel Stouffler, *Communism, Conformity, and Civil Liberties* (Garden City, NY: Doubleday, 1955); Gabriel A. Almond and Sidney Verba, *The Civic Culture: Political Attitudes and Democracy in Five Nations* (Boston: Little, Brown, 1965).

76. This paraphrases Michael McCarthy's astute observations on Aspinall's career in "He Fought for His West," *Colorado Heritage* 1 (1988): 35.

77. Ibid., 38.

78. Philip L. Fradkin, *A River No More: The Colorado River and the West* (Berkeley: University of California Press, 1996), 3–4.

79. Peter Iverson, *Barry Goldwater: Native Arizonan* (Norman: University of Oklahoma Press, 1997), 192–193.

80. Donald Worster makes this argument, or variations on it, in several places. Particularly, see his notable *Rivers of Empire: Water, Aridity, and the Growth of the American West* (New York: Pantheon Books, 1985). He makes the argument more succinctly in "Water as a Tool of Empire," a chapter in Donald Worster's *An Unsettled Country: Changing Landscapes of the American West* (Albuquerque: University of New Mexico Press, 1994), 44–46.

81. U.S. Department of the Interior, Bureau of Reclamation, *Collbran Project, Colorado*, Project Planning Report No. 4-8a.5-2 (1949), Box 48, no file, Wayne Aspinall Papers, UDA; *Daily Sentinel*, November 11, 1948.

82. Bradley F. Raley, "The Collbran Project and the Bureau of Reclamation, 1937–1963: A Case Study in Western Resource Development" (M.A. thesis, University of Houston, 1992), 32–35.

83. Wayne N. Aspinall to Michael Straus, January 10, 1951, Box 21, fd: "Precinct Voting Record, 1952," Wayne Aspinall Papers, UDA.

84. Wayne N. Aspinall to Adolph Sabath, March 20, 1952, Box 21, fd: "Precinct Voting Record, 1952," Wayne Aspinall Papers, UDA; *Congressional Record*, May 19, 1952, 5510-5511; Raley, "The Collbran Project," 41-43.

85. See Christine Jasper, "The Collbran Project: Influences Within the Grand Valley upon a Federal Reclamation Project" (paper prepared for History 404, Mesa State College, Grand Junction, CO), 18-19; Raley, "The Collbran Project," 44-54.

86. Wayne N. Aspinall to Fred G. Aandahl, February 27, 1953, Box 21, fd: "Precinct Voting Record, 1952," Wayne Aspinall Papers, UDA.

87. John Opie, *Nature's Nation: An Environmental History of the United States* (Fort Worth, TX: Harcourt Brace College Publishers, 1998), 333; Russell Martin, *A Story That Stands Like a Dam: Glen Canyon and the Struggle for the Soul of the West* (New York: Henry Holt, 1989), 48; Richard Allan Baker, *Conservation Politics: The Senate Career of Clinton P. Anderson* (Albuquerque: University of New Mexico Press, 1985), 65.

88. Chester J. Pach, Jr., and Elmo R. Richardson, *The Presidency of Dwight D. Eisenhower* (Lawrence: University of Kansas Press, 1991), 56-67.

89. This was a draft news story written by the *Daily Sentinel's* Washington correspondent, George Sanford Holmes, n.d., 1952, Box 3, fd: 41, William Nelson Papers, Special Collections, Mesa State College, Grand Junction, CO (hereafter cited as MSC). Several other Holmes telegrams and stories reinforced these perspectives.

90. See Harvey, *Symbol of Wilderness*; Cosco, *Echo Park*; and Elmo R. Richardson, *Dams, Parks, and Politics: Resource Development and Preservation in the Truman-Eisenhower Era* (Lexington: University Press of Kentucky, 1973).

91. Richardson, *Dams, Parks, and Politics*, 58.

92. *Daily Sentinel*, August 17, 1951.

93. Hal K. Rothman, *The Greening of a Nation? Environmentalism in the United States Since 1945* (Fort Worth, TX: Harcourt Brace, 1998), 41-42. The material on DeVoto is from Mark W.T. Harvey's analysis of DeVoto's contribution to the Echo Park campaign in *Symbol of Wilderness*, 94-96.

94. Harvey, *Symbol of Wilderness*, 183-184; Wayne N. Aspinall to Frank Delaney, May 11, 1953, Box 168, fd: 15, Frank Delaney Papers, UCAUCB.

95. Sierra Club news release, December 17, 1953, Box 4, fd: 10, William Nelson Papers, MSC.

96. *Colorado River Storage Project*, Hearings, Subcommittee on Irrigation and Reclamation, House Committee on Interior and Insular Affairs, 83d Cong., 2d Sess., on H.R. 4449 et al., 1954; Wayne N. Aspinall to Frank Delaney, May 11, 1953, Box 168, fd: 15, Frank Delaney Papers, UCAUCB.

97. *Colorado River Storage Project*, 134-135.

98. Ibid., 336-337.

99. Ibid.

100. Harvey, *Symbol of Wilderness*, 191-194; Stephen Fox, *The American Conservation Movement: John Muir and His Legacy* (Madison: University of Wisconsin Press, 1981), 284-285; *Colorado River Storage Project*, 824-825.

101. *Colorado River Storage Project*, 235-237, 831-832.

102. Ibid., 433-434; Fox, *American Conservation Movement*, 284-285.

103. Richardson, *Dams, Parks, and Politics*, 142-144.

104. Cosco, *Echo Park*, 76-77.

105. Ibid.; Fox, *American Conservation Movement*, 285-286; Wallace Stegner, "Battle for the Wilderness," *The New Republic* 130 (February 15, 1954), 13-15; Robert K. Cutter, "Hetch Hetchy—Once Is Too Often" (San Francisco: The Sierra Club, 1954), copy in Box 4, fd: 10, William Nelson Papers, MSC.

106. See Stephen Paul Sayles, "Clair Engle and the Politics of California Reclamation, 1943-1960" (Ph.D. dissertation, University of New Mexico, 1978), 53. Sayles argues that Engle "bears some attention from historians for his role in California's and the western region's postwar natural resources development policies."

107. *Colorado River Storage Project*, 1097-1098.

108. Wayne N. Aspinall to Horace M. Albright, April 14, 1955, and Wayne N. Aspinall to Allyn H. Tedmon, April 26, 1955, Box 69, fd: "Echo Park Project, 1955," Wayne Aspinall Papers, UDA.

109. Wayne N. Aspinall to John Dingell, June 6, 1955, Box 69, fd: "Echo Park Project, 1955," Wayne Aspinall Papers, UDA.

110. Clifford Kester to Wayne N. Aspinall, July 21, 1955; Wayne N. Aspinall to Clifford Kester, July 26, 1955; and Wayne N. Aspinall to Delert Ralphs, May 24, 1955, all in Box 69, fd: "Echo Park Project, 1955," Wayne Aspinall Papers, UDA.

111. Harvey, *Symbol of Wilderness*, 260-262.

112. Ibid., 270-273.

113. Ibid., 273; "Memo on Status of Power and Reclamation Projects," June 13, 1955, Box 72, fd: "Public Works 1-S.300 Correspondence, 1955-56," Series VI, Gordon Allott Papers, UCAUCB; see also Ival V. Goslin to the Upper Colorado River Commission, August 17, 1955, Box 4, fd: "Colorado River Storage Project (1954-55), 3," William Nelson Papers, MSC, which offers a perspective that is sympathetic to the proposed Echo Park Dam.

114. Harvey, *Symbol of Wilderness*, 272-274; Arthur Hawthorne Carhart to Wayne N. Aspinall, July 2, 1955, Box 69, fd: "Echo Park Project, 1955," Wayne Aspinall Papers, UDA.

115. Goslin to Upper Colorado River Commission, August 17, 1955; Harvey, *Symbol of Wilderness*, 270-276.

116. Wayne N. Aspinall to Frank Delaney, July 9, 1955, Box 82, fd: 11, Frank Delaney Papers, UCAUCB.

117. Wayne N. Aspinall to James Cinnamon, July 29, 1955; Wayne N. Aspinall to Maury Teague, July 30, 1955; and the United Press International news reports on the Aspinall-Engle anti-Echo Park pledge from late July 1955, all in Box 69, fd: "Echo Park Project, 1955," Wayne Aspinall Papers, UDA.

118. Wayne N. Aspinall speech in *Proceedings of the Upper Colorado River Commission*, September 19, 1955, Box 3, fd: 28, William Nelson Papers, MSC.

119. Ibid.

120. David R. Brower, "Environmental Activist, Publicist, and Prophet," oral history conducted by Susan R. Schrepfer, Regional Oral History Office, the Bancroft Library,

University of California at Berkeley, 1974–1978, 134–137; Harvey, *Symbol of Wilderness*, 280–282.

121. Harvey, *Symbol of Wilderness*, 281–282.

122. Howard Zahniser to Wayne Aspinall, February 1, 1956, Box 5: 100, fd: "NWPS-Wilderness Bill Advocacy, Correspondence, 1956," Papers of The Wilderness Society, Denver Public Library.

123. Harvey, *Symbol of Wilderness*, 284–285; Cosco, *Echo Park*, 89–90; Wayne N. Aspinall to Upper Colorado River Commission, March 29, 1956, Box 82, fd: 11, Frank Delaney Papers, UCAUCB.

124. Rothman, *The Greening of a Nation?*, 34.

125. Cosco, *Echo Park*, 112.

126. Brower, "Environmental Activist," 130–131. The four major dams authorized by the CRSP were Glen Canyon (on the Colorado River), Flaming Gorge (on the Green River), Curecanti (on the Gunnison River), and Navajo (on the San Juan River).

127. Tommy Neal interview with author, Grand Junction, CO, January 4, 1997.

128. "Report on Audit of the Outdoor Recreation Resources Review Commission . . . ," Box 202, fd: "FG 710 ORRRC," White House Central Subject Files, John F. Kennedy Presidential Papers, JFKPL; "Legislative Accomplishments of Wayne N. Aspinall, Representative from Colorado's Fourth Congressional District," Box 8, fd: 37, Wayne N. Aspinall Papers, UCAUCB.

129. Wayne N. Aspinall interview with Joe B. Frantz, June 14, 1974, Lyndon B. Johnson Presidential Library, Austin, TX (hereafter cited as LBJPL); Carl M. Brauer, *John F. Kennedy and the Second Reconstruction* (New York: Columbia University Press, 1977), 56, 64, 138.

130. Aspinall's involvement with the admission of Alaska and Hawaii to the Union is well documented. Aspinall claims it was he who devised the strategy of seeking Alaskan admission first, calming congressional fears over the admission of noncontiguous states. See Wayne Aspinall interview, February 15, 1979. Many of Aspinall's other actions with regard to Alaska and Hawaii are documented in *Records of the House Interior and Insular Affairs Committee*, 85th Cong., 2d Sess., Minutes, May 14, June 4, June 25, July 9, July 10, July 23, and August 6, 1958, Box 1004, fd: HR 85A–F9.5, National Archives, Washington, DC (hereafter cited as NA); *Records of the House Interior and Insular Affairs Committee*, 86th Cong., 1st Sess., Minutes, Full Committee, January 23, 1959, Box 793, fd: HR 86A–F9.3 (1 of 3 boxes), NA; *Records of the House Interior and Insular Affairs Committee*, 86th Cong., 1st Sess., Wayne N. Aspinall to Howard Smith, Chairman, House Rules Committee, February 12, 1959, and Howard Smith to Wayne N. Aspinall, February 16, 1959, Box 153, fd: HR 86A–D6-HR 4221, NA; *Records of the House Interior and Insular Affairs Committee*, 86th Cong., 1st Sess., Minutes, March 11, 1959, Box 795, fd: HR 86A–F9.3, unpublished hearings, NA; Larry Brown, *Aspinall* (Gunnison, CO: Western State College Foundation, 1996), 36.

131. *Congressional Quarterly Fact Sheet* (January 23, 1959): 109.

132. According to Michael Malone and Richard Etulain, *The American West*, 282, Engle won the Senate seat by defeating California governor Goodwin Knight, and Aspinall defeated Wells by more than 18,000 votes. Baker, *Conservation Politics*, 235.

133. Wayne N. Aspinall to Frank C. Layton, n.d., Box 14, fd: 2, Wayne N. Aspinall Papers, UCAUCB; Wayne N. Aspinall to James K. Carr, n.d., Box 12, fd: 1, Wayne N. Aspinall Papers, UCAUCB; Wayne N. Aspinall to Carson F. Lyman, n.d., Box 14, fd: 2, Wayne N. Aspinall Papers, UCAUCB.

134. Wayne Aspinall interview, January 10, 1978.

135. Sayles, "Clair Engle," 253; Fenno, *Congressmen in Committees,* 5.

136. Fenno, *Congressmen in Committees,* 7. Fenno notes that between 1947 and 1967, twenty-two Interior Committee members transferred from Interior to more prestigious committees—sixteen to Appropriations, three to Ways and Means, and three to Foreign Affairs.

137. Fenno, *Congressmen in Committees,* 57; "Legislative Accomplishments of Wayne N. Aspinall."

138. Fenno, *Congressmen in Committees,* 60–61.

139. Fenno, *Congressmen in Committees,* 58–59; Wayne N. Aspinall interview, February 15, 1979.

140. Baker, *Conservation Politics,* 7; Fenno, *Congressmen in Committees,* 62. In his study of membership of the House Interior Committee from 1955 to 1966, Fenno found that 50 percent of all members hailed from the western states; an additional 18 percent were from midwestern states.

141. See, for example, "Rules of the Committee on Interior and Insular Affairs," U.S. House of Representatives, 90th Cong., Box 274, fd: "1967 Legislative Interior and Insular Affairs Committee, General," Wayne Aspinall Papers, UDA; Wayne N. Aspinall interview, June 14, 1974; William Morrow, *Congressional Committees* (New York: Charles Scribner's Sons, 1969), 38–39, 48.

142. Fenno, *Congressmen in Committees,* 60, 120–121; Robert Tweedell, "Wayne Aspinall: A Man to Remember," in "Empire" (Sunday magazine supplement), *Denver Post,* May 4, 1980.

143. Ibid.

144. Fenno, *Congressmen in Committees,* 136, 199.

145. Fenno, *Congressmen in Committees,* 136, 173; Tommy Neal interview, January 4, 1997.

146. Patrick Gormley interview with author, Grand Junction, CO, August 23, 1994.

147. Tommy Neal interview, January 4, 1997; Patrick Gormley interview, August 23, 1994.

148. *Wall Street Journal* article quoted in Carol Edmunds, "Wayne N. Aspinall Biographical Sketch," Box 1, fd: 1, Wayne N. Aspinall Papers, UCAUCB; Fenno, *Congressmen in Committees,* 118.

149. *Rocky Mountain News,* May 2, 1965.

CHAPTER THREE

NEW FRONTIERS:
KENNEDY, UDALL, AND FRYINGPAN-ARKANSAS

By the early 1960s, Wayne Aspinall had emerged as one of the leading congressional forces in conservation policy. His role in the Echo Park controversy and the compromise legislation that became the Colorado River Storage Project of 1956 attested to the Colorado congressman's rising political influence. Yet it is clear that no single event tested Aspinall's political skills or helped define his attitude toward the West's future more than the ten-year-long controversy over the Wilderness Act. Aspinall's interaction with the Kennedy administration on Wilderness, however, was preceded by a decade-long struggle to authorize the Fryingpan-Arkansas Reclamation Project, a complex, transmontane water diversion that transferred water from Colorado's Western Slope to increasingly populous south-central Colorado.

The Kennedy administration's desire to capitalize on the political potential of the nation's new conservation awareness placed Wayne Aspinall in some uncomfortable political situations as the Wilderness battle was heating up. But though the Kennedy administration favored Wilderness legislation, it continued to view reclamation projects as a positive means of linking western support to other administration policies. Reclamation, in the early 1960s, was still recognized as vital to the nation's future, and the politics of reclamation still had not been seriously challenged by the environmental movement.

ASPINALL, UDALL, AND PRESIDENT KENNEDY

Wayne Aspinall and John Kennedy were old congressional friends. Though Kennedy had been elected two years earlier than Aspinall, the two men had become acquainted due to the proximity of their House offices and maintained

Wayne Aspinall speaking at the unveiling of his portrait in the House Interior Committee hearing room, 1960. The members of the committee commissioned the portrait to honor him. Courtesy, UDA.

a good relationship after Kennedy vaulted to the U.S. Senate in 1952. By 1956 and 1957, it was well known that Kennedy was contemplating a presidential bid in 1960.[1] During the 1956 Democratic National Convention in Chicago,

Aspinall, as a leader of the Colorado delegation, had played an important role in swinging the state's vice presidential votes away from Kennedy and toward the eventual nominee, Senator Estes Kefauver of Tennessee.[2] After the 1956 election, Kennedy invited Aspinall to a catered lunch, brought to the Capitol in warming pans from Kennedy's Georgetown residence. The purpose of the luncheon immediately became clear to Aspinall when Kennedy asked why he had failed to win more Colorado votes for the vice presidential nomination. Aspinall bluntly informed his old friend that Kennedy "did not know anything about the West." Aspinall went on to suggest that Kennedy knew the affairs of Europe better than he knew the issues affecting western Colorado, an assertion difficult for the young senator to refute.[3]

Looking ahead four years, Kennedy seized the opportunity to gain Aspinall's ear, and maybe his support, by asking if he could call upon Aspinall before voting against any future reclamation projects. By offering to check with Aspinall, Kennedy was acknowledging a major mistake he had made during Senate consideration of the Colorado River Storage Project, when he had voted for a crippling amendment offered by Senator Paul Douglass (D-IL). This vote, long remembered and lamented by western reclamation advocates, had not enhanced Kennedy's candidacy for national office. Kennedy then asked Aspinall to advise him on reclamation and agricultural matters. Aspinall agreed to assist the New England senator on reclamation issues but demurred to serve as an agricultural consultant, advising Kennedy to find an acknowledged Democratic expert on agricultural policy.[4]

Kennedy's willingness to consult with Aspinall could only mean one thing. As Aspinall concluded, "I knew right then that he was running for President of the U.S." In meetings such as this, Kennedy was laying the groundwork for his 1960 presidential bid.[5]

To be taken seriously in Colorado and the West, Kennedy needed to do some important fence mending. His vote on the Colorado River Storage Project had undermined his credibility. To repair the damage, Kennedy made an effort to court Aspinall and paid a series of pre-1960 campaign visits to Colorado. Kennedy's Colorado point man, Denver attorney and Democratic state representative Joseph F. Dolan, termed Kennedy's May 1957 visit "an unqualified success," noting in a memorandum to Kennedy aide Theodore (Ted) Sorensen that the senator had met most of the key Colorado Democrats and that Kennedy had agreed to come back to the state to speak in 1959.[6] By early 1959, a strong Kennedy-for-President movement had taken off in Colorado. Byron "Whizzer" White, former University of Colorado football hero, Rhodes scholar, and Denver attorney, agreed to head Kennedy's Colorado campaign. White, Dolan discovered, was an old friend of Kennedy's, having met Jack in France prior to World War II and again in the Solomon Islands during that conflict.[7]

Though organized early, Kennedy's Colorado campaign lacked visible support from high-profile Democrats. A mid-1959 survey of prominent Colorado Democrats found Wayne Aspinall leaning toward Adlai Stevenson or Hubert Humphrey, though Kennedy campaign sources believed that Aspinall had privately promised to support their candidate. Colorado Democratic governor Steve McNichols was said to be leaning toward Stevenson, as was Senator John Carroll. Always a political force, retired former governor and senator "Big Ed" Johnson favored Texas senator Lyndon Johnson. A March 1959 article in the Pueblo *Star-Journal* concluded that Aspinall and Carroll favored Stevenson, but John Kennedy seemed to be almost every Colorado Democratic politician's choice for the vice presidential slot. The *Star-Journal* also observed that where western reclamation was concerned, Kennedy seemed a changed man. According to Senator John A. Carroll, the Massachusetts senator now understood reclamation and other water matters "much more clearly" and knew what the Fryingpan-Arkansas Project was all about. Apparently, Kennedy's plan to seek Aspinall's advice had begun bearing fruit.[8]

By late November 1959, Kennedy was back in Colorado, appearing in Denver, Pueblo, and Grand Junction. Asked in advance of Kennedy's Grand Junction appearance to suggest themes that the senator could address, Dolan listed "Aspinall," "water as the key to America's survival," and the importance of western Colorado's oil-shale deposits. Dolan noted that oil shale's seemingly bright future could inspire a "population explosion" in the area, underscoring the importance of a reliable water supply.[9]

Kennedy did not disappoint the huge crowd that jammed the Cafe Caravan. Climbing up on his chair to address the Democratic throng, Kennedy sounded the themes that his western Colorado audience wanted to hear. In 1960, he predicted, one "sharp difference" between Democrats and Republicans would be over water. As Aspinall had done on many occasions, Kennedy flayed the Eisenhower administration's "no new starts" policy for reclamation projects because it halted and "hamstrung" the "dynamic long-range requirements of an expanding population." Eisenhower's policy, he concluded to the delight of his audience, "must be promptly reversed." During his late 1959 Colorado appearances, Kennedy proved that he had done his homework on the West, convincing many observers that his candidacy should be taken seriously.[10]

In a letter to an old friend, Aspinall described Kennedy's Grand Junction appearance as the "largest dinner we ever held" in western Colorado. Candidate Kennedy "lost no ground here" while making many friends. "Whether or not he made any votes is something else," Aspinall wryly concluded.[11]

The 1960 campaign would go well for Kennedy. The West, however, would continue to present problems for the New Englander. Kennedy's western supporters worked furiously to sell their candidate to a region that still did not fully believe he understood their need for a comprehensive reclamation program.

One early western convert to the Kennedy effort was Arizona Democratic congressman Stewart L. Udall. Born in 1920 in St. John's, Arizona, Udall was a descendant of an influential Mormon pioneer family. After attending the University of Arizona, serving in World War II, and earning his law degree from the University of Arizona, Udall started a law practice with his younger brother, Morris. In 1954, at the age of thirty-three, Udall won election to the U.S. House of Representatives, where he quickly sought appointment to the House Interior Committee. As a junior congressman from the West, Udall routinely voted for reclamation projects, supporting Wayne Aspinall and the Upper Colorado Basin's CRSP in the hope that one day, the Upper Basin congressman could repay the favor by supporting a Central Arizona Water Project. Later, Udall would confess that although he admired Aspinall's ability as a western spokesperson, he found the Colorado congressman's tight grip on the Interior Committee both personally and professionally stifling. Udall would not be alone in that conclusion, but in the late 1950s, the rising congressman tactfully confined his criticism of Mr. Chairman to the ears of his brother, Morris, and other like-minded young Democratic Party radicals.[12]

Declaring himself for Kennedy in September 1959, Udall worked feverishly for the candidate in Arizona, writing letters, giving speeches, and attempting to organize the Arizona campaign for the Massachusetts senator. Still, selling a New England Democrat, even the charismatic Kennedy, was an imposing task when the Democratic Party had been dominated for decades by the wishes of the aged but still influential Carl Hayden, an octogenarian who backed fellow senator Lyndon B. Johnson's candidacy. Udall's persistent efforts paid off when the young Arizona congressman delivered the Arizona delegation for Kennedy at the 1960 Democratic National Convention in Los Angeles.[13]

By contrast, Colorado's Democratic delegation presented nothing but frustration for Kennedy supporters. Although the state's Kennedy campaign remained visible and energetic, most prominent Colorado Democrats were split between Lyndon Johnson and Missouri senator Stuart Symington. Some, like Aspinall, hoped Adlai Stevenson would express renewed interest in the presidency.[14] Kennedy's campaign responded to high-level Democratic indifference with a barrage of letters, phone calls, and arm-twisting in an attempt to harvest national-convention delegates. Aspinall and his longtime campaign manager, Grand Junction attorney Charles Traylor, both likely 1960 convention delegates, received phone calls and visits from Kennedy admirers. Kennedy's 1959 Cafe Caravan speech was, in part, an attempt to corral potential convention delegates. Despite Aspinall's independent public posture, the Kennedy camp believed that Aspinall, who had close ties to Kennedy, would never deliberately undermine their candidate's chances. Still, Aspinall's insistence on remaining uncommitted while hoping for a Stevenson draft annoyed the Kennedy campaign.[15]

In May 1960, Aspinall told *Daily Sentinel* editor Preston Walker that Kennedy had "sent word" that the candidate wanted Aspinall to serve as his "advisor on conservation matters." What this might entail was not spelled out. Was Aspinall to merely offer natural-resources advice, or was this a potential tender of a future position, such as secretary of the interior? If the door to such an appointment had opened slightly, Aspinall quickly slammed it shut. He told Walker that by insisting on remaining uncommitted, he was undermining his chances for an eventual official relationship with Kennedy. This conclusion did not bother Aspinall. "I have considered that it would be better for western Colorado if I didn't get tied too closely to any particular candidate."[16]

Kennedy's final Colorado appearance before the presidential election took place in June 1960 at the Colorado State Democratic Convention in Durango. Though Aspinall and Traylor continued to feel Kennedy campaign pressure to commit as Kennedy delegates, both emerged from the Durango meeting and headed to the National Convention in Los Angeles undeclared. Still, the Kennedy campaign had handled Aspinall with skill. By not applying too much pressure, they allowed him, an avowed Kennedy friend, to retain the political independence his Fourth District constituents admired. By this point, Aspinall seemed to have begun reconciling himself to a possible Kennedy administration—a bright prospect, Aspinall asserted, for the West. He predicted nothing but a "most cooperative" relationship with Kennedy if the Massachusetts senator prevailed in the November election.[17]

The glittering Los Angeles Democratic National Convention, with Stevenson's substantial shadow looming over it, turned into a Kennedy first-ballot triumph. Even though Stevenson's name was submitted in nomination via an enthusiastic speech by Minnesota senator Eugene McCarthy, his last-minute candidacy could not shake years of unofficial campaigning and delegate hunting by aggressive Kennedy supporters. About half of Colorado's delegates had committed to Kennedy prior to the convention. Kennedy even met with Traylor and Aspinall in a last-minute effort to officially gain their convention votes. When it became clear that Kennedy would be the party's nominee, Aspinall and Traylor climbed aboard the bandwagon, giving him the majority of Colorado's votes.[18]

During the fall campaign, Aspinall regularly endorsed Kennedy but focused on his own re-election. Kennedy swept to a dramatic victory over Richard Nixon in November 1960, winning the popular vote by a razor-thin margin of 118,000 votes but sweeping the electoral college by 303–219. If election results provided a reliable guide, Kennedy faced a difficult challenge selling his message in the American West. He had lost not only Colorado but every mountain state with the exception of Nevada and New Mexico.[19]

Within days of the election, the inevitable speculation surrounded the president-elect. Who would be appointed to which cabinet post? Who would advise him on certain matters? In the case of the American West, one cabinet position

At the 1960 Democratic National Convention in Los Angeles. Delegates (left to right) Charles J. Traylor, Charles Conklin, and Aspinall. Traylor and Aspinall arrived at the convention uncommitted but eventually climbed on the Kennedy bandwagon. Courtesy, UDA.

mattered in particular: secretary of the interior. The interior secretary oversaw the vast federal empire, including lands belonging to Native American tribes, as well as such crucial land-management agencies as the National Park Service, the Bureau of Land Management, and the Bureau of Reclamation. The secretary of the interior, working with the chairs of the House and Senate Interior Committees, molded the future of the American West.

Tommy Neal, an Aspinall aide, later remembered that the day after the 1960 election, Arizona representative Stewart Udall telephoned Wayne Aspinall at his Grand Junction office. After their long phone conversation, Aspinall told Neal that Udall had asked for Aspinall's support in the Arizona congressman's bid to become John F. Kennedy's secretary of the interior. For months, informed speculation had pointed to Aspinall, or even Clinton Anderson, as likely choices for the Interior Department post. But Udall had positioned himself closely to Kennedy by supporting the senator's late-1950s crusade against labor racketeering and by being one of the first western politicians to embrace his presidential campaign. During the summer of 1960, Udall had strengthened his conservation credentials by leading a House Interior Committee expedition to Rainbow Bridge National Monument to inspect the site and consider various ways to protect it from imminent flooding by the Glen Canyon Dam.[20] Neal's remembrances indicate that the ambitious Udall was jockeying for the post, but it must be remembered that the Aspinall aide's observations came from someone who sat at the chairman's side and, like many others in Colorado, thought that the best candidate for interior secretary was Wayne Aspinall.

In the months leading up to the election, rumors had circulated that Aspinall would be Kennedy's choice.[21] A *Daily Sentinel* reporter contacted Kennedy spokesman Pierre Salinger in May 1960, asking him to confirm rumors that Aspinall was about to be named JFK's chief natural resources advisor—a role Aspinall had unofficially been filling for several years. Though Kennedy had made no official overtures to Aspinall in 1960, there is evidence to sustain the assertions of both Stewart L. Udall and author Russell Martin that Aspinall still entertained hopes of being named secretary of the interior if Kennedy prevailed over Nixon. The rumors followed both Aspinall and Kennedy to the Los Angeles convention. On Charles Traylor's agenda for his meeting with the hopeful candidate was reminding him that Colorado "has a potential Secretary of the Interior in Aspinall if there is a Democratic victory in November."[22]

Rumors also surrounded Arizona congressman Stewart Udall. A July 1960 *U.S. News and World Report* story had identified Udall as a possible cabinet choice in a Kennedy administration. Udall's early endorsement of Kennedy and strong seconding speech of vice presidential nominee Lyndon B. Johnson had enhanced the young Arizonan's stature with the national Democratic Party. Following the Los Angeles convention, the *Arizona Daily Star* referred to Udall as "of cabinet stature," noting that from a purely political standpoint, he deserved first-refusal rights for the Interior post because of his widely recognized labors on Kennedy's behalf.[23]

Most observers believed that Aspinall would receive strong consideration. Several factors, however, worked against the chairman's candidacy. Aspinall had done little to pursue the job, leaving it to others to advance his cause. Furthermore, Aspinall had only belatedly aligned himself with the Kennedy campaign. Nevertheless, the Coloradan's friendship with the president-elect, coupled with Aspinall's chairing of the powerful House Interior and Insular Affairs Committee, made him the natural subject of speculation for the Interior position. In the election's immediate aftermath, it is clear that Aspinall had not totally discounted the possibility that Kennedy would turn to him. Udall's post-election call to Aspinall and the Arizonan's subsequent political positioning must have rankled the veteran Colorado congressman.[24]

Both Robert and Ted Kennedy promoted Stewart Udall's candidacy to brother Jack. Udall clearly desired the job. In mid-November, Kennedy aide Hyman (Hy) B. Raskin informed Udall that he was under strong consideration for the Interior post. From Kennedy's perspective, one obstacle remained in the path of Udall's appointment: Senate Interior Committee chair Clinton Anderson (D-NM), who was rumored to be interested in the job. Kennedy's advisors believed the president-elect should delicately sound Anderson out on the depth of his interest. A call to Anderson confirmed it was only mild, and Kennedy easily flattered the New Mexican by pointing out that he did not want a veteran senator to give up his seat and valuable seniority. The way was now clear for Udall. President-elect Kennedy made his first cabinet appointment, Stewart L. Udall as secretary of the interior, on December 8, 1960. During his long tenure, Udall would face a fundamental dilemma: how to balance rising preservation sentiment with traditional demands for resource development.[25]

Wayne Aspinall's reaction to Udall's appointment is more difficult to discern. Though he might have conceded that others stood ahead of him based on the length of their political loyalty to Kennedy, Aspinall firmly believed that no one had his overall grasp of natural-resource issues. A *Daily Sentinel* news report one week after the election still predicted that Aspinall would likely take a high-profile role in the new administration, either as interior secretary or in his ongoing position as chair of the Interior Committee. Aspinall, the *Daily Sentinel* article proclaimed, would become "the spokesman for the Kennedy Administration on resource matters in the House."[26]

Though many western Coloradans envisioned such a role for their beloved congressman, it would not come to pass. Aspinall's relations with the Kennedy administration and Udall would remain uneasy, fluctuating between cordial and strained. Never a star in Kennedy's Camelot, Aspinall continued to value his political independence.

Aspinall did not readily embrace Udall's appointment, as the former interior secretary vividly remembered: "Congressman Aspinall thought he was the best qualified person and perhaps he was." Historian Russell Martin asserted that Udall's appointment "miffed" Aspinall, who "openly wondered whether Udall had amassed enough experience" to handle the job. In the years ahead, as the Udall-Kennedy conservation program took shape, Aspinall would find many more reasons to maintain a safe distance from official administration policies.[27]

ASPINALL'S RELATIONS WITH THE KENNEDY ADMINISTRATION

"I think Wayne [Aspinall] thought that he was more experienced and wise, and that Kennedy had made a mistake in picking a young squirt" to be secretary of the interior, Stewart Udall later recalled. Kennedy conservation initiatives depended on Aspinall's political interest and skills. Faced with a potentially tense political situation, Stewart Udall began devising strategies to salve the hurt feelings of his former Interior Committee boss. Udall made an early decision to do what it took to "assuage Wayne." One small but highly significant and symbolic action Udall took was to always visit the Coloradan in his office. "That was my way of paying my respects to him." Udall did not extend the same courtesy to Senate Interior Committee leaders such as Clinton Anderson or, later, Henry "Scoop" Jackson.[28]

If indeed miffed over Udall's appointment, Aspinall did not betray anything but optimism about the impending administration. At this juncture, Aspinall had no reason to fear a Udall-led Interior Department. Over the next few years, the Arizonan would slowly begin moving away from utilitarian conservation to embrace a greater preservationist vision, but in 1961, Udall remained squarely in the tradition of Theodore Roosevelt and Gifford Pinchot. In a post-election interview, Aspinall predicted that Kennedy would quickly reverse the "no new starts" policy of the Eisenhower years and implement an energetic reclamation program for the American West. Aspinall delighted many Front Range Coloradans by forecasting that within two years, Congress would approve the long-sought Fryingpan-Arkansas Reclamation Project.[29] In this new Washington atmosphere, with a president friendly to western resource-development interests, Fryingpan-Arkansas and other western water projects had a much greater chance of being authorized.

What Aspinall did not anticipate was the growing national sentiment against rapid resource development, and the Udall-Kennedy administration's responsiveness to this segment of public opinion, most of it located outside the American West. In the new administration's first month, Stewart Udall's emerging conservation vision became apparent. Udall would always feel a tension between the poles of resource development and preservation, but as his administrative tenure wore on, he seemed to move more toward the environmentalist end of the spectrum.[30] As he told his new Interior Department staff upon taking office, they faced a "unique opportunity" and could reach a "high water mark in conservation" in the years ahead. If Udall had his way, the near future would be nothing less than the "greatest decade in the conservation history of the United States."[31]

At House Speaker Sam Rayburn's funeral, 1961. A photograph featuring President Kennedy, Vice President Johnson, and Presidents Eisenhower and Truman. Aspinall sits in the third pew, fourth from the left. Courtesy, Sam Rayburn Library, Bonham, Texas.

Over time, Aspinall would frequently find himself at odds with the Udall-Kennedy-Johnson conservation vision. As a result, his political reputation would undergo a rapid change. By 1964, which many consider his year of greatest accomplishment, Aspinall's resistance to key conservation initiatives would brand him, in the eyes of its emerging proponents, as the nascent environmental movement's greatest foe. At the start of the Kennedy years, his status as a natural-resources insider was legendary; by the mid-1960s, Udall was referring to him as "the brakeman," an almost unmovable obstacle in the path of vital environmental initiatives.[32]

Aspinall gave early signs that he was not comfortable with the Kennedy administration's brand of conservation. By the early 1960s, as he opposed the various versions of the proposed Wilderness Act, Aspinall was pilloried and vilified by the national press corps—a fast fall for someone who had recently been regarded as the one of the nation's greatest natural-resource experts. What had happened? Had Aspinall changed? Or was it the nation's attitude toward the land that had undergone a transformation?

Friends and rivals. Stewart L. Udall (left) served as interior secretary under both Kennedy and Johnson. Udall's plans sometimes conflicted with Aspinall's, though the two men needed each other to achieve their respective legislative goals. Courtesy, SCUAL.

Udall convinced close Kennedy advisors that an active, nationally visible conservation agenda could lead to political gains. Americans, in larger numbers, were becoming "cognizant of the importance of conservation." Historian Hal K. Rothman referred to this era as the start of a "changing cultural climate" that would ultimately elevate "a new environmentalism" to the forefront of mainstream U.S. politics by the late 1960s.[33] Although the full-fledged protest associated with the counterculture and radical environmentalism still lay in the future, Aspinall would soon find himself labeled an obdurate foe of environmental progress and an apologist for corporate interests bent on destroying the West's remaining natural beauty.

In the first months of the Kennedy administration, Udall and his Interior Department staff made genuine attempts to consult with Aspinall on a regular basis. Three weeks after the inauguration, congressional liaison Lawrence O'Brien, who was scheduled to meet with Aspinall, received some advice from Kennedy deputy special counsel Lee White. White told O'Brien that Aspinall would be pleased that one-third of the nation's reclamation budget had been allocated to Upper Basin water projects; the Curecanti Project, in Aspinall's home district, was reported to be in particularly good financial condition. Aspinall, according to White, desired an "orderly, sustained reclamation program," not the starts and stops that had characterized the late Eisenhower years. White also suggested discussing the possibility of reopening the navy's oil-shale pilot plant near Rifle, Colorado. Aspinall, who had a lifelong romance with oil-shale development, could not help but be pleased at such a notion.[34]

Aspinall's political marginalization began during the early years of the Kennedy administration, despite attempts by Udall and administration congressional liaisons to keep constructive political avenues open to him. Secretary Udall did not glance Aspinall's way when he sought political or philosophical inspiration. Instead, he looked to such notable conservationists and social activists as author Wallace Stegner and scientist Rachel Carson. Udall asked Stegner to assist him with speeches and writing projects, including his 1963 conservation best-seller, *The Quiet Crisis*.[35] Udall was the first high government official to support Carson's well-publicized exposé of the synthetic pesticide industry, published in 1962 as *Silent Spring*. His ban of such chemicals from Interior Department use earned Carson's admiration. At his final press conference as interior secretary in January 1969, Udall remarked that the measure of a leader "is whether he is educable, whether he is capable of growing." He was undoubtedly thinking of his own growth as a conservationist. Udall's eight-year tenure saw the implementation of an aggressive national conservation program, sometimes in conjunction with Wayne Aspinall's support, and sometimes in spite of the chairman's indifference or opposition.[36]

Udall began his secretaryship by suggesting several policy initiatives. In June 1961, he sent the president a "Proposal for a Kennedy Administration

Parks Conservation Program," which argued that a "major new conservation program" would complement other administration legislative proposals and would ultimately rank as "one of the landmark accomplishments of the Kennedy Administration." Udall's report reviewed the nation's dismal conservation record since World War II, indicating that the time was at hand to aggressively add new national parks, develop green space, acquire lands for wildlife refuges, and increase recreational opportunities on federal lands. "There has been a steady upsurge of interest in conservation in this country," Udall observed.[37] But the centerpiece of the Kennedy administration's conservation initiative would be the creation of a national wilderness preservation system. It was on this proposal that Udall and the Kennedy administration allied themselves with the growing environmental movement and parted ways with Congressman Wayne Aspinall.

Though Aspinall and Udall would disagree vociferously over wilderness, their relationship in the early 1960s was on much sounder footing when reclamation was discussed. The Kennedy administration never hesitated to advocate a strong reclamation program to help court public support for policy goals in the West. It had witnessed the political damage incurred by the Eisenhower administration for its "no new starts" policy and related budgetary stinginess. In the early 1960s, with the environmental movement only in its infancy, it did not seem incongruous for Kennedy or Udall to advocate a federal wilderness system and a strong reclamation program in the same speech. Both were viewed as cornerstones of the same conservation program. In his 1962 "White House Message on Conservation," President Kennedy discussed water resources as a basic element of his conservation program. "In no resource field are conservation principles more applicable," according to Kennedy. In his message, the president recommended the immediate enactment of several large reclamation projects, including Colorado's Fryingpan-Arkansas. It is worth emphasizing that reclamation and conservation were considered one and the same in the early 1960s—a point Aspinall would continue to assert long after it became fashionable to argue to the contrary.[38]

Aspinall's skills as a master of water politics were never on display more conspicuously than during the Fryingpan-Arkansas authorization ordeal. Aspinall learned many lessons from the ten-year struggle, including how to harmonize the interests of both eastern and western Colorado while building a successful coalition to achieve House passage. Fryingpan-Arkansas had no chance of authorization until the Kennedy administration came to the White House, two years after Aspinall became chair of the House Interior and Insular Affairs Committee. In many ways, Aspinall's reputation as a supreme water politician reached its apex in 1962, before the environmental movement coalesced into a force capable of damaging his reputation and the federal reclamation program he became so closely identified with.

THE FRYINGPAN-ARKANSAS PROJECT

By the time Wayne Aspinall became deeply engaged in the debate over the Fryingpan-Arkansas Reclamation Project, he had already achieved success as the author of the Collbran Project and was embroiled in the struggle for the CRSP. The CRSP experience taught Aspinall that both individual states and the larger American West needed to present a unified front when making the case for a reclamation project. In the battle for CRSP, Aspinall also learned, to his consternation, that water projects could easily be blocked or delayed by any House combination of eastern, urban, and California opposition. Overall, the sparsely populated West's power in the House was limited. Thus, a strong presence on the House Interior Committee was deemed essential by Aspinall and most western state and regional leaders.

After CRSP's enactment, the House Interior Committee would prioritize CRSP projects, recommend funding, and study additional reclamation proposals. On many levels, it guided western economic development. Because the CRSP impacted several Colorado River Basin states, Aspinall always gave implementing its projects precedence over enacting Fryingpan-Arkansas, a Colorado-only project.

The Colorado–Big Thompson Project (C-BT) first brought Western Slope water to the Front Range. Political leaders from Colorado Springs to Pueblo looked with envy at C-BT and began planning ways to supplement the Arkansas River valley's limited water supply from Western Slope sources. After experiencing severe drought cycles and the Dust Bowl years, regional civic leaders believed that only by supplementing the Arkansas River system could a strong and predictable economic future be ensured. Early drafts of what would become the Fryingpan-Arkansas Project (then known as the Gunnison-Arkansas Project) emphasized using Gunnison River Basin water and diverting it via transmontane tunnels to the Arkansas River valley.[39]

Political momentum for the project had begun building in the 1940s but was stunted by the predictable opposition of Western Slope Fourth District congressman Edward Taylor and by the nation's involvement in World War II. In addition, the Bureau of Reclamation's extensive commitment to C-BT delayed serious consideration of yet another costly Colorado project.[40] At this point, Fryingpan-Arkansas crossed the political sights of Third District congressman John Edgar Chenoweth (R-CO), who needed a strong local issue to champion. Though he had long been an opponent of the New Deal and federal spending, Chenoweth, like many western politicians, fell silent on the subject when expensive water projects were mentioned. Reclamation projects have been justified for many reasons, but Chenoweth, Aspinall, and others publicly maintained that the projects more than paid for themselves in repayment contracts, power produced and sold, and crops grown.[41] Fryingpan-Arkansas also enjoyed the unstinting support of Pueblo's major newspapers, the *Chieftain* and the *Star-Journal*. The energetic support of editor Frank S. Hoag and his son would figure prominently in debates over the project.

By the early 1950s, Fryingpan-Arkansas was being presented to a rapidly changing and at times hostile political world. Western Slope leaders blanched at the prospect of another diversion to the Front Range. Not only was C-BT about to go on-line, but the powerful Denver Water Board had managed to gain the approval of the Blue River–Dillon Reservoir diversion. The huge Roberts Tunnel channeled 47,000 acre-feet of water to growing, post–World War II Denver.[42] Wayne Aspinall, political protégé of Edward T. Taylor, would play a significant part in the delicate negotiations between the Western and Eastern Slopes that led up to the bill's 1962 passage. Following his rise to the chairship of the House Interior Committee, Aspinall found himself in a position first to shape the bill to overcome Western Slope opposition, then to command the necessary committee, House, and Administration support to gain its passage.

Like many other western bills put before the House and Senate Interior Committees, Fryingpan-Arkansas would face little opposition in the Senate, where it enjoyed the bipartisan support of Colorado senators Edward Johnson (Democrat, 1937–1955), Eugene Milliken (Republican, 1942–1957), Gordon Allott (Republican, 1955–1973), and John Carroll (Democrat, 1957–1963). A different story greeted Fryingpan-Arkansas in the House, where U.S. Representatives from eastern and urban states cast wary eyes at such an expensive project. Many eastern members of Congress saw the project as both costly and unwieldy, an example of what would come to be called pork-barrel legislation. Some California politicians opposed the project, fearing it would threaten that state's share of the Colorado River. The Fryingpan-Arkansas Project exposed, in stark outline, a basic lesson in reclamation geopolitics. As one Bureau of Reclamation official remarked, reclamation "is a Western problem and most of the House is from the East. The [House Interior] Committee has to sell every reclamation project to the House . . . but in the Senate, we [the West] have nineteen states. It's much easier."[43]

The story of the Fryingpan-Arkansas Project is a classic tale of reclamation politics. It also highlights the political conflict not only between the Upper and Lower Colorado River Basins, but between Colorado's Eastern and Western Slopes. The Front Range and Western Slope had feuded intermittently for decades over water issues. The most spectacular instance was Edward Taylor's insistence on compensatory water storage for the Western Slope before he would bless C-BT. Wayne Aspinall's conspicuous involvement in Fryingpan-Arkansas began in 1954, when strong opposition to the project emerged from California, the Western Slope, and eastern urban interests.

Aspinall's role in the project almost became a serious liability during his re-election campaign in the fall of 1954. After being favorably reported from the

Interior Committee that year, the bill failed (188–195),[44] disappointing and angering many Eastern Slope Coloradans. By the same token, the project's near passage scared many Western Slope residents, who feared yet another Front Range raid on their water. That fall, Wayne Aspinall got caught in the political middle, blamed for the bill's last-minute failure in the House and castigated by some Western Slope residents who feared losing western Colorado water.

Aspinall had supported the Fryingpan-Arkansas bill but was not sad to see it voted down by the Eighty-third Congress. In a lengthy memorandum to Frank Delaney, a former Democratic candidate for Congress and a recognized authority on Colorado water issues, Aspinall justified his position and outlined why the bill had failed. Aspinall blamed Republican J. Edgar Chenoweth for not adequately explaining to congressional colleagues why the bill deserved support. To Aspinall, who already had a reputation as a strong legislative technician, this was unforgivable. Instead of selling the project on its technical merits, Chenoweth had attempted to garner support from congressional friends as a personal political favor.

Aspinall also was against considering Fryingpan-Arkansas while CRSP and Echo Park were still being formulated and debated. Non-western members of Congress seemed "unable to differentiate between the contents of the Fryingpan-Arkansas and the Upper Colorado, which includes the Echo Park Dam," Aspinall reported to Delaney. Aspinall also discussed the vociferous opposition presented by Congressman John Saylor (R-PA), who saw Fryingpan-Arkansas as technically deficient and too much of a deviation from federal reclamation law. Saylor would play a significant role as both a critic of western reclamation policy and an advocate of new environmental attitudes in the years to come. Aspinall also emphasized to Delaney what would become his maxim throughout the Fryingpan-Arkansas ordeal: the Upper Colorado River program of CRSP needed to take precedence because its benefits would accrue to the entire state and region, not just the Colorado Front Range.[45]

Because of his stand on Fryingpan-Arkansas, Aspinall faced a difficult re-election challenge in 1954 from his Republican opponent, Charles E. Wilson. Large numbers of Pitkin County residents flocked to Wilson's candidacy, which was short on specifics but certain on one point: Wilson opposed Fry-Ark. This position struck *Daily Sentinel* reporter William Nelson as "like being against sin at a Billy Graham revival." In forum after forum across the Western Slope in October 1954, Aspinall carefully qualified his support for Fryingpan-Arkansas,[46] using a campaign tactic against Wilson that he would employ in succeeding elections. He stressed the tangible benefits his increasing seniority on the Interior Committee brought to the Fourth Congressional District. Aspinall believed that this ritualistic assertion would prove an effective election charm.

The Republicans had controlled both the House and the Senate during the Eighty-third Congress (1953–1954), but most political pundits believed the

Democrats would regain control following the 1954 election. If that occurred, Aspinall, who had begun his congressional career fourteenth in seniority on the Interior Committee, would then become second—only one person stood in the way of his meteoric climb to the chairship.

If Aspinall and the Democrats prevailed in November, the Palisade legislator would ascend to the chairship of the key House Subcommittee on Irrigation and Reclamation. As a *Daily Sentinel* reporter told the story, the election stakes for western Colorado were high, because if the Republicans retained House control, Representative Saylor would chair the subcommittee. Well-known in western Colorado for his opposition to Fryingpan-Arkansas and CRSP, Saylor was considered, perversely, somewhat of a hero in Pitkin County. As George Sanford Holmes—the *Daily Sentinel*'s Washington correspondent—phrased it, a Saylor chairship was "a contingency that should scare the daylights out of Colorado voters interested in developing their own water resources."[47] As election day neared, Aspinall frequently equated his mission in Congress to that of the late Edward T. Taylor—not to give away one drop of Western Slope water. Colorado River-system water, Aspinall asserted, should be used in western Colorado, "where the water falls and the snow melts."[48]

At the time, Aspinall believed the 1954 election campaign contained more "mistruth, half-truth, and untruth" than his previous sixteen state and national election contests. Aspinall experienced firsthand the volatile nature of Colorado's water politics. He would never make the mistake of putting himself in a position to be labeled by an opponent as less than 100 percent committed to retaining Western Slope water. Despite the confusion over his position, Aspinall still won an impressive victory over Charles E. Wilson, beating his opponent by more than 4,500 votes. Not surprisingly, Aspinall took a severe beating in Pitkin County, where he was trounced by two candidates—Wilson and, in a raucous last-minute write-in campaign, Pennsylvania's John Saylor, the staunch foe of Fryingpan-Arkansas.[49]

Aspinall's 1954 victory signified, in many ways, a turning point in the West's reclamation history. In January 1955, Aspinall took control of the House Interior Subcommittee on Irrigation and Reclamation, where he would engineer the compromise that led to the passage of the CRSP in 1956. As the second-ranking Democratic member, Aspinall was in a position to take the reins of the Interior Committee four years later and influence the West's reclamation future, including shaping the final form of the Fryingpan-Arkansas Project.

With Aspinall chairing the Subcommittee on Irrigation and Reclamation, Fryingpan-Arkansas would, at his insistence, take a backseat to work on the CRSP. Die-hard Fry-Ark activists in southeast Colorado chafed under Aspinall's reclamation priorities, hoping to move their project forward despite his well-known position. In 1956, with CRSP on the verge of authorization, Pueblo newspaper editor Frank S. Hoag, Jr., still lamented Aspinall's stranglehold over

Fryingpan-Arkansas's fate. Because his colleagues considered him an expert on reclamation, Aspinall's opposition to Fry-Ark's bid for a rule in the summer of 1956 hurt the project's chances. The rule's margin of defeat in 1956 was even greater than 1954, 179–194. Aspinall's failure to speak in support of the measure from the House floor inspired uncertainty in many members of Congress who took their reclamation voting cues from him. Following its 1956 defeat, Fryingpan-Arkansas was sent back to the drawing board again.[50]

Fryingpan-Arkansas would languish in Congress into the early 1960s, never really gaining legislative momentum until after Aspinall had begun consolidating his power as chair of the full Interior Committee. The project seemed particularly vulnerable to charges first expressed by *Newsweek* writer and former New Dealer Raymond Moley that it had a poor cost-benefit ratio and was generally "unsound"—a Rube Goldberg contraption for the Rockies, as Moley put it. Unsound political strategy by the bill's chief sponsor, Colorado Republican congressman J. Edgar Chenoweth, also routinely plagued Fry-Ark.[51]

Motivated to placate Western Slope opposition to the measure, Aspinall, as chair of the full Interior Committee, would be in a strong position to influence the bill's passage after 1959. Until it became law in 1962, project advocates from the Front Range routinely blamed Aspinall for not "aggressively assisting us." Aspinall, to many, became a scapegoat for Fryingpan-Arkansas's lack of legislative progress.[52]

House hearings on the bill in the late 1950s did not go smoothly for project proponents. According to Charles T. Biese, an attorney and longtime Fry-Ark booster, project opponents were granted far too much time to air their concerns during hearings by Irrigation and Reclamation Subcommittee chair Aspinall. Biese believed this pattern would continue as long as the committee (or subcommittee) was chaired by a Western Slope member of the House. Western Slope opposition to the project actually increased during the late 1950s as residents demanded a guarantee against future Front Range diversions. The precipitating crisis was the Denver Water Board's plans to build the Dillon Reservoir to supply Denver's growing population. Chief Fryingpan-Arkansas House sponsor J. Edgar Chenoweth had promised that his pet project would be the last transmontane diversion in Colorado, a promise he was never in a position to make or keep.[53]

To further complicate matters, in the 1950s, the Western Slope was experiencing a major population boom of its own. The 1950s "uranium frenzy" created new towns, swelled the population of others, and led to anxiety over the region's future water supply. Western Slope boosters envisioned the area becoming a major energy-producing hub based upon its massive but unrealized reserves of oil-bearing shale formations. Western Slope leaders believed that these resources would be developed in the near future, requiring massive water reserves. Because of these pressures and his commitment to CRSP, Aspinall maintained a generally safe distance from Fry-Ark in the late 1950s. He and others had come to the conclusion that Fryingpan-Arkansas's basic features needed alteration before the Western Slope would support the project.[54]

After becoming Interior Committee chair following the 1958 elections, Aspinall was at liberty to shape Fry-Ark's future. Hoping to effect a compromise that would unite the state behind the project and yield positive returns for the Western Slope, Aspinall became a major force behind a substantial revision of the bill. In particular, he favored scrapping Fry-Ark's Aspen Reservoir in exchange for the new Ruedi Reservoir, which had almost four times the capacity. The Ruedi Reservoir's waters would be used for replacement and regulatory purposes in both the Fryingpan and Roaring Fork Rivers. Retaining adequate stream flows had been a long-standing concern of Pitkin County residents. In the revised 1959–1960 drafts of the project, 69,200 acre-feet of water would be diverted annually from the Western Slope across the Continental Divide into the Arkansas Valley. More importantly for Aspinall and the Western Slope, Ruedi Reservoir, slated for construction before any water could be diverted to the east, would provide the Western Slope with crucial water-storage capacity. Additionally, existing Western Slope water rights on the Fryingpan and Roaring Fork Rivers would be decreed as senior to project water.

The new compromise version of Fry-Ark, the result of years of study, wrangling, and political turmoil, brought a degree of peace and cooperation between Colorado's contending Eastern and Western Slopes. The new tranquillity characterizing Colorado's water politics stemmed from Aspinall's increased political leverage after becoming chair of the House Interior Committee. The basis for the resolution of this thorny political question had been achieved during Aspinall's first term in that position. Fry-Ark's passage now awaited only a more propitious time for congressional consideration, and support from a strong president.[55]

Always a believer in careful political timing, Aspinall continued to insist that Fry-Ark's authorization follow the budgeting of crucial CRSP components. In 1960, Aspinall still sought additional appropriations for the CRSP-authorized Curecanti Project, located on the Gunnison River in the heart of his district. In 1959 Aspinall and other western reclamationists had fought the Eisenhower administration's "no new starts" policy toward water projects. After the president vetoed a public-works bill, Congress overrode the veto, allowing money to flow to authorized projects. Still, Aspinall wanted to proceed cautiously and wait until construction on Curecanti had started.[56] Once assurances of Curecanti funding had been received and the 1960 elections were over, Aspinall felt free to devote more attention to Fry-Ark. His deliberate and methodical approach to its authorization continued to frustrate the project's advocates, some of whom insisted that the Western Slope congressman did not have his heart in it.[57]

In a *Denver Post* feature article on New Year's Day 1961, Congressman Aspinall pledged to "carry the fight" for Fry-Ark's passage in the Eighty-seventh Congress, set to convene by the end of the month. Pledging early Interior Committee consideration in 1961, Aspinall's statement—his strongest expression of support for the project—was regarded as "highly significant" by Fry-Ark supporters. The *Post* pointed out that Aspinall's backing increased Fry-Ark's chances because he was "regarded as one of the most influential Western members of the House." Aspinall based his optimism on a favorable political climate, advantageous timing, and direct conversations with a supportive president-elect, John F. Kennedy.[58]

Despite Aspinall's support, it quickly became evident that Fryingpan-Arkansas would not be enacted in 1961. Too many unresolved questions remained, including the disposition of the new secretary of the interior, Stewart Udall, toward the project. Udall had called the project "a two-time loser" in Congress and was known to dislike J. Edgar Chenoweth, the project's chief House sponsor, because of the Pueblo congressman's conservative stand on many social issues. But with Aspinall promoting Fry-Ark in the Eighty-seventh Congress, Udall was forced to be more circumspect for fear of endangering other Kennedy administration conservation initiatives that needed to clear the House Interior Committee.

Senator Clinton Anderson (D-NM) erected another hurdle to passage—an ironic twist in that the Senate had quickly passed other versions of Fry-Ark with little difficulty. However, in 1961, with the New Mexico senator now installed as chair of the Senate Interior Committee, the older Senate dynamics no longer operated; Colorado's water projects might be subjected to a higher price for passage. One month after Anderson's Navajo–San Juan–Chama water project had passed the Senate, Aspinall, hoping to see his agenda advanced on the Senate side, scheduled hearings on Navajo–San Juan. Less than a month later, Aspinall's committee had favorably reported the bill. Though Colorado's Ute residents regarded Aspinall with approval, the House Interior chair would be held in less esteem by other western Native American tribes. In his consideration of Navajo–San Juan, Aspinall had insisted that the Navajos waive their Winters Doctrine water rights in order to gain access to project water. In addition, Aspinall inserted an amendment into the House bill, requiring that any water shortages be shared by all users. Historian Peter Iverson asserted that in the years ahead, the San Juan–Chama portion of the project moved toward completion while the Navajo irrigation project "continually faced inadequate funding and support."[59]

Aspinall and other congressional strategists made a decision not to press for Fry-Ark's passage in 1961. Targeting 1962, Fry-Ark's congressional supporters concentrated on building political momentum. Public opinion in the old center of resistance to Fryingpan-Arkansas, the mountain resort town of Aspen, had even reversed itself. A May 26, 1961, *Aspen Times* editorial sheepishly admitted that it had been wrong about the project. Two weeks later, the *Times* attempted to calm any lingering fears about Fryingpan-Arkansas by discussing the project's benefits to Aspen, the Western Slope, and Colorado at large. "We in Aspen," the *Times* proclaimed, "are not living in a vacuum."[60] With Fry-Ark reconfigured, Aspinall felt free to defend the project in committee deliberations over whether to send the bill to the House floor.

On the day of the committee vote, Aspinall observed that Fry-Ark had been studied and revised many times, mostly to overcome opposition from the Western Slope. During the long discussion prior to the 19–4 committee vote, Aspinall and Pennsylvania Republican John Saylor engaged in a classic parliamentary debate, with Aspinall ably defending the project's integrity. Aspinall's strong influence upon his committee helped the bill win this important vote.[61]

Aspinall set the stage for final congressional action on Fry-Ark during the fall of 1961 by noting that it would be the "top piece" of Interior Committee legislation for 1962. The first year of the Kennedy administration, 1961, had seen no reclamation projects authorized, but Aspinall expected a major harvest of authorizations and appropriations in 1962, an election year. In a letter to a Colorado water official, Aspinall insisted that Fry-Ark's authorization remained his "highest priority." The Colorado delegation's strategy to begin by seeking House approval reversed the old pattern of moving it through the less difficult Senate first. The wisdom of this decision would be tested in 1962.

Proclaiming that he was ready to "do or die" in 1962 for Fryingpan-Arkansas and New Mexico's Navajo–San Juan Project, Aspinall took charge of both bills in the House. In the process, his strategy illustrated some of the nuances of western water politics. By agreement with Senate Interior chair Clinton Anderson, Aspinall gave the New Mexico project priority over Fry-Ark. In considering both bills individually, Aspinall flaunted the wishes of Secretary Udall, who was moving toward proposing an omnibus water-development package that might include the Colorado and New Mexico projects but would most certainly include what was to be known as the Central Arizona Project. Udall would propose this controversial measure without the New Mexico and Colorado projects in 1963 as the Pacific Southwest Water Plan.[62]

The Navajo–San Juan Project sailed through the House on May 23, 1962, by voice vote after a strong lobbying campaign by New Mexico officials and a delegation of Navajo leaders. Navajo–San Juan and Fryingpan-Arkansas, paired together to this point, now went their separate ways because of the New Mexico project's one advantage—as Aspinall succinctly phrased it, "Indians." In the early 1960s, Native American water rights were beginning to be considered in larger western water-allocation formulas. New Mexico's Anglo-American political leaders realized that it might be possible to achieve larger reclamation goals by using the cover of a "Navajo blanket."[63] Heading into June 1962, Fryingpan-Arkansas did not enjoy the political advantage of a Native American constituency, though

Colorado senator Gordon Allott recognized that passing the New Mexico project would, in his words, "smooth the way for easier passage of the Fryingpan-Arkansas Project." After another difficult but successful struggle to obtain a rule, debate on Fry-Ark was scheduled for June 10, with a House vote the following day.[64]

In remarks prepared for House floor delivery, Wayne Aspinall gave Fry-Ark unequivocal support. Aspinall's reclamation philosophy emerged with stark clarity in this address. Not only was Fry-Ark a worthy project, he explained, it was needed to continue a "sound and orderly" reclamation program. Federal reclamation "is a program for turning the waters of the West to their maximum usefulness. It is oriented toward full economic development of the West—development which is largely dependent upon the availability of water." Fryingpan-Arkansas, Aspinall conceded to its critics, was not a simple project. The West had already run out of easy-to-utilize dam sites and water projects. Fry-Ark was "designed to make maximum use of Colorado's limited water resources." Blessed with the support of Colorado's full congressional delegation, Aspinall urged the enactment of this project, which he believed had been subjected to more study and debate than any in the history of western reclamation.[65]

The Kennedy administration also gave Fry-Ark strong, if belated, support. Reluctant to fully approve the bill until 1962 in part because of its identification with Republican J. Edgar Chenoweth, the Kennedy administration changed its attitude at the last minute because of Aspinall's full embrace of the project, not to mention the administration's absence of a reclamation record to campaign on in the West in the looming 1962 elections. As Interior Secretary Udall told President Kennedy the day before the House Fry-Ark vote, passing the project would help re-elect Colorado Democratic senator John Carroll, perhaps unseat J. Edgar Chenoweth, and, combined with Navajo–San Juan, "provide us with an excellent record of reclamation new starts for the fall campaign." A strong reclamation record still guaranteed any administration a substantial number of western votes, although the growing environmental movement, still in its infancy in 1962, would soon change things.[66]

After a ten-year struggle, on June 13, 1962, the House of Representatives passed the Fryingpan-Arkansas Project. On the same day, President Kennedy signed into law New Mexico's Navajo–San Juan Project. Aspinall, still fearing a voter backlash for his strong support of Fry-Ark, went to great lengths to identify the project's benefits for his Fourth District constituents. Among the many features Aspinall touted were increased Western Slope water-storage capacity with the Ruedi Reservoir, and the project's "far-reaching impact on development in western Colorado." To Aspinall, one of the most exciting uses for the water would be would be in starting up a vibrant oil-shale mining industry, a longtime dream of the Western Slope congressman. Finally, the Ruedi Dam and Reservoir would enable western Colorado's streams to be kept alive and flowing during the summer and fall diversion periods. Aspinall believed Fry-Ark, in its 1962 form, offered many tangible benefits for the Western Slope.[67]

Aspinall's congressional office files contain an abundance of testimonials praising his astute handling of the difficult Fry-Ark before the House. His reputation for deliberate politics and fairness persuaded many non-western representatives to support this bill and other legislation reported by his committee. At the time of the House vote, Pennsylvania representative Daniel Flood told Aspinall, "If you are for Fryingpan, then I'm for it." Hawaii representative Daniel Inouye, who had once served on Aspinall's Interior Committee, addressed Aspinall as his "Professor" and confessed that he knew little about the project but would still vote in favor of its construction. "I shall do so because I have the greatest of confidence in my teacher. I have never known my teacher to lead me down the wrong path." Before the House-floor vote on Fry-Ark, Al Ullman (D-OR), chair of the powerful House Ways and Means Committee, indicated to Aspinall that he would "be glad to follow your lead" in doing whatever he could to obtain its passage. It is clear that when Aspinall made Fry-Ark's passage a priority, however belatedly in the eyes of the project's longtime supporters, the bill moved steadily toward passage.[68]

By mid-July, the Senate Interior Committee had approved Fryingpan-Arkansas; the bill passed the Senate on August 7. The Kennedy administration had discussed the possibility of exploiting the bill's political potential by having the president sign it in Colorado during a proposed western political tour that fall. During the summer, Secretary Udall leaked this plan to Aspinall, who reacted unfavorably, as he always did when not consulted first on administration plans affecting his congressional district and state. Aspinall feared that if Kennedy signed the bill during a political tour, it would frame Fryingpan-Arkansas in a partisan light. Like most reclamation legislation, Fry-Ark had been a bipartisan effort. Colorado governor Steve McNichols lauded Aspinall's tireless work for Fry-Ark, noting that Colorado would "always be indebted to you for the fact that you have always placed loyalty to your state ahead of political advantage." While both the Eastern and Western Slopes benefited in tangible ways from the legislation's passage, McNichols knew that Aspinall's political opponents could "make capital" of his support for the project because those who did not understand it saw only that it appeared to give away Western Slope water.[69]

The Fryingpan-Arkansas Bill, ready for President Kennedy's pen, was signed into law at the White House on August 16, 1962. Kennedy did include Pueblo, Colorado, on his fall western tour in an attempt, at Udall's steady urging, to excite Colorado's Democrats to defeat Republican Fry-Ark warhorse J. Edgar Chenoweth and other western Republicans. As it turned out, neither Aspinall nor Chenoweth would experience difficulty from their respective electorates on election day 1962. This would be the last time Aspinall's constituency was strictly

Western Slope; in 1964 the Colorado Legislature would reapportion his district to include several Eastern Slope counties.

The Fryingpan-Arkansas story illustrates the precarious water politics practiced by Aspinall as he attempted to balance the water needs of his district with those of the entire state. In particular, Aspinall learned that the state and region needed to present a united front when asking the rest of the nation to support their peculiar reclamation needs. As Aspinall said of Colorado during the House debate over Fry-Ark, "if you can find any more unanimity in a state, I would like to know about it." Aspinall's ability to lead and persuade was on display throughout the Fryingpan-Arkansas saga. During the final floor debates, project opponent John Saylor offered five amendments that, collectively, would have compromised Fry-Ark significantly. Aspinall supported two of Saylor's amendments, the only two that passed. By 1962, Aspinall had become guardian of the West's water and arbiter of any disputes pertaining to it.[70]

Aspinall's relations with the Kennedy administration illustrate the central place he occupied in its ambitious conservation plans. Through 1962, a strong reclamation program and a conservation agenda were viewed as compatible. Despite supporting limited programs of environmental protection and wilderness legislation, Kennedy and Udall "adhered to a traditional agenda which emphasized the efficient use of natural resources."[71] In the years ahead, balancing calls for preservation with the need for resource development would represent the most difficult task facing Udall, Aspinall, and others concerned with public lands.[72] Udall and Aspinall would gravitate increasingly to opposite poles of the conservation spectrum, with Udall moving toward the ranks of the preservationists while Aspinall became known as the country's leading voice for utilitarian land use. The event that would separate the two men more than any other was the long fight for the Wilderness Act. Aspinall's struggle to shape the ultimate form of Wilderness legislation earned him the eternal enmity of the nation's growing environmental movement.

ENDNOTES

1. Herbert S. Parmet, *Jack: The Struggles of John F. Kennedy* (New York: Dial Press, 1980), 388–389.

2. Wayne Aspinall interview with Al Look, Mesa County Oral History Program (OH-120, Part 1), Research Center and Special Library, Museum of Western Colorado, Grand Junction, CO (hereafter cited as MWC), January 10, 1978.

3. Wayne Aspinall interview, January 10, 1978; Wayne N. Aspinall interview with Nancy Whistler, Association of Former Members of Congress Project, Manuscript Division, Library of Congress, Washington, DC, February 15, 1979; Wayne N. Aspinall interview with Charles T. Morrisey, John F. Kennedy Presidential Library, Boston, MA (hereafter cited as JFKPL), November 10, 1965.

4. Ibid.

5. Ibid.

6. Joseph F. Dolan to Ted Sorensen, n.d., Box 928, fd: "Colo–Jos Dolan, 5-22-57–12-16-57," John F. Kennedy Pre-presidential Papers, JFKPL; Ted Sorensen and Bob Wallace to John F. Kennedy, July 14, 1959, Box 928, fd: "1960 Campaign File, Colorado Organization, 7-14-59," John F. Kennedy Pre-presidential Papers, JFKPL.

7. Joseph F. Dolan to Ted Sorensen, April 28, 1959, and Joseph F. Dolan to Ted Sorensen, April 30, 1959, Box 928, fd: "1960 Campaign Files, Colorado, Jos. F. Dolan, 1-22-59–6-29-59," John F. Kennedy Pre-presidential Papers, JFKPL; "Colorado Unit Formed to Back Kennedy," n.d., ca. 1959, Box 928, fd: "1960 Campaign File, Colo. Clippings," John F. Kennedy Pre-presidential Papers, JFKPL.

8. Sorensen and Wallace to Kennedy, July 14, 1959; Pueblo (CO) *Star Journal* and Pueblo *Chieftain*, March 15, 1959, Box 928, fd: "1960 Campaign Files–Colorado Public Relations, 3-15-59," John F. Kennedy Pre-presidential Papers, JFKPL.

9. Joseph F. Dolan to Ted Sorensen, November 22, 1959, Box 928, fd: "1960 Campaign file–Colo. Jos Dolan–10/8/59–12-17-59," John F. Kennedy Pre-presidential Papers, JFKPL.

10. "Remarks of Senator John F. Kennedy, Grand Junction, CO, November 30, 1959," Box 905, fd: "Senate Files–Speech File, Democratic Dinner, Grand Junction, CO, November 30, 1959," John F. Kennedy Pre-presidential Papers, JFKPL.

11. Wayne N. Aspinall to Watters Martin, December 21, 1959, Box 14, fd: 13, Wayne N. Aspinall Papers, University of Colorado Archives, University of Colorado at Boulder, Boulder, CO (hereafter cited as UCAUCB).

12. Stewart L. Udall, interview with author, Grand Junction, CO, March 31 and April 1, 1998; F. Ross Peterson, "The Creation of an Environmental Agenda: Stewart L. Udall Takes Charge, 1961–64" (paper presented at the meeting of the Western History Association, St. Paul, MN, October 17, 1997), 3–4.

13. Stewart L. Udall to John F. Kennedy, November 24, 1959, Box 78, fd: 1, Stewart L. Udall Papers, Special Collections, University of Arizona Library, Tucson, AZ (hereafter cited as SCUAL); Stewart L. Udall to J. K. Evans, July 1, 1960, Box 72, fd: "Correspondence June, 1960," Stewart L. Udall Papers, SCUAL.

14. Aspinall seemed to be among those who hoped that Stevenson would actively seek the Democratic nomination again in 1960. Short of that, Aspinall and many other Democrats hoped Stevenson would be the candidate a deadlocked convention would turn to. After the spring of 1960, when Kennedy appeared to have the nomination secured, Aspinall would likely still have been more comfortable with a Stevenson-Kennedy ticket. As late as May 1960, Stevenson still appeared interested in rumors of an impending presidential draft. When talk of a Stevenson-Kennedy ticket swirled around, Stevenson, according to Arthur M. Schlesinger, Jr., did little to discourage it. Kennedy saw Stevenson as the obstacle in his path to a clear-cut convention victory; if Stevenson would publicly announce that he was not interested in the presidency, Aspinall and others would be free to support Kennedy. See discussions about Stevenson's 1960 "shadow candidacy" in John Bartlow Martin, *Adlai Stevenson and the World: The Life of Adlai E. Stevenson* (Garden City, NY: Anchor Books, 1978), 496–498.

15. Joseph F. Dolan interview with Charles T. Morrisey, December 1, 1964, JFKPL; Charles J. Traylor interview with author, Grand Junction, CO, November 18, 1994;

Charles Traylor speaking on Wayne Aspinall 100th Birthday Anniversary Videocassette, April 3, 1996, Archives and Special Collections, Mesa State College, Grand Junction, CO (hereafter cited as MSC).

16. Wayne N. Aspinall to Preston Walker, May 11, 1960, Box 22, fd: "Very Personal Correspondence, P–Z," Wayne Aspinall Papers, University of Denver Archives, Denver, CO (hereafter cited as UDA).

17. Ibid.

18. For a good overview of the Los Angeles convention from the perspective of a Kennedy supporter, particularly for its observations of the last-minute Stevenson push, see Arthur Schlesinger, Jr., *A Thousand Days: John F. Kennedy in the White House* (Boston: Houghton Mifflin, 1965), 33–61; Charles J. Traylor interview, November 18, 1994; Wayne N. Aspinall interview by Joe B. Frantz, June 14, 1974, Box 1, fd: 15, Wayne N. Aspinall Papers, UCAUCB; Grand Junction *Daily Sentinel*, July 12, 1960.

19. Jim F. Heath, *Decade of Disillusionment: The Kennedy-Johnson Years* (Bloomington: Indiana University Press, 1975), 43–44.

20. Russell Martin, *A Story That Stands Like a Dam: Glen Canyon and the Struggle for the Soul of the West* (New York: Henry Holt, 1989), 215–231, discusses Udall's inspection trip to Rainbow Bridge.

21. See, for example, Martin, *Story That Stands Like a Dam*, 215–216.

22. Martin, *Story That Stands Like a Dam*, 215–216; Mary Louis Giblin to Pierre Salinger, May 7, 1960, and Pierre Salinger to Mary Louise Giblin, May 24, 1960, Box 1038, fd: "1960 Campaign File—Colorado, September 23, 1959–June 27, 1960," John F. Kennedy Pre-presidential Papers, JFKPL; Stewart L. Udall interview, March 31 and April 1, 1998; Stewart L. Udall, interview with Charles T. Morrisey, March 15, 1979, Box 10, Association of Former Members of Congress Project, Manuscript Division, Library of Congress, Washington, DC; Stewart L. Udall, comments at the meeting of the Western History Association, St. Paul, MN, October 17, 1997; Traylor's comments quoted in *Daily Sentinel*, July 12, 1960. The same issue also contains rumors of Aspinall's likely candidacy for the Interior post if Kennedy prevailed in November.

23. "If Kennedy Wins White House—Look for the 'Young Deal,'" *U.S. News and World Report* 49, no 4 (July 25, 1960): 58; *Arizona Daily Star* article quoted in the *Yuma* (AZ) *Sun*, July 31, 1960, Box 79, fd: 1, Stewart L. Udall Papers, SCUAL.

24. Stewart L. Udall interview, March 31 and April 1, 1998; Tommy Neal interview with author, Grand Junction, CO, January 4, 1997; Udall comments at Western History Association meeting, October 17, 1997.

25. Richard Allan Baker, *Conservation Politics: The Senate Career of Clinton P. Anderson* (Albuquerque: University of New Mexico Press, 1985), 129–130; Arthur Schlesinger, Jr., *Robert Kennedy and His Times* (Boston: Houghton Mifflin, 1978), 225–226; Stewart L. Udall interview, March 31 and April 1, 1998; Peterson, "Creation of an Environmental Agenda," 5.

26. *Daily Sentinel*, November 15, 1960.

27. Udall, comments at Western History Association meeting, October 17, 1997; Martin, *Story That Stands Like a Dam*, 223–224; Stewart L. Udall interview, March 31 and April 1, 1998.

28. Stewart L. Udall interview, March 15, 1979; Stewart L. Udall interview, March 31 and April 1, 1998.

29. *Daily Sentinel,* November 17, 1960.

30. Hal K. Rothman, *The Greening of a Nation? Environmentalism in the United States Since 1945* (Fort Worth, TX: Harcourt Brace, 1998), 72, asserts that Udall "walked a delicate line between development and preservation."

31. I am indebted to Charles Coate, "Vision, Politics, and Compromise: Stewart L. Udall and the Department of the Interior" (paper presented at the meeting of the Western History Association, St. Paul, MN, October 17, 1997), 1–2. Coate cites Udall's remarks before Interior Department meetings on the National Park Service, February 23, 1961, and a press release from March 9, 1962.

32. Coate, "Vision, Politics, and Compromise," 8; Stewart L. Udall interview, March 31 and April 1, 1998.

33. Martin, *Story That Stands Like a Dam,* 233, is the source of the "cognizant" quote; Rothman, *Greening of a Nation?,* 79–85.

34. Lee White to Larry O'Brien, February 9, 1961, Box 49, President's Office Files, Legislative Files, John F. Kennedy Papers, JFKPL. The Rifle Naval Oil Reserve is discussed in Andrew Gulliford, *Boomtown Blues: Colorado Oil Shale, 1885–1985* (Niwot: University Press of Colorado, 1989), 6, 49, 62.

35. Stewart L. Udall, *The Quiet Crisis* (New York: Holt, Rinehart and Winston, 1963). Writers Alvin Josephy and Wallace Stegner both contributed to the book's genesis. See Peterson, "Creation of an Environmental Agenda," 13–14.

36. Coate, "Vision, Politics, and Compromise," 2–3.

37. All the Udall quotes are from Peterson, "Creation of an Environmental Agenda," 11–13.

38. John F. Kennedy, "White House Message on Conservation," February 28, 1962, Box 98, fd: "Conservation," President's Office Files, Subject Files, John F. Kennedy Presidential Papers, JFKPL.

39. Carol Jean Drake Mehls, "Into the Frying Pan: J. Edgar Chenoweth and the Fryingpan-Arkansas Reclamation Project" (Ph.D. dissertation, University of Colorado at Boulder, 1986), 117.

40. Mehls, "Into the Frying Pan," 119.

41. Marc Reisner challenges this dubious assertion throughout his provocative study, *Cadillac Desert: The American West and Its Disappearing Water,* rev. ed. (New York: Penguin Press, 1993), passim.

42. Duane Vandenbusche and Duane A. Smith, *A Land Alone: Colorado's Western Slope* (Boulder, CO: Pruett Publishing, 1981), 265.

43. Richard F. Fenno, Jr., *Congressmen in Committees* (Boston: Little, Brown, 1973), 263.

44. Ibid., 261.

45. Wayne Aspinall to Frank Delaney, August 8, 1954, Box 168, fd: 15, Frank Delaney Papers, UCAUCB.

46. *Daily Sentinel,* October 15 and 17, 1954.

47. *Daily Sentinel,* October 18, 1954.

48. *Daily Sentinel*, October 29, 1954.

49. *Daily Sentinel*, November 3, 1954; *Daily Sentinel*, September 4, 1960; Stewart Udall phone interview with author, November 10, 1997; Stewart Udall interview, March 31 and April 1, 1998.

50. Frank S. Hoag, Jr., to Senator Eugene D. Milliken, December 8, 1954, Box 74, fd: 24, J. Edgar Chenoweth Papers, UCAUCB; see undated editorial, ca. March 1956, from Pueblo *Star-Chieftain*, Box 75, fd: 22, J. Edgar Chenoweth Papers, UCAUCB; Fenno, *Congressmen in Committees*, 261; Mehls, "Into the Frying Pan," 172.

51. Raymond Moley, "Rube Goldberg in the Rockies," *Newsweek* 43, no. 21 (May 24, 1954): 100. Moley called Fryingpan-Arkansas "one of those curious, complicated Rube Goldberg contraptions," equating it with the Colorado–Big Thompson Project that was being finished "just to the north."

52. Ibid.

53. Charles T. Biese to Gordon Allott, May 5, 1957, Box 72, fd: "Public Works I–Legislation—Fryingpan-Arkansas, 1957," Series VI, Gordon Allott Papers, UCAUCB; Mehls, "Into the Frying Pan," 187–190.

54. "Uranium frenzy" is Raye C. Ringholz's phrase. See Raye C. Ringholz, *Uranium Frenzy: Boom and Bust on the Colorado Plateau* (New York: W. W. Norton, 1989). Frank S. Hoag, Jr., to Gordon Allott, January 9, 1957, Box 72, fd: "Public Works I–Legislation—Fryingpan-Arkansas, 1957," Series VI, Gordon Allott Papers, UCAUCB.

55. Pueblo *Star-Journal*, April 8, 1959, and January 13, 1960; Daniel Tyler, *The Last Water Hole in the West: The Colorado–Big Thompson Project and the Northern Colorado Water Conservancy District* (Niwot: University Press of Colorado, 1992), 294. Colorado's entire congressional delegation, in a show of unity, introduced the "new" Fry-Ark proposal in 1959.

56. Pueblo *Star-Journal*, January 13, 1960.

57. Gordon Allott to Frank S. Hoag, Jr., February 3, 1960, Box 73, fd: "Public Works 1–Fryingpan–1960," Series VI, Gordon Allott Papers, UCAUCB. Contracts to build Curecanti were put to bid on April 5, 1962. Curecanti is one of four major CRSP units, the others being Glen Canyon (Arizona), Flaming Gorge (Utah), and Navajo (New Mexico). Construction of the Curecanti unit, renamed the Wayne N. Aspinall unit in 1980, included three dams—Blue Mesa, Crystal, and Morrow Point. The unit was completed in 1968. See Bureau of Reclamation news releases, April 5, 1962, and January 30, 1968, Box 1, fd: 41, William Nelson Papers, MSC.

58. *Denver Post*, January 1, 1961.

59. *Denver Post*, February 8, 1961; Baker, *Conservation Politics*, 247–248; Mehls, "Into the Frying Pan," 208–209; Peter Iverson, *The Navajo Nation* (Westport, CT: Greenwood Press, 1981), 112–114.

60. *Aspen Times*, May 26, 1961, and June 9, 1961; Pueblo *Star-Chieftain*, June 2, 1961.

61. *Fryingpan-Arkansas Project, Colorado*. House Interior and Insular Affairs Committee, Committee Papers, Unpublished Transcripts, Hearings, June 21, 1961, on H.R. 2206, Box 923, fd: "87A-F8.5, Minutes of Full Committee, last Session, 2 of 2," Center for Legislative Archives, National Archives, Washington, DC.

62. *Denver Post*, January 10, 1963.

63. Pueblo *Star-Journal*, September 10, 1962.

64. Gordon Allott, "Statement for Fryingpan-Arkansas Project," May 23, 1962, Box 78, fd: "Public Works, Fryingpan-Arkansas, 1961," Series VI, Gordon Allott Papers, UCAUCB.

65. Wayne N. Aspinall, "Remarks on H.R. 2206," Box 49, fd: "Fry-Ark History," Wayne Aspinall Papers, UDA; Wayne N. Aspinall to Congressional Colleagues, June 6, 1962, Box 49, fd: "Fry-Ark History," Wayne Aspinall Papers, UDA.

66. Mehls, "Into the Frying Pan," 209; Stewart Udall, "Report to the President," June 12, 1962, Box 980, fd: 7, Stewart L. Udall Papers, SCUAL.

67. Wayne N. Aspinall, "Capital Comments," June 16, 1962, Box 102, fd: 50, Wayne Aspinall Papers, UDA.

68. Daniel J. Flood to Wayne N. Aspinall, June 13, 1962; Daniel K. Inouye to Wayne N. Aspinall, June 8, 1962; and Al Ullman to Wayne N. Aspinall, June 7, 1962, all in Box 49, fd: "Fryingpan-Arkansas History—Correspondence," Wayne Aspinall Papers, UDA.

69. Claude DeSautels to Larry O'Brien, July 23, 1962, White House Staff Files, Lawrence O'Brien, Box 1, fd: "Aspinall, Wayne," John F. Kennedy Presidential Files, JFKPL; Steve McNichols to Wayne Aspinall, August 10, 1962, Box 49, fd: "Fryingpan-Arkansas History—Post Passage," Wayne Aspinall Papers, UDA.

70. Mehls, "Into the Frying Pan," 251–252; Fenno, *Congressmen in Committees*, 262.

71. Thomas G. Smith, "John F. Kennedy, Stewart Udall, and New Frontier Conservation," Pacific Historical Review 64 (August 1995): 337.

72. Peterson, "Creation of an Environmental Agenda," 6.

CHAPTER FOUR
FROM THE NEW FRONTIER TO THE WILDERNESS: ASPINALL AND EARLY ENVIRONMENTALISM

EARLY WILDERNESS BILL STRUGGLES

Wayne Aspinall's attitude toward Wilderness legislation helps elucidate western politics in mid-twentieth-century America. For almost a decade, Aspinall opposed the idea of creating federally protected wilderness areas. A utilitarian conservationist, Aspinall viewed wilderness protection as a violation of his belief in the right of the people to make use of natural resources. To Aspinall, Wilderness legislation favored a narrow interest group, those who used public lands recreationally. Aspinall's eventual endorsement of the Wilderness Act occurred only after he had shaped and reconfigured the original legislation into something that he and other western resource users could live with. In the long struggle for Wilderness legislation, Aspinall emerged in the public's view as the leading foe of the growing environmental movement.

The dream of a Wilderness bill reached back to the 1920s, when National Forest Service employee Aldo Leopold first convinced his bureaucratic masters to set aside portions of the Gila National Forest as wilderness. The idea of federally designated wilderness was kept alive by private conservation groups such as The Wilderness Society (founded in 1935) and the Sierra Club, and by government supporters such as Franklin D. Roosevelt's secretary of the interior, Harold Ickes. In 1950, Howard Zahniser, executive director of The Wilderness Society, reviewed Aldo Leopold's classic meditation on the environment, *A Sand County Almanac*. Zahniser admitted that Leopold's influence upon his own ideas was great and that his sudden death in 1948 came as a "shock to us all." To Zahniser's generation, the book imparted the author's rich knowledge and understanding of "the wild things of our world" and bequeathed "a sense of belonging to the whole community of life."[1] By the early 1950s, Zahniser had fashioned a proposed draft of the Wilderness Bill and began lobbying Congress for its introduction.[2]

Aldo Leopold, as much as anyone, deserves to be called the father of wilderness preservation in the United States. From the 1920s until his death, Leopold consistently argued for the importance of setting aside land as wilderness. Leopold biographer Curt Meine wrote that the national leaders who formed The Wilderness Society in the 1930s "found much of their inspiration in Leopold's early efforts and words." In his first letter to Leopold, Wilderness Society founder and zealot Robert Marshall called him "the Commanding General of the Wilderness Battle." There is no doubt that Leopold's influence upon the movement for Wilderness was profound.[3]

After several decades of discussion, the plan for federally designated wilderness finally crystallized in the early 1950s at the Sierra Club's biennial wilderness conferences. National Forest land was being managed as wilderness, but Wilderness advocates feared that land protected by one secretary of agriculture could be wiped out by his or her successor. David Brower recalled that conservationists "wanted something that would give wilderness a stronger kind of protection." The Wilderness movement was buoyed by the successful defeat of the Echo Park Dam proposal in 1956. For the first time, in historian Hal Rothman's words, Americans faced a "pivotal movement" in which they questioned "the course of their society." Progress, traditionally measured in terms of programs for rapid economic growth, had been temporarily thwarted. Many scholars believe that the modern environmental movement arose from the ashes of the Echo Park Dam proposal.[4]

Popular attitudes toward wilderness and the outdoors were changing throughout the United States in the post–World War II era. Increasing numbers of urbanites sought the solace of the great outdoors. Establishment of a national wilderness preservation system would gain increasing support over the years. As a product of the West's post-frontier era and a supporter of the region's extractive industries, Wayne Aspinall saw the land as a source of capital and never understood the nation's desire to lock it up as wilderness.

An initial version of the Wilderness Bill was introduced into the second session of the Eighty-fourth Congress immediately after the defeat of the Echo Park Dam when Howard Zahniser persuaded Minnesota Democratic senator Hubert Humphrey and Pennsylvania Republican representative John Saylor to sponsor it. Over the next eight years, seemingly endless hearings would be held on the legislation in both houses of Congress. The bill, however, would always face a tougher road in the House of Representatives, where it had to pass through the domain of Wayne Aspinall, chair of the House Interior and Insular Affairs Committee. To claim that Aspinall, more than any other individual, both delayed and shaped the ultimate form of the Wilderness Act is no exaggeration.

Aspinall paid little attention to Humphrey and Saylor's early drafts of the Wilderness Bill. As chair of the House Reclamation and Irrigation Subcommittee, he was busy shaping the final form of the Colorado River Storage Project of 1956. Introduced in Congress less than two months after the Colorado River Storage Act finally passed into law, the Zahniser-Humphrey Wilderness Bill faced an uphill battle. Written largely by Zahniser, the first Wilderness Bill declared that it was the intent of Congress "to secure for the American people of present and future generations the benefits of an enduring reservoir of wilderness." The bill went on to itemize more than 160 areas of national forests, national parks, national monuments, national wildlife refuges, and Native American reservations that would constitute the heart of a national wilderness preservation system.[5]

In addition, Zahniser hoped to create a National Wilderness Preservation Council consisting of key federal resource administrators and citizen conservationists who would gather information on other potential Wilderness areas and make recommendations for expansion of the system. Zahniser believed that the executive branch of the federal government should be responsible for maintenance and expansion of the Wilderness system. This in itself would prove a controversial provision in early drafts of the bill. Earlier National Forest Service efforts at wilderness preservation had been subject to the caprice of bureaucrats. Some key lands would be approved, while others, equally meritorious, would be rejected. The Forest Service simply made a recommendation to the secretary of agriculture, who, usually without exception, agreed. No appeals followed a secretary's unilateral decision. Of course, the wishes of timber companies could influence Forest Service wilderness recommendations or later decisions to shrink protected areas.[6] Howard Zahniser's proposal was an attempt to "capitalize on the momentum of the Echo Park decision even at the risk of engendering opposition that less ambitious proposals would have avoided."[7]

Perhaps the first bill was flawed. Maybe it was too soon after the draining Echo Park fight. Whatever the case, Congress was in no mood to yield another clear victory to the growing conservation movement. Aspinall, Senator Clinton Anderson, and other concerned western leaders employed a time-tested tactic to delay serious consideration of the measure: they suggested waiting until Congress had created an Outdoor Recreation Resources Review Commission (ORRRC) to review the proposal. As sponsor of the House version of the ORRRC, Aspinall envisioned the commission as a forum to study, among other topics, the place of wilderness within the nation's recreational future. Any congressional action on Wilderness legislation would, of course, have to await the ORRRC's final report and recommendations.[8]

The Outdoor Recreation Resources Review Commission, signed into law on June 28, 1958, had a September 1961 deadline to complete its work. Charged with conducting a nationwide study of recreational lands, as well as assessing future recreational resource needs, the ORRRC, as Aspinall, Anderson, and others argued, could conceivably, through its findings, impact the final form any potential Wilderness legislation might take.[9]

In 1957 and 1958, both the Senate and House Interior Committees held hearings on various versions of the Wilderness Bill, but all variants died with the end of the Eighty-fifth Congress. The immense obstacles facing the legislation were readily detectable from the bill's first foray in front of congressional committees. Aspinall took some of his earliest public stands against the Wilderness Bill in 1957 while serving as acting chair of the House Interior and Insular Affairs Committee and as an ex-officio member of the House Public Lands Subcommittee. In his usual forthright manner, Aspinall pointed out that many congressional Wilderness advocates, like California congressman George P. Miller, championed the cause because their home districts did not contain any potential Wilderness areas. Miller represented California's Fifth District, near Oakland. By contrast, Aspinall's district was heavily targeted for Wilderness designation. His hostility to the proposed National Wilderness Preservation Council emerged during these hearings. Aspinall, along with witnesses from the American Pulpwood Association and the American National Cattleman's Association, feared that the Preservation Council would be, in Aspinall's words, "loaded" with members friendly to "wilderness area values" and opposed to most nonconforming uses.[10]

During the hearings, Aspinall greeted opponents of the Wilderness Bill almost gleefully while scorning or casting aspersions on bill supporters. Aspinall timed the pro-Wilderness testimony of such notable conservationists as David Brower, Howard Zahniser, and Sigurd Olson precisely and raised a point of order, asking that half the committee's time be occupied with the bill's opponents. In a testimony submitted to both the House and Senate Interior Committees in 1957, close Aspinall friend Ival V. Goslin, secretary of the Upper Colorado River Commission, anticipated many of Aspinall's later public objections to the measure. According to Goslin, the bill espoused the notion that "preservation of the wilderness shall be paramount" and would therefore be "unreasonable," not to mention "unrealistic, monopolistic, and contrary to the real American philosophy of multiple or joint use of our natural resources for the benefit in the long run of the most people for the longest period of time." Goslin particularly blasted the proposed Wilderness Preservation Council as legally incorporating a special-interest political perspective. The council would usurp functions carried out by federal administrative agencies and their trained staffs. Over the next several years, Aspinall would voice many of the same objections to various versions of the Wilderness Bill.[11]

By the end of the 1957–1958 congressional session, Aspinall had established himself as a staunch foe of Wilderness legislation. Thus, it is not surprising that when he became chair of the House Interior and Insular Affairs Committee at the start of the Eighty-sixth Congress in 1959, Wilderness Society strategists targeted the U.S. Senate for initial passage of the Wilderness Bill. Though the Senate was not completely friendly territory, Wilderness advocates did not have to face Aspinall and other western members of the House who had to answer to their constituents every two years. Many western politicians feared that any discussion of the Wilderness Bill could be viewed as a threat to vested economic interests. Still, the bill would need to pass the House eventually, so advocates like Howard Zahniser regularly went out of their way to engage Aspinall in friendly Wilderness-related conversation. In 1959, Zahniser could report to the Sierra Club's David Brower that he was working hard for Aspinall's "constructive consideration" of the measure. "We have been considering his wishes and anticipating his concurrence."[12] Events would prove Zahniser a poor prophet. Aspinall was not averse to discussing the bill in a theoretical way, but his concurrence was a long way off.

The first set of congressional hearings in 1957 had demonstrated that the bill needed substantial alteration. Over the next three years, it underwent revision after revision but still was not close to passage when the Kennedy administration took office in January 1961. In 1958, the final year of the Eighty-fifth Congress, Howard Zahniser and other Wilderness advocates had reworked the measure in light of the many objections made against it during the 1957 hearings. One Zahniser strategy was to gain the support of Senator Clinton Anderson (D-NM), former secretary of agriculture under President Truman and an influential senior member of the Senate Interior and Insular Affairs Committee chaired by Montana Democrat James E. Murray. Anderson, the ranking Democrat behind the aged Murray, was a longtime friend of conservation causes but had not yet thrown his support behind the Wilderness Bill. Anderson and other potential supporters had been alienated by the militant, uncompromising tone of the early Wilderness Bill drafts.[13]

By 1959, Wayne Aspinall had begun formulating his long-term Wilderness Bill strategy. Many of the ideas he proposed at this time would be refined, redeveloped, and repeated like a mantra over the long course of the fight. In 1958, the enormous publicity surrounding the Wilderness initiative had alerted westerners to the possibility of another conservationist coup. Grand Junction's *Daily Sentinel,* always the voice of the conservative Western Slope, screamed on November 9, 1958: "CONSERVATIONISTS CLUTCHING AGAIN." The same gang of conservationists who had "bushwhacked" the West's hopes for water and power development at Echo Park were "on the prowl again." The article reported Congressman Aspinall's speech to the Colorado Cattleman's Association meeting in Montrose, where he revealed his Wilderness strategy. Demonstrating that he had learned valuable political lessons from the loss of Echo Park, Aspinall counseled western resource users to first realize that they represented a political minority when up against the political power of East and West

Coast-based conservation organizations. "The wisest course," Aspinall proclaimed, "is to give a little and seek to get into the bill those safeguards deemed necessary to protect regional interests of stockmen, lumbermen, miners, and proper provisions for water development." Speaking in late December 1958 to a small group of Western Slope farmers and ranchers, Aspinall affirmed his belief in the multiple-use philosophy of public-land management while reiterating his developing position on wilderness. Aspinall informed the gathering that he could hold off the bill in his committee for at least two more years, giving western land interests "time to prepare defenses" against the proposal. Once again, fearing another Echo Park fight, Aspinall predicted that some compromise would be inevitable because the seventeen western states rich in public land lacked political power.[14]

By 1959, foes of the Wilderness Bill had discovered strategies to both delay and sidetrack the measure. To Aspinall's pleasure, by the start of the Eighty-sixth Congress, the bill had been safely placed on the "back burner."[15] Particularly useful to Wilderness opponents was the 1958 enactment of the ORRRC, which enabled them to argue, "often with less than complete sincerity," that Wilderness Act passage should await the outcome of ORRRC deliberations.[16] Even young Arizona congressman Stewart L. Udall, still a dedicated utilitarian conservationist, echoed Aspinall, his Interior Committee chair, urging delay of the measure until at least the start of the next congressional session, in 1961. "The bill has stirred up more controversy in the West than any in recent years," Udall remarked. The issue, he continued, demanded more study and the incorporation of multiple-use language into the measure.[17]

Though the Wilderness Bill did not pose an immediate threat to Aspinall and his constituents, he continued to refine his arguments against it during the Eighty-sixth Congress. Writing to David Brower, a frank Aspinall advised the Sierra Club chief of his continued antagonism and what it might take to gain his constructive cooperation. He told Brower he would oppose the bill until its sponsors were "able to get together with the other users of public lands in the West and assure them that the Wilderness Bill supporters are not endeavoring to destroy already established uses (which include water resources development, mining, grazing, etc.)."[18]

Not surprisingly, during the Eighty-sixth Congress, Wilderness legislation foundered in Aspinall's House Interior Committee, where it faced an Aspinall-erected stone wall. Still, some Wilderness advocates in the House grew increasingly impatient with Aspinall's delaying tactics. California congressman Clem Miller informed David Brower that many of the House Interior Committee's members were concerned that Aspinall intended to "defer all decisions on recreation and wilderness" until the ORRRC report was complete. Miller recognized Aspinall's tactic as an attempt to delay full consideration of the Wilderness Bill. Brower, Miller, and other Wilderness advocates were buoyed by a letter from California Republican senator Thomas H. Kuchel, who informed Brower that the Senate would work on Wilderness legislation regardless of any impending ORRRC deliberations.[19]

In the Senate, little headway was made toward passing Wilderness legislation during the Eighty-sixth Congress, but a few developments foreshadowed eventual positive action. Responding to criticism voiced during the 1958 Senate hearings, Zahniser and Brower worked to reshape the bill's language to make it more acceptable to wary western senators. Other supporters, like original bill sponsor Hubert Humphrey, worked to convert New Mexico senator Clinton P. Anderson to their cause. Anderson, warming slightly to the bill but still reluctant to join the crusade, continued to advocate a wait-and-see approach pending publication of the ORRRC report. Anderson's reticence may have stemmed from his inkling that a full-scale western political revolt against the Wilderness Bill was under way by 1959. Senators Gordon Allott (R-CO) and Joseph C. O'Mahoney (D-WY) were attempting to reshape the bill into one that, in Allott's words, "we in the West could live with without foreclosing on our own."[20]

Allott later pointed out that although the 1959 bill was an improvement over earlier versions, it still had "a long way to go . . . before the West could live with it." Many of Allott's objections echoed Aspinall's initial problems with the bill. Since most of the Wilderness Bill's Senate support came from midwestern and eastern senators, they had "very little concept of the historic development of the use of public lands in the West." Most reassuring to Allott was the fact that the bill, in whatever form, still had to run the gauntlet of the Interior Committees of the House and Senate, which were composed largely of western members who appreciated "the complexity and scope of such uniquely Western problems as the continuing shortage of water, as well as other problems confronting cattlemen and other users of public lands."[21]

Allott introduced a series of amendments in the summer of 1959 designed to reshape the bill in accordance with the desires of western resource users. In particular, Allott tackled the thorny problem of who would recommend and approve Wilderness areas. Wilderness advocates favored administrative establishment of Wilderness areas, followed by a 120-day waiting period during which Congress could veto administrative action. The sites selected by the executive branch would likely be those recommended by a controversial body proposed in early Wilderness drafts, the National Wilderness Preservation Council, which Allott, Aspinall, and others believed usurped the powers of Congress and discounted the professional expertise of existing executive-branch agencies like the Interior and Agriculture Departments.[22]

The Allott Amendments, as they quickly became known, were instant anathema to conservationists. The Citizens Committee on Natural Resources, a coalition of Wilderness advocacy groups led by Zahniser, Charles Callison of the National Wildlife Federation, and William Zimmerman of the Trustees for

Conservation, called the Wilderness Bill with the Allott Amendments "worse than no bill from the standpoint of Wilderness advocates." Allott's amendments removed national parks, monuments, and wildlife refuges from potential Wilderness protection status. Conservationists also objected to granting Congress the sole right to designate Wilderness areas. According to an analysis of Allott's amendments prepared by Zahniser and other conservationists, the Colorado senator had vitiated the "central purpose of the Wilderness proposal" by making wilderness "subservient" to other land uses, including mining and grazing. If enacted, the Allott Amendments would provide a legal basis for the destruction of wilderness.[23]

Before the addition of the Allott Amendments, a real possibility had existed that the Senate would report a Wilderness Bill during the summer of 1959. The conservation community believed it had the political votes and momentum to get a favorable report from the Senate Interior Committee.[24] Colorado senator Allott, who received strong encouragement from Wyoming's O'Mahoney, used his amendments as the basis for a substitute Wilderness Bill, which he proposed in August 1959. The Senate Interior Committee now had several versions of the bill, ranging from the reworked original (with Brower and Zahniser's careful changes) to Allott's decidedly public land–user–friendly draft. In fact, Wilderness advocates referred to Allott as the "spokesman for groups with commercial interests." Amidst all the controversy generated by Allott's actions, and with the Senate session's fall recess looming, Interior and Insular Affairs chair James Murray elected to postpone further action on the measure until the 1960 session.[25]

Hospitalized following a stroke, O'Mahoney nevertheless fought vigorously for Allott's amendments, sending letters to all Interior Committee members, urging them to fight for the principles embodied in the Allott Amendments.[26] The energetic counterattack by Allott, O'Mahoney, and representatives of western resource interests kept the Wilderness Bill bottled up in the Senate Interior Committee for the rest of 1959, buying crucial time for the legislation's opponents. As the anti-Wilderness Colorado Water Congress observed, supporters of the Wilderness Bill knew that they had lost a great opportunity in 1959 and that more delays awaited them because Chairman Aspinall wouldn't consider the bill until it had passed the Senate. At that point, Aspinall and the House would "insist on extensive hearings in the West." Thus, it was unlikely that any House action on Wilderness would occur until the Eighty-seventh Congress, when the bill's advocates would have to start all over again in the Senate.[27]

Amid the rancor of debate over Allott's actions, it was difficult to envision grounds for future compromise, but they were already taking shape, albeit dimly. In a revealing letter to David Brower from early 1960, Aspinall struck a pose that would characterize his Wilderness strategy for the next several years. Aspinall told Brower what he had been telling resource-user groups all over the Western Slope for two years: a Wilderness Bill was inevitable because of the national political strength of the conservationists. Thus, the ranchers, miners, and water users needed to make their wishes known to their representatives, who would "try to work out programs and procedures which will satisfy as nearly as possible all interests." Aspinall admitted that his idea for a fair bill would fail to satisfy "the extreme conservationists." By the same token, the chairman also believed that he would have trouble gaining the cooperation of "the most selfish and gouging" resource users. The timing of controversial legislation such as Wilderness, Aspinall lectured Brower, would be as important to the bill's success as its merits. With that out of the way, Aspinall delivered the main thrust of his message: "Personally, I am sure that this is not the time for the consideration of this bill," though he promised not to postpone its consideration indefinitely.[28]

By May 1960, with the presidential election capturing most of the nation's attention, Aspinall could safely predict that the Wilderness Bill would not escape the Senate Interior Committee in the waning days of the Eighty-sixth Congress. Once again, Senate Wilderness opponents led by Colorado's Gordon Allott and Wyoming's Joseph C. O'Mahoney had slowed the bill's progress by proposing land user–oriented amendments. If by chance the Wilderness Bill passed the Senate Interior Committee, it had "even less chance" of passing the entire Senate, and if indeed it made it that far, it would "not be acted upon by the House this year." As Aspinall informed his constituent and strong supporter, Judge Dan H. Hughes of Montrose, Colorado, "this gives us the fall and winter to prepare for whatever battle lies ahead." Aspinall reiterated his stance that simple opposition to the bill would not work; the bill, in some form, would pass. Strategy, then, dictated trying to shape it into something acceptable to the interests of western resource users.[29]

By the end of 1960, the Wilderness Bill had already faced a difficult trial in Congress. Aspinall summarized the bill's status in a speech to an understandably nervous American Mining Congress in mid-October: "Many [Wilderness] bills were introduced," he observed, "but there was very little action."[30] Despite Aspinall's less-than-enthusiastic rendering of the Wilderness Bill's progress, several decisive events had occurred in 1960, setting the stage for the final battle over its fate. Senator Hubert H. Humphrey's decision to enter the 1960 presidential race left him little time to be the bill's principal Senate advocate. In addition, Senate Interior Committee chair James Murray (D-MT) announced in April 1960 that he would retire following the November election, thus vaulting New Mexico's Clinton P. Anderson into the chairship. The bill's fate in the Senate would depend on Anderson's leadership and the unproven conservation agenda of the incoming Kennedy administration. It should be noted that Anderson's feelings about the bill, at least until 1960, could only be characterized as "lukewarm."[31]

In the immediate aftermath of the November 1960 election, conservationists began pressuring Anderson to become the Senate's chief Wilderness advocate.

Apparently, Anderson had indicated through his legislative assistant Claude Wood that if a revision of the bill could be "responsive to the Allott-O'Mahoney proposals," he would consider co-sponsoring it. Anderson's representatives met several times with Wilderness advocates between election day and the start of the Eighty-seventh Congress in early January 1961. Wood worked closely with Zahniser and others to redraft an acceptable bill that the new chairman could support. On January 5, 1961, Anderson introduced Senate Bill 174, completing his political turnabout on the Wilderness Bill. To the editor of the *Atlantic Monthly*, Anderson justified his about-face by saying that S. 174 was a vastly improved bill that answered many of the criticisms aimed at previous versions. Anderson also sensed a change in public mood regarding Wilderness. "The public has grown sufficiently alert to the need for preservation of primitive areas," Anderson wrote. With a growing realization that he might not suffer political damage for his efforts, Anderson became one of the wilderness movement's strongest supporters.[32]

The new national mood Anderson sensed might have arisen with the arrival of the Kennedy administration, which ushered in an era that, in historian Hal Rothman's words, "advanced the cause of wilderness preservation." Though it may have taken its time in addressing other national issues such as civil rights, the Kennedy administration wasted no time in establishing an ambitious conservation program. On February 23, 1961, President Kennedy delivered a "Special Message on Natural Resources" to Congress and advocated passage of the Wilderness Bill. With the Kennedy administration's strong support, the bill seemed to have a better chance than ever for Senate passage in 1961.[33]

In February 1961, Kennedy administration congressional liaison Lawrence O'Brien met separately with Aspinall and Clinton Anderson, the respective chairs of the House and Senate Interior Committees. Tactfully, O'Brien's agenda with Aspinall emphasized the administration's interest in oil-shale development and user-oriented programs. The Anderson agenda looked much different. In notes prepared for the Anderson meeting, presidential aide Lee C. White wrote of Anderson's deep interest in the Wilderness Bill, "which should have Administration support," especially since the bill "will cost no money" and "has the support of all naturalists." White did note that lumber and mineral interests opposed the legislation. The driving force behind the Kennedy conservation program was Secretary of the Interior Stewart L. Udall, who at the first cabinet meeting in January 1961 had urged the establishment of a conservation program "worthy of two Roosevelts." Kennedy's positive response to Udall's enthusiasm led to the February 23 conservation special message. Aspinall, though in a key position to determine much of the conservation agenda's fate, would never prove receptive to much of the program's aesthetic emphasis, though he would heartily support more utilitarian programs like reclamation.[34]

With Kennedy and Udall's support, coupled with Anderson's leadership, the Wilderness Bill began to make headway in the Senate. Predictably, Senator Allott opposed much of Anderson's S. 174, arguing that its simple procedure for designating Wilderness areas made it too difficult for states to oppose designation of specific land parcels. Anderson's bill required only the recommendation of the secretary of the interior or the secretary of agriculture to the president to designate a Wilderness area. The site was then added to the wilderness preservation system one day after the adjournment of Congress unless the recommendation was voted down by both houses through a concurrent resolution. Allott believed that the interests of western states were not protected in Anderson's bill.[35]

Aspinall's growing alarm over the advancing Wilderness Bill could also be detected. Writing to a Western Slope wool grower, Aspinall reminded his constituent that he had asked the wool growers to suggest the type of Wilderness legislation they could live with. "When we present flat opposition, and are so out-numbered as we are in this particular matter," Aspinall wrote, Congress would enact a bill "adverse to our own interest." The matter in 1961 had become complicated, Aspinall argued, because a credible westerner—Clinton Anderson—from a large public-domain state had sponsored the legislation. "That makes this rigid opposition that much more difficult," Aspinall concluded.[36]

In late February, Anderson's Wilderness Bill was favorably recommended by Interior Secretary Udall, with only minor suggested revisions. Udall's report noted that Anderson's bill "resolves many, if not all," of the previous objections. A Wilderness Act, Udall noted, was not only "in the public interest" but "in accord with the President's program." By contrast, in March 1961, when the House Interior Committee requested reports on the various versions of the Wilderness Bill before it, the Interior Department came to much different conclusions about the legislation. Acting interior secretary James Carr recommended that the House Wilderness Bills be amended and shaped "in conformance" with Anderson's S. 174. After several years of successful delay, the Wilderness gauntlet had been thrown down to Aspinall. If a Wilderness Bill was to pass, the pressure existed to make it conform to the vision of both the Senate and the Kennedy administration.[37]

In early 1961, the Wilderness Bill had become a central component of the developing Kennedy-Udall conservation program. However, one potential trouble spot loomed—the slow work of the ORRRC, which did not appear to be on target to meet its 1961 deadline. Anticipating this difficulty, both David Brower and Senator Anderson argued that deferring action on Wilderness for fear of duplicating the commission's work was, in Brower's words, "a search for time and not information." In the late February 1961 hearings on his Wilderness Bill, Senator Anderson now maintained that a Wilderness Bill would help facilitate the labors of the ORRRC.[38]

Despite the growing tide of Wilderness support in 1961, strong objections to the bill still emanated from the western states. In the Senate, the indefatigable Allott continued to lead the opposition.[39] Working with a small group of western senators, including Alan Bible (D-NV) and Henry Dworshak (R-ID), Allott presented another series of amendments in a last-minute attempt to derail Anderson's measure. Among Allott's 1961 amendments was a proposal to make all National Forest areas subject to federal mining laws, thus opening National Forest wilderness areas to mining operations. Wilderness advocates charged that mining was not compatible with wilderness preservation. Senate Interior Committee aide Ben Stong informed Chairman Anderson that a committee "test vote" had revealed that nine of seventeen senators, including Allott, were prepared to support a "wide open" mining amendment like Allott's. Frank Church (D-ID) intervened at this point, proposing a compromise amendment to permit mining surveys and the gathering of information in wilderness areas of National Forests by means that did not violate the character of those areas.[40] Though other amendments were presented to the committee, it became apparent by the summer of 1961 that a strong Senate Wilderness Bill would be reported and passed.

Allott's final attempt to shape (or kill, according to supporters) the Wilderness Bill occurred during the legislation's final markup in committee, behind closed doors on July 13, 1961. Allott introduced an amendment requiring the House and Senate to take "separate affirmative actions" on each Forest Service primitive area. Under Anderson's bill, 45 million acres fit this classification. As Anderson biographer Richard Allan Baker narrates the story, Allott's amendment first passed the Senate committee 9–8. A distraught Anderson, dismayed at seeing half a year's work ruined, announced that "as far as he was concerned," the Wilderness Bill was dead. During the committee's noon recess, Anderson took heart from Senator Frank Church, who told the chair that he would stand with him in ditching the amended bill, "rather than report to the Senate a butchered version of what already was somewhat of a compromise." As the committee reconvened in the afternoon, it quickly became apparent that Anderson and other bill supporters had been applying a great deal of pressure to wavering senators. In a reconsideration of Allott's measure, Senators Jack Miller (R-IA) and Frank Moss (D-UT) changed their votes. Allott's amendment was defeated by an 11–4 margin. The bill was now cleared for the consideration of the Senate at large.[41]

For some time, Howard Zahniser had been quietly confident that the Senate Interior Committee would report the bill to the full Senate. In addition to strong editorial support from the *New York Times* and *Washington Post*, the executive director of The Wilderness Society believed that a "barrage of telegrams" sent to wavering senators could prove the difference in a close vote. An avalanche of public support, including the asked-for telegrams, hit the Senate in

July 1961, undoubtedly influencing the committee's positive action on the bill. The conservation movement had once again demonstrated its ability to impact the nation's public-land agenda.[42]

By late August, the Wilderness Bill had reached the Senate floor, where Senator Anderson's remarks established the context for its successful passage a week later. Though he never delivered the remarks himself, having had to return to New Mexico for medical treatment, they nonetheless outlined for reluctant substitute floor manager Frank Church a series of strong arguments to make on the legislation's behalf. Emphasizing the bill's modest aims, Anderson highlighted the roles of Humphrey, former Interior Committee chair James Murray, and other longtime Senate champions of the bill. Not wishing to alienate members of the "loyal opposition," Anderson conceded that Allott, O'Mahoney, and other bill critics had "helped improve the measure" with their amendments and close scrutiny. Finally, Anderson noted that his own commitment to wilderness preservation dated back more than thirty years to a discussion he had had with the great conservationist Aldo Leopold, who sold Anderson on the importance of setting aside wilderness parcels.[43]

The Senate floor debate lasted two days, September 5 and 6. The Kennedy administration, through its conservation leader, Interior Secretary Stewart Udall, gave the legislation vigorous support. In a report to President Kennedy, Udall remarked that enacting Wilderness "would be a landmark conservation accomplishment of the Kennedy Administration." During floor debate, several last-ditch attempts to delay or derail the bill emanated from both familiar and unfamiliar sources. Allott introduced a potentially crippling amendment requiring both houses of Congress to affirm including any of the 45 million acres of "primitive" National Forest Service lands. Allott also attempted to give the secretary of agriculture (rather than the president) the authority to grant exceptions to rules against mining in the national wilderness preservation system. Once again, Allott's amendments failed. Perhaps more threatening was an attempt by the chair of the Agricultural and Forestry Committee, Allen Ellender (D-LA), to stall the bill by referring it to his committee for further study. The Ellender Amendment also failed by a narrow margin.[44]

The full Senate vote on September 6, 1961, saw the measure pass by an overwhelming (78-8) margin. The Wilderness Society, a multitude of other environmental groups, and Senate supporters breathed a deep, collective sigh of relief. Howard Zahniser and other conservation leaders felt that their six-year effort, though not yet completed, was approaching vindication. A pleased Stewart Udall immediately shifted the spotlight to the next legislative arena: the House Interior Committee. In a report to President Kennedy, Udall indicated that he was "already attempting to soften up Chairman Aspinall and his colleagues." Udall predicted the bill would represent "one of the towering conservation landmarks of American history," and recommended that the Kennedy administration give its passage "high priority" in its 1962 legislative program. With Congress about to take its fall recess, most Wilderness supporters were optimistic that the bill would become law the following year.[45]

The Senate's favorable consideration of the Wilderness Bill in 1961 reveals several interesting lessons about the politics of the post–World War II West. Accountable to the electorate every six years rather than every two, senators are better positioned to take more principled stands on controversial legislation than their House counterparts. Because of the long interval between elections, senators remain more insulated from pressure groups. Thus, it is not surprising that Wilderness supporters targeted the Senate for their first success. The Wilderness Bill confronted a difficult route to Senate passage, but when several prominent western senators became identified as supporters, success was only a matter of time. Clinton Anderson's strong leadership was certainly decisive, as was the support of California's Thomas Kuchel, Montana's Lee Metcalf and Mike Mansfield, and Idaho's Frank Church. Supporting Wilderness legislation in the early 1960s always entailed some degree of political risk for western politicians.

The senator who took the greatest political gamble was Frank Church. Church's journey on the Wilderness Bill illustrates the precarious danger Wilderness legislation posed for western politicians. Where Anderson could embrace the bill more openly because of his lengthy Senate tenure and service, Church had no such luxury. Most Idahoans, living in a state dependent on mining, timbering, and control of irrigation water, failed to see any value in Wilderness legislation. Church also faced the prospect of a tough re-election battle in 1962. Only reluctantly did Church accede to the wishes of his senior colleague, Anderson, and take the Wilderness Bill floor leadership thrust upon him at the last minute. Church knew that he embraced Wilderness at "considerable risk" to his career, feeling that he had "thrown a handful of dirt on his political grave every time he spoke" on the bill's behalf. Church knew he had given his 1962 Republican opponent, John T. Hawley, a strong weapon to use against him during the election. In the eyes of many Idahoans, Church had sided with out-of-state conservation groups and had worked to undermine Idaho's natural resource-based economy.[46]

THE CENTER OF ATTENTION: ASPINALL AND WILDERNESS

Aspinall would never risk the ire of his district's anti-Wilderness constituents. Painfully aware that he now basked in the national conservation spotlight, Aspinall kept his promise that House consideration would follow Senate action, scheduling a series of field hearings for Representative Gracie Pfost's (D-ID) Subcommittee on Public Lands during the fall 1961 recess. House hearings were a step that The Wilderness Society's Howard Zahniser had hoped to avoid. Aspinall, however, a firm believer in House prerogative, would not consider skipping full House consideration, especially on legislation as controversial as the Wilderness Bill. Zahniser had been attempting to whet Aspinall's appetite for the bill, pointing out in July 1961 that the logic of recent events seemed to favor a Wilderness Bill in the near future. "With Senate passage, Presidential recommendation, and increasing public support," a bill was all but inevitable. Aspinall, of course, saw nothing inevitable about it and did not feel bound in any way by the Senate's actions.[47]

After the Senate had passed the bill, Frank Church remarked to Howard Zahniser with more than a little understatement that "a big fight looms ahead in the House." In the fall of 1961, Wilderness proponents began devising a strategy to speed the bill through the House of Representatives. Charles Callison of the National Audubon Society warned Wilderness advocates that like the Senate Interior Committee, the House Committee was composed primarily of westerners, from states where "industrial or commercial users of the public lands exercise political power far greater than the proportion of voters they can pretend to speak for." Callison pointed out that in the successful Senate Wilderness drive, some of the bill's leading advocates hailed from western states. Clinton Anderson, Thomas Kuchel, and Frank Church come quickly to mind. Still, Callison predicted vigorous House opposition from timber, mining, and livestock interests and warned that a determined House member "skilled in parliamentary procedure" could delay committee action "almost indefinitely." He did not mention Aspinall by name, but he was clearly predicting the bill's course in the House. Callison remained certain of one thing: the path to House passage would not be easy, and the bill that emerged would be different from the one that had passed the Senate.[48]

The House Public Lands Subcommittee hearings were scheduled for McCall, Idaho (October 30 and 31); Montrose, Colorado (November 1); Sacramento, California (November 6); and Washington, D.C. (January 1962). Howard Zahniser urged supporters of the Wilderness program to flood the House with both in-person and written testimony to counter what he termed the "opponents of wilderness." Mining, timber, and other commercial interests had been active in the summer and fall of 1961, Zahniser reported, urging House Committee members to "kill the measure in Committee." He noted that one commercial foe of the Wilderness Bill distributed its attack with a dividend notice.[49]

Aspinall did not attend the hearings in McCall, Idaho. But the chairman was present the following day for the hearings in Montrose, Colorado, sixty miles south of his Palisade home, in the heart of the Fourth Congressional District. "The sword hangs heavy over the Montrose area," the *Montrose Daily Press* proclaimed the day before the hearing. Assessing the public's mood, the *Daily Press* predicted catastrophic consequences for western Colorado if a Wilderness Bill were signed into law. Not only would the mining and timber industries be destroyed, but the "end of many things you now enjoy" would surely result. Painting with a far-reaching, sensational brush, the *Daily Press* envisioned an economic blow so severe that it was doubtful "a televised booster station could survive. Your daily newspaper could not survive and many of your local business houses would have to close their doors. This town, the area would die—murdered economically by legislation. We would be legislated out of existence."[50]

It is no surprise that of the 424 people attending the Montrose hearing, 401 registered as opponents of the Wilderness Bill. A smart and savvy politician who prided himself on knowing his constituents, Aspinall put on a skilled show for western Colorado's voters, who above all feared serious consequences to their rural, public land–based economy if the Wilderness Act cleared the House of Representatives. Aspinall's congressional district was a huge, desolate region, with high, mountainous National Forest lands surrounded by parched Bureau of Land Management deserts, and only two cities of more than 10,000 people. Aspinall identified with those citizens who wrested their living from the West's public lands. Wilderness protection, to Aspinall, was a luxury his congressional district could ill afford to embrace, except at peril to its economic future—and his political career.[51]

Even though House Public Lands Subcommittee chair Gracie Pfost presided over the hearings in Montrose, Aspinall, playing the role of the Grand Inquisitor, dominated the questioning, which took place downtown in the crowded Fox Theater. Aspinall asked many witnesses, especially those opposing a strong Wilderness Bill, if Congress should "abdicate" its authority to the president to propose and establish Wilderness areas.[52] Aspinall took the liberty of summarizing the testimonies of many anti-Wilderness witnesses, then asked them if he had done so accurately. As Aspinall remarked to one witness, if he had understood that witness's statement correctly, then if new Wilderness areas were added to the system, "they should be surveyed and an affirmative action taken by Congress. Is that correct?"[53]

In testimony that clearly delighted Aspinall, geologist Ray E. Gilbert urged the legislators to exercise extreme caution before locking up potential sources of mineral wealth in Wilderness areas. A technological breakthrough in oil-shale research could almost overnight "change vast acreages of previously useless shale rock into a very valuable fuel."[54] Several of the Montrose witnesses remarked that national security demanded that the nation's future mineral needs not be hamstrung by restrictive Wilderness legislation. Aspinall agreed that before any legislation cleared his committee, the nation's future mineral needs and the needs of a healthy mining industry would be taken into account.

Almost every anti-Wilderness witness parroted not only Aspinall's and Allott's desire for affirmative congressional action on Wilderness-system additions, but also the need to await ORRRC findings. The few Wilderness advocates who dared venture to Montrose were virtually ignored by Aspinall, who saved most of his questions and remarks for those who agreed with him. A particularly well-rehearsed witness, H. G. "Si" Berthelson, former president of the Colorado Cattleman's Association, noted that his group favored vesting Congress with the right of affirmative approval of system additions. John B. Barnard, counsel for the Colorado River Water Conservation District, indicated why so many witnesses favored granting Congress—and not the executive branch—the right of Wilderness area approval, stating he did not want additions to the Wilderness system handled by presidentially appointed bureaucrats. He wanted them handled by Congress, "people we can whip when they come up for reelection, if we do not agree." The Fox Theater immediately burst into applause.[55] Grand Junction's *Daily Sentinel* reported that most of the crowd in attendance "expressed disapproval" of the Wilderness measure, a fact that would not be lost upon Aspinall and other western members of Congress.[56]

A few days later, parts of the subcommittee gathered again in Sacramento for additional hearings. Aspinall stayed home in Colorado to begin formulating his response to what he had heard in Montrose. In fact, both Wilderness proponents and foes spent the late fall and winter regrouping and assessing their positions. A representative for the Colorado Cattleman's Association who had been present in Montrose concluded that despite the overwhelming amount of testimony against the Senate Wilderness Bill, some form of Wilderness legislation would eventually pass Congress. Working on House versions of the Wilderness Bill from his Grand Valley home in November 1961, Aspinall confided to a correspondent that he hoped "we have something akin to Senator Allott's [amendments] and some protective provisions in other parts of the bill."[57] In its analysis of the House field hearings, The Wilderness Society warned of a campaign by stockmen, lumbermen, miners, local chambers of commerce, and representatives of other extractive industries to kill the bill in the House. Mining companies had been busy addressing letters to their stockholders, urging opposition to the Wilderness legislation. The Anaconda Company noted its support of a Wilderness Bill "in principle" but opposed any bill restricting mineral exploration in areas withdrawn for inclusion in a national wilderness preservation system. Both Anaconda and Phelps-Dodge Corporation urged stockholders to write Chairman Aspinall to express their desire to keep potential Wilderness areas open for mineral exploration and mining.[58]

The battle lines were drawn by the end of 1961. Supporting the Wilderness Bill were most U.S. senators, a confident and strengthened conservation lobby, and an increasing number of urban Americans sensitive to outdoor recreation values. On the other side sat Chairman Aspinall, joined by a small but powerful group of House colleagues and governors from the West, and supported by representatives of extractive industries who wanted continued and largely unregulated access to public lands. Citizens residing near potential Wilderness areas or working in the timber, mining, or cattle industries were highly critical of Wilderness legislation as well.

On December 21, 1961, Aspinall released a statement summarizing the Wilderness strategy he would follow for the next several years. He would try to harmonize the aspirations of conservationists with "the basic multiple-use principle of our federal land resources." Aspinall believed the fall hearings had brought to the fore what he considered the "real question" in the debate: "what shall the restrictions on use be within wilderness areas?"[59]

Public opinion, whether in the East, the halls of Congress, or the urban West, seemed to be climbing on the Wilderness bandwagon. Even the *Denver Post*, Colorado's leading daily newspaper and a barometer of western urban opinion, had switched its Wilderness position. As late as 1959, the *Post* had consistently editorialized against Wilderness. By the end of 1961, however, the *Post* had come to favor the Senate's Wilderness Bill. After "an examination of the overall picture," the *Post* wrote, "it is better to have this bill than no bill at all, or a weak one." Repeating an argument that had been made over and over in hearing after hearing and in dozens of Wilderness Society publications, the *Post* pointed out that once it was gone, wilderness regions were "lost forever." The *Denver Post*'s conversion to the Wilderness cause demonstrated that a new environmental awareness had begun seeping into the urban West.[60]

In May 1962, President Kennedy and Secretary Udall hosted the White House Conference on Conservation, a well-publicized event designed to generate political momentum for the Kennedy administration's legislative proposals, including the Wilderness Act. The conference followed Kennedy's March 1, 1962, "Message on Conservation," in which the president outlined the conservation accomplishments—and dreams—of his administration. In addition, the long-awaited ORRRC report had finally been published on January 31, 1962, heightening excitement over conservation. The ORRRC report urged the enactment of a Wilderness Bill, recommending "prompt and effective action" to preserve primitive areas, "since once destroyed, they can never be restored."[61] With the stage thus set, the White House conference provided a focal point for the nation's growing conservation awareness. President Kennedy's welcoming remarks highlighted what he hoped would be the distinctive conservation accomplishment of the 1960s—applying the "great discoveries of science to the question of conservation." Ironically, as the decade progressed, it would be the nation's faith in scientific and technological solutions that would often come under attack by the growing environmental movement. Still, President Kennedy went to great lengths to link his administration with the growing public concern over environmental problems.[62]

With massive publicity favoring positive action on Wilderness, continuing to oppose the bill meant inviting the wrath of much of the nation. That is exactly what Congressman Wayne Aspinall did in 1962 and 1963 by attempting to shape Wilderness legislation that his district and much of the rural West could live with. When his turn came to address the White House conference,

Aspinall argued that "string savers are not conservationists." Declaring that conservation meant developing the nation's resources in a responsible manner, Aspinall argued that the nation should not save "merely for the sake of saving." Congress, he admonished, should not enact Wilderness legislation that would create "mausoleum-like museums in which people can go see resources that cannot be utilized or, even worse, see the surface and be compelled to wonder as to what resources might be uncovered if we were allowed to look." With these words, and in front of a national audience, the chair of the House Interior and Insular Affairs Committee threw down the gauntlet to what he termed the "purist preservationist" faction.[63]

Aspinall conducted skirmish after skirmish with Wilderness advocates throughout 1962. Prior to the White House conference, the House Public Lands Subcommittee held hearings on the Wilderness Bill in Washington, D.C. Though they were chaired by Gracie Pfost (D-ID), Aspinall made his presence felt at every stage of the May 7–11 hearings. Not only did he take the lead in questioning witnesses, he also lashed out at the Anderson Senate bill while vigorously defending the "tradition" of multiple-use resource management.

Even before the Public Lands Subcommittee's Washington hearings, the Kennedy administration knew it was in for a fight to keep the primary features of the Senate Wilderness Bill intact in the House. An observer from the Interior Department predicted Aspinall's Interior Committee would attempt to emasculate the House version of the bill, whose chief sponsor was John Saylor (R-PA), the Interior Committee's ranking Republican. An Interior Department official, Sharon Francis, believed that under Aspinall's influence, the Interior Committee would, among other actions, redefine Wilderness to make multiple use part of its definition, continue timber sales, and allow for mining claims. Granting Congress the right to approve Wilderness areas (rather than simply permitting it to veto executive-branch recommendations, as the Senate bill called for) was also a central point. Francis warned Udall and his undersecretaries that a hard committee fight over the bill would "probably mean death" to the legislation in the Eighty-seventh Congress. Her predictions would prove accurate.[64]

The Washington hearings provided an opportunity for executive-branch officials to speak on behalf of the bill; no federal officials had weighed in for or against the legislation during the fall 1961 field hearings. On the eve of the Washington hearings, Chairman Aspinall predicted that a Wilderness Bill would pass the House during 1962. After the hearings, Aspinall planned on working with the Public Lands Subcommittee to redraft the bill to take into account information gathered during the 1961–1962 hearings. With more than a trace of sarcasm, the besieged chairman noted that he detected "a great throbbing emotion, a desire on the part of the United States" to implement a Wilderness policy. However, Aspinall quickly added, "I don't believe the people in my district want such a bill." Thus, Aspinall hoped to shape a Wilderness Bill that protected land-use rights already vested and provided for "a constitutional division of power." In Aspinall's mind, this meant keeping the power to determine resource policy with Congress, not the executive branch. Those close to the veteran Colorado lawmaker knew he was preparing for a major battle.[65]

With Chairman Aspinall and several other members of the full House Interior Committee present, Public Lands Subcommittee chair Gracie Pfost called the hearings to order. As chair of the full committee, Aspinall led the questioning of most witnesses. Almost every Wilderness advocate, including Secretary Udall, quoted the ORRRC report's recommendation that federal protection be granted to wilderness areas. Aspinall, who had been severely criticized by Wilderness proponents for delaying serious consideration of the bill until after the publication of the ORRRC report, asked Udall if he believed delaying House Committee action had been a wise decision. Udall, a former member of Aspinall's Interior Committee, knew how to answer: "The committee acted soundly in waiting." Proceeding logically, Aspinall then asked Udall if he agreed with critics who argued that the accumulated hearings and ORRRC report provided enough information for Congress to act on regarding the Wilderness question. Udall, of course, knew that the chairman was setting him up, so he wisely responded that he favored additional House hearings, the "normal congressional procedure of a congressional committee." Finally, Aspinall was ready for the big question: should resource policy be set in the "usual constitutional and traditional" manner by Congress or, as the Senate bill would have it, by bestowing that power on the executive branch?[66] In this matter, the interior secretary could not provide the answer desired by his former chairman, who well knew that Udall had come before the committee to advocate for the Anderson Wilderness Bill.

Howard Zahniser offered up a strong statement on behalf of the Wilderness Bill, giving what he hoped would be his final testimony for the legislation so close to his heart. In a lengthy but eloquent testimony, Zahniser pled for the Anderson Wilderness Bill, arguing that it would enlarge upon and make permanent existing Forest Service primitive areas, involve no new land-management agencies, and "safeguard these areas for the permanent good of the whole people."[67] Aspinall's admiration for Zahniser's single-minded determination emerged during this hearing. Perhaps the two men, leaders of opposite camps in the Wilderness debate, respected each other's differences and leadership styles, and above all else, realized that each needed to contribute to the resolution of what had become a national impasse. After welcoming Zahniser, Aspinall remarked that he felt Zahniser was "one of the most effective writers with regard to conservation values of the United States that we have." Though Zahniser and Aspinall frequently went round and round, Aspinall felt they had "come a lot closer together."[68]

Still, the two men had major differences to reconcile. In May 1962, the most visible conflict concerned the concept of multiple use. How would this traditional and formative conservation concept be applied to Wilderness areas? Earlier in his testimony, in an effort to build a semantic bridge, Zahniser had referred to the Wilderness Bill as essentially a multiple-use proposal. Though this statement pleased Aspinall, he quickly asked Zahniser how he would determine priority of uses in a Wilderness area. Just as quickly, Zahniser shot back, "The national interest."[69] Feeling pressure from Aspinall to elaborate, executives from The Wilderness Society listed several potential uses, including recreation, watershed protection, scientific research, and even grazing, "when it does not damage the basic resource." Wilderness areas, Zahniser continued, could still be places where many of the traditional multiple uses occurred, as long as the essential wilderness character was preserved. Not surprisingly, Aspinall, a close friend of the mining industry, wondered why, when Zahniser listed potential multiple uses, he had omitted mining, so dear to "us . . . in the West?" Would mining be permitted in Zahniser's vision for Wilderness areas?[70]

Zahniser's response illustrated the size of the chasm that had to be bridged if the nation were going to have a Wilderness Act. Though prospecting, or "fact-finding, gathering knowledge of what we have," could be tolerated, actual mining in a Wilderness region could not occur in an area "to be preserved as truly wilderness." Zahniser did note that in determining whether a potential Wilderness area should be designated as such or removed from the inventory, a major consideration should be whether the primitive lands were valuable primarily as wilderness or for their mineral resources.[71]

Seeing that Zahniser seemed open to not locking up valuable mineral finds, Aspinall moved on to another area of concern: which branch of government should bear the responsibility for making Wilderness determination—Congress or the executive branch? Recognizing he was under the chairman's close scrutiny, Zahniser stuttered without committing himself: "I have the deepest regard for Congress." After more stammering, Zahniser said what Aspinall had hoped but not expected the Wilderness advocate to say: "Yes, most certainly, the Congress should determine the areas which may be preserved as wilderness." Though the intent of Zahniser's vague answer was far from clear, Aspinall's long-standing hope of ensuring congressional prerogative in Wilderness designation seemed closer to reality.[72]

The Sierra Club's David Brower squared off against Aspinall on May 9. Brower began his testimony by asking if he and other well-known conservation advocates could save valuable subcommittee time (thereby speeding its consideration of the Wilderness Bill) by submitting written copies of their testimony. An incensed Aspinall immediately objected, seeing Brower's proposal as an attempt to circumvent normal committee procedure. Taking umbrage at the mere suggestion, Aspinall noted with pride his committee's historic ability to write a full record on each piece of legislation before acting upon it. Because of the importance of gathering all possible information before taking committee action, Aspinall saw no need to hasten the process. Far more vital to the chairman was following correct and orderly procedure—an Aspinall trademark.[73]

Aspinall's demeanor changed markedly when questioning representatives of the extractive industries so vital to his Fourth Congressional District's economy. Among those testifying were Floyd Beach, chair of the Western Colorado Cattlemen's Committee, and James Boyd, president of the Metallurgical Society of America. Boyd stated that if the Anderson Wilderness Bill were enacted, "the capacity of this nation to maintain its productivity of mineral raw materials" would be impaired. Aspinall appreciated Boyd's recommendations for protecting the mining industry's substantial interests in Wilderness legislation. The Boyd-Aspinall exchange laid the groundwork for the industry's advocacy of continuing mining operations in Wilderness areas, a stipulation that Aspinall would cling to in future deliberations.[74] By May 10, the committee had amassed almost 2,000 pages of testimony, hearing from both key Wilderness advocates and many of its staunchest foes. More importantly, Aspinall and other western members of the House had begun formulating some ideas about what citizens of the rural West could live with in a Wilderness Bill.

By the summer of 1962, Aspinall had become identified in the national press and by Wilderness supporters as the main obstacle to the bill's passage. In the ensuing months, Aspinall's actions would brand him as the most obdurate foe of an acceptable Wilderness proposal; few doubted that the chairman's intentions were to savage the Senate's Wilderness Bill. In House Public Lands Subcommittee sessions in June, July, and August, Aspinall succeeded in introducing a substitute Wilderness Bill, H.R. 776, in place of Clinton Anderson's Senate bill. In an early July report to President Kennedy, Interior Secretary Udall characterized Aspinall's bill as "anti-wilderness in its conception." He concluded that it was, in essence, "an anti-conservation measure."[75]

Aspinall's Substitute Wilderness Bill, as it was known, took shape in the House Interior Committee and Public Lands Subcommittee sessions over the summer of 1962. On August 9, the subcommittee favorably reported H.R. 776 to the full Interior Committee, presaging what a Colorado reporter from the *Durango Herald* predicted would be the fight of Aspinall's legislative career. Aspinall's substitute bill not only favored traditional users of public lands but made it more difficult to add parcels to the national wilderness preservation system. Anderson's bill included roughly the same amount of Wilderness acreage as Aspinall's but designated another 45 million acres to be added to the system within ten years unless Congress vetoed such inclusions by individual parcel in either the House or the Senate—an unlikely event. By contrast, Aspinall's bill required affirmative action by Congress to add any area greater than 5,000 acres.

Aspinall's substitute measure thus would substantially reduce future additions to the system, or at least make such additions politically difficult.[76]

Though displeased with Aspinall's bill, Secretary of the Interior Udall chose his words of condemnation carefully, not wishing to dash the entire Kennedy administration conservation edifice. The House Interior Committee chair would have to be dealt with carefully. Udall expressed the most concern with Aspinall's Title I proposal, which undercut the president's ability to be the creative force in conservation policy. If Aspinall's substitute bill were enacted, no longer would the president be able to designate wildlife refuges or utilize the Antiquities Act of 1906 to protect public lands. Some of the "great achievements" in twentieth-century conservation history had occurred through executive action, Udall asserted. Ever the optimist, the interior secretary continued to hold out hope that Aspinall's measure could be reworked to achieve a mutually acceptable Wilderness Bill. Aspinall, however, was in no mood to compromise. When asked if he would bargain with Wilderness advocates who wanted to keep primary power to designate Wilderness areas with the executive branch, Aspinall shot back a crisp "Not on your life!" Matters were heating up.[77]

On August 30, the full Interior Committee ended all hopes of enacting Wilderness legislation that would be acceptable to Udall, Zahniser, and other conservationists. In an action the *New York Times* termed "sabotaging the Wilderness Bill," the Interior Committee approved Aspinall's measure by voice vote, sending the bill to the floor of Congress. The bill, however, was encumbered with a rule limiting the full House to either taking the bill as written in committee or passing on it. No amendments or changes in language would be permitted. Calling it an "affront to the intelligence" of members of the House of Representatives, the *New York Times* opined that the Aspinall substitute bill's "defects," coupled with the Colorado congressman's "parliamentary" maneuvers, meant that the bill should be rejected in favor of the "strong but reasonable" Senate Wilderness Bill. "The Aspinall Bill is a betrayal of the proposal to establish a sound National Wilderness System." A series of articles and editorials about the Wilderness issue in August and September 1962 inaugurated a campaign against Aspinall, styling him in the national press as "a consistent opponent of effective wilderness legislation." In the years ahead, Aspinall's reputation as an environmental reactionary would grow, ultimately damaging his political effectiveness.[78]

The Aspinall Wilderness Bill was scheduled for brief debate on the floor of Congress on September 17. Under House rules, Aspinall's rare maneuver, which limited both debate and the possibility of amendments, was permitted only on alternate Mondays. The Sierra Club's David Brower urged all friends of Wilderness to quickly apply political pressure to fight Aspinall's rules suspension and insist on achieving "a normal ruling which will allow full debate on this important measure." Even Eleanor Roosevelt in her syndicated "My Day" newspaper column urged readers to actively oppose Aspinall's Wilderness Bill.[79] At the last minute, on Friday, September 14, Aspinall decided against bringing the bill to the House floor. House Speaker John McCormack (D-MA), besieged by outraged messages against Aspinall's actions, declined to schedule action on the chairman's bill under rules suspension because Aspinall could not guarantee the required two-thirds vote in favor of the legislation.[80]

A growing contingent of Aspinall foes, ranging from Wilderness advocates to local Colorado Republicans, took special delight in the powerful chairman's inability to push his own bill through Congress. With election season looming and Congress racing to adjourn, a tired and worried Aspinall prepared to hurry back to Colorado to begin his fall campaign.[81] Before leaving, however, Aspinall took to the House floor and offered his own analysis of what had transpired over the past few months. Not surprisingly, the Coloradan defended his actions, pointing out that they had been in good faith. He had promised that the House Interior Committee would seriously consider Wilderness legislation after the Senate had passed a bill and the ORRRC findings had been reported. Aspinall felt he had been true to his word that year, holding hearings on the legislation well in advance of the ORRRC's final recommendations.[82]

What perplexed Aspinall the most as he left Washington in the fall of 1962 was how the "purist preservationist" faction had become associated in the public's mind with the leading edge of the U.S. conservation movement. This phenomenon would bother Aspinall for the duration of his congressional career—indeed, until the end of his long life. Congress had historically pursued a policy of multiple use. When had this changed and why, Aspinall wondered. What he failed to comprehend was that the nation's attitudes toward the land had been changing since World War II. By the early 1960s, an important turning point had been reached. Though most Americans agreed with Aspinall that public lands should serve many uses, a growing number also believed that a portion of those lands should be set aside, forever, as wilderness.

In many ways, 1962 represented a turning point in the nation's attitudes toward the environment. Rachel Carson published her classic indictment of the pesticide industry, *Silent Spring*, which many observers believe jump-started the modern environmental movement. Interior Secretary Stewart Udall called Carson "the fountainhead of the ecology movement."[83] *Silent Spring* spent thirty-one weeks on the *New York Times* best-seller list. Carson sensitized the American public to the dangers of disrupting nature's balance through the use of synthetic pesticides, especially DDT.[84] Responding to a growing public awareness of and interest in the environment, the Kennedy administration began pursuing a more aggressive conservation agenda. For the first time, an active environmental stance could pay political dividends.

To critics who charged Aspinall with dragging his feet on Wilderness legislation, the chairman responded that although Wilderness remained "the most important overall conservation measure," it was by no means his busy committee's only concern during the Eighty-seventh Congress. To illustrate his point, Aspinall noted that the National Parks Subcommittee alone had considered thirty-nine pieces of legislation that had been enacted, including three proposed national seashores—all significant conservation achievements "on par and having a status equal to that of a national park." The passage of the Cape Cod National Seashore bill was especially dear to President Kennedy's heart.[85] Aspinall also defended his attempt to use the rules-suspension procedure to pass the bill, noting that the committee adopted the resolution 10–4 as a way to avoid what would have surely become an emotion-charged and time-consuming floor debate.[86]

An unapologetic Aspinall admitted on the House floor that he had withdrawn his bill after having doubts about his ability to muster the two-thirds vote required for passage. "Of course, my doubts had been stirred by the propaganda barrage" inspired by lobbyists representing the major conservation organizations who "deluged with criticism . . . our well-considered measure." Particularly irksome to Aspinall was the impression generated by his critics that few, if any, people and organizations favored his substitute Wilderness Bill. To refute this, he released a list of organizations supporting his version, including the U.S. Chamber of Commerce, the National Reclamation Association, the American National Cattleman's Association, the National Association of County Officials, the Colorado State Association of County Commissioners, the Board of Water Commissioners of the City and County of Denver, and numerous timber and mining groups. Aspinall's bill obviously had its share of advocates, particularly among traditional users of the West's public lands.[87] No conservation organizations, however, made Aspinall's list. In a fall 1962 newsletter, the Colorado Mining Association called Aspinall the "champion of western mining," particularly lauding the congressman's efforts to give mining locators twenty-five years to stake claims on prospective Wilderness lands.[88]

With the Eighty-seventh Congress drawing to a close, Aspinall left Washington for Colorado on September 22, citing as his reason the deteriorating health of his wife, Julia, who had recently experienced heart problems. One of his Washington secretaries noted that Aspinall had been "very worried about her this week." Back on friendly Colorado turf, Aspinall began defending himself against attacks from what he disdainfully called the "purist preservationist lobby." This group, which proclaimed itself "the exclusive voice of conservation in the United States today," had incited much of the vicious mail Aspinall received toward the end of the congressional session. "One would be led to think that it is un-American to advocate the conservation policies of Gifford Pinchot," Aspinall asserted to the Natural Resources Committee of the U.S. Chamber of Commerce at its Denver meeting in late September. Aspinall regarded the conservation lobby's tactics as patently unfair. Increasing numbers of newspapers, publications, lobbyists, and urban easterners saw conservation as standing for all that was good in America. Aspinall was being styled by these groups as anti-conservation, the chief roadblock to Wilderness action, and thus the bad guy.[89]

In late September, Wilderness advocates still entertained hopes that Aspinall's bill could somehow be brought back to the floor, amended, and passed in his absence. Some supporters believed that without Aspinall's threatening presence, a better Wilderness Bill could be shaped. Most learned observers, however, understood that the Wilderness Bill was dead in the Eighty-seventh Congress; proponents would have to wait for 1963 and the start of the Eighty-eighth Congress to resurrect it. As the Wilderness Bill was considered an administration measure, President Kennedy had been following its progress carefully. Though he applauded Anderson's Senate bill, Kennedy termed Aspinall's substitute bill "not very satisfactory."[90]

At the end of the Eighty-seventh Congress, rumors had begun flying about Aspinall's next tactic in the Wilderness battle. People close to the Coloradan frequently had heard him discuss the need to clarify legislative guidelines on the management and disposal of public lands, including jurisdictional issues that clouded the executive-congressional relationship where federal lands were concerned. This controversy, Aspinall believed, lay at the heart of the Wilderness battle. Colorado Western Slope journalist Helene Monberg predicted in late September that Aspinall "really has his back up" on this issue, and Wilderness supporters could "look forward to a long wait" before the Palisade congressman would allow Wilderness legislation to escape his jurisdiction. Monberg based this assessment upon Aspinall's similar behavior in the long battle to pass Fryingpan-Arkansas, which he delayed and ultimately shaped to his own wishes.[91]

Although Aspinall usually enjoyed strong support, or at least admiration, throughout Colorado for his positions, it was apparent by late 1962 that urban Coloradans were beginning to desert him based on his alleged anti-conservation attitudes. This did not pose an immediate political threat, as Aspinall's Fourth District continued to include the more than twenty counties west of the Continental Divide. Still, it was a harbinger of change in Colorado's political climate and would spell danger in the years ahead. By 1962, the *Denver Post*, a mild supporter of the Wilderness movement, blamed Aspinall for not passing the bill during the Eighty-seventh Congress. Too much wilderness "would be unwise," but the *Post* saw a "reasonable protection" of wilderness as justifiable on scenic, recreational, and scientific grounds. Sounding almost like Aspinall, the *Post* held that traditional multiple-use management need not rule out "preservation of some areas in their natural state." Citing the upcoming 1962 elections as a factor in the Wilderness proposal's lack of progress, the *Post* asserted that western politicians feared answering to their powerful public land–user constituents during a congressional election year.[92]

With the election looming, Aspinall wasted little time returning fire to Zahniser and other Wilderness advocates. In a lengthy letter to the chief of The Wilderness Society, Aspinall pointed out that the Senate Wilderness Bill staked an extremist conservation position he could never support. "I have found," Aspinall wrote, "that after thirty years of legislative experience, very few matters are all white or black." Clearly, some room existed for compromise on the Wilderness issue. It is interesting to note that even during the heat of battle, Aspinall's deep regard for Zahniser continued. During the final days of the Eighty-seventh Congress, Zahniser's health had failed and he had become bed-ridden. Aspinall was told that there was even a chance the wilderness leader would not recover. Pleased to hear of Zahniser's convalescence, Aspinall assured him of his continuing friendship and promised to work for a "fair and constructive" bill during the next congressional session.[93]

Aspinall's rumored public-lands initiative became the focal point of the next phase of the Wilderness controversy. In a letter to President Kennedy, Aspinall outlined his requirements for being fully cooperative toward the Wilderness Bill. "The core of the controversy" over the House and Senate versions of the bill was "the degree of responsibility and authority to be exercised by the legislative and executive branches." Aspinall argued that this needed clarification, due to overlapping agency responsibilities for public lands, conflicts between executive and legislative branches, a growing land scarcity, and the "parallel need to preserve some land as wilderness." After establishing guidelines for dealing with these pressing issues, "we can then immediately turn our attention to wilderness preservation." In other words, Aspinall's trying 1962 experience with the Wilderness Bill, which included a steady public flogging, had forced him to recalculate the cost of his cooperation. Aspinall's promise to Kennedy of taking action on Wilderness legislation now came with an additional burden: the assessment and clarification of historic controversies plaguing public-land policy. Aspinall would make the creation of the Public Land Law Review Commission the mechanism to resolve these questions.[94] In his reply, President Kennedy defended executive-branch expertise in public-land matters but admitted that the nation's land system might well "warrant comprehensive revision."[95]

A lengthy and comprehensive land-policy review might have appealed to the logical and orderly mind of Wayne Aspinall, but to Wilderness advocates, tired of struggling and waiting, his land-study proposal simply seemed another excuse to forestall action. In the final months of 1962, Aspinall was cudgeled in the national press, attacked by conservation lobbyists, criticized by many senators, and goaded toward action by the Kennedy White House. Ira N. Gabrielson, chair of the Citizens Committee on Natural Resources, argued that "a moratorium" on Wilderness legislation was not necessary simply because Aspinall had a sudden "notion that some new relationship between Congress and the

Executive is needed."[96] John P. Saylor, the ranking minority member of the House Interior Committee, sarcastically labeled Aspinall's substitute measure "a bill to protect miners, lumbermen, and other enterprising patriots against rampant conservationists trying to preserve two percent of the country as God has made it."[97]

In some small but significant ways, the 1962 congressional election foreshadowed Aspinall's future political difficulties—this time from a new direction. Republican opponent Leo Sommerville attacked Aspinall from a right-wing perspective, calling him a "rubber stamp representative" of a big-spending administration, who believed the people of western Colorado were not fit to run their own lives. People close to Aspinall knew that he would never trample the rights of individual Coloradans and few voters would be convinced by Sommerville's stock right-wing rhetoric. Ironically, Aspinall's most severe political troubles in the years ahead would come from the growing liberal end of his own Democratic Party. Many Western Slope Republicans would feel comfortable with Aspinall's moderate message and regularly vote for him until the end of his long career.[98]

Despite Sommerville's and the Republican Party's best efforts, Aspinall still prevailed by a comfortable margin, winning 59 percent of the vote, though this was considerably less than his usual 70 percent or better. Aspinall's tough road to victory may be attributed in part to Sommerville's able opposition, but also to the pounding Aspinall's reputation had taken in 1962 from outraged wilderness advocates. Clinton Anderson biographer Richard Allan Baker believes that Aspinall's reduced margin was directly attributable to conservationist outrage. In his own election postmortem, Senator Anderson hoped Aspinall might realize that his election difficulties were connected to the growing conservation fervor across the nation.

These are certainly plausible interpretations, but a sounder explanation would point out that Aspinall's diminished performance in 1962 could be attributed to a tremendous Colorado Republican resurgence, the greatest in years. The G.O.P., under gubernatorial candidate John Love, trounced incumbent governor Steve McNichols. Republican Peter H. Dominick overturned incumbent senator John A. Carroll by more than 55,000 votes. In Aspinall's Mesa County home, the Republicans swept the State House and Senate races as well. Carroll's mistake, it seems, was to identify too closely with President Kennedy's social welfare program. Running against Aspinall, candidate Sommerville attempted to paint Aspinall in the same light—as a reflexive Kennedy supporter. This tactic failed miserably because of Aspinall's well-known political independence, especially on matters affecting Colorado's Western Slope. Several days before the election, the lead editorial in Grand Junction's *Daily Sentinel* reminded voters of Aspinall's great wisdom and foresight in handling the Wilderness issue. Aspinall, the *Daily Sentinel* insisted, had fought the "restrictive" Senate

Wilderness Bill by arguing for legislation that included multiple use and congressional control. Aspinall had defended the West's interests against an army of "dreamy-eyed recreation enthusiasts" and an "empire-building" secretary of the interior (Stewart Udall), who together tried to pressure Aspinall for a bill that "would restrict usage of the public domain by anyone except vacationers." Aspinall, "bucking terrific pressures," had fought to preserve the West's multiple-use public-lands heritage. The *Daily Sentinel's* enthusiasm for the congressman from Palisade clearly had not abated.[99]

1963–1964: TOWARD WILDERNESS COMPROMISE

At the start of the Eighty-eighth Congress in January 1963, Aspinall was in a stronger position than ever to shape legislation vital to Colorado and the West. As the new year began, speculation over Aspinall's motives centered upon how he might utilize his public-land law-revision proposal or the Land and Water Fund Bill, a measure to finance federal park and recreation lands through park admission fees and a tax on recreational users, as "trading stock." Ben Stong, the Senate Interior Committee's staff member specializing in water and wilderness matters, pointed out that the choice facing Wilderness supporters heading into the new congressional session was to try to "roll" the bill over the Coloradan, which would require immense political pressure and "probably some unconventional parliamentary tactics," or to find some ground for compromise.[100]

Few congressional observers could be confused by Aspinall's position on Wilderness entering 1963. He despised the Senate bill for many reasons, but first and foremost because it favored executive over congressional authority. The Senate bill, in Aspinall's view, also gave preference to recreational wilderness uses over competing legitimate uses. Aspinall had begun viewing the Wilderness controversy as an opportunity to reformulate and clearly state what he believed had been and still remained the dominant conservation philosophy in the United States: multiple use. Aspinall and other westerners saw the Multiple Use–Sustained Yield Act (MUSY) of 1960, which set forth priority uses on public lands, including recreation, as a law making proposals like the Wilderness Bill unnecessary. MUSY located management authority for the nation's forests firmly in the hands of the National Forest Service in the face of increasing pressure from both timber companies and forest preservationists. As its name implies, Multiple Use–Sustained Yield reaffirmed the utilitarian orientation of timber management in the United States. As historian Paul W. Hirt assessed it, MUSY represented the Forest Service's last major victory in the battle to control its own destiny, free from political pressure exerted by conservationists and Wilderness advocates. "The act further symbolized the continued hegemony of the expanding pie ideology of politicians and agency leaders." In the post–World War II paradigm, production and prosperity equated with social stability and liberty. "Wilderness," Hirt remarked, "theoretically threatened full production—even if in fact no opportunities for commercial exploitation were present."[101]

Aspinall firmly believed in the land-management principle of multiple use. As pressure for environmental legislation mounted in the 1960s, the Coloradan turned increasingly to Gifford Pinchot's doctrines for intellectual ammunition and inspiration. At one point, Aspinall asked Library of Congress researchers to study and digest many of Pinchot's key tenets, ostensibly so he could better answer preservationist critics in Pinchotian terms. In a speech before a friendly body of BLM land advisors, Aspinall railed against advocates of "single-purpose use," which by 1963 had become an Aspinall code phrase for "wilderness recreation enthusiasts." Wilderness advocates, Aspinall declared, had proclaimed themselves "to be the only true conservationists." To Aspinall, a true conservationist was cast in the utilitarian mold of Pinchot, balancing the needs of society with available resources and managing them carefully over time. In a letter to a concerned constituent in December 1962, Aspinall styled himself as a conservationist "with the same philosophy as Gifford Pinchot, Theodore Roosevelt, and Franklin Roosevelt."[102] In a speech some months later, Aspinall argued that the conservation ideas of Pinchot and Theodore Roosevelt were "as valid today as they were fifty years ago." The only difference in public-land uses in the two eras was that the types of activities "have increased with the intensified needs of the 1960s."[103]

In early February 1963, Aspinall outlined his Interior Committee plans for the legislative session. Noting that he would not likely offer a substitute Wilderness measure in 1963, the chairman did not rule out the possibility that another committee member would introduce such a bill. In words that must have bothered Wilderness proponents, Aspinall indicated that if his committee reported a Wilderness Bill in 1963, "it probably would be along the same lines as the last one." Calling his enemies "extremists," Aspinall maintained that many citizens wanted to go "the whole hog or nothing. A Congressman finds himself caught between the selfish groups on both sides. There is as much selfishness for the exotic use [wilderness recreation] of the lands as there is from those seeking the land for monetary use." Aspinall reassured Wilderness advocates that he "had nothing against wilderness," but acceptable Wilderness legislation would need to include open mining and utilization of timber resources in the event of a national emergency.[104]

Aspinall's criteria for action on Wilderness seemed clear to him and to other western land users. To representatives of the growing environmental coalition, his intentions seemed hazy and ill-defined. What did the Colorado Representative really want? Was he only trying to delay constructive Wilderness consideration by injecting the public-land law-review question into the fray? Pro-Wilderness newspapers, congressional Wilderness advocates, and representatives of numerous conservation groups wasted no chance to educate the public about the Wilderness Bill. They also hoped to pressure the reluctant House Interior Committee chair to action. A steady barrage of pro-Wilderness articles and editorials emerged in the nation's press in late 1962 and early 1963. But the strongest attack on Aspinall's national reputation occurred in the March 1963 issue of *Harper's Magazine*. In "Congressman Aspinall vs. The People of the United States," writer Paul Brooks left little doubt that one stubborn man, representing corporate interests that profited from public-land use, had frustrated a strong national desire to save "our remaining wilderness." Right or wrong, the Brooks article marked a turning point in defining Aspinall's national reputation as an uncompromising enemy of thoughtful conservation legislation.[105]

Brooks had not acted alone. He had received ample encouragement and information from Howard Zahniser, who recognized that a hard-hitting piece in a national journal could help turn the tide in his favor.[106] Several weeks before the appearance of "Congressman Aspinall vs. The People," Zahniser reviewed a draft of the article, noting that it was unfortunate that this "excellent interpretation" of the Wilderness controversy had to deal with Aspinall "in such a personal way." However, Zahniser believed that a major reason the controversy existed lay with Aspinall's personality. In fact, he believed that Brooks had demonstrated admirable restraint in the piece; the Colorado congressman's perfidy was actually greater than Brooks had asserted. Though Zahniser would readily admit that Aspinall had many admirable qualities, on conservation matters the Wilderness Society director could not discover a basis for constructive engagement with the Coloradan.[107]

With the Wilderness debate set to resume in 1963, both sides seemed irrevocably locked into their positions. Stewart Udall listed the Wilderness proposal as the third priority of the Interior Department's 1963 legislative program but predicted continued resistance from an anticipated "Aspinall blockade." Udall did not expect the Wilderness showdown to be resolved until 1964. If anything, Aspinall approached 1963 more committed than ever to his key demands: legislation that would "respect multiple purpose uses" and accept the principle of affirmative congressional action for future Wilderness-area establishment. These principles, Aspinall argued, would be consistent with the nation's historic land-management ideals, first articulated by Gifford Pinchot, espousing "the greatest good of our natural resources for the greatest number" over the longest period of time.[108]

Returning to Washington in January 1963, Aspinall sought an audience with Udall and Kennedy, expressing a willingness to heal the rift that had grown between the administration's Wilderness plans and his requirements for action on Wilderness legislation. Downplaying the size of the breach, Aspinall told a reporter for the *Denver Post* that he was only trying to recoup the constitutional policy-making powers of Congress that previous Congresses had let be usurped by the executive branch. While preparing Kennedy for an early 1963 meeting with Aspinall, presidential advisor Lee White noted that the Coloradan's most pressing concern would be the Wilderness situation. "The Chairman regards himself as pro-wilderness areas and resents the attacks made against him," White told Kennedy. White believed that "considerable strain" had characterized Kennedy administration relations with Aspinall, much of it stemming from a failure to understand the Coloradan's desire to be constantly apprised of all issues within his legislative purview. Both sides vowed to maintain a more cooperative attitude heading into the Eighty-eighth Congress.[109]

In a letter to Wilderness supporter John Saylor, who was the ranking Republican on the House Interior Committee, presidential assistant Lawrence O'Brien summarized Aspinall's meeting with Kennedy, noting that "there was agreement that legislation of this type is important" and that the Interior Committee would turn its attention again to Wilderness "during this session of Congress." O'Brien left the meeting with Aspinall convinced that the chairman would uphold his end of the bargain, but only after every aspect of the bill had been carefully considered.[110]

The Senate wasted little time addressing the Wilderness Bill in early 1963. S. 4 sailed through the Senate on April 9, passing 73–12 after fighting off a series of amendments proposed by Colorado senators Gordon Allott and Peter Dominick. The Senate's rapid action neither surprised nor concerned Aspinall. The Coloradan only seemed doubly determined to have his way with the Wilderness issue. Aspinall knew that the Senate bill, as written, would never leave his committee, so he planned to stay calm and above the fray. Aspinall maintained that Wilderness supporters would need to "show some kind of understanding of my position and of my committee" to get the bill moving in the House.[111]

The Senate's fast action on the Wilderness Bill at the start of the Eighty-eighth Congress only riveted more attention on Aspinall's legislative intentions. The *Washington Daily News* urged the people to speak out and demand that the Colorado congressman take action on Wilderness.[112] The *Washington Post* viewed the passage of another Senate Wilderness Bill as an opportunity to profile the "grey-haired, slightly stooped man [who] has brought down on himself the wrath of garden clubs, hiking groups, and conservation societies." Aspinall had no intention of holding hearings on the Wilderness Bill in the near future. Nor would he allow himself to be moved by those "calling names and putting on pressures." If the conservation lobby believed it could force Aspinall into action, they were "mistaken," Aspinall told *Washington Post* reporter Julius Duscha, who believed that the Coloradan meant every word he said.[113]

Not surprisingly, Aspinall's local paper, the Grand Junction *Daily Sentinel*, jumped to his defense after passage of the Senate Wilderness Bill in April, denouncing the avalanche of verbal abuse heaped upon the chairman as "completely unwarranted" and "scurrilous." The fact that Aspinall continued to battle

Wilderness supporters, forcing them to resort to unfair tactics, was evidence "that he is representing the West and its future in this battle." The *Daily Sentinel* argued that the latest round of attacks could not hurt Aspinall in the West. "They prove to Westerners how vital to the West's very existence is the victory for which Aspinall is fighting."[114] However, the congressman needed support, and the newspaper reminded readers that Aspinall "should not be expected to fight the battle alone."[115]

Although it may have seemed at times like Aspinall stood alone against the Wilderness tide, his positions remained wildly popular in his Fourth Congressional District. Farrington Carpenter, one of Colorado's most influential ranchers and the man Congressman Edward Taylor chose to implement the Taylor Grazing Act during the New Deal years, called the Wilderness Bill "crank legislation" advocated by "extremists." Aspinall agreed with the Hayden, Colorado, rancher, noting that wilderness conservationists were difficult to work with because there was "no give from the position to which they religiously adhere." Judge Dan Hughes, a prominent Montrose, Colorado, rancher, pointed out that the "harder the conservationists jump on Wayne, the more we like him around our area." Hughes believed that Wilderness legislation, a single-use venture, would spell economic disaster for many western Colorado counties. Prominent Denver attorney Stephen H. Hart pronounced Aspinall one of the hardest-working members of Congress and expressed his deep regret that the chairman had been forced to endure the "worst and most unjustified campaigns of vilification" over the Wilderness issue. Writing to Aspinall, Hart remarked, "You and I know that you are not against conservation. You are fighting for the rights of Congress as against an encroaching executive [branch]. You are fighting for the rights of people who live in the area involved to have a say in how it [the local public land] should be used."[116]

In late April, Aspinall experienced some disturbing chest and arm pains, leading to a thorough physical examination, a cardiogram, and further tests at Bethesda Naval Hospital. After a couple of weeks' hospitalization followed by a period of physician-ordered rest, a rejuvenated Aspinall returned to Congress in early summer, seemingly more determined than ever to defend congressional prerogatives in public-land matters.[117] In late May, the Sierra Club's Washington representative observed that Aspinall's recent illness had not precipitated any changes in his attitudes toward Wilderness, noting that the Coloradan remained "adamant against the Senate procedure," which merely gave Congress "a veto power against future designations" of Wilderness areas. In a resounding pronouncement, Aspinall asserted that the Wilderness Bill might just be "the biggest land grab in history." Aspinall indicated, however, that if Wilderness advocates were willing to compromise, an act could yet be passed in 1963.[118]

Not surprisingly, after he returned to Congress, emissaries from the Kennedy administration paid the chairman a visit to sound him out on his Wilderness intentions. After meeting with Kennedy special counsel Lee White and Bureau of the Budget officers Elmer Staats and Philip S. Hughes, Aspinall told the press that he hadn't promised them anything about Wilderness. Still in an uncooperative mood, Aspinall recalled that all he had received for his labors from Wilderness advocates in 1962 was "abuse, some of it unprintable."[119]

There is little doubt that Aspinall's surly attitude toward Wilderness in 1963 stemmed from the harsh press barrage and personal attacks he had endured after introducing his substitute bill late in the Eighty-seventh Congress.[120] Yet just when the situation appeared the most hopeless, signs that the impasse might thaw began to appear. One indication was the improving personal relationship between Zahniser and Aspinall, which seemed more cordial than ever following Aspinall's illness.[121] Another major step toward compromise was the news that Zahniser, The Wilderness Society, and Representative John Saylor would no longer oppose Aspinall's demand for positive congressional action on proposed Wilderness-area additions. In mid-July, Saylor told Aspinall that the prospects for passing a "sound and effective" Wilderness Bill seemed "increasingly good." Aspinall's response was only mildly encouraging. The two Interior Committee leaders were good friends and as veterans of fourteen years of service together in Congress, could almost anticipate each other's thoughts and actions. Aspinall revealed to Saylor that the war of words had taken a great toll on him. The biggest barrier, however, remained the shape of the Senate Wilderness Bill. "After fourteen years of association with me, you know I am not an extremist." Aspinall would therefore not embrace a bill that bore the marks of environmental extremists.[122]

By late summer 1963, the national press reported that Senate Wilderness Bill supporters such as Clinton P. Anderson, White House officials, and President Kennedy himself had been revising the measure into a form more acceptable to Chairman Aspinall. Returning to Colorado for a round of speeches and visits in late July, Aspinall told the press that the bill still stood a chance for authorization during the Eighty-eighth Congress, though passage in 1963 seemed unlikely. For the first time, however, both sides in the Wilderness battle were speaking in optimistic tones. Aspinall declared himself open to discussion with the White House on the matter, and if the executive branch could convince Wilderness groups to reshape the bill into something more palatable to Aspinall, he would contact users of western lands to gauge their reaction. Aspinall made it clear that he was not caving in to public pressure, though he did seem to be tiring of the constant public name-calling. A reporter for the Scripps-Howard newspaper chain concluded that "there is new optimism for enactment both at the Capitol and the White House."[123]

The sense that the Wilderness logjam might finally break pervaded the environmental community during the late summer of 1963. By August, the *Washington Evening Star* reported that "Congressman Aspinall . . . is in a conciliatory mood. The formidable Coloradoan is talking of a compromise" Wilderness Bill that could "shake loose" the measure from the grasp of his committee.[124] A delighted Howard Zahniser contacted *Denver Post* editor Lee Olson for support. Olson had always promised Zahniser such help when needed. "We are now at such a time," Zahniser informed Olson. Inviting *Post* editorial support, Zahniser nevertheless cautioned Olson against antagonizing the powerful chair of the House Interior Committee.[125]

Aspinall's changed disposition might also have been related to another rumor, this one involving Senator Clinton P. Anderson. According to several sources, Anderson, tiring of Aspinall's stalling, was considering holding Aspinall's pet project, the Public Land Law Review Commission, hostage in the Senate Interior Committee in an attempt to force Wilderness action. Aspinall had introduced H.R. 8070 to establish the commission during the summer of 1963. More than one observer in the nation's capital had commented upon the speed with which Aspinall's public-land law-review plan had moved through the labyrinth of the House of Representatives while the Wilderness proposal remained stalled in the House Public Lands Subcommittee.[126]

By late August, Dixie Barton, a member of Aspinall's House Interior Committee staff, confirmed that members were "working something out" on the Wilderness issue. Though Barton was not willing to divulge details of the high-level discussion that was under way, it seems clear that intensive talks were continuing, maybe driven in part by Aspinall's interest in a massive public-land law-review procedure. Rumors also flew around the Capitol that Aspinall's desire to enact a strong public-land law procedure was so strong that he might decide to retire from Congress in order to direct the review commission.[127] In retrospect, this rumor seems rooted in the wishful thinking of Wilderness advocates.

The focus of the Wilderness debate shifted in the fall of 1963 to several new bill drafts. The latest revisions represented attempts at cooperation involving Aspinall, his staff, Zahniser, and several executive agencies, including the National Forest Service, the Bureau of the Budget, and the White House. Increasingly, bill revisions incorporated features more reflective of what the press now called Aspinall's "Western vision" for the Wilderness Bill.[128] Throughout the revision discussions, Aspinall continued to insist on several provisions that he considered vital. He was adamant that the numerous Forest Service primitive areas should not automatically become Wilderness areas, as the Senate bill proposed. Additionally, he continued to demand positive congressional action on future Wilderness-area additions. Finally, Aspinall insisted that Wilderness areas remain subject to the nation's mining laws for a period of time. Not surprisingly, Senator Clinton Anderson continued to champion the Senate bill, which protected a greater amount of primitive land, favored executive rather than congressional initiative for Wilderness inclusion, and banned all mining immediately.[129]

The momentum toward Wilderness compromise continued. Benton J. Stong, the Senate Interior and Insular Affairs water-policy expert, informed Secretary Udall that the Senate's Wilderness Bill sponsors had agreed to many of Aspinall's demands, including Wilderness-area approval by Congress, one of the oldest sticking points. Senate sponsors had hoped to force Congress to examine in a timely fashion all of the primitive lands originally slated for Wilderness status and make a final determination as to whether they met Wilderness criteria. The mining issue, according to Stong, still remained an imposing barrier to passage. Senate sponsors recognized that the bill would need to allow a period of wide-open mining in Wilderness regions, but they hoped to minimize that mining window during the House-Senate negotiations. Aspinall still hoped to win fifteen to twenty-five years of opportunity for the mining industry. Though obstacles to compromise remained, both sides seemed closer to agreement by late fall 1963.[130]

At Secretary Udall's behest, President Kennedy, attempting to capitalize on growing national conservation sentiment, undertook what was termed "a conservation tour" in late September 1963. After dedicating the Gifford Pinchot Institute for Conservation Studies in Milford, Pennsylvania, Kennedy flew to Duluth, Minnesota; Grand Forks, North Dakota; Cheyenne, Wyoming; and Grand Teton National Park. Over the next several days, Kennedy visited Montana, Seattle, Salt Lake City, California, and Las Vegas. Along the way, the president gave speeches, commented on conservation issues, and dedicated the Point Reyes National Seashore in California and the new Flaming Gorge Dam in Utah. Secretary Udall, who hoped the trip would boost the administration's conservation program, judged the president's enthusiasm for the cause as somewhat lackluster. Udall confided to his diary that Kennedy would not be another Theodore or Franklin Roosevelt when it came to conservation. "He doesn't respond to the land with their warmth or excited interest." To the many glories of nature witnessed on the trip, from bald eagles to the magnificent skyline of the Grand Tetons, Kennedy demonstrated about as much emotion as might be expected "from a Wall Street investment broker who felt no tug of elemental things." "Imagine a conservation trip," Udall exclaimed to himself, "where the leader never gets out of his suit or steps off the asphalt." Still, at the end of his tour, in a speech written partially by Udall, Kennedy called for a "new campaign to preserve a natural environment worthy of the wealthiest nation on earth." Despite Udall's disappointment, newspapers were quick to link Kennedy's remarks with calls for Representative Wayne Aspinall to give "a gift to the nation that will keep on giving forever," a national wilderness preservation system.[131]

By the late summer of 1963, the environmental movement had gained substantial momentum, which only increased the pressure on Aspinall to take action on Wilderness. Rachel Carson's 1962 allegations in *Silent Spring* had led to a Kennedy-appointed scientific commission to study the impact of pesticide use.

In 1963, the panel's findings "basically substantiated" Carson's findings.[132] In 1963, Stewart Udall's *The Quiet Crisis*, written with the assistance of noted author and historian Wallace Stegner, appeared. Udall hoped the book's publication would add momentum to the incipient environmental movement, and indeed *The Quiet Crisis* was well received, becoming a bellwether title for 1963. By 1964, the nation's growing commitment to environmental causes was beyond question; soon it would be a force capable of impacting the political culture of Colorado and the American West.

But in 1963, Wayne Aspinall did not fret over the future power of the environmental movement. Instead, with some glee, he revealed to longtime confidant and campaign manager Charles J. Traylor in Grand Junction that he believed "the wilderness people are about to come to my way of thinking." Anticipating a political triumph on the Wilderness question, Aspinall still did not envision final action on the matter until the end of the Eighty-eighth Congress in 1964. Interestingly, Aspinall predicted that the enacted bill would closely resemble the substitute Wilderness Bill he had taken so much political flack for in 1962.[133]

Yet another compromise bill was introduced in November 1963 by Wilderness champion John Saylor (R-PA). Aspinall immediately called Saylor's bill "an important step, very constructive," and promised hearings on it and similar bills early in the new year. Immediately, The Wilderness Society's Howard Zahniser expressed delight over Saylor's bill, finding reports of Wayne Aspinall's favorable reaction "especially satisfying." Meanwhile, the White House continued to press Aspinall for action. On November 12, presidential aide Lee White reminded Aspinall of President Kennedy's deep interest in the Wilderness Bill. After speaking with the chairman, White concluded that "the prospects of agreement on a wilderness bill are extremely bright."[134]

Driving home to Colorado during the Thanksgiving recess, Aspinall sensed impending vindication over his course of action on the Wilderness Bill. He and Kennedy had discussed the matter just before Aspinall left Washington and Kennedy boarded Air Force One for Dallas, Texas. During the conversation, Kennedy had asked his old congressional friend to try to move the bill to a speedy conclusion. Aspinall pointed out the impossibility of doing so in 1963, to which Kennedy simply replied, "All right, can't blame me for asking." Aspinall informed the president of his intention to give the Wilderness Bill early priority after returning from the Christmas recess. It was here that matters stood when Aspinall, rather uncharacteristically, turned on his radio in a driving snowstorm west of Decatur, Illinois, on the afternoon of Friday, November 22. Learning of the president's assassination, Aspinall sadly drove on to Colorado, thinking that he might have been one of the last members of the House, other than those who accompanied the president to Dallas, to have a conversation with Kennedy before his tragic death.[135]

1964: A WILDERNESS BILL TO LIVE WITH

President Kennedy's death altered the legislative atmosphere in Washington. The new president, Lyndon B. Johnson, a master legislative craftsman, understood the chaotic situation and poised his new administration to take advantage of Kennedy's political legacy. As historian and former Johnson aide Doris Kearns remarked, "By carrying out what his predecessor had started, Johnson argued that his call to continue was in effect John Kennedy's call. Johnson was but the dutiful executor of his predecessor's will." From November 1963 to the 1964 presidential election, Lyndon Johnson closely identified with Kennedy, not only as a means of gathering political support, but also because he believed that much of the former president's program was essential to the nation's welfare.[136] Major legislation like the Civil Rights Act of 1964 was signed into law as a monument to the fallen leader, but legislation of more regional significance, such as the Wilderness Act of 1964, also benefited from the national mood of healing and reconciliation.

Aspinall had always admired John F. Kennedy, and the president's death affected him deeply. Reflecting on the nation's mood two weeks after the assassination, Aspinall called the shock of Kennedy's death "worse than the declaration of the three wars that I have witnessed." To Aspinall, such an atrocity didn't "seem possible in this country. I think each of us has lost something and that we have received a permanent set-back to whatever progress we have otherwise made." Aspinall knew he had "lost an understanding leader and friend." Undersecretary of the Interior John Carver remembered the unusually good personal relationship that existed between Kennedy and Aspinall: "I can't emphasize too much . . . this feeling of respect and admiration and regard the Chairman had for the President."[137] It is not an exaggeration to argue that Aspinall's certain and steady handling of the Wilderness legislation in 1964 relates to promises he made to the former president.

Though Kennedy had hoped to talk Aspinall out of scheduling another round of hearings, he and other Wilderness supporters understood that this would not likely occur. Still, Aspinall held to his promise of fast consideration, scheduling field hearings for January 1964 in Olympia, Washington; Denver; and Las Vegas. A final round of House hearings would take place from April 27 to May 1 in Washington, D.C. In announcing the hearings, to be held before the House Public Lands Subcommittee chaired by Walter Baring (D-NV), Aspinall indicated that the subcommittee would consider three groups of Wilderness bills. Most environmentalists still favored S. 4 (the Anderson Senate Wilderness Bill) and House bills resembling it. The other groups of bills represented attempts at reaching a compromise and meeting objections articulated by Aspinall and other guardians of traditional western economic activities. On the eve of the House hearings, The Wilderness Society decided to focus its efforts on the more recent House compromise bills, such as that introduced by Representative John Saylor, since Aspinall and the Interior Committee did "not intend to act favorably on the Senate Act or House bills like it."[138]

Though Aspinall was not at the January 1964 House Public Lands Subcommittee hearings, his presence loomed large. The Colorado congressman did not hide the fact that he favored the compromise bill introduced by Michigan congressman John Dingell. The Dingell Bill gave Congress the power to designate Wilderness areas. In addition, it permitted mining operations to carry on for ten years on 6.1 million acres of primitive lands under review as possible Wilderness areas. Dingell's draft also allowed pre-existing grazing leases to continue. Aspinall felt that Saylor's compromise proposal was "closer to the mark" than previous bills emanating from Wilderness supporters, but it differed from Dingell's in two crucial ways: it immediately terminated the filing of new mining-permit and grazing leases and accelerated the timetable for review of primitive lands from ten to five years. Of course, S. 4, the Anderson Senate Bill, gave the power to designate Wilderness to Forest Service bureaucrats, leaving Congress with only the difficult-to-exercise veto power.[139]

At the January 1964 hearings in Olympia, Denver, and Las Vegas, proponents of each version of the Wilderness Bill were present. The Denver hearings demonstrated that Dingell's bill, H.R. 9162, had gathered a great deal of support, especially from western state politicians and representatives of the extractive industries. Colorado Republican governor John Love favored Dingell's approach but called for an extension of the mineral-search window to twenty years. Many western state politicians also used this opportunity to argue for Aspinall's public-land law-review proposal. Even the most adamant foes of Wilderness legislation—among them Leonard Horn, representing the American National Cattleman's Association—appreciated the attempt at compromise in the Dingell Bill, correcting S. 4's "grave weakness" of neglecting congressional action for area inclusion. Future Colorado governor Richard Lamm, representing the Young Democrats of Denver in 1964, appeared and testified in favor of a strong Wilderness Bill similar to S. 4. Lamm saw no reason to allow any further mining in Wilderness areas. At the conclusion of the Denver hearings, Representative John Saylor remarked that "there had been a complete change of attitude in the West" toward Wilderness legislation over the past few years. Saylor correctly pointed out that some of the bill's staunchest former foes had reconciled themselves to a compromise measure. Saylor told the *Denver Post* that he was confident that Wayne Aspinall would now "sit down with his committee and work out a reasonable solution, a satisfactory compromise" to the Wilderness controversy. Evidently, Saylor and other Wilderness supporters saw Aspinall as representing not just the sparsely populated Fourth Congressional District, but indeed public-land users in Colorado as a whole and the entire intermountain West.[140]

At the end of January 1964, Aspinall publicly announced that he would make a strong effort to pass a Wilderness Bill before the Eighty-eighth Congress adjourned. It had become evident that Senator Anderson's bill (S. 4) was all but dead; the Wilderness Act's final form would likely bear a closer resemblance to the Saylor or Dingell Bill—and conform to Wayne Aspinall's wishes. By February, The Wilderness Society seemed reconciled to using the Dingell Bill as the basis for House consideration. Wilderness Society strategy now shifted to shaping H.R. 9162 through altering its language and creating amendments against mining in primitive areas to protect potential Wilderness tracts from further damage. "It would be a tragic ending to the long Wilderness Bill struggle" if the Dingell Bill passed without strong amendment, according to Howard Zahniser, David Brower, Ira N. Gabrielson, and other national conservation officials.[141]

Evidently, Stewart Udall agreed. Though securing favorable Wilderness legislation had long been a Kennedy-Johnson administration priority, in a late January 1964 news conference, Udall expressed his hope that the Wilderness Bill, the Land and Water Conservation Fund, and the Public Land Law Review Commission would all pass Congress in 1964, making it a banner year in U.S. conservation history. "With a little statesmanship and a little give and take," Congress, Udall asserted, could approve a Wilderness Act. He quickly added that he would be very disappointed "if we don't have one, come July."[142] But other pressing national priorities threatened Udall's hopes. An inordinate amount of congressional attention would be focused on passing the milestone Civil Rights Act on July 2. Of course, 1964 was also a presidential election year, with Lyndon Johnson squaring off against Arizona Republican senator Barry Goldwater. The Wilderness Bill would need fortuitous timing to negotiate the congressional labyrinth before the Eighty-eighth Congress adjourned.

While the Wilderness Bill meandered along in the House Interior Committee, Aspinall's pet project, the Public Land Law Review Commission, took a fast track to passage in the House of Representatives in March 1964. In the meantime, Aspinall called for additional hearings on the Wilderness Bill, scheduling them for late April in the nation's capital. Director of the Bureau of Outdoor Recreation Edward Crafts predicted to Secretary Udall that Aspinall would be almost unmovable on three remaining Wilderness issues: the slow, not automatic, inclusion of Forest Service primitive areas into the Wilderness system; the requirement that Congress have the power to approve such areas; and the continuation of mining laws in Wilderness areas for some length of time. Crafts predicted trouble if Zahniser and other advocates tried to vigorously amend the Saylor and Dingell Bills to make them more compatible with Anderson's Senate measure. Crafts, a Wilderness advocate, favored a pragmatic strategy of conciliation. It was time to get a Wilderness Bill "on the books," and the Dingell Bill, however imperfect, stood the best chance for passage.[143]

As it turned out, the Washington, D.C., hearings (April 27 to May 1) were the final House hearings on the Wilderness Bill. Filled with drama, they included the final appearance of Wilderness warrior Howard Zahniser before Congress, another vigorous statement of support from Interior Secretary Udall, and some probing questions and emotional statements from Congressman Wayne Aspinall. Zahniser boasted of attending all eighteen previous House and Senate hearings on the bill and seemed to view his final testimony as an opportunity to restate his love of wilderness, a topic he seemingly never tired of. Zahniser asserted that the growing and increasingly urban U.S. population made Wilderness legislation a necessity. Without legislative action, "we cannot expect to see wilderness endure in our country." True to Edward Crafts's prediction, Zahniser did not openly object to Dingell's compromise measure, though he hoped that Congress would adopt certain amendments to bring it into closer agreement with the Saylor or Anderson version. Wilderness, Zahniser concluded, "perpetuates the choice that Americans have always had, the choice of going to a wilderness if they so wish." Young people, especially, "should know the wilderness."[144]

A week later Zahniser died, succumbing to a heart attack. The *New York Times* called him "a leader in U.S. conservation" and, quoting Stewart Udall, "'a lovable person with the character of the wilderness.'" David Brower wasted no time in using Zahniser's death to inspire the living. The morning after Zahniser's fatal heart attack, Brower sent a letter to Wilderness friends and each member of Congress, stating what would become a widely echoed refrain—that there could be "no finer memorial" to the fallen leader than enacting the Wilderness Bill, an effort Zahniser had "worked so hard for, shortening his life in the effort." A day later, on the floor of Congress, Wayne Aspinall memorialized his old friend and rival. "Even though he and I had our differences of opinion, I think we always understood each other and respected those opinions." Despite the fact that Zahniser was not able to "see the fulfillment of his lifetime work," he went to his death "knowing that the main battle had been won." Aspinall told his congressional colleagues that in his final conversation with Zahniser five days earlier, the Wilderness Society leader still feared that some "outside disruptive forces" might destroy the developing congressional consensus for Wilderness compromise. Aspinall agreed that a sound Wilderness Act would be "a lasting memorial to the work of Howard Zahniser."[145]

The Washington hearings set the stage for House passage of the Wilderness Bill. As chair of the House Interior and Insular Affairs Committee, Aspinall participated in subcommittee hearings only in an ex-officio capacity. But the chairman would not miss an opportunity to shape Wilderness legislation to conform to western land-user interests. Aspinall remained in Room 1324 of the Longworth Office Building for most of the hearings, taking the lead in asking questions, grilling witnesses, and nudging proceedings in the direction of the

Dingell Bill, H.R. 9162. For example, after Stewart Udall's testimony, which seemed a plea to enact a bill resembling the Saylor or Anderson scenario, Aspinall reminded the interior secretary that the delicate 1963 negotiations between Aspinall and the Kennedy administration had brought the Wilderness Bill "closer in form to the Dingell Bill than any other bill that has been presented." Aspinall also forced the interior secretary to admit that few mining claims would likely be filed in Wilderness areas. To illustrate this point, Aspinall asked Udall to provide the House Interior Committee with information on the number of mining claims and oil and gas leases in national park properties subject to the mining laws and in wildlife refuges since the first Wilderness bills were introduced in the mid-1950s. This tactic enabled Aspinall to deftly make his point: fewer than 100 mining claims and several hundred oil and gas leases had been awarded, principally in remote regions of Alaska.[146]

Representative John Dingell (D-MI) also appeared before the subcommittee on the second day of hearings, April 28, 1964. Immediately, the Michigan congressman reiterated that his H.R. 9162 had been written in close consultation with Aspinall and Kennedy administration officials. Not surprisingly, Dingell invoked the late president's wishes on the matter, noting that Kennedy had termed the bill "one of the most significant conservation landmarks in recent years." In his cross-examination of Dingell, Aspinall took issue only with Dingell's assertion that "people from all over the entire nation are urging" the bill's enactment. Instead, Aspinall pointed out that a recent poll had revealed that 72 percent of those interviewed had never heard of the Wilderness Bill, though he admitted that of the remaining 28 percent, the majority favored Wilderness legislation.[147]

On the penultimate day of the hearings, a remarkable event occurred, demonstrating how fragile Aspinall's will to cooperate really was. At the beginning of the day's hearings, Aspinall jumped up, asked subcommittee chair Walter Baring (D-NV) for recognition, and launched into an emotional tirade against the national press for its reporting on the Wilderness Bill. Aspinall charged that the press had little understanding of how the congressional committee system functioned. The press had consistently styled Aspinall as the sole roadblock in the path of a Wilderness Act. It was not Aspinall who had blocked the bill, but the controversial nature of the legislation itself. As Aspinall remarked, "Those people and those individuals who consider that the action of the last congress was the action of the Chairman of the Committee and not the action of the committee itself just do not know what they are talking about and never have, and if they continue in this mode of operation, my opinion is that we will end up without any legislation."[148] Aspinall's thunderous remarks, presented before a roomful of committee members, scheduled witnesses, and representatives of the press, concluded with a plea to Wilderness supporters to rein in their friends in the national media and stop blaming him for blocking the bill.

If the issues were not more fairly presented to the American people, "then we might as well shut the door and go on with something else." Aspinall's comments sent AP and UPI reporters scrambling from Room 1324 down the hall to the telephones, prompting fears of another Aspinall-inspired delay for the Wilderness Bill. More than anything else, Aspinall's remarks made it clear to many that the crusty Coloradan's cooperation needed to be carefully nurtured.[149]

Aspinall's outburst may have been calculated to discourage Wilderness supporters from trying to amend the Dingell Bill into a form more closely resembling S. 4. However, his heated remarks were more likely prompted by a *Washington Post* editorial that ran that morning (April 30, 1964), accusing him of standing "like a Druid ready to resume a familiar ritual"—delaying and destroying still more versions of the Wilderness Bill. Following Aspinall's tirade, the Interior Committee's ranking Republican, Wilderness supporter John Saylor, telephoned Robert C. McConnel of the Interior Department with the news that Aspinall was "absolutely livid" over the *Post* editorial.[150]

In an attempt to regain Aspinall's cooperation and goodwill, at the conclusion of the House hearings the following day, Public Lands Subcommittee chair Walter Baring and John Kyl (R-IA) went on record lauding Aspinall for his fairness and cooperation throughout the Wilderness hearings. "It has been my impression," Kyl remarked, "that the Chairman of the full committee has taken far too much personal abuse concerning this legislation." Both Kyl and Baring stressed Aspinall's impartiality in conducting the hearings. As it turned out, these remarks would essentially conclude almost a decade of House hearings on the Wilderness Bill.[151]

Aspinall's final outburst, coupled with Zahniser's untimely death and the conclusion of the House hearings, led to the last act in the drama of the passage of the Wilderness Act. With time running out for the Eighty-eighth Congress, Senator Clinton Anderson, long a key Wilderness supporter, assured David Brower he would do everything he could to bring about enactment of the Wilderness Bill. To prove his point, near the end of May, Anderson met with Aspinall in the New Mexican's private Senate office, where the two men agreed upon the essentials of a Wilderness Bill compromise. Anderson held a strong bargaining chip—Aspinall still awaited summer Senate action on the House-approved Public Land Law Review Commission. During the meeting, Anderson agreed to yield on the provision for affirmative action by both legislative chambers. In return, Aspinall agreed to move the bill forward. Anderson, in his memoirs, recalled that at this point, "Wayne smiled with pleasure and, somewhat to my surprise, took my offer, he seemed delighted that he could finally settle the dispute on terms favorable to himself and end the bitter antagonism of the conservationists." The route to passage had opened; all that remained were bill markups, committee approval, and the House-Senate conference committee. After decades, the Wilderness Act was almost reality.

On June 10, the same day that the Senate, by a four-vote margin, broke the two-month filibuster on the Civil Rights Bill, the House Subcommittee on Public Lands approved a version of the Wilderness legislation sponsored by Representative John Saylor. Since Aspinall had already won major concessions from Wilderness proponents, he believed he could shape Saylor's draft into a form that would make it acceptable to both Wilderness friends and foes. In the markup session on June 1 and 2, Aspinall introduced many wording changes and amendments to nudge the Saylor draft back toward conformity with the Dingell Bill. With the subcommittee's historic vote of approval on June 10, it became apparent, for the first time, that the full House would soon have a Wilderness Bill; by passing the Subcommittee on Public Lands, it had cleared its most difficult obstacle. A relieved Congressman Saylor told the subcommittee that the bill had passed because of hard work and good-faith bargaining. Representative Leo O'Brien (D-NY) took the floor and indicated that the Wilderness Bill, because of its controversial nature, "constitutes national law-making at its very best. I think it demonstrates that it is possible under our system to build a legislative house in which people of sharply conflicting views can live."[152]

A week later, the Wilderness Bill was considered by the full House Committee on Interior and Insular Affairs. Although the discussion centered principally on possible amendments and language changes, it moved along with a minimum of acrimony. On June 18, the full committee voted 27–0 to report the bill to the House of Representatives. Following the committee vote, Ed Edmondson (D-OK) pointed out that Aspinall's leadership through the Wilderness struggle had been a great example to committee members. His patience had been "biblical in its magnitude and I think he has done something of enduring value for the country." Finally, Aspinall rose to speak and assured those assembled that the bill would pass Congress "in its present form" or something very close to it. The House bill contained a twenty-five-year mining provision and allowed a ski area in the San Gorgino Wilderness Area in Southern California.[153]

Most Wilderness leaders praised the House Interior Committee's work on the bill, though they hoped to modify some of its more objectionable features either on the House floor or in conference committee with Senate representatives.[154] Aspinall predicted quick House approval if the Wilderness advocates were willing to accept a bill similar to the one reported by the full Interior Committee on June 18. On July 30, 1964, the Wilderness Act passed the House of Representatives by a 373–1 margin. In his news conference, Secretary of the Interior Stewart L. Udall indicated that "private conversations" between Senator Anderson and Congressman Aspinall augured well for the House-Senate conference on the bill. The *New York Times* lauded both Aspinall's and Anderson's work, indicating that "Mr. Aspinall deserves praise for bringing his committee's bill to the floor" in such a way that it can be amended. This was an obvious

President Lyndon B. Johnson signs the Wilderness Act into law September 3, 1964. Stewart Udall (to Johnson's far left) looks on with John Saylor (directly behind the president). Wayne Aspinall stands sixth from the right. Courtesy, LBJPL.

backhanded reference to Aspinall's clever parliamentary method of reporting his 1962 substitute Wilderness Bill. The *New York Times* editorial asked for Congress to delete both the mining provision and the San Gorgino ski area.[155]

The House passage of the Wilderness Act marked one of the greatest weeks in U.S. conservation history. On July 23, the House passed the Land and Water Conservation Fund. "If this Congress keeps up the way it is going," Representative Morris K. Udall told the House on July 30, "I think it's going to be known as 'the Conservation Congress,'" a label that many would indeed apply to the Eighty-eighth Congress.[156] The House-Senate conference committee met on August 14 and 15, 1964. Afterward, Congressman John Saylor observed that he knew of "no conference between the House and the Senate in which the versions

President Lyndon Johnson offers pens to Aspinall (left), *Clinton Anderson* (center), *and John Saylor* (right) *used to sign the Wilderness Bill into law on September 3, 1964. Courtesy,* UCAUCB.

of the two bills passed by the separate bodies have been as far apart." In presenting the *Conference Report*, Aspinall specifically thanked Saylor, noting, with some understatement, that "there have been times when the gentleman from Pennsylvania and the Chairman of the committee have been so much in opposition to each other on this legislation that it looked as if it would be impossible for us ever to get together." Finally, Aspinall mentioned another name that "stands out like a beacon light to all of you," friend "and co-worker" Howard Zahniser, a man who, like the "patriarch of old was denied to experience his moment of victory."[157]

Of course, the ultimate victory for Zahniser and other Wilderness supporters came in a splendid White House Rose Garden ceremony on the morning of September 3, 1964. President Lyndon B. Johnson, with Aspinall, Udall, and Senators Anderson and Henry Jackson (D-WA) at his side, signed into law not only the Wilderness Bill but the significant Land and Water Conservation Fund Act as well. To the assembled members of Congress, bureaucrats, cabinet officials, Wilderness supporters, and reporters, Johnson observed that the passage of the Wilderness Act "reflects a new and strong national consensus to look ahead." Singling out Aspinall and Senators Jackson (who had headed the Senate Interior and Insular Affairs Committee since 1963) and Anderson, Johnson noted that the Eighty-eighth Congress would be remembered as bringing about "another historic era" in U.S. conservation history worthy of the two Roosevelts. To further support this assertion, Johnson would, later in September, sign bills creating the Public Land Law Review Commission, Canyonlands National Park, and Fire Island National Seashore, as well as several other measures with conservation significance.[158]

THE WILDERNESS ACT—A CONSERVATION LANDMARK

Wayne Aspinall termed the Wilderness Act "a landmark" for the conservation movement. The Coloradan's intersection with the movement for a Wilderness Act provides astonishing testimony of how one well-placed member of Congress can safeguard his or her region's interests while shaping a piece of legislation's ultimate form. The final Wilderness Act conformed, in most respects, to Aspinall's western vision for public-land use. Included was his demand for affirmative congressional action on Wilderness-area additions. The final bill retained many existing multiple-use activities in named Wilderness areas. Most important to Aspinall, the bill allowed mineral exploration and mining until 1984. The final bill also demonstrated Aspinall's ability to compromise. The House version included a requirement that Wilderness areas contain at least 5,000 acres of land. The Senate bill had had no such requirement. The House-Senate conference committee agreement provided that an area have at least 5,000 acres, or be of sufficient size to "make practicable its preservation and use in an unimpaired condition." In addition, the *Conference Report* spelled out an orderly ten-year timetable for review of roadless areas, national parks, and wildlife refuges for possible inclusion in the Wilderness system. About 9 million acres were initially brought into the national wilderness preservation system, with another 50 million slated for possible inclusion in the ten-year review. The controversial San Gorgino ski area was also eliminated by the conference committee.[159]

At the conclusion of conference committee deliberations, Senator Clinton Anderson acknowledged that "there will be some disappointment that the Bill did not go further" in protecting wilderness, but he noted that the bill did bring "from concept to reality" a national wilderness preservation system. Anderson might have added that the system was created despite what seemed at times to be overwhelming political odds.[160] There is little doubt that from a Wilderness advocate's perspective, the law could have been much stronger. However, it was the only law possible at the time. Aspinall, acting on behalf of the West's public-land users, commanded the power through his Interior Committee chairship to protect powerful western economic interests. The nation demanded a Wilderness Act, but it would be, like many federal laws, imperfect and a product of substantial compromise.

Assessments of the Wilderness Act have almost universally lauded it as a milestone in U.S. environmental history. Roderick Nash, author of the seminal work *Wilderness and the American Mind,* observed that Congress had "lavished more time and effort on the Wilderness bill than any other measure in American conservation history." Advocates of Wilderness preservation took great encouragement from the bill's passage and "the knowledge that the United States had formally expressed its intent to keep a portion of its land permanently wild." Historian Stephen Fox argues that "seen in the light of history, Echo Park and the Wilderness Act of 1964 reversed the verdict of Hetch Hetchy." But perhaps the best way to evaluate the Wilderness Act is to examine what it was and what it was not. Historian Hal Rothman termed it "truly a victory for the environmental movement." There can be little doubt that the issues that spawned the bill gave birth to the environmental movement as a significant political force. Western politics, even in Wayne Aspinall's Colorado, would never resemble the pre-ecology political culture that the Colorado congressman had cut his teeth on and continued to adhere to religiously.[161]

Still, the Wilderness Act of 1964 was the product of political compromise, and as such, it was, as Stewart Udall later termed it, "watered down." Much of the original idealism expressed in Howard Zahniser and Hubert Humphrey's first draft was gone by 1964. But to say that Aspinall "wore the glasses of the mining industry," as Stewart Udall alleged, is far too simplistic an explanation for Aspinall's approach to the Wilderness Bill. Because of the importance of their products to modern, Cold War America, Aspinall believed that miners should be "first in line at the altar of wilderness." In assessing early drafts of the Wilderness Bill, he maintained that outdoor recreation enthusiasts had an unfair advantage over traditional users of western lands. Wayne Aspinall saw himself as a product of the post-frontier era, a member of the first generation of westerners to not only use nature's bounty, in the form of public lands, to build a civilization where little had existed before, but to use that land responsibly and in close cooperation with other users. Aspinall's conduct throughout the long Wilderness battle is best expressed in the outrage westerners felt when an increasingly urban civilization, buttressed by eastern political power and money, attempted to force its values on what they viewed as "their" land, values, and lifestyle. The same sense of outrage would later animate the Sagebrush Rebellion of the late 1970s.[162]

1964: AT THE APEX OF POWER

In many respects, 1964 was Representative Wayne Aspinall's greatest year as a member of Congress. He could rightfully claim credit not only as the ultimate shaper of the Wilderness Act, but as the driving force behind several more key measures, including the Land and Water Conservation Fund and the Public Land Law Review Commission. The latter was viewed by some senators as a throwaway, "the price that had to be paid for Aspinall's agreement to dislodge the Wilderness bill."[163] In late August 1964, Interior Secretary Udall described the end of the Eighty-eighth Congress as "far and away the most productive period I have ever seen in ten years of working in the conservation vineyard." Udall believed that the key to the "big bumper harvest" of 1964 conservation legislation was breaking the Wilderness Bill logjam. Udall recalled the bitterness surrounding Aspinall's substitute Wilderness measure during the fall of 1962. A fair Wilderness Bill seemed to have little chance at that time. The secretary credited the chairs of the House and Senate Interior Committees for crafting the legislative compromises that led to the bill's enactment.[164]

Well into the 1964 fall campaign season, Aspinall continued to receive accolades for his handling of the Wilderness compromise. His hometown newspaper, the Grand Junction *Daily Sentinel,* thanked Aspinall on behalf of "Colorado and the entire West" for modifying early drafts of the Wilderness Bill. If Aspinall had not "stood his ground," the "conservationist bloc" would have "rammed the legislation giving the executive branch of government the full say on additions to the system. The West," the *Daily Sentinel* argued, "would have been locked up tight." Not surprisingly, the Grand Junction paper offered a strong re-election endorsement of Aspinall for writing a Wilderness Bill the rural West could live with.[165]

For the first time in his congressional career, Aspinall faced a reconfigured congressional district. Under legal mandate from the U.S. Supreme Court (in the 1962 *Baker v. Carr* decision), the Colorado General Assembly approved a reapportionment plan in April 1964. Added to his already huge congressional district were six northeastern Colorado counties, all traditional Republican strongholds, and several more south-central Colorado counties in the San Luis Valley. The redistricting led to charges by Aspinall and his supporters that Colorado Republican governor Love, working with a Republican-dominated legislature, hoped to retire Aspinall. As the fall election season began, most political observers predicted Aspinall would have a difficult time winning the new Fourth Congressional District.[166]

The 1964 congressional campaign was easily Aspinall's most expensive to date—a far cry from the $4,000–$5,000 war chests of his 1950s campaigns. In 1964, Aspinall devoted almost $30,000 to advertising, nearly half of it earmarked for newspaper ads. The radio and television budget still remained small, not quite $5,000. The redistricting forced Aspinall to advertise with comparatively costly Front Range newspapers, radio stations, and television stations. He even bought time on Albuquerque, New Mexico's KOB radio to reach his new San Luis Valley constituents. The new district fostered other innovations. Though

Wearing his trademark Stetson, Aspinall receives some good election news at the Grand Junction Daily Sentinel office. Daily Sentinel editor Preston Walker is on Aspinall's left, in a plaid shirt, with his hand on the congressman's shoulder. Courtesy, UCAUCB.

Aspinall had always courted Republican support, in 1964 his campaign formed the Bipartisan Committee for Aspinall, inspired, in part, by the addition of the new, traditionally Republican northeastern Colorado counties.[167]

Aspinall made his record the central issue of the 1964 campaign. Specifically, he campaigned on his chairship of the House Interior and Insular Affairs Committee and its "value to the people of the Fourth District, the state, and the West." Aspinall called upon his old political friend "Big Ed" Johnson to campaign for him, "because the name of Ed Johnson is a magic word in all of Colorado, but particularly in the northeastern part of Colorado." Running his typical hard-driving campaign, Aspinall appeared in all thirty-five counties of his expanded district, beginning a whirlwind tour on September 18 that ended only on election day, November 3. The new Fourth Congressional District was not only larger geographically, it contained more than 200,000 new constituents for the sixty-eight-year-old congressman to win over.[168]

On election day, President Lyndon B. Johnson and the Democrats won a landslide victory over Arizona's Barry Goldwater. Aspinall surprised many political pundits by trouncing his Republican opponent, Edwin S. Lamm, by a 42,000-vote margin and carrying all thirty-five counties. Aspinall ran ahead of President Johnson's strong ticket by more than 10,000 votes in the Fourth Congressional District. A delighted Aspinall felt on top of his craft at the end of 1964. The Republican state legislature had tried—and failed—to gerrymander the chairman to, in his words, "give me the works," in a district "they thought I wouldn't be able to carry under any condition." Aspinall had once again prevailed.[169]

Indeed, 1964 was a banner year for the Colorado congressman. He had won several hard-fought victories, overcome stringent environmentalist and Republican opposition on several fronts, and emerged from it all seemingly in his strongest political shape ever. Earlier in 1964, environmental groups had hoped that Aspinall's Wilderness obstruction, coupled with the congressional redistricting, would spell his political demise. Sierra Club official William Zimmerman expressed surprise at the ease of Aspinall's November victory. Recognizing that he would need to continue dealing with the chairman, Zimmerman thanked Aspinall profusely for the harvest of conservation legislation in the Eighty-eighth Congress. Zimmerman also apologized for some of the "misunderstandings" of the past several years. On the eve of the 1964 election, the Grand Junction *Daily Sentinel* observed that the chairman had played a "key role" in what President Johnson called the "Conservation Congress"—environmentalist shorthand for the Eighty-eighth Congress and its many legislative achievements.[170]

At the end of 1964, the National Wildlife Federation, a moderate conservation organization, named Aspinall its "Conservationist of the Year." This award, coming from a group that included such conservation luminaries as Ira N. Gabrielson and Spencer Smith, meant a great deal to Aspinall. He had often fought the National Wildlife Federation, but he also agreed with many of its positions. Aspinall felt invincible at the end of 1964, and as Greek tragedy often tells us, such hubris brings doom. In Wayne Aspinall's case, forces were already in motion that would embroil him in volatile national environmental disputes, sully his good reputation, and ultimately destroy his long and distinguished political career. As the nation's political culture changed over the next few years, the "Conservationist of the Year" would become known as the conservationists' most durable foe.

ENDNOTES

1. Draft of Howard Zahniser's review of Aldo Leopold, *A Sand County Almanac* (New York: Oxford University Press, 1949), in Howard Zahniser Collection, fd: 21, Denver Public Library, Denver, CO (hereafter cited as DPL).

2. See, for example, Howard Zahniser's memorandum for the files on this subject, January 30, 1952, in Box 5:100, fd: "NWPS Wilderness Bill Advocacy Correspondence, 1952–54," Papers of The Wilderness Society (hereafter cited as TWS), DPL.

3. Curt Meine, *Aldo Leopold: His Life and Work* (Madison: University of Wisconsin Press, 1988), 247–248; Susan L. Flader, *Thinking Like a Mountain: Aldo Leopold and the Evolution of an Ecological Attitude Toward Deer, Wolves, and Forests* (Madison: University of Wisconsin Press, 1974), 16, points out that although some scholars have argued that Colorado landscape architect Arthur H. Carhart deserves to be called the "father" of the wilderness preservation system, Leopold "seems to have had a more influential role than Carhart in formulating Wilderness concepts and policies on a national scale."

4. David R. Brower, "Environmental Activist, Publicist, and Prophet," oral history conducted by Susan R. Schrepfer, Regional Oral History Office, the Bancroft Library, University of California, Berkeley, 1974–1978, 64; Hal K. Rothman, *Greening of a Nation? Environmentalism in the United States Since 1945* (Fort Worth, TX: Harcourt Brace, 1998), 45; Stephen Fox, *The American Conservation Movement: John Muir and His Legacy* (Madison: University of Wisconsin Press, 1981), 286.

5. This analysis of the content of the first Wilderness Bill is from Roderick Nash, *Wilderness and the American Mind*, 3d ed. (New Haven, CT: Yale University Press, 1982), 221.

6. Paul W. Hirt, *A Conspiracy of Optimism: Management of the National Forests Since World War Two* (Lincoln: University of Nebraska Press, 1994), 37–38.

7. Nash, *Wilderness and the American Mind*, 221–222.

8. Richard Allan Baker, *Conservation Politics: The Senate Career of Clinton P. Anderson* (Albuquerque: University of New Mexico Press, 1985), 110–113; *New York Times*, May 5, 1957; "Aspinall, Wayne (Norviel)," *Current Biography Yearbook* (1968): 32–34.

9. Ibid.

10. *Records of the U.S. House of Representatives*, 85th Cong., 1st Sess., Committee Papers, House Interior and Insular Affairs Committee, Public Lands Subcommittee, June 20, 1957, Box 137, fd: "HR 85A-D8—HR 1960, 5 of 5," Center for Legislative Archives, National Archives, Washington, D.C. (hereafter cited as NA).

11. *Records of the U.S. House of Representatives*, 85th Cong., 1st Sess., Goslin Statement, House Committee on Interior and Insular Affairs, on S. 1176, June 19–20, 1957, 416–420, NA; *Records of the U.S. House of Representatives*, 85th Cong., 1st Sess., Goslin Statement, Papers Accompanying Bills, Unpublished Hearings Before the House Irrigation and Reclamation Subcommittee, Box 137, fd: "HR 85A-D8—HR 1960, 5 of 5," Center for Legislative Archives, NA.

12. Howard Zahniser to David R. Brower, January 9, 1959, Box 5:200, fd: "NWPS—Legislation, 1959, Drafts and Bills, House, 86th Congress, 1st Session," Papers of TWS, DPL.

13. Clinton P. Anderson to Howard Zahniser, July 1, 1958, Box 622, fd: "Interior—Wilderness Bill, S. 1176 and S. 4028," Clinton P. Anderson Papers, Manuscript Division, Library of Congress, Washington, DC (hereafter cited as LC); Claude Wood, memorandum to Senator Anderson, April 8, 1958, and July 1, 1958, Box 622, fd: "Interior—Wilderness Bill, S. 1176 and S. 4028," Clinton P. Anderson Papers, LC.

14. Montrose (CO) *Morning Sun and Record*, December 20, 1958, Box 45, fd: 1, Series X, Gordon Allott Papers, University of Colorado Archives, University of Colorado at Boulder, Boulder, CO (hereafter cited as UCAUCB).

15. This is Richard Allan Baker's term for the situation. See Baker, *Conservation Politics*, 113.

16. Ibid.

17. Unidentified newspaper clipping, March 24, 1959, Box 72, fd: 5, Stewart L. Udall Papers, Special Collections, University of Arizona Library, Tucson, AZ (hereafter cited as SCUAL).

18. Wayne N. Aspinall to David R. Brower, January 2, 1959, Box 5:101, fd: "NWPS–Wilderness–Advisory–Correspondence, January-July 1959," Papers of TWS, DPL.

19. Clem Miller to David Brower, July 1, 1959, Box 5:101, fd: "NWPS–Wilderness–Advocacy–Correspondence, January-July 1959," Papers of TWS, DPL; Thomas H. Kuchel to David R. Brower, June 29, 1959, Box 5:101, "NWPS–Wilderness–Advocacy–Correspondence, January-July 1959," Papers of TWS, DPL.

20. Claude Wood memorandum to Senator Clinton P. Anderson, February 2, 1959; Clinton P. Anderson to Hubert H. Humphrey, February 3, 1959; Hubert H. Humphrey to Clinton P. Anderson, February 9, 1959; Clinton P. Anderson to Hubert H. Humphrey, February 18, 1959; and Clinton P. Anderson to Odd S. Halseth, May 20, 1959, all in Box 619, fd: "Interior and Insular Affairs, Wilderness Bill, 86th Congress," Clinton Anderson Papers, Manuscript Division, LC; "From the Office of Gordon Allott," October 20, 1959, Box 45, fd: "Parks and Forests, Wilderness Source Material," Series IV, Gordon Allott Papers, UCAUCB.

21. Gordon Allott to Richard Hoyt, December 31, 1959, Box 45, fd: "Parks and Forests, Wilderness Source Material," Series IV, Gordon Allott Papers, UCAUCB.

22. Gordon Allott to Douglas Ayers, Jr., September 10, 1959, Box 5:101, fd: "NWPS–Wilderness Bill–Advocacy–Correspondence, August-December 1959," Papers of TWS, DPL.

23. Howard Zahniser, Charles Callison et al., "Analysis of the Allott Amendments to S. 1123, Wilderness Bill," and Charles Callison, William Zimmerman, and Howard Zahniser telegram to Clinton P. Anderson, August 13, 1959, Box 622, fd: "Interior, Wilderness Bill, CEW's File," Clinton P. Anderson Papers, Manuscript Division, LC.

24. Conservationist optimism can be sensed in Paul Brooks to Howard Zahniser, May 15, 1959, and Howard Zahniser to Paul Brooks, May 21, 1959, Box 5:101, fd: "NWPS–Wilderness–Advocacy–Correspondence, January to July 1959," Papers of TWS, DPL. Before the Senate Interior Committee hearings in August 1959, Zahniser personally wrote to every member of the committee, imploring each to keep an open mind about the bill, in hopes of undercutting the Allott Amendments. Allott wrote Zahniser that he was not opposed to Wilderness areas as long as the legislation did not "infringe on the legitimate uses of others in the West." See Gordon Allott to Howard Zahniser, August 8, 1959, Box 5:101, fd: "NWPS–Wilderness Bill–Advocacy–Correspondence, August-December 1959," Papers of TWS, DPL.

25. Joseph C. O'Mahoney to James E. Murray, August 27, 1959; Henry Jackson to Howard Zahniser, September 1, 1959; Joseph C. O'Mahoney to Howard Zahniser, September 1, 1959, all in Box 5:101, fd: "NWPS–Wilderness Bill–Advocacy–Correspondence, August-December 1959," Papers of TWS, DPL; Colorado Water Congress *Newsletter* 2, no. 9 (September 1959): 3-4, Box 45, fd: 1, Series IV, Gordon Allott Papers, UCAUCB; Baker, *Conservation Politics*, 120-121.

26. Colorado Water Congress *Newsletter*, 3–4.

27. Ibid., 4–5.

28. Ibid.; Wayne N. Aspinall to David Brower, February 10, 1960, Box 83, fd: "L-11-a-1," Wayne Aspinall Papers, University of Denver Archives, Denver, CO (Hereafter cited as UDA).

29. Dan H. Hughes to Wayne N. Aspinall, May 5, 1960, and Wayne N. Aspinall to Dan H. Hughes, May 10, 1960, Box 83, fd: "L-11-a-1," Wayne Aspinall Papers, UDA.

30. Wayne N. Aspinall, "Statement by Representative Wayne N. Aspinall at American Mining Congress, October 11, 1960," Box 16, fd: 2, Wayne N. Aspinall Papers, UCAUCB.

31. Baker, *Conservation Politics*, 123–126.

32. Howard Zahniser to Claude Wood, November 4, 1960, Box 642, fd: "Senate Bill No. 74, Claude's Senate Bill No. Folder," Clinton P. Anderson Papers, Manuscript Division, LC; Claude Wood to Clinton Anderson, n.d., ca. December 1960, and Claude Wood to Howard Zahniser, December 29, 1960, Box 642, fd: "Co-sponsored S. 174, General Legislation Material, 87th Congress," Clinton P. Anderson Papers, Manuscript Division, LC; Baker, *Conservation Politics*, 132–133.

33. Rothman, *Greening of a Nation?*, 52; Stewart L. Udall interview with William Moss, February 16, 1970, John F. Kennedy Presidential Library, Boston, MA (hereafter cited as JFKPL).

34. Lee C. White to Lawrence O'Brien, February 9, 1961, and Lee C. White to Lawrence O'Brien, February 13, 1961, Box 49, Legislative Files, President's Office Files, John F. Kennedy Presidential Papers, JFKPL; Thomas G. Smith, "John Kennedy, Stewart Udall, and New Frontier Conservation," *Pacific Historical Review* 64 (August 1995): 336–337. At this point, 1961, the two Roosevelts were identified, in the public's mind, with national conservation activity. Conservation, it should be noted, retained a strong, utilitarian orientation that could still encompass Stewart Udall, Aspinall, and many others.

35. Allott statement in press release, n.d., ca. 1961, Box 45, fd: "Wilderness," Series IV, Gordon Allott Papers, UCAUCB.

36. Wayne N. Aspinall to William E. Bray, February 28, 1961, Box 93, fd: "L-11-a-1," Wayne Aspinall Papers, UDA.

37. Stewart Udall to Clinton Anderson, February 24, 1961, and Stewart Udall to James K. Carr, March 17, 1961, Box 135, fd: "HR 87A-D7," Papers Accompanying Bills and Resolutions, House Interior and Insular Affairs Committee, 87th Congress, Center for Legislative Archives, NA.

38. Baker, *Conservation Politics*, 133.

39. Clinton Anderson to Gordon Allott, March 13, 1961, Box 44, fd: "Parks—Forests—1—Special Interest Mail," Series IV, Gordon Allott Papers, UCAUCB. Colorado Republican congressman J. Edgar Chenoweth, who represented southern Colorado, also opposed early versions of the bill, pointing out to one correspondent that he believed "very strongly in the multiple use of our lands." See J. Edgar Chenoweth to J. Paul Harrison, March 16, 1961, Box 81, fd: 26, J. Edgar Chenoweth Papers, UCAUCB.

40. Baker, *Conservation Politics*, 139; Ben Stong to Clinton Anderson, May 5, 1961, Box 642, fd: "S-174, Claude's Folder," Clinton P. Anderson Papers, Manuscript Division, LC.

41. Baker, *Conservation Politics*, 140-141; Clinton P. Anderson to Frank Church, July 14, 1961, Box 641, fd: "Co-sponsored S. 174 General Correspondence, 87th Congress," Clinton P. Anderson Papers, Manuscript Division, LC.

42. Howard Zahniser to Ernest E. Day, June 21, 1961, Box 5:102, fd: "Correspondence to Legislators, July-December 1961," Papers of TWS, DPL; Howard Zahniser to Hubert H. Humphrey, July 14, 1961, Box 5:102, "NWPS–Wilderness Bill–Advocacy–Correspondence, July-October 1961," Papers of TWL, DPL; Baker, *Conservation Politics*, 140-141.

43. Clinton P. Anderson, "Opening Remarks on the Wilderness Bill," August 24, 1961, Box 642, fd: "S. 174, Senator Anderson's Material for July 1961," Clinton Anderson Papers, Manuscript Division, LC; Baker, *Conservation Politics*, 141-142.

44. Baker, *Conservation Politics*, 142-143; Stewart L. Udall, "Report to the President," August 29, 1961, Box 88, fd: 6, Stewart L. Udall Papers, SCUAL.

45. Stewart L. Udall, "Report to the President," September 12, 1961, Box 88, fd: 6, Stewart L. Udall Papers, SCUAL.

46. Clinton P. Anderson, "Opening Remarks"; LeRoy Ashby and Rod Gramer, *Fighting the Odds: The Life of Senator Frank Church* (Pullman: Washington State University Press, 1994), 145-155. Church won the 1962 election, capturing nearly 55 percent of the vote. Ashby and Gramer credit Church's victory to his ability to turn the Cuban Missile Crisis to his political advantage.

47. Howard Zahniser to Wayne Aspinall, July 18, 1961, Box 5:102, "NWPS–Wilderness Bill–Advocacy–Correspondence to Legislators, July-December 1961," Papers of TWS, DPL.

48. Frank Church to Howard Zahniser, September 23, 1961, Box 5:102, fd: "NWPS–Wilderness Bill–Advocacy–Correspondence to Legislators, July-December 1961, Papers of TWS, DPL; Charles Callison, memorandum on Wilderness Bill, undated, ca. autumn 1961, Box 5:102, fd: "NWPS–Wilderness Bill–Advocacy–Correspondence, July-October 1961," Papers of TWS, DPL.

49. Howard Zahniser, "Memorandum for Members and Cooperators," October 16, 1961, Box 5:203, fd: "NWPS–Campaign–Releases–From TWS, 1960s," Papers of TWS, DPL.

50. *Montrose* (CO) *Daily Press*, October 31, 1961.

51. *Delta* (CO) *Independent*, November 2, 1961.

52. See Aspinall's questioning of witnesses, *To Establish a National Wilderness Preservation System*, Hearings, Subcommittee on Public Lands, House Interior and Insular Affairs Committee, 87th Cong., 1st Sess., Hearings on S. 174 et al., Part 2, 1961, 477-478.

53. Ibid., 487.

54. Ibid., 491.

55. Ibid., 549-554.

56. *Daily Sentinel*, November 1, 1961.

57. Wayne N. Aspinall to Ralph Faxon, n.d., ca. November 1961, Box 16, fd: "1961 Correspondence E-L," Wayne N. Aspinall Papers, UCAUCB.

58. The Wilderness Society, "Wilderness Field Hearings Stir Opponents," Box 5:102, "NWPS–Wilderness Bill–Advocacy–Correspondence to Legislators, January-June

1956," Papers of TWS, DPL; Clyde Wood (Anaconda) to Stockholders, November 6, 1961, and Robert G. Page (Phelps Dodge) to Shareholders, December 7, 1961, Box 5:102, "NWPS–Wilderness Bill–Advocacy–Correspondence, November–December 1961," Papers of TWS, DPL.

59. "Statement by Hon. Wayne N. Aspinall (D-CO), Chairman of the Committee on Interior and Insular Affairs of the House of Representatives," December 21, 1961, Box 16, fd: 45, Wayne N. Aspinall Papers, UCAUCB.

60. *Denver Post*, December 10, 1961. A sampling of earlier anti-Wilderness *Denver Post* statements may be found in *Denver Post*, May 29, 1958, and June 11, 1959.

61. Outdoor Recreation Resources Review Commission, *Outdoor Recreation for America* (Washington, DC: GPO, 1962), 131.

62. John F. Kennedy, "The White House Message on Conservation," March 1, 1962, Box 98, fd: "Conservation," President's Office Files, John F. Kennedy Presidential Papers, JFKPL.

63. "Remarks of Hon. Wayne N. Aspinall to White House Conference on Conservation," May 24, 1962, Box 85, fd: "House of Representatives, 88th IIA News Releases," Papers of the House Committee on Interior and Insular Affairs, Center for Legislative Archives, NA.

64. Sharon F. Francis to James Carr, April 3, 1962, Box 162, fd: "Wilderness Bill, 1961–62," Stewart L. Udall Papers, SCUAL.

65. "Wilderness Hearings Set for May 7 by House Committee," news release, House Committee on Interior and Insular Affairs, April 6, 1962, Box 117, fd: "Pub 4," Wayne Aspinall Papers, UDA; *Daily Sentinel*, April 22, 1962.

66. *To Establish a Wilderness Preservation System*, Hearings, Subcommittee on Public Lands, House Interior and Insular Affairs Committee, 87th Cong., 2d Sess., on S. 174 et al., 1962. See, for example, the testimony of Representatives Robert R. Barry, Edward P. Boland, Dominick V. Daniels, and Robert N. Giaimo, 1121–1127, 1142–1145.

67. Ibid., 1285.

68. Ibid.

69. Ibid., 1285–1286.

70. Ibid., 1286.

71. Ibid.

72. Ibid., 1287–1289.

73. Ibid., 1366–1367.

74. Ibid., 1571.

75. Stewart L. Udall, "Report to the President," July 3, 1962, Box 980, fd: 7, Stewart L. Udall Papers, SCUAL; Committee Papers, Minutes, Subcommittee on Public Lands, July 2, 1962, Box 924, fd: "HR 87A-F8.5," Center for Legislative Archives, NA. Aspinall had asked for the unanimous consent of the Public Lands Subcommittee to use his version of H.R. 776 as "the bill on which the Committee works," a request adopted by the subcommittee without objection.

76. *Durango Herald*, August 10, 1962.

77. Ibid.; Stewart L. Udall, "Excerpts from Stewart Udall's Press Conference," August 23, 1962, Box 162, fd: "Wilderness Bill, 1961–62," Stewart L. Udall Papers, SCUAL.

78. *Daily Sentinel,* August 30, 1962; *New York Times,* August 31 and September 14, 16, and 19, 1962; *Records of the U.S. House of Representatives,* 87th Cong., 1st Sess., Committee Papers, Minutes, House Interior and Insular Affairs Committee, August 28–30, 1962, Box 923, fd: "HR 87A-T8.5," Center for Legislative Archives, NA.

79. *New York Times,* September 16, 1962; David Brower to Friends of Wilderness, September 13, 1962, Box 5:203, fd: "NWPS—Campaigns, releases by other organizations, 1962–64," Papers of TWS, DPL; Eleanor Roosevelt, "My Day," September 17, 1962, Box 20, fd: 38, Wayne N. Aspinall Papers, UCAUCB.

80. *Daily Sentinel,* September 15, 1962.

81. Dixie D. [Aspinall secretary] to Pat [Aspinall staff member], September 17, 1962, Box 18, fd: "1962–63 Correspondence, S–T," Wayne N. Aspinall Papers, UCAUCB.

82. *Congressional Record,* September 20, 1962.

83. For assessments of Carson's significance, see John Opie, *Nature's Nation: An Environmental History of the United States* (Fort Worth, TX: Harcourt Brace College Publishers, 1998), 413–415; Rothman, *Greening of a Nation?,* 85–90. Udall's assessment comes from his comments to a session at the annual meeting of the Western History Association, October 17, 1997, in St. Paul, MN.

84. Ibid.

85. Baker, *Conservation Politics,* 144.

86. *Congressional Record,* September 20, 1962.

87. Ibid.

88. *Atomic Minerals News and Views,* September 24, 1962, Box 6, fd: 22, Wayne N. Aspinall Papers, UCAUCB.

89. Pat to Dixie D. [Aspinall secretaries], September 22, 1962, Box 20, fd: "1962 Wilderness & HR 776," Wayne N. Aspinall Papers, UCAUCB; "Remarks of Honorable Wayne N. Aspinall to Meeting of the Natural Resource Committee of the Chamber of Commerce of the United States, Denver, Colorado," September 27, 1962, Box 110, fd: "L-11-a-1," Wayne Aspinall Papers, UDA.

90. Press release, Citizens Committee on Natural Resources, September 28, 1962, Box 5:203, fd: "NWPS Campaign Releases by Other Organizations, 1962–64," Papers of TWS, DPL.

91. Sharon F. Francis, memorandum to the secretary, September 29, 1962, Box 98, fd: 10, Stewart L. Udall Papers, SCUAL.

92. *Denver Post,* September 30, 1962.

93. Wayne N. Aspinall to Howard Zahniser, October 1, 1962, Box 20, fd: 38, Wayne N. Aspinall Papers, UCAUCB.

94. Wayne N. Aspinall to John F. Kennedy, October 15, 1962, Box 489, fd: "LE/NR-1-LE/NR 6-1," White House Central Files, John F. Kennedy Presidential Papers, JFKPL.

95. John F. Kennedy to Wayne N. Aspinall, January 17, 1963, Box 489, fd: "LE/NR-1-LE/NR 6-1," White House Central Files, John F. Kennedy Presidential Papers, JFKPL.

96. Ira N. Gabrielson to John F. Kennedy, October 29, 1962, Box 20, fd: 37, Wayne N. Aspinall Papers, UCAUCB.

97. Press release, Citizens Committee on Natural Resources, October 29, 1962, Box 20, fd: 37, Wayne N. Aspinall Papers, UCAUCB.

98. Advertisement, "Leo Sommerville in Congress," *Daily Sentinel*, November 3, 1962. The assertion of consistent Republican support for Aspinall is verified by numerous conversations the author has had with Grand Valley citizens in the course of his research.

99. *Daily Sentinel*, November 3, 1962.

100. Ben Stong to Clinton P. Anderson, November 14, 1962, Box 670, fd: "88th Congress, 1st Session, S. 4," Clinton P. Anderson Papers, Manuscript Division, LC; Baker, *Conservation Politics*, 131, 194–195. Title I of Aspinall's Substitute Wilderness Bill had prohibited all executive-branch land withdrawals of more than 5,000 acres except to serve the limited needs of a government agency for a year or less for defense purposes. Even in those cases, notification of Congress was required. Aspinall was acting to prevent any executive action on Wilderness creation. In addition, he was clearly trying to limit the size of potential Wilderness parcels.

101. Hirt, *A Conspiracy of Optimism*, 190–191; Baker, *Conservation Politics*, 98–99.

102. "Remarks of Hon. Wayne N. Aspinall to BLM, National Advisory Board Council, Las Vegas, NV, November 15, 1962," Box 20, fd: 22, Wayne N. Aspinall Papers, UCAUCB; "Remarks of Hon. Wayne N. Aspinall to Routt National Forest Advisory Council, Craig, CO, November 17, 1962," Box 20, fd: 22, Wayne N. Aspinall Papers, UCAUCB. For the Aspinall request for information on Pinchot, see Tom Wilder to Wayne N. Aspinall, May 13, 1963, Box 139, fd: "L-11-a-1," Wayne Aspinall Papers, UDA. Wilder was chief of the Natural Resources Division of the Library of Congress's Legislative Reference Service. Aspinall was interested in learning about Pinchot's controversy with Interior Secretary Richard Ballinger in 1909–1910.

103. Wayne N. Aspinall speech to Utah State University Conservation Banquet, May 3, 1963, Box 139, fd: "L-11-a-1," Wayne Aspinall Papers, UDA.

104. *Rocky Mountain News*, February 12, 1963.

105. Paul Brooks, "Congressman Aspinall vs. The People of the United States," *Harper's Magazine* 226 (March 1963): 60–63. Brooks received both encouragement and assistance on his article from Howard Zahniser of The Wilderness Society. Zahniser told Brooks that he wished personal references to Aspinall's role could be removed but added, "it does seem impossible to understand the situation without such personal understanding of Congressman Aspinall." See Paul Brooks to Howard Zahniser, December 11, 1962, and Howard Zahniser to Paul Brooks, December 19, 1962, Box 5:102, fd: "NWPS–Wilderness Bill–Advocacy–Correspondence, June–December 1962," Papers of TWS, DPL; Howard Zahniser to John Fisher, February 21, 1963, Box 131, fd: "1963 Legislation, Interior, Public Lands," Wayne N. Aspinall Papers, UDA.

106. Stewart L. Udall interview with author, Grand Junction, CO, March 31 and April 1, 1998.

107. Howard Zahniser to John Fisher, February 21, 1963, Box 139, fd: "L-11-a-1," Wayne Aspinall Papers, UDA. See also the letters cited in note 105.

108. *Denver Post*, January 6, 1963.

109. Lee C. White, memorandum to the president, n.d., Box 1, fd: "Aspinall, Wayne," White House Staff Files, Lawrence O'Brien Files, John F. Kennedy Presidential Papers, JFKPL.

110. Lawrence F. O'Brien to John P. Saylor, March 6, 1963, Box 139, fd: "L-11-a-1," Wayne Aspinall Papers, UDA. Saylor left little doubt that he believed that Aspinall's recent interest in studying public-land laws related to the chairman's interest in "obstructing passage of the Wilderness Bill."

111. Wayne N. Aspinall to William H. Nelson, April 1, 1963, Box 139, fd: "L-11-a-1," Wayne Aspinall Papers, UDA; *Washington Daily News*, April 10, 1963; *Washington Evening Star*, April 10, 1963.

112. *Washington Daily News*, April 11, 1963.

113. *Washington Post*, April 12, 1963.

114. *Daily Sentinel*, April 14, 1963.

115. Ibid.

116. F. R. Carpenter to Wayne N. Aspinall, March 11, 1963, and Wayne N. Aspinall to F. R. Carpenter, March 14, 1963, Box 139, fd: "L-11-a-1," Wayne Aspinall Papers, UDA; Pueblo *Star-Journal*, March 17, 1963; Stephen H. Hart to Wayne N. Aspinall, May 7, 1963, Box 24, fd: "P-10," Wayne Aspinall Papers, UDA.

117. Even Aspinall's political enemies seemed taken aback by his health scare of May 1963. Howard Zahniser wrote to Wilderness Society colleague Harvey Broome that "I do hope he is all right and will remain on the scene, for I have faith that we are going to be able to work things out with him." See Howard Zahniser to Harvey Broome, May 3, 1963, Box 5:102, fd: "NWPS—Wilderness Bill—Advisory—Correspondence, January–March 1963," Papers of TWS, DPL. Upon hearing of Aspinall's illness, Zahniser immediately wrote to the chairman, enclosing a book as a gift. When he finally sent his thank-you notes two months later, Aspinall wrote Zahniser that "the fact that we may be divided on a piece of legislation does not, I hope, cause any strain on a friendship that is very valuable to me." Aspinall and Zahniser maintained a relationship of dignity and mutual respect even during extremely tense periods of the Wilderness legislation battle. See Howard Zahniser to Wayne Aspinall, May 3, 1963, and Wayne Aspinall to Howard Zahniser, July 18, 1963, Box 139, fd: "L-11-a-1," Wayne Aspinall Papers, UDA.

118. "Sierra Club Report," May 24, 1963, Box 5:102, "NWPS—Wilderness—Advocacy—Correspondence—From Sierra Club, 1962–64," Papers of TWS, DPL. The report's author is not identified but is likely to have been either William Zimmerman or David Brower. *Daily Sentinel*, June 3, 1963.

119. *Daily Sentinel*, June 3, 1963.

120. *Albuquerque Journal*, May 31, 1963.

121. Howard Zahniser to Wayne N. Aspinall, July 19, 1963, Box 139, fd: "L-11-a-1," Wayne Aspinall Papers, UDA.

122. Draft letter, John Saylor to Aspinall, ca. July 20, 1963, and Wayne N. Aspinall to John Saylor, July 24, 1963, Box 139, fd: "L-11-a-1," Wayne Aspinall Papers, UDA.

123. *Daily Sentinel*, July 22, 1963; *Rocky Mountain News*, July 27, 1963; *Washington Daily News*, July 27, 1963.

124. *Washington Evening Star*, August 6, 1963.

125. Howard Zahniser to Lee Olson, August 1, 1963, Box 5:102, "NWPS—Wilderness—Advisory—Correspondence, June–December 1963," Papers of TWS, DPL.

126. *Albuquerque Journal*, August 25, 1963; see Representative John Saylor's remarks and comments from two Washington, D.C., newspapers in the *Congressional Record*, September 10, 1963.

127. *Albuquerque Journal*, August 25, 1963; memorandum from Senator Gordon Allott's office, n.d., "Status of H.R. 3846, S. 2, S. 4," Box 8, fd: "Associations and Committees, 3-1 Outdoor Recreation 5.858, 1963," Series IV, Gordon Allott Papers, UCAUCB.

128. Lee C. White to President John F. Kennedy, November 12, 1963, Box 1, fd: "Chronological Files, 1963, June–December," White House Staff Files, Lee C. White Files, John F. Kennedy Presidential Papers, JFKPL; Lee C. White interview with William Moss, JFKPL, March 17, 1970; Carol Edmunds, "Wayne N. Aspinall Biographical Sketch," Box 1, fd: 1, Wayne N. Aspinall Papers, UCAUCB.

129. Edward Crafts to Stewart L. Udall, September 27, 1963, Box 162, fd: "Wilderness Bill, 1963-66," Stewart L. Udall Papers, SCUAL; Howard Zahniser to Harvey Broome, October 2, 1963, Box 5:102, fd: "NWPS—Wilderness—Advisory—Correspondence, June–December 1963," Papers of TWS, DPL. An example of the compromise Wilderness legislation from this period includes Congressman John Dingell's H.R. 2001. Dingell (D-MI) offered to broker the Wilderness controversy, and Aspinall encouraged his efforts, which provides further evidence of Aspinall's changing attitude toward the Wilderness issue. See John D. Dingell to Wayne N. Aspinall, October 4, 1963, and Wayne N. Aspinall to John D. Dingell, October 8, 1963, *Records of the U.S. House of Representatives*, 88th Cong., 1st Sess., Committee Papers, Minutes, House Interior and Insular Affairs, Box 10, fd: "HR 88th IIA, HR 2001," Center for Legislative Archives, NA.

130. Benton J. Stong to Stewart L. Udall, October 8, 1963, Box 162, fd: "Wilderness Bill, 1963-66," Stewart L. Udall Papers, SCUAL.

131. Stewart L. Udall, "Some Impressions of the President on the Conservation Trip of September 24-29, 1963," Box 112, fd: 4, Stewart L. Udall Papers, SCUAL; editorial, Scripps-Howard newspapers, October 1, 1963, Box 9, fd: "Legislation—Wilderness Bill, January 9, 1963–November 12, 1963 and undated," White House Staff Files, Lee White General Files, John F. Kennedy Presidential Papers, JFKPL; Edward Meeman to Lee White, October 3, 1963, in preceding box and file.

132. Smith, "John Kennedy, Stewart Udall, and New Frontier Conservation," 348.

133. Wayne N. Aspinall to Charles J. Traylor, November 4, 1963, Box 5, fd: 35, Wayne N. Aspinall Papers, UCAUCB.

134. *Washington Daily News*, November 8, 1963; Carol Edmunds, "Aspinall Biographical Sketch"; Wayne N. Aspinall interview with Joe B. Frantz, Lyndon B. Johnson Presidential Library, Austin, TX, June 14, 1974; Lee C. White to John F. Kennedy, November 12, 1963, Box 1, fd: "Chronological Files, 1963–6/63-12/63," White House Staff Files, Lee C. White Files, John F. Kennedy Presidential Papers, JFKPL.

135. For background on Kennedy's trip to Texas in November 1963, see William Manchester, *The Death of a President: November 1963* (New York: Harper and Row, 1967), passim; David Burner, *John F. Kennedy and a New Generation* (Boston: Scott Foresman/ Little, Brown College Division, 1988), 150; Wayne N. Aspinall interview, June 14, 1974.

136. Doris Kearns, *Lyndon Johnson and the American Dream* (New York: Harper and Row, 1976), 180; Robert M. Dallek, *Flawed Giant: Lyndon Johnson and His Times, 1961–1973* (New York: Oxford University Press, 1998), 59–62; Paul K. Conkin, *Big Daddy from the Pedernales: Lyndon Baines Johnson* (Boston: Twayne, 1986), 172–207; Irving Bernstein, *Guns or Butter: The Presidency of Lyndon Johnson* (New York: Oxford University Press, 1996), 1–113.

137. Wayne N. Aspinall to Dan Hughes, December 4, 1963, Box 140, fd: "L-11-a-3," Wayne Aspinall Papers, UDA; John Carver interview with William Moss, JFKPL, November 18, 1969.

138. News release, The Wilderness Society, December 19, 1963, Box 5:203, fd: "NWPS–Campaign–Release from TWS–1960s," Papers of TWS, DPL; Press release, Committee on Interior and Insular Affairs, "Wilderness Hearings Announced by House Interior Committee," n.d., ca. 1/1/64, Box 167, fd: "L-11-e-3-c," Wayne Aspinall Papers, UDA.

139. *Rocky Mountain News*, January 10, 1964; Wayne N. Aspinall to Arthur H. Carhart, January 3, 1964, Box 167, fd: "L-11-3-b," Wayne Aspinall Papers, UDA.

140. *Denver Post*, January 12, 1964; *Wilderness Preservation System*, Hearings, Subcommittee on Public Lands, House Interior and Insular Affairs Committee, 88th Cong., 2d Sess., on H.R. 9070 et al., 1964, 353–354, 405–406.

141. *Denver Post*, January 30, 1964; The Wilderness Society, "Memo for Members and Cooperators," February 13, 1964, Box 167, fd: "L-11-e-3-c," Wayne Aspinall Papers, UDA.

142. Stewart L. Udall, press conference transcript, January 31, 1964, Box 116, fd: 8, Stewart L. Udall Papers, SCUAL.

143. Edward C. Crafts to Stewart Udall, April 15, 1964, Box 162, fd: "Wilderness Bill, 1963–66," Stewart L. Udall Papers, SCUAL.

144. *Wilderness Preservation System*, Hearings (1964), 1182, 1199.

145. Paul H. Oehser, "Howard Zahniser," *The Cosmos Club Bulletin* (November 1964), 2–4; Aspinall's remarks are contained in *Congressional Record*, May 6, 1964, 8892; *New York Times*, May 6, 1964; David Brower to Members of Congress, May 5, 1964, fd: 1, Howard Zahniser Collection, DPL.

146. *Wilderness Preservation System*, Hearings (1964), 1096, 1106.

147. Ibid., 1126, 1133.

148. Ibid., 1291.

149. Ibid., 1292; Robert C. McConnel to Stewart L. Udall, April 30, 1964, Box 162, fd: "Wilderness Bill, 1963–66," Stewart L. Udall Papers, SCUAL.

150. *Washington Post*, April 30, 1964; McConnel to Udall, April 30, 1964.

151. *Wilderness Preservation System*, Hearings (1964), 1393–1394.

152. *Records of the U.S. House of Representatives*, 88th Cong., 2d Sess., Transcripts, House Interior and Insular Affairs Committee, Public Lands Subcommittee, June 10, 1964, Legislative Files, Box 49, fd: "H.R. 88th IIA, H.R. 9070, 7 of 16," Center for Legislative Archives, NA.

153. *Records of the U.S. House of Representatives*, 88th Cong., 2d Sess., Committee Hearing Transcript, House Interior and Insular Affairs Committee, June 17, 1964, Legislative Files, Box 50, fd: "H.R. 88th IIA, HR 9090," Center for Legislative Archives, NA; *Records of the U.S. House of Representatives*, 88th Cong., 2d Sess., Committee Hearing

Transcript, House Interior and Insular Affairs Committee, June 18, 1964, Legislative Files, Box 56, fd: "88th IIA, H.R. 9070, 9 of 16," Center for Legislative Archives, NA.

154. See Charles Callison to Audubon Society Leaders, June 18, 1964, Box 5:204, fd: "NWPS–Campaigns–Clippings–1964," Papers of TWS, DPL.

155. *Albuquerque Tribune*, June 19, 1964; *New York Times*, July 29, 1964; Stewart Udall press briefing, July 30, 1964, Box 116, fd: 9, Stewart L. Udall Papers, SCUAL.

156. *Washington Post*, July 31, 1964.

157. Baker, *Conservation Politics*, 219; Saylor's and Aspinall's remarks are in *Congressional Record*, August 20, 1964, 20630. In addition, see *Conference Report to Accompany S. 4*, U.S. House of Representatives, 88th Cong., 2d Sess., Report No. 1829, August 19, 1964.

158. Baker, *Conservation Politics*, 220; "Remarks of President Johnson upon Signing S. 4," September 3, 1964, Box 119, fd: 3, Stewart L. Udall Papers, SCUAL.

159. *Conference Report to Accompany S. 4*, 9–11.

160. Clinton Anderson, press release, August 17, 1964, Box 670, fd: unlabeled, Clinton Anderson Papers, Manuscript Division, LC.

161. Nash, *Wilderness and the American Mind*, 226; Fox, *The American Conservation Movement*, 289; Rothman, *The Greening of a Nation?*, 54.

162. Stewart L. Udall interview, March 31 and April 1, 1998; Carol Edmunds, *Wayne Aspinall: Mr. Chairman* (Lakewood, CO: Crown Point, 1980), 211.

163. Baker, *Conservation Politics*, 220.

164. Stewart L. Udall, press conference transcript, August 21, 1964, Box 116, fd: 9, Stewart L. Udall Papers, SCUAL.

165. Harry R. Woodward to Wayne N. Aspinall, September 9, 1964, Box 167, fd: "L-11-e-3-b," Wayne Aspinall Papers, UDA; John B. Bernard, Jr., to Gordon Allott, September 17, 1964, Box 46, fd: "Parks and Forests 1, Wilderness," Series V, Gordon Allott Papers, UCAUCB; *Daily Sentinel*, October 23, 1964.

166. Hugh Kingery to Howard Zahniser, April 30, 1964, Box 5:200, fd: "NWPS–Advocacy–Correspondence–1964," Papers of TWS, DPL; *Rocky Mountain News*, April 30, 1964.

167. See "1964 Campaign Financial Statement," Box 8, fd: 4, Wayne N. Aspinall Papers, UCAUCB; see correspondence relating to "Bipartisan Committee for Aspinall," Box 7, fd: 22, Wayne N. Aspinall Papers, UCAUCB.

168. Wayne Aspinall to Ed Johnson, September 8, 1964, Box 21, fd: 27, Wayne N. Aspinall Papers, UCAUCB; "Campaign Schedule for Congressman Aspinall, 1964," Box 8, fd: 22, Wayne N. Aspinall Papers, UCAUCB; Wayne Aspinall interview, June 14, 1974. During the campaign, Aspinall avoided direct engagements with his opponent, preferring instead to emphasize his record of service to the Fourth District.

169. Wayne N. Aspinall to Paul Shriver, November 23, 1964, Box 20, fd: 54, Wayne N. Aspinall Papers, UCAUCB; Wayne Aspinall interview, June 14, 1974.

170. On the "Conservation Congress," see Baker, *Conservation Politics*, 191–228; Smith, "Kennedy, Udall, and New Frontier Conservation," 360–361. In his speeches during the 1964 campaign, Aspinall, too, referred to the Eighty-eighth Congress as "the greatest conservation Congress in history." See "1964 Clippings," Box 48, Wayne N. Aspinall Papers, UCAUCB.

CHAPTER FIVE
GUARDIAN of WESTERN WATER

RECONFIGURING the CENTRAL ARIZONA PROJECT

In 1963, Wayne Aspinall briefly halted proceedings on the House floor to commemorate a momentous event. On March 13, a milestone "of significance in the history of water resource development in this great nation" had occurred: the closing of the left diversion tunnel of the Glen Canyon Dam, the crown jewel of the 1956 Colorado River Storage Project. Aspinall, who saw the CRSP as his greatest legislative achievement, marked the birth of Lake Powell in March 1963 with "great pleasure," viewing it as a "source of satisfaction."[1]

Not sharing Aspinall's joy that day was Sierra Club leader David Brower, who had recently eulogized the canyon in his book, *The Place No One Knew: Glen Canyon.* The diversion tunnel's closing marked the end of one of the most magnificent and pristine canyons in the American West. In a last-minute attempt to halt the tunnel closing, Brower had sent a copy of the book to all members of Congress, including Wayne Aspinall. Brower may also have been trying to assuage his own guilt for having not fought the dam in the original CRSP of 1956. Brower believed that the conservation movement, which had first emerged as a national political force when it eliminated the Echo Park Dam from early drafts of the CRSP, should have persisted in opposing the CRSP as a whole. Brower believed that he and other Echo Park opponents had been so blinded by their victory on behalf of Echo Park that they overlooked and sacrificed magnificent Glen Canyon in the process. At that time, Brower recalled, the conservation movement had believed only "in the principle of protecting the national parks." The Glen Canyon Dam site had been proposed as part of a huge national monument in the late 1930s, but World War II intervened, and by the postwar era, the canyon's geological features had attracted the attention of Bureau of Reclamation engineers. Part of what made it so appealing, of course, was that it was not under the protection of the National Park Service. When the legislative CRSP horse-trading was going on, Brower had only heard rumors of Glen Canyon's beauty. Soon after 1956, he would visit the doomed canyon and see what he and the nation's other leading conservationists had bargained away. Almost immediately, the Sierra Club formulated a new policy: never to give away an inch of any site until the organization had looked at it.[2]

Brower alleged that *The Place No One Knew* moved Aspinall to tears. Though Aspinall admitted to Brower that the book's "artistry is magnificent," he quickly recovered his senses, pointing out that although Glen Canyon was beautiful, places like it were a dime a dozen in the West. "I wish you would let me have [the book's] photographer-artist, and I could take him into numerous canyons in my district where he could get similar pictures with like narrations." In the fight to retain the Echo Park Dam, Aspinall had said the same thing about Dinosaur National Monument and Echo Park. Earlier, when the *New York Times* had somewhat belatedly editorialized against the Glen Canyon Dam as an "unnecessary impediment" on the Colorado River, Aspinall had told the press that the newspaper was simply "opening up old wounds." He noted, "I have got 10,000 areas in my district as beautiful as Glen Canyon which are available to people who want to see them."[3]

Wayne Aspinall thus could both rationalize and celebrate the loss of Glen Canyon as its second gate closed, dooming it to a watery destruction on March 13, 1963. The canyon's death, according to Aspinall's utilitarian principles, was for a greater good: humanity's gain. The water the dam would soon impound, the power it would generate, and the multitude of recreational uses it would provide seemed well worth the loss of but one of the West's many canyons.

Glen Canyon's slow, agonizing demise had actually begun on January 21, 1963, when the first, or right, diversion tunnel slammed shut, causing water to rise toward the higher, or left, diversion tunnel, which would be sealed in March. By coincidence, on that same January day, Interior Secretary Udall, with Bureau of Reclamation commissioner Floyd Dominy at his side, met the press to disclose a new, larger reclamation plan that would dominate Wayne Aspinall's political career until 1968. From the podium, Udall unveiled the outlines of the Pacific Southwest Water Plan, an integrated approach to reclamation meant to unite Arizona, California, and the rest of the Southwest, hopefully overcoming decades of political hostility while providing for the region's hydraulic future.[4]

Since the early twentieth century, Arizonans had dreamed of securing additional water for their desert state. The method and plans for doing so changed over the years, but the basic outline remained the same: to bring supplemental water to the parched but growing population corridor of south-central Arizona. Whereas Arizona's need for water only increased with time, many of the political dynamics remained stationary through the decades: California would continue to resist Arizona's claims to its Colorado River Compact-specified 2.8 million acre-feet of water; Arizona would continue to have a strong political player in powerful but aging Democratic senator Carl Hayden, who could get almost any form of a Central Arizona Project (or CAP, as it would come to be known) authorized in the U.S. Senate; and the House of Representatives would remain the largest obstacle to passage, as it had for most post-World War II reclamation dreams. As chair of the House Interior and Insular Affairs Committee, Wayne Aspinall would again occupy center stage over most phases of the CAP deliberations.

Arizona's early struggles to obtain a reliable water supply, including its protracted legal struggle with California, are well documented elsewhere.[5] Arizona shared with the Upper Colorado River Basin states a deep-seated fear of California's water machinations, especially that state's penchant for capturing and using more than its legal share. Like the states of the Upper Basin, Arizona boomed during and after World War II: the population of Phoenix swelled from a modest 65,000 in 1940 to 439,000 by 1960. Between 1920 and 1960, Arizona's overall population quadrupled. Rapidly depleting its groundwater, Arizona desperately sought ways to supplement the supplies that nature had shortchanged.[6]

As a young congressman, Carl Hayden had talked about some form of Central Arizona Project in the early 1920s,[7] but it was not until after World War II that the State of Arizona actually proposed constructing the massive reclamation project. After Arizona's legislature refused to fund the plan, the state's congressional delegation introduced a bill in the late 1940s to authorize a CAP. Soon a pattern emerged: the bill would pass the Senate, where influential Arizona senators Carl Hayden and Ernest F. McFarland could push the bill through, only to fail in the House of Representatives, where sparsely populated Arizona proved no match for California's large delegation. By the early 1950s, CAP legislation had become entangled in a legal morass over a final determination of Arizona's and California's shares of the Colorado River.[8]

By 1952, California was already using more than 5.3 million acre-feet of Colorado River water per year—almost 1 million more than its legal allotment. After several failed attempts, in 1952 Arizona finally convinced the U.S. Supreme Court that the state's future would be compromised if the Court did not intervene and determine its claims to Colorado River water.[9] The ensuing legal case, *Arizona v. California*, proved, in Norris Hundley's words, "to be among the most complicated and hotly contested in Supreme Court history." Lasting more than eleven years and requiring the work of a special master, Simon Rifkind of New York, the trial entailed testimony from 340 witnesses. The opinion, announced on June 3, 1963, upheld Arizona's position on almost every issue. Most significantly, Arizona's claim to 2.8 million acre-feet was affirmed, and water from the Salt-Verde-Gila watershed would not count against Arizona's Colorado

River entitlement. The Court also ruled that responsibility for apportioning water during drought years would lie with the secretary of the interior. Arizona, whose native son, Stewart Udall, was firmly ensconced as head of the Interior Department, felt especially secure on this point in 1963. Finally, the decision examined an issue that was cropping up with increasing frequency in the 1960s— the riddle of Native American water rights. *Arizona v. California* helped inspire Native American tribes to proactively assert their water rights by invoking the Winters Doctrine. In 1908, the Supreme Court had asserted in the case *Winters v. U.S.* that when the federal government established Native American reservations, those reservations were not limited to land "but included water as well." Disappointing to the state of Arizona, however, was the Court's assertion in the 1963 case that Native American water usage be charged against the state in which the reservation was located.[10]

Although *Arizona v. California* significantly strengthened the Native American legal position in the chase for western water, it did not automatically provide the precious substance. In most instances, years of costly litigation would follow any attempt to assert these water rights. Still, after 1963, Native Americans could, as Hundley put it, "no longer be ignored in future planning for the Colorado River."[11]

Not surprisingly, Arizonans greeted the Court's decision with jubilation. Along with the announcement of *Arizona v. California*, Arizona's congressional delegation almost simultaneously introduced legislation for a Central Arizona Project. Meanwhile, disappointed Californians hoped to resist and delay Arizona's water claims in Congress, which would still have to authorize any CAP. Arizona's capabilities in the Senate, where Carl Hayden continued to hold sway, might be strong, but a more troubled path awaited population-sparse Arizona in the House of Representatives, where Wayne Aspinall would help determine whether a CAP would see legislative light and what shape such a project might take.

Aspinall's disposition toward the Central Arizona Project provides insight into the Coloradan's great influence not only on post–World War II reclamation policy, but on the larger issues shaping western water politics as well. Aspinall, of course, feared that a series of extensive Lower Basin water projects would endanger the Upper Basin's share of the Colorado River. The timing of the CAP also presented problems for Aspinall. Though the CRSP had been authorized in 1956 and Fry-Ark in 1962, many of the components or supporting projects still needed to be either funded or built. A fast commitment to an expensive CAP might provide competition for limited federal reclamation dollars. Still, Aspinall was not reflexively adverse to meeting Arizona's water needs. As a junior member of the House Interior Committee in the early 1950s, Aspinall had "listened intently" to Arizona's earlier failed bids for a Central Arizona Project. From 1963 to 1968, Aspinall would be a key legislative designer of the Central Arizona Project, as well as its main obstacle.[12]

A hint of Aspinall's intent may be gleaned from the chairman's letter to Interior Secretary Udall in late November 1962. Anticipating the Supreme Court's decision in *Arizona v. California*, Aspinall indicated that the time had come to start discussing the "broad parameters" that would guide future Lower Colorado River development. Aspinall revealed the direction he felt this planning might take. Although the situation facing the Lower Colorado was not as dire as the one confronting the Upper Basin prior to CRSP passage, Aspinall believed that the basinwide CRSP approach might be the most politically viable mechanism for addressing the Southwest's water needs. In short, Aspinall believed Udall should begin formulating a plan to address the entire region's water future and projected power needs.[13]

Udall's response to Aspinall in January 1963 contained the seeds of what would soon be called the Pacific Southwest Water Plan (PSWP). Specifically, the interior secretary argued for the inclusion of the long-planned dams in the Grand Canyon at Bridge and Marble Canyons. Both units, in Udall's estimate, would be necessary to fully utilize the region's water and power potential. Present water and power supplies were "inadequate." Instead, a "coordinated comprehensive plan involving a long-range program" would best meet the Pacific Southwest's water needs.[14]

In the immediate aftermath of the Supreme Court's June 1963 decision, there was no shortage of approaches to Arizona's and the Southwest's hydraulic future, with a political clash all but inevitable once the public began discussing the potential plans. Aspinall and Udall favored the comprehensive regional approach as the most politically salable. Arizona senator Carl Hayden believed that a bare-bones CAP should be constructed, free from the encumbrance of a regional plan. Congressman Morris Udall, walking a political tightrope as the interior secretary's brother, Aspinall's Interior Committee colleague, and Hayden's Arizona political associate, took a wait-and-see approach for the time being.[15]

Representative Udall, analyzing Arizona's political situation in June 1963, seemed certain of one fact: Wayne Aspinall would play a significant part in what would soon transpire. The leader of the House Interior Committee, "one of the most effective and respected House Chairmen" and a "superb legislative tactician with a passion for detail," had never lost a bill on the floor after it had met his committee's demanding standards. "Nearly all of the major reclamation projects of the last decade," Udall noted, "bear his imprint," including the massive CRSP, of which he was a "principal architect." Udall did not foresee great difficulty for a CAP in the Senate, where Hayden continued to exert his influence, but he predicted a "major fight" in the House.[16] *Arizona Republic* political correspondent Ben Cole depicted Aspinall in 1963 as "fiercely dedicated" and fair, "neither liberal nor conservative, neither pro- nor anti-administration." Aspinall made it clear on the eve of congressional CAP consideration that "nobody puts the bee on this congressman."[17]

Invited to address the Arizona Reclamation Association in the fall of 1963, Aspinall further hinted at what his cooperation would require from both southwestern water planners and the state of Arizona. Aspinall made it clear that he had supported and would continue to support Arizona's water needs, provided they were brought to his committee "in a timely manner." Political and economic conditions had changed in Arizona and the West since CAP legislation had been brought before Congress in the early 1950s. New studies were needed, and they would take time. To Aspinall's orderly mind, the Interior Committee could not be expected to lay aside all other reclamation projects to "give immediate attention to Arizona's desire." Arizona would need to be patient and get in line.[18] Aspinall's long experience with western water politics had taught him that states needed to work out their differences far from the public view and come to Congress as a united front: "unity and cooperation are imperative if the water needs of the Pacific Southwest, the fastest growing area of the nation, are to be met." Controversy, Aspinall stressed, would benefit no one.[19]

Arizona's congressional delegation would differ over which approach to take well into 1964. Carl Hayden continued favoring a simple CAP-alone approach. "If we involve other projects in our bill, I feel certain that we will meet new arguments and new delays," the senator maintained. Secretary Udall had told Hayden that there was "not the faintest chance" that Congress would authorize a CAP in any form in 1963–1964. Udall's Pacific Southwest Water Plan, hastily cobbled together, was released in August 1963 on the eve of Senate hearings on the Hayden-Goldwater CAP bills. Many in Arizona resented Udall's comprehensive approach, feeling that the large plan would only distract Congress and the nation from the business of slaking Arizona's thirst. As Udall told an impatient Hayden, he had to serve the president "as Secretary of the Interior of the United States, and not Secretary of the Interior for Arizona."[20]

Burdened with too much detail that made it an easy target for congressional critics, the Pacific Southwest Water Plan nonetheless focused attention and strategy on the regional approach to water development. The advantage of the regional approach lay in its ability to muster many states behind it, in effect maximizing the West's diluted political power. A large plan could also be dissected and reshuffled; portions could be sacrificed and compromised. Aspinall, of course, favored this approach and, over the next several years, would add to it his ideas and concepts, not all of them pleasing to Arizona water interests.

But there still remained the problem of Carl Hayden, the powerful dean of the Senate, and his desire to see a CAP-only plan presented to Congress. On January 7, 1964, a group of Arizona politicians and numerous Bureau of Reclamation and Department of the Interior officials met in Stewart Udall's Washington office to discredit Hayden's plan. Of course, Hayden was not present. At this point, Congressman Morris Udall dropped all pretense of objectivity, emerging as a strong supporter of the regional approach. This was the only plan, he maintained, that could muster enough votes to pass the House. Even Hayden's immense prestige could not bludgeon a CAP-only bill through the lower house. As far as Mo Udall was concerned, the decisive factor in formulating strategy remained the attitude of Congressman Wayne Aspinall. The Coloradan "would be willing to support the larger plan," but Udall doubted Aspinall "would support a separate CAP." At this early point in the CAP discussions, the exact form of any regional plan remained hazy.[21]

Buoyed by seemingly increasing support, on February 7, 1964, Stewart Udall announced a revised Pacific Southwest Water Plan to the nation, signaling the beginning of an all-out campaign for a regional approach. A central feature of the plan was a high dam at Bridge Canyon that would generate power for sale to enhance project repayment and lift water from the deep recesses of the Grand Canyon so gravity could bring it to thirsty south-central Arizona. The high dam would back water into the Grand Canyon's inner gorge for about thirteen miles. Although this may seem like a repudiation of National Park Service policy, which had protected parklands since the Echo Park fight, the Grand Canyon's enabling legislation, written in 1919 by none other than Congressman Carl Hayden, had foreseen such a possibility. The 1919 law stated that "whenever consistent with the primary purposes of said park the Secretary of the Interior is authorized to permit the utilization of areas therein which may be necessary for the development and maintenance of a Government reclamation project."[22] Udall's PSWP included political inducements for every Lower Basin state, including the immediate authorization of reclamation projects in Arizona, California, Nevada, and Utah. The water plan guaranteed the Lower Basin 7.5 million acre-feet annually, thus eliminating the need for the interior secretary to act as a water broker in times of shortage.[23]

Overlooked amidst the fanfare surrounding Udall's water spectacular was Carl Hayden's opposition. The Arizona senator continued to press Udall for long-overdue Interior Department reports on the simple CAP introduced in conjunction with Senator Barry Goldwater in the aftermath of the Supreme Court decision. Hayden also feared that the PSWP would "play into the hands" of those who continued to want to deny Arizona its share of the Colorado River. Hayden made noises about threatening more extreme political measures if Udall did not issue immediate and favorable CAP reports, something the senator would ultimately resort to, but against Wayne Aspinall, not Stewart Udall. Hayden's position was born of a fifty-year career in politics, during which he had attempted to bring about a federal reclamation program to supplement Arizona's dismal water supply.[24]

Udall, not wanting to attack the infirm octogenarian, chose to blame the senator's young, intelligent, and ambitious legislative assistant, Roy Elson, not only for Hayden's inflexibility, but for poisoning much of Arizona against a regional approach. After learning of Udall's charges, Hayden took offense at

Udall's implication that he could not control his office staff. Finally, after an angry exchange of letters, Hayden in effect said that the two men should withdraw their remarks and work toward unity for the sake of Arizona. In late February 1964, not only did Hayden and Udall agree not to disagree, but Hayden assented to including the CAP as part of a regional plan—a significant compromise for the old senatorial water warrior.[25]

The next step toward Lower Basin unity was dealing with California's insistence upon a guarantee of its annual allotment of 4.4 million acre-feet. Senator Thomas Kuchel (R-CA) saw this as the cornerstone for Arizona-California cooperation. Kuchel, however, would only consider supporting a CAP with the proviso that any bill must first be passed by the touchier and more difficult House of Representatives. This marked the beginnings of a constructive hydraulic dialogue between Arizona and California. Soon, members of Congress from California were introducing their own versions of a regional water plan, something unheard of several years earlier.[26]

Senate hearings took place on Udall's Pacific Southwest Water Plan in 1964. Dissected thoroughly, the plan failed to win overall support, though many of its particulars were appealing. Though the PSWP did not win approval, it did provide a conceptual framework for those favoring a broad, regional approach to the Southwest's water problems. But to the restless citizens of Arizona, it seemed little progress had been achieved during the first year following the state's Supreme Court victory. Congress, in 1964, was tied up with the great debate over civil rights legislation. Aspinall's House Interior Committee was also busy refining a Wilderness Bill and other significant conservation legislation. Additionally, both political parties were about to hold their national conventions in anticipation of November's presidential election. Behind the scenes, however, the warring factions, taking Aspinall's advice, worked toward a resolution of their differences in preparation for a strong authorization drive when the new Eighty-ninth Congress convened in January 1965.

Much to the delight of most Arizonans, Aspinall brought his House Irrigation and Reclamation Subcommittee to Phoenix after the November elections. At a hearing on November 9, 1964, the pattern was established for future House hearings on Lower Colorado River Basin water legislation. Aspinall appeared receptive and sympathetic to Arizona's needs. At the same time, the Coloradan left no doubt that the route to House passage would be a difficult one, with the rules set by him and him alone. For example, when Wayne Akin, chair of Arizona's Interstate Stream Commission, asserted in his testimony that Arizona's "turn" for water had finally arrived, Aspinall took immediate umbrage. The House Interior Committee, the chairman thundered, was punctilious about "considering reclamation project authorizations only when their feasibility could be proved to the committee . . . there isn't any political turn in this operation."[27]

At the conclusion of the Phoenix hearing, Aspinall made a flyover across the Grand Canyon to view the sites of the proposed Bridge and Marble Canyon Dams, which were integral components of most water plans for Arizona and the Southwest. After his trip, Aspinall indicated that he favored the lower Bridge Canyon Dam, though he believed that a high dam would cause only minimal harm to the Grand Canyon. To another friend, Aspinall confided that he believed at least one of the proposed dams should be constructed. According to Aspinall, a dam would be built, but one that did "not back water up into the Grand Canyon National Park." It should be noted that the Grand Canyon is 277 miles long; of those scenic miles, only 100 were actually protected by national-park or national-monument status at the start of the controversy. In the year ahead, the question of placing dams in the Grand Canyon would once again raise the ire of the nation's growing environmental movement, ultimately forcing Aspinall and other reclamation advocates to modify their plans.[28]

Arizona's senators, Hayden and the recently elected Republican Paul Fannin, introduced S. 75 in January 1965. The new bill demonstrated that Arizona had learned from its divisiveness in 1963–1964. Hayden's new plan, the Lower Colorado River Basin Project, resembled a trimmed-down version of Udall's Pacific Southwest Water Plan but retained a CAP as its most prominent feature. Hayden's support of a regional approach represented a significant compromise and step forward for the Southwest's water interests. Hayden's plan asked the secretary of the interior to study sources for augmenting the Southwest's water supplies and included dams at both Marble and Bridge Canyons in the Grand Canyon, but not in Grand Canyon National Park as it was then constituted. To broaden its support, S. 75 also contained a Southern Nevada Project to deliver water for the rapidly growing Las Vegas area. The major difference between Hayden's bill and those introduced by the California delegation was a provision in California's versions limiting CAP diversions when necessary to guarantee California's 4.4 million acre-feet. This issue would become a flashpoint in 1965 between Arizona and California. On the House side, the CAP, reconfigured as the regional Colorado River Basin Project, was introduced by Morris Udall as H.R. 4671.[29]

After 1965, Wayne Aspinall's relationship with Central Arizona Project proponents became distinctly strained. From 1962 to 1965, the chair of the House Interior Committee had encouraged Arizona's hydraulic efforts, but in so doing, he had supported the broad regional approach to the Southwest's water future. The more politically viable regional approach might also allow Upper Basin states to weave more storage facilities into the final legislation. After 1965, Aspinall became a guardian of the Upper Colorado River Basin's water, ensuring that any legislation contained adequate protection for Colorado and other Upper Basin states. Working with Felix (Larry) Sparks, director of the Colorado Water Conservation Board, Aspinall asked if enough water existed in the river system to build any version of the Lower Colorado River Basin Project. Aspinall and Sparks contended that a CAP could only be successful if it utilized some of the Upper Basin's allotted water. Aspinall, a master water strategist, was building the foundation for additional protection of Upper Basin water. One way to accomplish this goal was to advocate augmentation of the Colorado River's waters. "The most probable source is the Columbia River system," Sparks concluded. Of course, if the Pacific Northwest's representatives were to resist this plan, other sources of water would need to be found: additional Upper Basin reclamation projects would be the most likely solution.[30] Such projects could be grafted onto a CAP as a condition of Aspinall's support.

On February 1, 1965, Carl Hayden accepted California senator Thomas Kuchel's requirement that Arizona guarantee California's 4.4 million–acre-foot share of river flow. The Arizona-California agreement contained the significant provision that any CAP bill must first pass the House of Representatives. This action focused the political spotlight squarely on Aspinall's House Interior Committee.[31] Rich Johnson, president of Arizona's CAP Association, tried to motivate Aspinall to schedule hearings by calling the chairman's 1963 Phoenix address a "turning point in our struggle for water." Johnson also reminded Aspinall that his professed criterion of intrastate and interbasin unity had finally been achieved: the path to significant Interior Committee action was clear. Other Arizonans, including Assistant Interior Secretary Orren Beaty, believed that Secretary Udall needed to remind Aspinall, before he called for hearings, of Arizona's past water statesmanship, including its support for the CRSP and Fryingpan-Arkansas. "Arizona has a right to expect that the Upper Basin will not resort to legalities or court tests to stall Arizona's project." Aspinall was never pleased when Arizona or any other state felt that it was entitled to particular consideration from his committee, which, he liked to believe, evaluated water projects on their merits only.[32]

Despite the fact that they were not in open disagreement anymore, Arizona's congressional contingent was still plagued by a lack of political unity. The delegation still had not organized itself to press Aspinall to schedule hearings on the CAP legislation. Realizing he might be attacking his brother Morris, Secretary Udall nevertheless continued to assert that Arizona lacked "any meaningful united leadership in Washington." As he remembered from the years before the CRSP's enactment, the political background work was strenuous but necessary for legislative success. The long effort to enact the CRSP could serve as a model for CAP's authorization. The highlight of his first term as an Arizona congressman was "the opportunity to participate in the congressional strategy sessions—with Representative Wayne Aspinall acting as our captain and quarterback—which led to the passage of the Upper Colorado Storage Project. Our strategy sessions were frequent and once decisions were thrashed out we followed the leadership of our captain and carried them out."[33]

In May 1965, the White House endorsed the Pacific Southwest Water Plan, which was by then routinely referred to as the CAP or the Lower Colorado River Basin Project. The Bureau of the Budget also endorsed the legislation but recommended constructing only the Marble Canyon Dam. The Bridge Canyon Dam, already opposed by a swelling contingent of environmentalists, would back water into Grand Canyon National Park, and the White House did not want to challenge this increasingly vocal and influential group.[34] With strong executive-branch support for the plan, Aspinall might now consider scheduling hearings.

In May, Senator Hayden and other CAP advocates asked Aspinall to do just that. However, a less-than-enthusiastic Chairman Aspinall continued to bide his time, formulating a strategy of delay to better strengthen the Upper Basin's bargaining position. On May 22, Aspinall asked the governors of the Colorado River Basin states to provide data on their projected water needs and Colorado River water supplies. Aspinall argued that the information was a prerequisite for constructive House Interior Committee action on the Southwest's water problems. Though Aspinall's logic was sound, most project proponents saw his request as not only cumbersome but a delaying tactic as well. The evidence suggests that is exactly what Aspinall envisioned. At the time, Ival Goslin, executive director of the Upper Colorado River Commission, was studying future Upper Basin water needs, especially as they might be impacted by Lower Basin reclamation endeavors.[35]

At the same time, Arizona congressman Mo Udall was busy assessing Arizona's chances for its water project, in particular Aspinall's intentions toward it. In an analysis prepared for his staff and fellow Arizona political operatives, Udall called Aspinall "a sincere, capable, knowledgeable technician—dedicated to placing before the House sound projects that have been scrutinized in every aspect. He is deliberate and sometimes seemingly arbitrary and immovable. He is a champion of the Upper Basin." As Udall viewed it, Aspinall seemed to be stalling at the behest of Goslin's Upper Colorado River Commission to gain both time and leverage. The commission hoped to release the Upper Basin from responsibility for supplying water to Mexico via the Mexican Water Treaty of 1944 and even aspired to additional Upper Basin water projects. Viewed from this perspective, Aspinall's request to the state governors was indeed an attempt to move the CAP debate at a snail's pace and limit the House hearings, when scheduled, to a restrictive agenda: the Basin's available water supply. At that rate, actual CAP authorization could still be years away.[36]

To compound Arizona's fears, during the summer of 1965 a national water commission, the Water Resources Council, was established as part of the Water Resources Planning Act of 1965 to devise approaches to and anticipate future water problems.[37] Arizonans, wanting a CAP in any form, saw this council as an additional excuse to delay redress of their water needs. Their fears were compounded when Senator Henry Jackson (D-WA), Representative Thomas Foley (D-WA), and other Pacific Northwest politicians began to publicly discourage legislation targeting the Northwest as a potential source for southwestern water-importation schemes. To Senator Jackson, chair of the Senate Interior and Insular Affairs Committee, a broad national commission seemed less threatening to his region's future.[38]

As late as July 30, 1965, Aspinall still had not scheduled LCRBP hearings. Arizonans blamed Aspinall for plotting to kill the legislation by delay, but they might just as well have pointed the finger at northwestern politicians (who feared interbasin water transfers) or their traditional foes from California.[39] Aspinall's foot-dragging may have resulted from a sincere fear that not enough water was available in the Colorado River Basin or a belief that with the passage of time, Colorado and the Upper Basin's political position to influence the final shape of CAP legislation would improve. The latter interpretation seems most likely, though Aspinall was intellectually supple enough to delay legislation, as the Wilderness case study makes clear, for a variety of reasons.

In a revealing personal letter to former Colorado governor and senator Ed Johnson, Aspinall indicated that he had no plans to move the LCRBP through his committee during the Eighty-ninth Congress. Though he intended to hold hearings in August 1965 (but had not publicly announced this fact), Aspinall told Johnson that after the hearings, he would allow the bill to languish until January 1966, when the Upper Basin's bargaining position should be enhanced. Aspinall concluded this letter with a brutally realistic assessment of his power and ability to shape this legislation: "I can say in all modesty that the Central Arizona Project legislation cannot pass the House without my support."[40]

After much delay, the House Irrigation and Reclamation Subcommittee opened hearings on the LCRBP on August 23, 1965. It was too late in the legislative year for the bill to pass, but the hearings nonetheless offered all sides an opportunity to state their positions and demands for an LCRBP bill. Although not the subcommittee chair, Aspinall essentially presided over most of the August hearings. In his opening statement, he indicated that his overriding concern, which he had expressed in a May letter to the Basin's governors, was to determine the availability of enough Colorado River Basin water to sustain *any* form of an LCRBP. Only three days before the House hearings began, a seven-state accord—the result of Aspinall's letter to the governors—was reached on the water-availability question. The agreement's foundation envisioned the ultimate need to import water into the Basin to sustain the Southwest's hydraulic dreams. The most likely source of water would be the Columbia River Basin of the Pacific Northwest. This would prove a major stumbling block and source of controversy for the LCRBP in the years ahead.[41]

Wayne Aspinall opened the hearings with a sly understatement: "The history of the Colorado [River] as to the amount of waters is a matter of much controversy." The chairman's standard for action on the LCRBP was simple, yet difficult to attain—the Upper Basin required firm assurance that it would have the water it was entitled to under the Colorado River Compact of 1922 after the CAP was built. With this assurance, Aspinall would favorably report a bill that benefited the Lower Basin. As Aspinall would say many times over the next three years, he did not want the Lower Basin building water projects using the Upper Basin's precious water allotment. The legislation under consideration, H.R. 4671, was a scaled-down version of Secretary Udall's Pacific Southwest Water Plan. However, its centerpiece remained a large and expensive CAP, with at least one "cash register" dam in the Grand Canyon to generate power, thus ensuring the project's financial viability.[42]

Four issues developed during the August 1965 House hearings that would prove major hurdles to CAP passage. The notion of interbasin water transfers, or water augmentation, as it was frequently referred to, quickly emerged as something eagerly promoted by project supporters and greatly feared by northwestern politicians.[43] In addition, early in the hearings, the Upper Basin states, led by Aspinall, revealed their price for positive action on CAP—the assurance that Lower Basin development would not come at the expense of legitimate Upper Basin water claims. A third issue involved the role of the growing environmental movement in the West's water deliberations. When the Interior Department's revised LCRBP plans dropped one of the Grand Canyon dams, Aspinall began fearing that Secretary Udall and the Johnson administration were surrendering to the wishes of what he labeled "a minority group," the preservationists. Their objections to the Grand Canyon dams were the same ones "we quarreled over in the upper Colorado river program with Echo Park." Aspinall did not yet fear their political power, but he was wary of the impact environmental groups might have on the political resolve of other supporters of federal reclamation.[44] Finally, the water claims of Native Americans emerged and, over the next several years, would threaten to cloud or destroy all forms of CAP legislation.

Usually genial and friendly to witnesses, Aspinall nevertheless could explode almost without warning and lash out at witnesses who exhibited little understanding of the nuances of western water politics or respect for the Upper Basin's rights. One such unfortunate was Arizona governor Sam Goddard, who testified on August 24, 1965. The official minutes record that "Congressman Aspinall questioned Governor Goddard quite closely."[45] The hearing transcripts and newspaper accounts, however, reveal what "quite closely" actually meant. Aspinall verbally bludgeoned the hapless and shocked Arizona governor. A UPI reporter characterized Aspinall's interrogation as "blistering," especially after the Coloradan accused the governor of not giving satisfactory answers to his questions about Arizona's future water needs. According to newspaper accounts, the chairman demonstrated no respect for Goddard, often gazing off at the ceiling during his testimony and cutting off his answers. At one point Aspinall—

born in Ohio—accused Goddard of not being a "native son" of the West and therefore being incapable of understanding the region's water problems. Goddard, who had moved to the West after World War II, was certainly not alone in being a relative newcomer to fast-growing Arizona. An Arizona newspaper came to the governor's defense, admitting that the governor could have been better prepared for Aspinall's questions but maintaining that Goddard did not deserve the full-fledged schoolmasterly humiliation Aspinall dished out. At one point, a flustered Goddard called the chairman "Congressman Aspinwall," to which Aspinall responded with a thunderous, "There is no 'w' in my name!" Based on such episodes, the *Arizona Republic* deduced that the CAP was in political trouble once again. The newspaper speculated, quite correctly, that Aspinall and other foes would delay the legislation until new water sources were discovered or until sufficient guarantees were inserted into the bill to safeguard the Upper Basin's legal water entitlement.[46]

Near the end of the hearings, Aspinall allowed representatives of various conservation organizations to testify. Many of the conservation groups had already expressed opposition to the Grand Canyon dams, but the August House hearings marked the first significant public condemnation of the plan. The Sierra Club's David Brower appeared on August 30 and served notice that the American public would not "tolerate such an invasion of the Grand Canyon and the national park system," especially if they knew that alternatives to damming the canyon existed. Brower had in mind nuclear power plants, perceived by many in 1965 as efficient, clean, and more environmentally friendly than building dams and destroying one of the world's most magnificent natural sites.[47]

Brower's opposition had been anticipated by the release of a beautiful photo-filled Sierra Club book, *Time and the River Flowing*, published in 1964. Brower mailed the book to the major actors in the CAP controversy. He also sent letters imploring the West's water politicians to consider the strong visual evidence in the book before passing a death sentence on the Grand Canyon. Even before the 1964 House hearings, conservation organizations like the Sierra Club had begun mobilizing opposition to the proposed dams. Anticipating such a movement, Floyd Dominy, commissioner of the Bureau of Reclamation, penned a publicity tract, *Lake Powell: Jewel of the Colorado*, to demonstrate that the works of humankind could actually enhance nature and improve upon God's handiwork, so to speak. Dominy argued that before the dam, Glen Canyon had been nothing but an inaccessible gorge. Following the dam's construction, the beautiful blue reservoir was now a haven for boaters, fishermen, and recreationists of all types. The publication date of *Lake Powell* was not coincidental; its release was timed to combat the expected anti-dam hysteria that would follow anticipated CAP House hearings sometime in 1965. In the book, Dominy used prose, poetry, photographs, and the Bureau's technical information to make the case for a Glen Canyon enhanced by its dam. By implication, an even "grander" Grand Canyon would be the outcome of Bureau of Reclamation dams erected there.[48]

Interior Secretary Udall, still a strong CAP advocate, expressed pleasure in the aftermath of the August hearings that a "head-on clash" between Aspinall and the Lower Basin's water leaders had not erupted. Udall also seemed to discount the strength of environmental-group opposition. After the hearings, the interior secretary's imagination was fired by proposals to augment the Southwest's water supply. "If Western water politics is played wisely and well during the next decade, I predict the world's longest aqueduct will one day run from Portland to Lake Mead."[49] Other observers believed that emerging opposition to the Grand Canyon dams was the most significant outcome of the August 1965 hearings. The preservationist message even began seeping into Wayne Aspinall's home base. Future Colorado governor Richard Lamm, then an idealistic leader of Colorado's Young Democrats, implored the House Interior chair not to build dams in the "irreplaceable" Grand Canyon. According to Lamm, "the dams serve no practical purpose whatsoever, and are sure to be a 3/4 of a billion dollar boondoggle if built."[50]

Through the fall and winter of 1965–1966, LCRBP proponents continued to hold discussions, cut deals, and redraft the bill based upon sentiments expressed at the August hearings. Not party to these discussions were the growing number of environmentalists, coordinated by the Sierra Club's David Brower, who continued to enlarge his program to save the Grand Canyon. The evidence suggests that the preservationist campaign to stop the dams was making strong headway by the end of 1965. In late October, Congressman Mo Udall even felt obliged to respond to the deluge of anti-dam mail he and other members of Congress were receiving by sending, to his colleagues, a rejoinder to the preservationists' arguments. Udall maintained that as an Arizonan, he, too, loved the canyon, but the dream of a Central Arizona Project was now three generations old—not a recent "brain-child" of the Bureau of Reclamation, as some opponents had claimed. Udall noted that the original CAP had been broadened to address the future water needs of other parts of the region as well. Udall also attempted to refute charges made by Brower and others during the hearings that the dams would destroy the canyon's natural beauty. The Grand Canyon, Udall argued, had ceased to contain a natural, flowing river many years ago when the first dams on the Colorado River were built. Drawing upon his best Dominy-esque prose, Udall argued that the proposed dams would transform the Canyon from a muddy stream with a fluctuating flow into a clear, predictable river highway, "a superb habitat for fishing and a safe course for thrilling visits to the innermost reaches of the canyon."[51]

Articles against the dams began appearing in many publications in late 1965 and on into 1966, including Life, Newsweek, Reader's Digest, and that staple of schoolchildren's reading in those days, the *Weekly Reader*. Growing environ-mentalist criticism of the LCRBP with Grand Canyon dams was more than background noise by May 1966, when the second round of House hearings convened.

"BLACKMAIL" AND THE GRAND CANYON

After the 1965 House hearings, it was not clear whether additional hearings would take place or when they might occur. Many issues had emerged from the August hearings that required discussion and negotiation. Almost immediately, the major parties began a mind-numbing barrage of memorandums and meetings to draft and revise H.R. 4671.[52] Aspinall turned his attention to shaping the LCRBP into a piece of legislation he could support in the fall of 1965. After a series of discussions and memos, Aspinall and Felix (Larry) Sparks, director of the Colorado Water Conservation Board, added five western Colorado water projects to the bill. This would constitute Aspinall's price for passage. Several of the projects had been authorized for study in the 1956 CRSP but had yet to be considered by Congress for authorization. Aspinall envisioned this as the perfect political opportunity to secure Colorado and the Western Slope's legal share of the Colorado River. As Sparks succinctly phrased it, "the main object in all the discussions and work on this legislation was to build projects in Colorado." Aspinall's dream for the LCRBP was now out in the open.[53]

In mid-October, Sparks apprised Aspinall of an impending Colorado water war between Eastern and Western Slope interests over the Colorado projects to be included in the LCRBP. Sparks reported that Aspinall's old University of Denver law-school friend Byron Rogers, now a congressman representing Denver, was particularly incensed over the five projects. In addition, the Denver Water Board believed that the Western Slope was "getting too much." The five projects, of course, were all located in Aspinall's congressional district, on the Western Slope: Animas–La Plata, Dallas Creek, Dolores, San Miguel, and West Divide. The board feared that if the five Western Slope projects were authorized and built, Colorado would use its entire Colorado River Compact allotment and "there would come a time when there would be no more water for Denver." Replying to Sparks, Aspinall emphasized the importance of both state unity and haste in making the project selections. The Upper Basin, Aspinall asserted, had but a small window of opportunity to secure some water guarantees in the form of new projects inserted into the LCRBP legislation. Aspinall denied conspiring to help only the Western Slope: "I have no set personal position on what should be done," he told Sparks. "I also realize the conflicting interests in the Upper Basin and the State of Colorado." Aspinall concluded on a lighter note in an obvious attempt to assuage Sparks: "The trouble with members of Congress, and that includes all of us, is that we are prima donnas. Each and every one thinks that he should be taken into consideration on any matter that involves him, even going to the 'john.'"[54]

Preparing for what Arizonans hoped would be their final CAP authorization drive in 1966, the state's water planners met on January 4, 1966, to discuss campaign strategy. The group feared that Aspinall had the ability to delay CAP consideration by scheduling additional hearings on each of the five western Colorado projects. Congressman Morris Udall, anticipating this move, checked with his brother the interior secretary, who ruled that individual hearings would not be necessary—the five projects could be considered as part of the overall LCRBP procedure. Congressman Udall expressed other concerns to Arizona's water planners, not the least of which was the Vietnam War, raging out of control by 1966. The war was already draining the financial life from President Johnson's ambitious domestic agenda. The Pacific Northwest's fear of water-importation plans and the Sierra Club's campaign against the Grand Canyon dams also threatened the project as 1966 began. Interestingly, Congressman Udall and other project advocates seemed to discount or underestimate the growing power of the environmental movement. Udall believed that the environmentalists' bid to stop the dams could be overcome "by presentation of the facts and adequate national publicity."[55]

On March 9, 1966, Arizona congressmen Udall and John Rhodes met with Aspinall in the chairman's office to discuss the Coloradan's plans for H.R. 4671, the revised LCRBP. Aspinall indicated that he hoped to convene hearings on the bill on April 18 but would do so only if favorable Interior Department and Bureau of the Budget reports were back in his hands on the five Colorado water projects. Without the favorable reports, according to Rhodes, Aspinall would withdraw Colorado's support from the entire project. Though Aspinall did not explicitly say so, "the implication was very clear that if Colorado did this, the whole affair would grind to a complete halt" as far as the Interior Committee was concerned.[56]

While the House of Representatives postured, revised, and made deals, the Senate sat and quietly waited for the contentious House to act, confident that the aged but still potent Carl Hayden had the prestige to drive the bill to authorization. As Hayden's top assistant, Roy Elson, recalled, "Carl Hayden always knew that he could get the [CAP] bill through the Senate at will, anytime he wanted to." During the March conference in Aspinall's office, the Coloradan indicated that if the Senate wanted to act on the bill at the same time the House did, he had no objection, as long as the Senate acted upon the revised H.R. 4671—with the five western Colorado water projects. If, however, Senate deliberations revealed a lack of Arizona unity or a rupture over the revised bill, "it would seriously embarrass" Aspinall and "probably result" in the chairman's dropping the entire project. There is little doubt that in the spring of 1966, Aspinall controlled congressional deliberations on the Lower Colorado River Basin Project.[57]

Roy Elson later recalled that in early 1966, Arizonans believed that Aspinall, California, and the Pacific Northwest were doing whatever they could to delay constructive consideration of the LCRBP legislation. Proposals for long-term interbasin water-transfer studies, for example, would only result in "further and further delay." According to Elson, "everyone was trying to blackmail us, from the Upper Basin, it was just a nightmare going on all the time." The "blackmail" that Elson referred to, of course, was Aspinall's requirement of positive action on his five Western Slope water projects. Even Utah and New Mexico had their own prices for support. In March 1966, Orren Beaty, Stewart Udall's assistant secretary, chief confidant, and fellow Arizonan, characterized Aspinall's and the Upper Basin's behavior in regard to the LCRBP as "Operations Blackmail."[58] Ironically enough, behind the scenes, it was the specifications of several of Aspinall's Colorado projects that threatened the entire LCRBP. Although they had acceptable cost-benefit ratios, several of the projects had development costs ranging from $1,400 to $1,600 per acre, and Udall's Interior Department had a rule to never endorse projects with development costs of more than $1,000 per acre. Even taking this into account, Beaty and Mo Udall continued to regard favorable reports from the Interior Department as "imperative if there are to be hearings this year in the House." Rules would need to be disregarded to meet Aspinall's expectations.[59]

Arizona's water brain trust, desperate for action, convinced Aspinall to try to expedite favorable reports from the Bureau of the Budget. To this end, Aspinall wrote a forceful letter to President Johnson's budget director, Charles L. Schultze. Aspinall informed Schultze that "we are nearly ready to bring peace among the Colorado River states with regard to the use and development of the water resources of the Colorado River." He quickly added that although not every controversy would cease, the time to settle many festering issues seemed "opportune." Admitting that the Bureau of the Budget might have some question about the "benefits" of "one or two of the Colorado projects," Aspinall nevertheless brushed any potential criticism aside by saying that "there can be no question as to the engineering feasibility or the financial feasibility of the projects, nor can there be any final decision other than a decision that they should be authorized and constructed."[60]

For several months, hearings on the revised H.R. 4671 had been scheduled for April 18, 1966. Lacking a full complement of favorable executive reports on the five Colorado projects, Aspinall decided to postpone the hearings until May 9, much to the disappointment of Arizona's water strategists. When Aspinall had demanded the executive-branch reports in late February, few water-policy experts believed that five major reclamation-project studies could be completed in time for the April hearings. However, the Interior Department ordered the Bureau of Reclamation to drop other project plans and produce the reports with all deliberate speed. Initially, the Bureau of the Budget failed to approve the Animas–La Plata Project. Aspinall responded by calling for the positive approval of all five projects, threatening nonaction on the entire LCRBP otherwise. The revised reports still had not cleared the Bureau of the Budget by April 6, so Aspinall decided to stall hearings until at least May 9. Most Interior Department officials who had worked fast and hard on the studies were understandably furious about the delay.[61] When the reports finally arrived, only two Colorado projects received unconditional executive-branch clearance.

By the spring of 1966, reclamation promoters had begun sensing the dimensions of the environmental community's challenge to the LCRBP. Legislation had been introduced in Congress to expand Grand Canyon National Park's boundaries, thereby hindering dam construction in both Marble and Bridge Canyons. In response, most project advocates supported building one dam at Bridge Canyon, a site generally favored by the Bureau of Reclamation, but changing the structure's name to Hualapai Dam to honor the Native American nation living near the site. An additional bonus of this strategy was that it would help upset anti–Bridge Canyon Dam propaganda. Aspinall, who approved of the name change, asked Morris Udall to find a Hualapai, "preferably the Chief," and have him testify for the dam at the hearings. Aspinall, according to Udall, wanted to put dam foes "in the position of being anti-Indian and suggested that we might have the Indians do some lobbying along the lines that this project will end their poverty problems and assure the success of their reservation." The chairman understood earlier than many western politicians what would later be termed the "Indian blanket" strategy—taking advantage of white guilt to gain the moral advantage in the battle for reclamation authorizations.[62]

At long last, Aspinall consented to begin the subcommittee hearings on the afternoon of May 9. The main focus would be consideration of Aspinall's five Colorado Western Slope water projects. Aspinall had hoped that this round of hearings would consist of a fast-paced affirmation of the revised bill, but a large number of witnesses wanted to testify both for and against the project. The less-than-enthusiastic executive-branch reports had guaranteed that the hearings would not proceed smoothly. The first round saw Colorado Republican governor John Love and Ival Goslin, executive director of the Upper Colorado River Commission, offer their complete satisfaction with the revised H.R. 4671. At the conclusion of Love's testimony, Aspinall seized an opportunity to summarize what was apparently both Colorado's and his own position on the bill. Colorado would support the revised H.R. 4671—with the five projects included—provided that the legislation also called for a river augmentation study. Aspinall then issued a stern warning to the subcommittee: Colorado would withdraw its support "if any one of these important parts of the legislation are left out."[63] In short, Aspinall did not care that the executive branch had written reports unfavorable to his five-project package.

Many of the witnesses at the May hearings supported Aspinall's five Colorado water projects. Several proponents of the West Divide Project had connections to Colorado's nascent oil-shale industry, including Edward Morrill, president of

Colony Development Company, who argued that oil shale's future was tied to water projects such as West Divide.[64] When Assistant Secretary of the Interior Kenneth Holum appeared, Aspinall questioned him closely about the contents of the five executive-branch reports. Aspinall's anger over the reports' conclusions was readily apparent. At one point, Aspinall argued that Colorado, not the executive branch, should determine which water projects were "best for Colorado."[65]

One of the tensest moments of the May 1966 hearings occurred when Sierra Club leader David Brower testified. Of course, Brower's main goal was to cast shadows over any form of the project containing dams in or near the Grand Canyon. Before Brower was allowed to speak, Aspinall took the floor to answer charges that the scheduled hearing witnesses had been packed in favor of an LCRBP with Grand Canyon dams. Aspinall argued that he had allowed people of all viewpoints to testify. Before Brower could even begin speaking, Representative Craig Hosmer (R-CA) objected to including some of Brower's supporting material in the hearing record because Hosmer deemed it "repetitive." Rising in Brower's defense was Representative John Saylor (R-PA), a consistent Brower and Sierra Club supporter and western reclamation critic. Saylor found the prohibition on Brower's evidence hypocritical because so much repetitive pro-LCRBP material had already been admitted before the hearings. "But the first time a witness appears who is opposed to this legislation, objection is raised that they are putting in material which, in the opinion of one of the members, is repetitive." To avoid the appearance of a packed hearing, Chairman Aspinall had to agree with Saylor's charge and allow the Sierra Club director to continue with his original testimony. In his appearance, Brower alleged that the Interior Department had suppressed information about possible damage to the Grand Canyon's scenic resources if the dams were built.[66]

On balance, the May House hearings likely produced more confusion than clarification. Assistant Secretary of the Interior Kenneth Holum reported that the Bureau of the Budget could only support two of the five Colorado projects, which only increased Aspinall's indignation. The Johnson administration added to the disorder by recommending against the construction of the Bridge Canyon (Hualapai) Dam. Finally, the environmentalists cast doubts over the desirability of the entire project by arguing for a nuclear alternative to the hydroelectric dams. The hearings ended on May 18 with little resolved.

Before the House Irrigation and Reclamation Subcommittee could meet to mark up and vote on H.R. 4671, Aspinall indicated that he still believed that dams in the Grand Canyon were a viable source of project power and income. "If built," he told a constituent, "neither of the reservoirs will be visible from any present viewpoint along the banks of the Canyon." Calling himself an "exponent" of the outdoors, Aspinall believed that Lake Powell's great success with the recreation-minded public demonstrated that the many should be able to enjoy wild places, "not just a few of us." "I think that is what is involved more than anything else in regard to the controversy between the preservationists and the rest of the conservationists in these matters." The two dams would make the dramatic beauty of a hard-to-reach place accessible to the many without substantially damaging its natural integrity.[67]

Before H.R. 4671 was voted out of subcommittee, three key motions revealing the nature of the criticism surrounding the bill were voted down. One, sponsored by Representative Thomas Foley (D-WA), asked to curtail all discussion of water importation. Another motion hoped to delete both Bridge (Hualapai) and Marble Canyon Dams from the bill, and a third, introduced by Saylor, attempted to eliminate both dams and Aspinall's five Colorado projects as well. The motions were easily defeated, and the largely intact but still controversial bill was sent to the full House Interior and Insular Affairs Committee, where it could expect to receive strong and timely consideration.

In the aftermath of the May hearings, an aroused national environmental movement led by the Sierra Club leapt into action. Employing arguably the most radical and innovative tactics in the history of U.S. conservation, on June 9 the Sierra Club unleashed a national advertising campaign against the Grand Canyon dams.[68] Using expensive full-page spreads in the *New York Times, Los Angeles Times, Washington Post,* and *San Francisco Examiner,* the Sierra Club proclaimed, "Now Only You Can Save the Grand Canyon From Being Flooded . . . For Profit." The advertising copy asserted that the canyon would be submerged beneath 500 feet of water used primarily to make electric power to fuel Arizona's growth. The canyon would be forever disfigured, its once-beautiful walls caked with horrible mud scars due to fluctuating water levels. The advertisement encouraged the public to clip and mail prewritten and addressed letters to President Johnson, Interior Secretary Udall, and Chairman Aspinall, who could halt committee proceedings and "seek expert testimony from the many Interior Department agencies that have not appeared." Letters could be sent to other senators and House members. Brower asserted that various Interior Department agencies, including the National Park Service, U.S. Fish and Wildlife Service, Bureau of Outdoor Recreation, and U.S. Geological Survey, all had testimony that could impact the deliberations and decisions of the Interior Committee. Chairman Aspinall had "discouraged" them from presenting their findings. Only the pro-dam voice of the Bureau of Reclamation had been heard. The ad concluded on a strong emotional note: "Remember, with all the complexities of Washington politics and Arizona politics, and the ins and outs of committees and procedures, there is only one simple, incredible issue here: This time it's the Grand Canyon they want to flood. *The Grand Canyon.*"[69]

A furious Morris Udall took to the floor of Congress on June 9 to denounce the environmentalist campaign. Expressing "shock and indignation," Udall termed the advertisements a "flagrant hatchet job." In House hearings,

Udall had already attacked Sierra Club assertions over the visual impact of reservoir flooding on the Grand Canyon's scenic beauty. From the floor of Congress, the Arizona congressman contended that the Sierra Club's reservoir-impact photo was actually of Lake Mead, the reservoir behind Hoover Dam, in the desert region east of Las Vegas.[70] But the damage had been done. Soon, what had been a large number of angry letters, telegrams, and phone calls to Congress became an avalanche. The public outcry only increased after three more Grand Canyon "battle ads," as David Brower termed them, appeared in the weeks ahead. The most famous advertisement—one that many Americans recall—ran late in the summer of 1966. Its banner headline asked the question, "Should we flood the Sistine Chapel so tourists can float nearer the ceiling?"[71]

Brower's plea for a letter-writing campaign had worked; hundreds of thousands of letters poured into the nation's capital. The day after Brower's initial ad, a "small faceless man in a dark blue suit from the Internal Revenue Service" hand-delivered a letter to Sierra Club headquarters, indicating that because of the organization's blatant political activity, the IRS would no longer consider contributions to the organization tax-deductible.[72] The official history of the Sierra Club theorizes that Morris Udall, in a fit of anger over the advertisements' attack on his brother, approached the undersecretary of the Treasury to revoke the Sierra Club's tax-exempt status. Other historians have identified different culprits. Stephen Fox's history of the American conservation movement speculates that it was either Mo Udall or Aspinall but leans toward Aspinall, "the old nemesis of conservation." Mo Udall, in his book *Too Funny to Be President*, took no credit for inspiring the IRS but admitted that the maneuver failed miserably, creating, in the public's eyes, a "David versus Goliath" aspect to the conflict.[73]

With the Grand Canyon issue echoing as loudly as the rushing waters of the Colorado River, the House Interior Committee began considering H.R. 4671 on July 13. As committee members deliberated and debated, the bill grew, becoming increasingly complex, cumbersome, and expensive. For example, almost every Colorado River Basin state now wanted future water projects authorized for study. Aspinall attempted to alter or delete the provision for the interbasin water-transfer study, hoping to derail objections from the Pacific Northwest. This move was foiled in committee by a coalition of Upper Basin House members, Californians, and Arizonans who feared that scuttling the importation study might endanger California's guaranteed 4.4 million acre-feet of water per year. The full committee insisted upon retaining a National Water Commission provision directing the interior secretary to conduct reconnaissance of possible water-transfer options by 1969. If the initial study found some projects feasible, a second, more comprehensive study would be completed by June 30, 1972. The committee debate over water planning was characterized by many "complex parliamentary maneuverings," with more than fourteen committee votes on various provisions. This episode demonstrated some of the major hurdles the bill had yet to overcome.[74]

Once again, Representative John Saylor tried to redirect the committee proceedings by introducing a motion to kill both Grand Canyon dams. Saylor's motion was defeated by an 18–8 vote. Saylor moved closer to his goal on July 27 when his amendment to overturn the Bridge Canyon (Hualapai) Dam failed by a narrow margin (16–13), with two members voting "present." Finally, on July 28, the controversial legislation was passed and ordered reported by a 22–10 vote, with Saylor again leading the opposition, along with Representatives from the Pacific Northwest. On August 11, the House report was received, and the following day a rule was requested. Thus, the bill's fate lay in the hands of the House Rules Committee; a favorable rule was required for House floor action.[75]

To pry the bill from the Rules Committee would take concerted action from LCRBP proponents. Furthermore, with the campaign season about to begin, H.R. 4671 faced a critical time shortage. General support for the bill was also eroding because of the effective conservationist campaign against it. With most members of Congress eager to return home to begin their fall campaigns, few politicians wanted to be associated with what environmentalists styled as a plot to destroy one of the nation's greatest natural treasures. At this point, efforts to obtain a rule were, in political scientist Helen Ingram's words, "abandoned" as futile.[76]

By late August 1966, Morris Udall had all but arrived at the same sad conclusion. Although Udall's overall House-vote head count revealed strong support for the bill, the LCRBP remained stalled in the Rules Committee and was likely dead, at least for the remainder of the Eighty-ninth Congress. At the same time, Interior Secretary Udall admitted in a news conference that H.R. 4671 was "in the ninth inning now," with little prospect of passage that year. Rationalizing the bill's impending defeat, the interior secretary reflected upon the lessons learned from an earlier controversial water project, Fryingpan-Arkansas. It had taken Congress nearly a decade to authorize that project, Udall remembered. Out of H.R. 4671, he believed, would "ultimately come compromises that will enable legislation to be enacted." By the end of August, newspapers routinely referred to the LCRBP as "dead." Aspinall, scheduled to adjourn his committee by September 1 to return to Colorado for the fall campaign, had tried to attach some compromises to the bill during full committee consideration. But the bill stood little chance of leaving the Rules Committee, where California's large House delegation helped lock it up.[77]

Other bill supporters feared that in the hysteria over the Grand Canyon dams, Representative Saylor might conceivably introduce amendments to delete the two dams, substitute a coal-powered CAP, or threaten California's 4.4 million-acre-foot annual water guarantee. After Arizona's experience in 1966, it is understandable why a substantial "go-it-alone" mentality that favored building a state-funded CAP re-emerged in Arizona in late 1966.[78]

In a fall 1966 postmortem over H.R. 4671, Clinton Anderson, Mo Udall, and John Rhodes discussed the bill's shape and direction for 1967. Anderson, not only a powerful and influential senator, but a western leader who specialized in the art of the politically possible, said he was against an LCRBP with Colorado River dams, but he could be persuaded to support a single structure in Marble Canyon. Anderson seemed certain that Washington senator Henry Jackson, chair of the Senate Interior and Insular Affairs Committee, would never support a study of Pacific Northwest water diversions to the Southwest. As Anderson pointedly remarked, "this would be felt by Senator Jackson to be inimical with his political survival." Anderson favored a "bare-bones" CAP and agreed to work for it beginning in 1967. During the discussion, held in Anderson's Senate office, Congressman Udall said he believed that the bill would not have passed the Senate in 1966. Carl Hayden had been ill for much of that summer, and Jackson's vigorous opposition to any water-importation study would have doomed the Senate bill. The Sierra Club's "misleading national campaign to 'save the Grand Canyon'" also deserved a share of the blame. Many members of Congress had told the Arizonan that they had received more mail on this subject than on any matter facing the Eighty-ninth Congress.[79]

Near the end of the year, it became evident that the assorted parties interested in the LCRBP were looking ahead to the next Congress, thinking about revisions and possible ground for compromise. In several key letter exchanges, the various water groups attempted to find common ground and meet the standards of the "Sierra Clubbers and/or Saylor." In past years, the environmentalists had not been factored into early drafts and revisions of reclamation legislation, but after the environmentalist publicity barrage of 1966, no serious politician could now overlook their clout. In one proposal, Congressman Udall suggested deleting the two Grand Canyon dams, delaying the three unfavorably reported Colorado projects, and creating a nonthreatening National Water Commission to defuse much of the bill's opposition. A week later, Udall reported to Arizona colleague John Rhodes that Saylor, speaking for the environmental community, said he might be willing to accept a CAP with one low dam at Bridge Canyon, the two approved Colorado projects, California's 4.4 million–acre-foot guarantee, and an enlargement of Grand Canyon National Park to include Marble Canyon. Crucially, this proposal would ask the Senate Interior Committee to write a non-threatening National Water Commission Bill that would pass Senator Henry "Scoop" Jackson's muster. The pathways for compromise were taking shape from the wreckage of H.R. 4671.[80]

Aspinall's continued insistence upon at least one Grand Canyon dam would frighten project supporters and animate the environmental opposition over the next several months. During his 1966 fall campaign tours, Aspinall continued to envision a CAP essentially the same as H.R. 4671. Aspinall held firm to his assertion that the five Western Slope projects must be authorized, despite the adverse reports on Dallas Creek, San Miguel, and West Divide. The chairman argued that the provisions of the CRSP Act of 1956 entitled Colorado to these projects, subject to the will of Colorado's governor and Water Conservation Board.[81]

Speaking in Cortez, Colorado, Aspinall outlined the reasons why the bill had failed in 1966, laying most of the blame at the door of Interior Secretary Udall and the Johnson administration. The Grand Canyon dams suffered from administrative "disinterest" in the same way that Aspinall's Western Slope projects did. The Colorado congressman also blamed the Sierra Club "and other so-called conservation organizations for contributing to H.R. 4671's 1966 demise. Such groups were not "conservationists," they were "preservationists," Aspinall hissed. They conducted a "misleading" campaign, "aided and abetted" by influential national publications like the New York Times, Life, and Reader's Digest. Aspinall also cited the national economy as a factor; because the Vietnam War enjoyed priority budgetary status, many domestic programs, including reclamation, had been scaled back.[82]

Two events in the fall of 1966 offer a microcosmic view of the LCRBP's fate to this point. The renowned naturalist Joseph Wood Krutch wrote to Stewart Udall to express his dismay at how emotional the battle over the Grand Canyon dams had become. Krutch, a Udall friend, was not afraid to tell the secretary that even though he was wrong to insist upon the dams, the Arizonan was still "a good friend of conservation." Udall, like many LCRBP advocates, had taken a hard public line toward Brower and the Sierra Club's 1966 actions. Udall admitted to Krutch that he had been "somewhat aggrieved" by Brower's assertion that "I inspired the Internal Revenue reaction." Yet the interior secretary was pleased that the controversy had helped the Sierra Club attract members, because "the Sierra Club is the one indispensable national conservation organization." Udall predicted that over the next year, a compromise would develop "that all of us can live with." Udall was already exploring directions this compromise might take.[83]

The other event also involved David Brower, this time more directly. Brower had been invited to address the November 1966 annual meeting of the National Reclamation Association in Albuquerque. In the lobby of the Sheraton Hotel, a photographer for the Albuquerque Tribune spied Brower and Aspinall and tried to arrange a photograph of the two men who, in many ways, represented opposite extremes in the nation's approach to natural resources. When Brower moved toward Aspinall to oblige, Aspinall bellowed at Brower, "You've been telling a bunch of damn lies to the newspapers and now you want your picture taken with me!" When a reporter asked Aspinall how the Sierra Club director had lied, Aspinall responded that the proposed dams would not impact Grand Canyon National Park.[84]

The following day, Brower wrote to Aspinall, demanding that the chairman "specify and document" the lies the Sierra Club leader had allegedly told.

Aspinall replied that he resented being "played for a sucker" by the photographer and reporter and did not have time to enlarge upon his allegations. He did tell Brower that he had lost confidence in the environmentalist's credibility. "When I lose confidence in an individual, sooner or later he is going to know it."[85]

Brower, increasingly alarmed by Aspinall's tone, stressed to the congressman the importance of "clarifying your charges" and "documenting the lies you have publicly charged me with." Brower reminded Chairman Aspinall of his influential position—"you hold a position of eminence . . . and of great power with respect to what conservation legislation is to be written; your influence is enormous in what is going to happen to the face of this land." After flattering Aspinall, Brower again reiterated his request for a documented charge. This was important, because a public incident like the one in the lobby could damage Brower's career. If Aspinall's charges were on target, Brower conceded, "then my career needs damaging." Brower concluded his plea with a reminder of earlier, more civil meetings between the two men. Both had been present when President Kennedy signed the Point Reyes National Seashore bill into law. At that time, Aspinall turned to Brower and remarked that "at least we agree part of the time, Dave."[86]

In the face of such earnestness, Aspinall could no longer postpone a letter documenting the environmentalist's falsehoods. Plunging to the heart of the matter, Aspinall reminded Brower of the distortions, misrepresentations, and errors of omission in the Sierra Club's 1966 advertising campaign. The result, according to Aspinall, had been to lead a naive American public into believing that the Grand Canyon National Park would be "totally flooded from rim to rim." Aspinall also contested Brower's charge that the chairman had prevented Interior Department witnesses from presenting information that would have reflected negatively upon the proposed dams. "All Congressional Committee members have ready access to this information," which "was included as an appendix in the project feasibility report," Aspinall responded. After listing several more lies and distortions, Aspinall closed with a warning: if Brower continued to exaggerate and "mix opinion and fact without distinguishing one from another," the Sierra Club leader risked losing all credibility as a congressional hearing resource. In the years ahead, Aspinall's committee would be reluctant to consider Brower's approach on such questions as Wilderness-area additions and national-park and wild-rivers legislation.[87]

By the end of 1966, the issue of wilderness preservation had been injected into the debate over the LCRBP. Brower and the Sierra Club had struck a chord with the national conscience and succeeded in broadening many Americans' definition of conservation. No longer would it mean simply efficient or multiple resource use. To borrow Irving Bernstein's graphic phrase, because of Brower, Rachel Carson, and others, the conservation "stream" was growing wider, encompassing an increasing number of causes and crusades.[88] Only a year before, water experts from Congress and the American Southwest had revised and drafted Pacific Southwest Water Project legislation without considering either the broader wishes of the American public or the feelings of so-called conservation groups. Looking toward 1967, Secretary Udall and others realized that the only way an LCRBP could pass Congress would be without dams in or near the Grand Canyon. After the Sierra Club's spectacular 1966 defense of the Grand Canyon, environmental concerns would need to be taken into account. Udall's sensibilities were clearly widening, but his sense of what was politically possible also figured into his LCRBP strategies for 1967–1968.[89]

TOWARD COMPROMISE

After the failure of H.R. 4671, Secretary Udall and his staff operated from the perspective that a CAP could only be authorized without dams in the Grand Canyon. With the option of hydroelectric power off the table, Udall began studying the possibility of using coal-fired plants. Between the end of the Eighty-ninth and the start of the Ninetieth Congress, the Interior Department continued to be concerned about Aspinall's attitude, which remained fastened upon building at least one dam in the Grand Canyon to power the Central Arizona Project. Aspinall would view any compromises on the dam question as a sign of weakness or capitulation to environmentalist criticism. After Aspinall's public feud with Brower, chances of the congressman's cooperation had diminished. Animated by a spirit of pragmatism and the willingness to compromise, Udall ventured forward, planning yet another version of the CAP, this one without hydroelectric power. "By eliminating the Grand Canyon dams," he told President Johnson, "I am optimistic that we can put together a new Lower Colorado Project bill which can successfully 'run the rapids' on the hill."[90] To this end, near the conclusion of the Eighty-ninth Congress, Secretary Udall had directed his department to begin studying "all feasible alternatives to the hydroelectric power dams" that had attracted so much controversy, negative publicity, and national criticism.[91]

Aspinall did not wait long to unveil his own Lower Colorado River Basin Project strategy for 1967, introducing H.R. 3300 on January 10. The bill contained, among other features, a CAP, his five Western Slope projects, and a dam in Bridge Canyon, well outside the Grand Canyon National Park border. Aspinall proposed moving the national park's borders, shifting the western boundary to the east, thus undercutting predictable charges that the Bridge/Hualapai Dam would back water far into the national park. He also proposed extending the eastern boundary to include some of Marble Canyon. To gain support from the Pacific Northwest, Aspinall called only for a preliminary study of the water-importation question. Aspinall's strategy for dealing with David Brower and the growing environmental movement also seemed clear. Aspinall hoped to isolate the Sierra Club leader by eliminating the Marble Canyon Dam and constructing only a low dam at Bridge Canyon. This tactic, Aspinall believed, would erode Brower's public support and draw wavering House members from the East to Aspinall's position. Aspinall also seemed to be losing patience with the bill and hoped that his new strategy would bring the LCRBP to authorization. The chairman surmised that until the CAP was resolved, other western states, including Colorado, could expect little in the way of reclamation legislation. It was this necessity of action and compromise that drove Aspinall as the new year and the new Congress began.[92]

At the end of January 1967, Secretary Udall reported to President Johnson that he had indeed developed a new plan for the Lower Colorado. Unveiled in February, Udall's proposal separated the National Water Commission from the main bill, authorized the CAP, contained no Grand Canyon dams, and included only two of Aspinall's Colorado projects, leaving the other three to the findings and recommendations of the National Water Commission. Udall surprised many water experts by scrapping the hydroelectric dams in favor of privately built coal-fired plants to be constructed near Page, Arizona, where they could readily take advantage of Navajo and Hopi coal deposits. After much discussion and some arm-twisting of Carl Hayden, the main Senate version of the bill came to resemble the interior secretary's bill more closely than Aspinall's. Hayden had hoped to retain the Bridge Canyon Dam, but the ancient senator, now eighty-nine years old, wanted the legislation more than he needed to adhere to his convictions. Both the interior secretary's and the Senate's versions scrapped California's 4.4 million–acre-foot water guarantee on the assumption that the combined support of the Pacific Northwest and environmentally minded members of Congress would more than compensate for the lost support of the predictably angry Californians.[93]

Aspinall had told a reporter in February that he did not believe the Interior Committee would reject his lead and pass a bill that failed to include a Colorado River dam. Other observers who knew Aspinall predicted that if he did not get his way on H.R. 3300, he might attempt another Wilderness Bill–type stall. With several different versions of the LCRBP in play, Aspinall's early scheduling of hearings for mid-March did not befit a lawmaker attempting to slow legislative consideration. Introduced on February 27, Aspinall's bill to change Grand Canyon National Park's boundaries to include Marble Canyon may have further confused LCRBP friends and foes who were trying to discern the chairman's true intentions. Once again, Aspinall hoped to seize the initiative from the environmentalists, who targeted Aspinall's H.R. 3300 for criticism because it still retained Bridge Canyon Dam. Aspinall wanted to show his water statesmanship and silence his growing number of critics. According to Aspinall, H.R. 3300 and his bill to expand the national park were in the "longstanding American tradition of compromise and fair play to try to bring two sharply opposed interests—the water development advocates and the conservation groups—together."[94]

Aspinall seemed confident that he could assert his will heading into the March House hearings. His bill closely resembled H.R. 4671, which had nearly been authorized late in the Eighty-ninth Congress. He had refined the bill and dropped the Marble Canyon Dam, yet retained the strengths of the regional approach that both he and Secretary Udall had long favored. Called to order on March 13, the House Irrigation and Reclamation Subcommittee, now chaired by Harold T. "Bizz" Johnson (D-CA), opened the various versions of the bill, including Aspinall's H.R. 3300 and the administration-approved plan of Interior Secretary Udall, to consideration. Early in the hearings, California senator Thomas H. Kuchel expressed shock and dismay at Udall's apparent change of heart on the dam issue. Californians, Kuchel testified, were united against the interior secretary's plan, favoring instead bills like Aspinall's and the old H.R. 4671. H.R. 4671 had been the product of several years' careful compromise among California, Arizona, and the Upper Basin states. Kuchel could not resist pointing out that H.R. 4671 had been, in part, formulated by Stewart Udall and was "warmly endorsed" by him last year. The Californian then identified other shortcomings of Udall's measure—its failure to investigate ways to supplement the river basin's shrinking water supply, and the lack of a dam on the Colorado River. What Kuchel failed to say was implicit in every word of his passionate criticism: the administration's proposal did not mention California's 4.4 million-acre-foot water priority.[95]

On March 14, Interior Secretary Udall defended his report on Aspinall's H.R. 3300 and enlarged upon his own plan for the Colorado River's future. Udall spent much of his time before the House subcommittee justifying the substitution of a coal-fired generating plant for the pair of hydroelectric dams in earlier proposals. Udall's plan recommended the immediate authorizations of the Central Arizona Project and the Dolores and Animas–La Plata Projects in Colorado. As for the other projects, including the remaining three Colorado Western Slope projects, Udall expressed confidence that the National Water Commission would "give urgent attention to the problems of the Colorado River Basin." After recommending that the Marble Canyon Dam site be added to Grand Canyon National Park and deferring a final decision on the Bridge/Hualapai Dam until the National Water Commission's final report, Udall spent the remainder of his time fielding questions, many of them asking him to explain his sudden shift in direction over the question of the Grand Canyon dams. Aspinall's questioning left little doubt that the Coloradan felt betrayed by the interior secretary and was now more committed than ever to the Hualapai Dam as part of H.R. 3300. With Udall's shift, Representative John Saylor found himself in the odd position of arguing before the subcommittee that the administration was on the right track with this proposal. Udall left the House hearings believing that legislation "similar to the Administration compromise bill" he had presented would pass Congress. Udall believed he had strong support (including Senators Hayden, Anderson, and Jackson) in the Senate. Perhaps most importantly, Udall believed—incorrectly as it turned out—that Aspinall was "wavering" and would not "risk going to the House floor with a controversial dam in the bill."[96]

Once again, the indefatigable David Brower led the opponents of the Bridge/Hualapai Dam. Pleased that the Senate bill contained no dams, Brower and his environmental cohorts trained their energy and resources against H.R. 3300. At the hearings, Brower reiterated many points made in previous committee appearances and reported that the Sierra Club had grown to 40,000 members—with a spectacular increase of 10,000 in the eight months since the Internal Revenue Service had "singled out the Sierra Club for special attention." In his statement, Brower tried first to explain his own 1949 vote with the Sierra Club to endorse a dam at Bridge Canyon. Brower indicated that the club's vote was rescinded the following year and had been made in the first place based on the same arguments and logic that LCRBP proponents were using in 1967: the reservoir would be removed from Grand Canyon-rim view, would flood nothing of significance, and might make the difficult-to-reach area more accessible to tourists. With great eloquence, Brower reminded his listeners that the national civilization was still in its infancy. Generations to follow should have "the freedom to see unspoiled wilderness, to know that it exists"—and "to know that it exists in the Grand Canyon." Perhaps thinking of Glen Canyon's sad fate, Brower concluded by pointing out that most dams and reservoirs had a lifespan of only 100 to 200 years; they would then fill with silt and die. The Grand Canyon deserved a better fate. It remained "a place to stop, look and always have a river to listen to—two hundred and forty miles of river, all of it alive."[97]

Colorado's position was ably presented by Governor John Love, accompanied by Aspinall friend and co-laborer Felix (Larry) Sparks, director of the Colorado Water Conservation Board. Love's message was simple: Colorado supported Aspinall's H.R. 3300 and was strongly against Interior Secretary Udall's new proposal. Not surprisingly, Love endorsed the five Western Slope projects, noting that all had been authorized for feasibility studies in the 1956 Colorado River Storage Project. Each had been analyzed carefully for more than twenty years. The state of Colorado, which contributed 70 percent of the river's flow, had only been able to realize a small portion of its Colorado River Compact allotment. Wrapping up, Love argued that it seemed as though Colorado had been "singled out" by Interior Secretary Udall and the administration in a proposal that left three of its projects subject to the caprice of a National Water Commission study. Sounding suspiciously like Wayne Aspinall, Love remarked that "to suggest that a National Water Commission should determine the internal allocation of water within a state is to perpetuate a cruel hoax upon our people."[98]

Aspinall, who had been conspicuously silent through most of the May hearings, jumped to second Love's statement, focusing on Colorado's burden in being forced to wait to develop its rightful water resources until the National Water Commission report had been prepared. In an obvious criticism of Stewart Udall, Aspinall remarked, "I cannot understand the mind processes of an individual who would write that into a report." Throwing down the gauntlet to Secretary Udall and the preservationists, Aspinall emphasized that "as far as I am concerned, there won't be any legislation if we don't have Hualapai Dam in the bill." With these words, Aspinall triggered another critical battle over the Colorado River that would lead to one of the greatest political miscues of his career.[99]

Whereas Aspinall seemed to retreat and sulk after the March hearings, the Senate, impatient with House inaction, moved toward enacting a CAP bill. S. 1004, which was debated and reported by the Senate Interior and Insular Affairs Committee in July 1967, had "something for everyone."[100] The bill's centerpiece remained a coal-powered CAP, but it also upheld California's 4.4 million–acre-foot water priority for twenty-seven years and included Utah's Dixie Project, New Mexico's Hooker Dam, and Aspinall's five Western Slope projects, inserted at Hayden's insistence in an obvious attempt to gain Aspinall's cooperation. The bill was notable, as well, for what it did not contain: there were no water-augmentation studies to threaten the Pacific Northwest, and, more importantly, no dams in the Grand Canyon. By simplifying the LCRBP and alienating fewer interest groups, S. 1004 sailed through the Senate on August 8 by a vote of 70–12.[101]

Though the Senate had obviously accepted many of Secretary Udall's and the administration's designs for a CAP, Aspinall remained insistent that his H.R. 3300 with the Hualapai Dam provided the only certain path to a successful water future for the Southwest. It is likely that many members of Aspinall's Interior and Insular Affairs Committee would gladly have dropped the dam in exchange for House action on the bill. Aspinall's stubbornness was leading to his isolation. Secretary Udall confided to New Mexico senator Clinton Anderson that Arizona's congressmen, Morris Udall and John Rhodes, continued to publicly support the Grand Canyon dam only to "appease Aspinall." Privately, "they would be tickled to death" to have the Senate's bill. Furthermore, the interior secretary remained "dead certain" that President Johnson, not wanting to fight both the Vietnamese and the growing environmental community, would "veto any bill with a dam in it."[102]

In a private off-the-record discussion with President Johnson during the summer of 1967, Wayne Aspinall registered his disgust with the administration's (i.e., Secretary Udall's) CAP plan. Always an advocate of congressional prerogative, Aspinall viewed Udall's initiative as a usurpation of accepted procedure.

The chairman also complained to Johnson about the general state of Congress. To Aspinall, whose penchant for order was by now legendary, it was "drifting without any direction," and, according to one presidential aide, the Colorado congressman had "never seen it so bad."[103] Aspinall, at this point in his career, was still an effective legislator by any measure, but a growing tendency to take refuge in his self-righteousness had begun undermining his effectiveness. This penchant, on display during some critical junctures in the battle for the Wilderness Act, would display itself with increasing frequency in the late 1960s.

Isolated by Secretary Udall's initiative and the Senate's rapid action, Aspinall and Colorado Water Conservation Board director Felix (Larry) Sparks both indicated that they would fight the Senate bill and refuse to act upon it in 1967. For Aspinall, the specific blow that had killed the bill was the Senate Interior Committee's deletion of the Hualapai Dam on a motion from Senator Hayden. "This is the death knell for the basin project," Aspinall announced on June 25. "I am saddened to hear about this. I denounce this. I reject it. I will fight against it." Aspinall insisted that the Central Arizona Project could not stand on its own merits; without Colorado River augmentation, the CAP would be forced to utilize portions of the Upper Basin's water allotment. In addition, a cash-register dam like Hualapai was needed to make it feasible. Pledging his resistance to the Senate bill "to the very end," Aspinall expressed confidence that he could "bottle the measure up" in his committee and prevent House floor action. Earlier in June, Director Sparks had predicted that the CAP was dead for 1967, arguing that the Johnson administration had completely capitulated to Arizona, the Pacific Northwest, and the Sierra Club.[104]

With his measure making steady progress in the Senate but stalled in the House, Interior Secretary Udall dropped out of sight for two weeks beginning in mid-June, taking a float trip down the Colorado River through the Grand Canyon. Ostensibly to form "some final opinions on dams in the Grand Canyon controversy," Udall kept a journal wherein he reacted to the scenery and reflected on the controversy that had occupied so much of his time. Udall's journal reveals a public figure increasingly drawn to the environmental perspectives of Joseph Wood Krutch and David Brower, but also someone who understood that the political power he had been entrusted with made him accountable to several different constituencies. Criticizing the "short term outlook of the reclamation engineers," Udall lamented the "muddy legacy" of Lakes Mead and Powell as both slowly filled with silt. Floating near the projected site of Bridge Canyon Dam, Udall was struck by the magnificent canyon scenery. "Only the most overpowering economic considerations should force serious consideration of Hualapai Dam now, and such are not present today." In prose that would have thrilled Brower but brought Aspinall to apoplexy, Udall concluded, "There is only one Grand Canyon on this planet. We hold it in trust for all who reside on it.[105]

After his return from the Grand Canyon, the interior secretary hoped to improve the Senate bill's chances with Aspinall in the House. Working behind the scenes, Udall attempted to bring Aspinall and Senate Interior Committee chair Henry Jackson together to resolve some differences in the two bills. Aspinall did not appear eager to negotiate at this point; he had taken a stand on the Senate bill and believed that the Senate version demanded serious alteration before the House committee could consider it. As S. 1004 sped toward passage in early August, Aspinall told anyone who would listen that his committee was about to complete its business for the year—it was time to get back to Colorado for his annual tour of the Fourth Congressional District. The House Interior Committee adjourned for 1967 on August 28 without considering the Central Arizona Project.[106]

In the months—and years—ahead, Aspinall would be roundly condemned for his inaction in 1967. How could he so cavalierly ignore S. 1004 after it had passed the Senate? Furthermore, how could he ignore a bill that Carl Hayden had devoted more than fifty years of his public life to obtaining? Hayden—and, by this reckoning, Arizona—deserved the bill because they had cooperated with Upper Basin politicians like Aspinall in the battle for the Colorado River Storage Project of 1956. Now it was time for Hayden to "call in his chits for having supported other members' projects in the past."[107]

Aspinall's action—or lack thereof—should not have surprised anyone. People close to him had predicted his 1967 stall. What is more difficult to explain is what the chairman hoped to accomplish with this tactic. Aspinall believed that S. 1004's hybrid origins as both an administration and a Senate measure contributed to its weakness as a piece of legislation. He believed that Secretary Udall had abandoned and dishonored earlier agreements that called for a regional approach to the Southwest's water problems. Though some may see this as evidence of Udall's political pragmatism, to Aspinall S. 1004 seemed like a capitulation to the demands of Brower and the environmentalists, making it anathema to the Colorado congressman, especially following his November 1966 altercation with Brower.[108]

Though Aspinall's refusal to constructively engage S. 1004 struck his contemporaries as arrogant and dictatorial, congressional committee chairs in the 1950s and 1960s routinely used their power to schedule action on a measure to gain concessions or to better shape a bill's outcome. As Helen Ingram notes, "the control exercised by committee chairs in the 1960s was far greater than they were to have after [congressional] reforms in the 1970s."[109] Aspinall could reasonably expect his committee members to follow his lead; his control over the Interior and Insular Affairs Committee was legendary. He indeed felt betrayed by Secretary Udall's reversal, but many of his objections to the Senate bill were based on content. Felix L. Sparks, always in close communication with Aspinall, indicated that the bill would only be acceptable to Colorado if it included a high dam at Bridge Canyon, California's 4.4 million–acre-foot guarantee "in perpetuity," water-importation provisions, and most importantly, guaranteed completion of the five Colorado projects "concurrently with CAP, which has a ten-year construction schedule." After the bill cleared the Senate, Aspinall recognized that S. 1004's passage was a tribute to Hayden, "the grand old man from Arizona." Not waxing sentimental for long, Aspinall quickly added that the bill still would not stand up before his committee. Although he had no intention of acting on it "this late in the session," he did not rule out action in 1968.[110]

Aspinall's objections to S. 1004 were, on balance, substantive and not personal, though it is difficult to deny that personal disappointments had colored his perspective and actions. Arizonans, naturally, were incensed by Aspinall's inaction. Rich Johnson of the Central Arizona Project Association believed Aspinall had acted "almost petulantly" toward Arizona. Arizona governor Jack Williams accused Aspinall of obstructing the bill, calling him a "rugged, tough curmudgeon." Aspinall, Williams remarked, was "afraid people in Colorado will say 20 years from now, 'there's the SOB who gave our water away.'" Representative John Rhodes bemoaned Aspinall's "amazing lack of gratitude, mainly toward Senator Carl Hayden." Rhodes believed Aspinall, Sparks, and Upper Colorado River Basin Commission head Ival Goslin were trying to "get their last pound of flesh" in the legislation. "I thought for a long time that if we got the Central Arizona Project it would be over Wayne Aspinall's dead body and it practically was," Rhodes declared in a later interview.[111]

When it became apparent in late August and early September that Aspinall really was going to abandon S. 1004 and return to Colorado, Arizona's water strategists began urging Carl Hayden to use his enormous power—the power of the purse as chair of the Senate Appropriations Committee—to gain Aspinall's attention and perhaps force the Coloradan into action. Aspinall, in the words of Rhodes, believed he still "had the upper hand and would do whatever he wanted to." Aspinall's confidence was apparent in a discussion he had with Arizona representative Morris Udall several days after the Senate had passed S. 1004. When Udall tried to explain the tremendous political pressure Arizona's politicians labored under, Aspinall said he would understand if a move were undertaken to override him and force him into action, but "you will have a hard time meeting without me." It was Aspinall's arrogance that had prompted water strategists to approach Hayden about bringing his power to bear on the Coloradan.[112]

Soon, Aspinall began to feel pressure from several directions. Morris Udall briefed House Speaker John McCormack (D-MA) on Aspinall's actions. Not mincing words, Udall asked for the Speaker's assistance in inspiring Aspinall to action, perhaps by expressing personal interest in the bill's fate to the chairman. Carl Hayden also approached Michael J. Kirwan (D-OH), the powerful chair of the House Public Works Appropriations Committee, to explore other avenues for motivating Aspinall. Kirwan exercised great discretion in the funding of reclamation projects, including Fryingpan-Arkansas, which was, by 1967, approaching some early critical construction phases. When Kirwan asked why Carl Hayden's CAP bill was not moving forward in the House, Aspinall responded with a history lesson on the Upper Basin's struggles to realize its fair share of the Colorado River. As written, Aspinall declared, S. 1004's CAP would have to "borrow" Upper Basin water to be feasible.[113]

Hayden contemplated scrutinizing at least two pet Aspinall projects for funding cuts. Aspinall's Public Land Law Review Commission was being considered for reauthorization and refunding in 1967. Hayden asked the Appropriations Committee to take a good, long look at the PLLRC. Hayden also used the appropriations process to threaten stalling construction of the Fryingpan-Arkansas Project. In a statement prepared for the Senate Appropriations Committee, Hayden examined Aspinall's fears over the Colorado River Basin water supply. If the basin might experience future water shortages, why was Aspinall endorsing exporting Colorado River–system water east over the Continental Divide to Colorado's eastern plains? This water was being put to use "outside the Colorado River basin to the detriment of the Central Arizona Project," according to Hayden. While Hayden threatened to cut Fry-Ark's funding, Senator Gordon Allott, originally from southeastern Colorado and always a strong Fryingpan-Arkansas supporter, sat on the Appropriations Committee and shuddered over the water war that was developing. Hayden withdrew his Fryingpan-Arkansas budget-cut proposal when he realized he did not have the votes—or the taste—for this brand of politics.[114] But the threat had been made.

The final attempt to pressure Aspinall into action was the most serious and ultimately the most effective. It gained Aspinall's attention in distant Colorado and brought him hastily back to the nation's capital. Ironically, the successful tactic was suggested to Arizona congressman John Rhodes by reclamation commissioner Floyd Dominy, an Aspinall loyalist but someone who enjoyed building large-scale reclamation projects even more than maintaining friendships. Dominy had told Rhodes that the CAP could be authorized as part of an appropriation bill. Rhodes, unfamiliar with this procedure, protested, "Floyd, I didn't think you could do that." But Dominy insisted to the Arizona lawmaker that the procedure had been used many times over the years. After Aspinall had left Washington for Colorado, Rhodes, Morris Udall, Hayden, and his assistant, Roy Elson, huddled and decided to attempt the unusual parliamentary procedure. The tactic would work the following way: Hayden would attach the CAP rider to a Senate public-works appropriation bill by amendment. In a House-Senate conference committee session, the House conferees would adopt the Senate amendment, taking the bill to the House floor, where it would be voted upon. "I don't like to do things like that," Hayden protested at first, but Roy Elson and

Arizona's other House members talked him into it. Elson had commissioned some research on this procedure, which revealed that other reclamation projects—including, ironically, Colorado–Big Thompson in 1937—had been authorized using this technique. Elson's researcher, Wallace Duncan, concluded that the C-BT case "does pose a striking analogy to the situation facing Senator Hayden" and the CAP.[115]

On September 28, Hayden attached his CAP authorization bill as a rider to the $4.7 billion Senate public-works appropriation bill. Hayden's audacious threat quickly worked its magic. Back in Colorado, Wayne Aspinall understood he needed to return to Washington, D.C., and limit the political damage. Caught in a trap largely of his own making, the Coloradan would need to back down. The courtly Hayden, however, allowed Aspinall to save some face. Although most observers and members of Congress did not give Hayden's rider much chance for success, a few House members believed it had a fair shot at passage. One of them, Harold "Bizz" Johnson (D-CA), the House Reclamation and Irrigation Subcommittee chair, stated as much to the Grand Junction *Daily Sentinel*. Grumbling that the rider gambit "amounts to blackmail," Aspinall met with Hayden, called the House Interior Committee back into session on October 10, and agreed to consider the CAP legislation at the end of January or early February 1968. On the same day, Hayden went to the Senate floor to withdraw his amendment to the public-works appropriation bill. Senate Minority Leader Everett Dirksen (R-IL), who had been critical of Aspinall's early departure, expressed pleasure that Aspinall had thought better of his maneuver "by reason of the impulses of his own conscience and conduct or by some external force that might have been applied."[116]

Dirksen's analysis pointed to the end of what was perhaps Aspinall's greatest political miscalculation. Had Aspinall returned to Washington because of a crisis of conscience, the political thumbscrews that had been applied, or a higher concern for Carl Hayden's legacy? Aspinall's own memory of the event seems deliberately cloudy. In a later interview, Aspinall remarked that he did not feel pressured to return and compromise on the CAP. He saw it, as he did most everything, to be a question of timing and, as the bill moved forward in the months ahead, a question of political compromise. To Aspinall, two overriding concerns remained: the authorization of the five Western Slope projects and some guarantee that the overall Colorado River water-supply question was being taken seriously. As for the conflict with Hayden, the Coloradan would soon be spinning a different and more self-serving version of events that allowed him to better save face.[117]

Aspinall told almost anyone who would listen that his return to Colorado in September was normal: he usually adjourned his committee early in the fall; doing so was not meant to punish S. 1004 or its backers. In addition, Saylor, the ranking minority leader, had experienced severe health problems in August and would not be able to fully participate in committee deliberations for some time. Finally, Aspinall had told Saylor in August that he intended to consider Colorado Basin legislation in January or early February 1968, when he planned to take action on the Wild and Scenic Rivers Bill and measures creating Cascade and Redwoods National Parks. As Aspinall told Colorado governor John Love, his sudden return to Washington was motivated by concern for other legislative issues—not "solely for the purpose of the entanglement involving Arizona vs. the rest of the Colorado River Basin States." Whether Aspinall's explanation convinced anyone is doubtful. Those close to Colorado River Basin legislation appreciated his change of heart, but few believed his return had been a coincidence.[118]

Aspinall began the new year by meeting with Morris Udall to plot legislative strategy for H.R. 3300. The chairman was armed with a long, scholarly treatise on "The Colorado River Water Supply" given to him by Ival Goslin of the Upper Colorado River Commission. Udall's recollections of the meeting indicate that Aspinall seemed "reconciled" to the passage of Colorado River Basin legislation in 1968. Doing "most of the talking," Aspinall indicated that he planned a brief two-day hearing on H.R. 3300 to offer a redraft of the bill by Felix L. Sparks and work toward harmonizing his position with S. 1004. The hearings were scheduled to start on January 30.[119]

During the House hearings, Aspinall hoped to focus attention once more on the Colorado River Basin's water supply. In a letter sent to Secretary of the Interior Udall two weeks before the hearings, Aspinall indicated that he was reconciling himself to an H.R. 3300 in which "both of the Colorado River dams will be eliminated." He still believed, however, that the Interior Department needed to base the legislation on more accurate examinations of the river's historic flow patterns. Aspinall thought that the high-flow years that became the basis for the 1922 Colorado River Compact were especially misleading. Aspinall also seemed resigned to, though not comfortable with, the coal-fired power plant as the CAP's main energy source.[120]

Most of the 1968 House hearings consisted of Secretary Udall presenting information on a Lower Colorado project without the dams. Udall answered Aspinall's inquiries on stream flow and also discussed what impact the project might have on the region's Native American groups. Udall remained confident that the river would be augmented, either by interbasin transfer, desalinization of seawater, or weather modification. In his questioning of the interior secretary, Aspinall was a changed man. Less contentious, he truly seemed to be working toward shaping H.R. 3300 into something both he and the Senate could be comfortable with. No one in the hearing room, he stated, "wishes the authorization of a feasible Colorado River project with a CAP any more than the Chairman of the full committee." Aspinall had always seen hearings as essential for writing a complete historical record of any legislation. Trying to rehabilitate his public image after the Hayden rider fiasco, Aspinall made it clear through his questioning of Stewart Udall that the Lower Colorado House bills written since 1963 had been responses to the changing demands of the Interior Department: two dams, to one dam, to none. How could anyone consider him stubborn and unresponsive? Aspinall might wonder to his cronies and associates. Perhaps unconvincingly, Aspinall remarked that it made "no difference to me personally whether or not there are any dams on this river."[121]

With Native American and other minority groups calling for recognition of their rights, it is hardly surprising that the House hearings devoted a moderate amount of time to assessing the LCRBP's impact upon the Southwest's Native American groups. Aspinall had warned Secretary Udall that this would be a concern of the committee during the 1968 hearings. Under questioning, Udall revealed that the Orme Dam, part of the CAP, would provide valuable recreational benefits to Arizona's Fort McDowell American Indian community. Udall also indicated that Peabody Coal Company had already consummated a contract with the Navajos and Hopis to mine coal on their reservations for the projected Page, Arizona, power plant. Viewed as a great economic boon to the tribes, the Hopi mines at Black Mesa later became one of the most controversial and tragic federal Native American policy decisions of the 1960s.[122]

After only three days, the House hearings concluded. The Interior Committee's next task was to revise H.R. 3300 to reflect concerns articulated during the hearings. Above all, the legislation needed to meet the exacting standards of Chairman Aspinall, who had a reputation for never taking a piece of legislation to the House floor unless he had secured its approval. From February 26 to March 1, the House Irrigation and Reclamation Subcommittee revised, marked up, and debated H.R. 3300. An Arizonan who kept close watch over the proceedings noted that it went smoothly and passed 17–5 because "Chairman Aspinall worked from his bill" and led the proceedings. His redrafted H.R. 3300 dropped the Grand Canyon dams, favored a coal-fired power plant, and omitted all mention of the National Water Commission, now to be authorized in a separate bill. Aspinall, out of his deep concern for Colorado River water supply, retained a carefully worded section that asked for feasibility studies on "the most economic means of augmenting the water supply by 2.5 million acre-feet annually." The proposed studies would examine such techniques as seawater desalinizing and weather modification but would only allow the interior secretary to recommend interbasin water transfers with the approval of the affected states. Aspinall's redrafted bill also retained the CAP, the five Colorado water projects, and California's 4.4 million–acre-foot water guarantee.[123]

Though Aspinall moved forward with the bill, his mind still harbored doubts about the legislation's content and the political events and compromises that had created it. On March 8, President Johnson delivered a major conservation address, "To Renew a Nation." In this strong environmental message, Johnson remarked upon the "Central Arizona Project." Aspinall was apoplectic after hearing this, castigating Secretary Udall, who had helped Johnson draft the speech, for leaving the impression that the Lower Colorado River Basin Project was only a Central Arizona Project. Unable to restrain himself in a March 8 letter, Aspinall lectured the secretary that anyone who knew the river and its history knew that the CAP would not be feasible without one of two developments: "The first is that the Central Arizona Project takes water that rightfully and legally belongs to other Basin states. The second is that the [water] supply of the River Basin is increased by some means or the other." Aspinall's anger seemed to build as the letter continued. Reverting to the old Aspinall of fall 1967, he warned the secretary that he was "in a good position to dump the Project right now" because of the content of the president's address. The preceding autumn, after his war with Arizona, Aspinall had been willing to let bygones be bygones, even though he had plenty of strong reasons for not trusting Secretary Udall. "You dumped the dams," he reminded Udall, without consulting the chairman first. Though Aspinall did not publicly release this letter, he reminded Udall that he reserved the right to as "I deem necessary."[124]

A contrite and weary Udall realized his error, remarking that Aspinall "had good reason to be aggrieved" and resent the language in the president's message. Admitting that his department sometimes made "stupid mistakes," Udall said what Aspinall hoped to hear—that the president's references should have been to H.R. 3300 "as amended" and not to the Central Arizona Project alone. As this story illustrates, Aspinall's hard feelings over the way Secretary Udall, the Arizona congressional delegation, and the environmentalists had dealt with him over the past two years had not abated. This letter to Stewart Udall served notice of Aspinall's ability and willingness to continue obstructing the long-sought project.[125]

On March 20, 1968, the full House Interior Committee began consideration of H.R. 3300. Several days later, voting 22–10, they sent it on to the Rules Committee, its graveyard of two years earlier. The bill faced many challenges before the Interior Committee, and many from Congressman John Saylor, who proposed twenty-nine amendments. All of them failed, but some by close votes. For the most part, Aspinall's H.R. 3300 emerged from full Interior Committee consideration as it had passed through the subcommittee, with only minor changes. Notably, the full committee defeated motions to delete three of the five Colorado water projects, while affirming a key Aspinall provision to make the Mexican Water Treaty a "national obligation," theoretically giving the Southwest's water experts more precious acre-feet to divide up.[126]

How did H.R. 3300 differ from S. 1004? Aspinall's bill confirmed California's 4.4 million–acre-foot-priority guarantee in perpetuity, whereas the Senate bill awarded it for only twenty-seven years. Aspinall's bill was also more concerned with the question of an adequate Southwest water supply; he therefore took a strong stand on making the Mexican Water Treaty a national, not regional, issue. Contrary to S. 1004, Aspinall's measure insisted on a program of studies and investigations that could lead to the augmentation of the Colorado River Basin's limited water supply. The Senate bill, shaped by Washington senator "Scoop" Jackson's fears, avoided the touchy subject of interbasin transfers and augmentation altogether. Other differences existed, mainly in the realm of project finance. H.R. 3300 authorized two basin funds, one to pay for the CAP and one for river-augmentation projects. Both versions contained a moratorium on power generation at the Bridge Canyon site, but the House bill contained a moratorium for Marble Canyon as well. Of course, both bills could be amended from the floor of Congress, but the chances of significant alteration before a floor vote were slim.[127]

H.R. 3300 had no difficulty clearing the Rules Committee this time. Four hours of floor debate were scheduled over a two-day period, May 15 and 16. Meanwhile, the Arizona delegation and other key supporters remained busy securing House votes, twisting some arms, and calling in old political debts. The preliminary vote count heading into the floor debates looked good for the project: 221 in favor, with the total of strong commitments rising daily. In the House debates, Aspinall, according to one observer, "was in his chosen element." Explaining the legislation's painstaking path to the present, the Coloradan demonstrated how H.R. 3300 fit into the history of congressional attempts to develop the Colorado River. The Colorado River, Aspinall asserted, had "been a river of trouble and controversy from the beginnings of its development. It has been undependable, unruly, and wasteful because of the vagaries of nature." Aspinall's reputation as a committee chair who never pushed ill-prepared legislation to the House floor enhanced the bill's support.[128]

Only one small floor amendment was added. Even Saylor, who always had crippling amendments ready for attachment to reclamation bills, understood that such efforts would be futile with H.R. 3300. When the House Speaker called for the vote, H.R. 3300 passed with overwhelming voice approval. Aspinall's leadership in the process was immediately lauded and recognized by many, including Arizonans John Rhodes and Mo Udall. Aspinall, according to Rhodes, had "quarterbacked the whole team," with "the skill and sense of timing we have all come to expect and appreciate." Congressman Udall recognized Aspinall's "superb" floor "generalship," noting that as the bill moved to the conference stage, he and Rhodes would follow Aspinall's guidance and strategy. Udall called the bill "Arizona's most important legislation since statehood" and volunteered to serve on the House conference team with the Senate. However, Udall loyally added to Aspinall: "You will be my leader, as always."[129]

The bill remained in a delicate state of balance, and Arizona's political leaders ordered all of its pressure groups and supporters to refrain from attempting to influence conference committee preparations and proceedings. Aspinall wanted to do much of the preliminary conference work out of the public spotlight, in one-to-one sessions with Senate conference committee chair Henry M. Jackson. After years of attempting to influence the legislation and push it forward, Arizona's political leaders had to place full trust in the House Interior chair.

In July, Morris Udall was still lobbying for appointment to the conference committee. After taking a congressional excursion for the Interior Committee to inspect the area that might become North Cascades National Park, Udall wrote to Aspinall, commenting on what he believed the major conference committee issues would be. Udall, who was from a famous Mormon pioneer family, could not resist a humorous reference to his heritage. With the inspection tour over, he noted, and the conference committee not yet ready, and "after carrying out all my maximum leader's [Aspinall's] current marching orders, I withdraw to my tent to rest, to kneel on my prayer rug facing Salt Lake City to await further revelations." A couple of days later, Udall's dreams were realized when Aspinall named the Arizonan as a House conferee on H.R. 3300.[130]

On August 1, after six intensive sessions, an agreement was reached between House and Senate conferees on what was now being called S. 1004. In the midst of the conference committee proceedings, a frustrated Aspinall wrote to his brother, Ralph, in Palisade, telling him that the Colorado River conference was proving to be "almost impossible" because of the Northwest's fear of water importation. The bill's language stepped delicately around this issue. Senator Frank Church (D-ID) in particular had gotten himself "out on a limb and it may be necessary to cut down the tree," Aspinall told Ralph. Still, two major compromises were crafted. Investigations of water augmentation from every possible source would occur, but in deference to the concerns of the Pacific Northwest, a ten-year moratorium on interbasin diversions was declared. Aspinall also imposed his will in regard to the Mexican Water Treaty. Fulfilling its terms would be a national obligation, not one to be met only by the Colorado River Basin, with its limited water supply.[131] Overall, Aspinall was pleased.

At long last the battle was over. Little remained to be done. On September 5, the House conference report on what was now commonly called the Colorado River Basin Project (CRBP) was approved by an overwhelming voice vote. A little over a week later, the Senate followed suit. The bill awaited only President Johnson's signature. With great fanfare and ceremony, Johnson signed S. 1004 in the East Room of the White House on September 30, 1968. Senator Hayden, stooped but proud, accepted bill-signature pens from the president, who credited Hayden, "that great statesman and beloved human being" now in the "twilight of his career," for persisting in his vision. Johnson also singled out Senator Henry "Scoop" Jackson and Wayne Aspinall for making the day possible.[132] Earlier in September, Carl Hayden had announced his retirement from the Senate, effective at the end of the Ninetieth Congress; his more than fifty-year quest for Arizona's water had been fulfilled. Though Hayden deserves credit for maintaining his commitment to the CAP, others understood that the most difficult and skillful politics in the affair had been played by Aspinall. As Morris Udall later said of the Colorado congressman, he "was a mean, tough customer. Aspinall understood force, he understood power."[133]

Arizona congressman John J. Rhodes believed that the CAP had slipped through a "very narrow window" that was about to close.[134] The era of large-scale reclamation projects, launched by the booming U.S. economy that had surged after World War II, was coming to an end by the late 1960s. No new significant reclamation projects would be authorized after the Colorado River Basin Project of 1968; a combination of changing environmental attitudes and inflationary difficulties forced Americans to rethink their dam-building binge. The enactment of the CAP in 1968 also represented Aspinall's last significant contribution on the national stage. His remaining years in Congress would contain more frustrations than accomplishments.

ENDNOTES

1. Statement of Wayne N. Aspinall to Congress, n.d., ca. March 1963, Box 130, fd: "62A," Wayne Aspinall Papers, University of Denver Archives, Denver CO (hereafter cited as UDA).

2. Russell Martin, A Story That Stands Like a Dam: Glen Canyon and the Struggle for the Soul of the West (New York: Henry Holt, 1989), 45–47; David R. Brower, "Environmental Activist, Publicist, and Prophet," oral history conducted by Susan R. Schrepfer, Regional Oral History Office, the Bancroft Library, University of California, Berkeley, 1974–1978, 269.

3. Brower, "Environmental Activist," 209; Grand Junction (CO) Daily Sentinel, July 22, 1963; New York Times, July 5, 1963; Wayne N. Aspinall to David Brower, July 23, 1963, and Wayne N. Aspinall to Jack Foster, August 2, 1963, Box 139, fd: "L-11-a-1," Wayne Aspinall Papers, UDA.

4. Jared Farmer, Glen Canyon Dammed: Inventing Lake Powell (Tucson: University of Arizona Press, 1999), 146–147, contains information on the closing of the diversion tunnels; Martin, Story That Stands Like a Dam, 253–254.

5. See Marc Reisner's rich detail in Cadillac Desert: The American West and Its Disappearing Water, rev. ed. (New York: Penguin Books, 1993), 257–264; see also many sections of the following studies: Philip L. Fradkin, A River No More: The Colorado River and the West (Berkeley: University of California Press, 1996); Norris Hundley, Jr., Water and the West: The Colorado River Compact and the Politics of Water in the American West (Berkeley: University of California Press, 1975); Rich Johnson, The Central Arizona Project: 1918–1968 (Tucson: University of Arizona Press, 1977); Jack L. August, Jr., Vision in the Desert: Carl Hayden and Hydropolitics in the American Southwest (Fort Worth: Texas Christian University Press, 1999); Byron E. Pearson, "People Above Scenery: The Struggle over the Grand Canyon Dams, 1963–1968" (Ph.D. dissertation, University of Arizona, 1998); and Donald W. Carson and James W. Johnson, Mo: The Life and Times of Morris K. Udall (Tucson: University of Arizona Press, 2001).

6. The population statistics are from Reisner, *Cadillac Desert*, 259–260.

7. Ross R. Rice, *Carl Hayden: Builder of the American West* (Lanham, MD: University Press of America, 1994), 131; Pearson, "People Above Scenery," 25–68.

8. Johnson, *Central Arizona Project*, 24–25, 28–29, 33, 61–62.

9. Reisner, *Cadillac Desert*, 260–261; Johnson, *Central Arizona Project*, 87; Norris Hundley, Jr., "The West Against Itself: The Colorado River—An Institutional History," in *New Courses for the Colorado River: Major Issues for the Next Century*, ed. Gary D. Weatherford and F. Lee Brown (Albuquerque: University of New Mexico Press, 1986), 30–31. Johnson asserts that Arizona filed suit in 1931, 1934, and 1936, whereas Reisner states that 1952 represented Arizona's third attempt to seek Supreme Court redress.

10. Useful for understanding *Arizona v. California*'s impact on Native American tribes are Hundley, "The West Against Itself," 30–34; Reisner, *Cadillac Desert*, 260–262; Martin, *Story That Stands Like a Dam*, 250.

11. Hundley, "The West Against Itself," 30–34.

12. Johnson, *Central Arizona Project*, 75; Rice, *Carl Hayden*, 34.

13. Wayne N. Aspinall to Stewart L. Udall, November 27, 1962, in "Further Water Resources Development in the Lower Colorado River," Box 141, fd: "L-11-b," Wayne Aspinall Papers, UDA.

14. Stewart L. Udall to Wayne N. Aspinall, January 18, 1963, "Further Water Resources Development in the Lower Colorado River," Box 141, fd: "L-11-b," Wayne Aspinall Papers, UDA.

15. Byron E. Pearson, "The Plan to Dam Grand Canyon: A Study in Utilitarianism" (M.A. thesis, Northern Arizona University, 1992), 50; Rice, *Carl Hayden*, 133–156.

16. Morris Udall, "Arizona's Water Fight Shifts to Congress," Box 166, fd: 10, Stewart L. Udall Papers, Special Collections, University of Arizona Library, Tucson, AZ (hereafter cited as SCUAL).

17. *Arizona Republic*, July 28, 1963.

18. *Denver Post*, September 29, 1963; Wayne N. Aspinall, "Speech to the Arizona State Reclamation Association," September 28, 1963, Box 147, fd: "Pub 7," Wayne Aspinall Papers, UDA.

19. Aspinall, "Speech to Arizona Reclamation Association."

20. Carl Hayden, memorandum, May 10, 1963, Box 5, fd: 10, Carl Hayden Papers, Special Collections, Arizona State University Library, Tempe, AZ (hereafter cited as SCASUL); Stewart L. Udall to Carl Hayden, June 12, 1963, Box 5, fd: 11, Hayden Papers, SCASUL; Johnson, *Central Arizona Project*, 146–147.

21. "Memorandum for the File, Meeting, January 7, 1964, re: Pacific Southwest Water Plan," Box 21, fd: 3, Hayden Papers, SCASUL.

22. Stewart L. Udall to President Lyndon Johnson, February 14, 1964, Box 74, fd: "PSWP," Bill Moyers Papers, Office Files, Lyndon B. Johnson Presidential Library, Austin, TX (hereafter cited as LBJPL).

23. "PWSP," n.d., ca. February 1964, Box 74, fd: "PSWP," Bill Moyers Papers, Office Files, LBJPL.

24. August, *Vision in the Desert*, 10–11, argues that Hayden's primary concern in his long career was bringing water to his arid region.

25. Carl Hayden to Stewart L. Udall, February 2, 1964, Box 2, fd: 2, Hayden Papers, SCASUL; Stewart L. Udall to Carl Hayden, February 12, 1964, Box 167, fd: "February–March 1964," Stewart L. Udall Papers, SCUAL; Carl Hayden to Stewart L. Udall, February 20, 1964, Box 167, fd: "February–March 1964," Stewart L. Udall Papers, SCUAL.

26. Johnson, *Central Arizona Project*, 152.

27. *Central Arizona Project*, Hearings, Subcommittee on Irrigation and Reclamation, House Committee on Interior and Insular Affairs, 88th Cong., 2d Sess., on H.R. 6796 et al., November 9, 1964, 37–38.

28. Wayne N. Aspinall to Elenor Mueller, November 19, 1964, Box 165, fd: "L-11-b-1-B," Wayne Aspinall Papers, UDA; Wayne N. Aspinall to Mike Perko, February 5, 1964, Box 165, fd: "L-11-b," Wayne Aspinall Papers, UDA.

29. Johnson, *Central Arizona Project*, 150–151.

30. See veteran journalist Bert Hanna's writing on this topic in the *Denver Post*, "Aspinall Vows to Guard Upper Basin's Water Rights," ca. early 1965, Box 196, fd: "L-11-b-1-A," Wayne Aspinall Papers, UDA.

31. Carl Hayden, memorandum for Senator Kuchel, Box 5, fd: 11, Hayden Papers, SCASUL; Johnson, *Central Arizona Project*, 152.

32. John Rhodes, George F. Senner, Jr., and Morris Udall, memorandum, February 9, 1965, Box 184, fd: "39H (3)," Wayne Aspinall Papers, UDA; Rich Johnson to Wayne N. Aspinall, March 5, 1965, Box 8, fd: 8, Hayden Papers, SCASUL; Orren Beaty, memorandum to the secretary, March 24, 1965, Box 121, fd: 11, Stewart L. Udall Papers, SCUAL.

33. Stewart L. Udall to Lawrence Mehren [board chair, CAP Project Association, Phoenix, AZ], April 1, 1965, Box 184, fd: "39-H," Wayne Aspinall Papers, UDA.

34. *Wall Street Journal*, May 11, 1965.

35. Carl Hayden to Wayne N. Aspinall, May 18, 1965, Box 5, fd: 22, Hayden Papers, SCASUL; Johnson, *Central Arizona Project*, 158; Wayne Aspinall to Morris Udall, June 11, 1965, Box 476, fd: "April–June 1965," Morris K. Udall Papers, SCUAL.

36. Morris Udall, memorandum for the file, May 29, 1965, Box 476, fd: "April–June 1965," Morris K. Udall Papers, SCUAL.

37. Robert G. Kaufman, *Henry M. Jackson: A Life in Politics* (Seattle: University of Washington Press, 2000), 165.

38. Johnson, *Central Arizona Project*, 159–160. This is also my assessment after reading several volumes of 1965 and 1966 CAP hearings.

39. John Rhodes, "The Arizona Water Situation as of July 22, 1965," Box 893, fd: 2, John Rhodes Papers, SCASUL.

40. Wayne N. Aspinall to Edwin C. Johnson, July 30, 1965, Box 196, fd: "L-11-b-1-A," Wayne Aspinall Papers, UDA.

41. Johnson, *Central Arizona Project*, 163.

42. *Lower Colorado River Basin Project*, Hearings, Subcommittee on Irrigation and Reclamation, House Interior and Insular Affairs Committee, 89th Cong., 1st Sess., on H.R. 4671 et al., August 23, 1965, 35–36.

43. See, for example, the arguments of Representative Thomas Foley (D-WA) against interbasin transfers from the Pacific Northwest in *Lower Colorado River Basin Project*, Hearings (August 1965), 202–203.

44. Ibid., 166, 232.

45. *Records of the U.S. House of Representatives*, 89th Cong., 1st Sess., Committee Papers, House Subcommittee on Irrigation and Reclamation, Minutes, August 24, 1965, Box 71, fd: "Minutes, Subcommittee on Irrigation and Reclamation," Center for Legislative Archives, National Archives, Washington, DC (hereafter cited as NA).

46. See UPI dispatch, August 24, 1965, Box 196, fd: "L-11-b-1-A," Wayne Aspinall Papers, UDA; *Arizona Republic*, August 26, 1965; *Lower Colorado River Basin Project*, Hearings (August 1965), 245.

47. *Lower Colorado River Basin Project*, Hearings (August 1965), 245, 767.

48. Farmer, *Glen Canyon Dammed*, 149.

49. Stewart L. Udall, "Weekly Report to the President," September 7, 1965, Box 121, fd: 7, Stewart L. Udall Papers, SCUAL.

50. Richard Lamm to House Interior Committee, November 15, 1965, Box 476, fd: "October–December 1965," Morris K. Udall Papers, SCUAL.

51. Mo Udall to Colleagues, October 22, 1965, Box 196, fd: "L-11-b-1-A," Wayne Aspinall Papers, UDA; see also Mo Udall's speech to the House in *Congressional Record*, September 15, 1965.

52. Johnson, *Central Arizona Project*, 175.

53. Minutes, Colorado River Advisory Committee, September 28, 1965, Box 3, fd: "Colorado River Advisory Committee," William Nelson Papers, Archives and Special Collections, Mesa State College, Grand Junction, CO (hereafter cited as MSC).

54. Felix L. Sparks to Wayne N. Aspinall, October 11, 1965, and Wayne N. Aspinall to Felix L. Sparks, October 13, 1965, Box 184, fd: "39-H," Wayne Aspinall Papers, UDA.

55. Arizona Water Leaders Meeting, minutes, January 4, 1966, Box 476, fd: "January–March 1966," Morris K. Udall Papers, SCUAL.

56. John J. Rhodes, memorandum for the files, March 9, 1966, Box 476, fd: "January–March 1966," Morris K. Udall Papers, SCUAL.

57. Rhodes, memorandum, March 9, 1966; Roy Elson interview by U.S. Senate Historical Office, Washington, DC, SCASUL, April 27–August 21, 1990.

58. Elson interview, April 27–August 21, 1990; Orren Beaty to Stewart L. Udall, March 9, 1966, Box 127, fd: 1, Stewart L. Udall Papers, SCUAL.

59. Beaty to Stewart Udall, March 9, 1966.

60. Wayne N. Aspinall to Charles L. Schultze, March 14, 1966, Box 89, fd: 3:4, John Rhodes Papers, SCASUL.

61. *Durango* (CO) *Herald*, April 11, 1966.

62. Morris K. Udall to Les Alexander, n.d., Box 476, fd: "January–March 1966," Morris K. Udall Papers, SCUAL; for a discussion of the "Indian Blanket" strategy, see Daniel McCool, *Command of the Waters: Iron Triangles, Federal Water Development, and Indian Water* (Tucson: University of Arizona Press, 1994), 140–141. McCool's study was originally published by the University of California Press in 1987.

63. *Lower Colorado River Basin Project*, Hearings, Subcommittee on Irrigation and Reclamation, House Interior and Insular Affairs Committee, 89th Cong., 2d sess., on H.R. 4671 et al., May 9, 1966, 1071; Pearson, "The Plan to Dam Grand Canyon," 185–186.

64. *Lower Colorado River Basin Project,* Hearings (May 12, 1966), 1262.

65. Ibid., 1362–1363.

66. Ibid., 1428–1429, 1431, 1435–1436.

67. Wayne N. Aspinall to William H. Anderson, Jr., May 11, 1966, Box 245, fd: "L-11-b-1-A," Wayne Aspinall Papers, UDA.

68. See Pearson, "People Above Scenery," 390–456, for a thorough analysis of the Sierra Club's anti-dam campaign.

69. *New York Times,* June 9, 1966; Farmer, *Glen Canyon Dammed,* 152–153.

70. Udall's remarks in House of Representatives, June 9, 1966, reprint in Box 8, fd: 7, Carl Hayden Papers, SCASUL.

71. Aspinall's copy of this ad was found in Box 245, no file, Wayne Aspinall Papers, UDA; also see Michael P. Cohen, *The History of the Sierra Club, 1892–1970* (San Francisco: Sierra Club Books, 1988), 362–364; Pearson, "People Above Scenery," 415–416.

72. Cohen, *History of Sierra Club,* 360–361, tells the story of the IRS man.

73. Stephen Fox, *The American Conservation Movement: John Muir and His Legacy* (Madison: University of Wisconsin Press, 1981), 320; Morris K. Udall, *Too Funny to Be President* (New York: Henry Holt, 1988), 55; Pearson, "People Above Scenery," 399, seems similarly puzzled about who inspired the IRS to change the Sierra Club's tax status, admitting that "it has never been determined definitively who precipitated the IRS action."

74. Helen Ingram, *Water Politics: Continuity and Change* (Albuquerque: University of New Mexico Press, 1990), 58–59; Chuck [Allott staff member] to Senator Allott, August 1, 1966, Box 83, fd: "Official Correspondence," Series VI, Gordon Allott Papers, University of Colorado Archives, University of Colorado at Boulder, Boulder, CO (hereafter cited as UCAUCB).

75. *Congressional Quarterly,* "Committee Roundup," August 5, 1966, 1697–1698 in Box 215, no file, Wayne Aspinall Papers, UDA.

76. Ingram, *Water Politics,* 59.

77. Morris Udall, memorandum to Les Alexander and John Rhodes, August 22, 1966, Box 245, fd: "L-11-b-1-A," Wayne Aspinall Papers, UDA; Stewart L. Udall, news conference transcript, August 25, 1966, Box 89, fd: 4/1, John Rhodes Papers, SCASUL; *Daily Sentinel,* August 29, 1966.

78. Johnson, *Central Arizona Project,* 190–192; "Joint Statement of Representatives John J. Rhodes and Morris K. Udall," ca. September 1966, Box 215, no file, Wayne Aspinall Papers, UDA.

79. John J. Rhodes, memorandum to CAP Task Force, September 1, 1966, Box 7, fd: 4, Carl Hayden Papers, SCASUL. Anderson believed that representatives from the Pacific Northwest would fight any and all diversion plans, even the gargantuan NAWAPA (North American Water and Power Alliance), which proposed taking water from the Yukon region and diverting it to the thirsty American West. Some of NAWAPA's water would go to ever-thirsty California, and Jackson and other northwestern politicians feared jobs from their region would follow water there. See also "Joint Statement of Rhodes and Udall."

80. Morris K. Udall, "Confidential Memorandum to Wayne N. Aspinall," August 29, 1966, Box 245, fd: "L-11-b-1-AZ," Wayne Aspinall Papers, UDA; Morris K. Udall to

John J. Rhodes, September 7, 1966, Box 476, fd: "September 1966, Morris Udall Papers, SCUAL.

81. *Daily Sentinel*, October 6, 1966; Wayne Aspinall, "Remarks to the Annual Meeting of the State Grange, Cortez, CO," October 1, 1966, Box 88, fd: 4/2, John Rhodes Papers, SCASUL.

82. Ibid.

83. Joseph Wood Krutch to Stewart L. Udall, August 6, 1966, and Stewart L. Udall to Joseph Wood Krutch, August 12, 1966, Box 169, fd: "June–August 1966," Stewart L. Udall Papers, SCUAL.

84. Reisner, *Cadillac Desert*, 288; *Albuquerque Tribune*, November 18, 1966.

85. David Brower to Wayne N. Aspinall, November 19, 1966, and Wayne N. Aspinall to David Brower, November 22, 1966, Box 274, fd: "L-11," Wayne Aspinall Papers, UDA.

86. David Brower to Wayne Aspinall, November 28, 1966, Box 274, fd: "L-11," Wayne Aspinall Papers, UDA.

87. Wayne N. Aspinall to David Brower, draft reply, ca. December 1966, Box 274, fd: "L-11," Wayne Aspinall Papers, UDA.

88. Irving Bernstein, *Guns or Butter: The Presidency of Lyndon Johnson* (New York: Oxford University Press, 1996), 265.

89. "Colorado River Basin Project," in *Administrative History of the Department of the Interior*, Box 1, fd: "Volume I, Part I," LBJPL. This history (pages 36–37) reflects Udall's perspective on these events, especially his crucial decision to scrap the Grand Canyon dams and seek an alternative power source for the Central Arizona Project; Byron Pearson, "People Above Scenery," consistently argues that throughout this issue, Udall was driven more by political pragmatism than by any deep environmental convictions. See, for example, pp. 36, 176, 221.

90. Orren Beaty to Secretary of the Interior Udall, November 28, 1966, Box 127, fd: 1, Stewart L. Udall Papers, SCUAL; Stewart L. Udall, "Weekly Report to the President," December 6, 1966, Box 126, fd: 7, Stewart L. Udall Papers, SCUAL. See Pearson's many references to Udall's pragmatism on this point in "People Above Scenery," passim.

91. "Colorado River Basin Project," in *Administrative History*, 36.

92. Edward Weinberg, Deputy Solicitor, Interior Department, to Secretary Udall, December 13, 1966, Box 169, fd: "December 1966," Stewart L. Udall Papers, SCUAL; see Aspinall's bill in Box 275, fd: "1967 Legislation, Interior and Insular Affairs, Colorado River Basin, bills, reports, etc.," Wayne Aspinall Papers, UDA; Pearson, "People Above Scenery," 444–445, points out that the Sierra Club voiced fast opposition to Aspinall's border-manipulation proposal, arguing that slack water from the Bridge Canyon Dam would still be present throughout Grand Canyon National Monument. Aspinall's solution to this dilemma was simple: abolish the national monument!

93. "Colorado River Basin Project," in *Administrative History*, 36; Stewart L. Udall "Report to the President," January 24, 1967, Box 133, fd: "Reports to the President," Stewart L. Udall Papers, SCUAL. The outline of Udall's new water plan is contained in his report on H.R. 3300, February 15, 1967, in *Colorado River Basin Project*, Hearings, Subcommittee on Irrigation and Reclamation, House Interior and Insular Affairs Com-

mittee, 90th Cong., 1st Sess., on H.R. 3300 et al., March 13–14 and 16–17, 1967, 58–59, 250–251.

94. Orren Beaty to Stewart L. Udall, February 4, 1967, and Orren Beaty to Stewart L. Udall, February 25, 1967, Box 134, fd: 11, Stewart L. Udall Papers, SCUAL; Wayne N. Aspinall, news release, February 27, 1967, Box 275, fd: "1967 Legislation, Interior and Insular Affairs, Colorado River Basin, bills, reports, etc.," Wayne Aspinall Papers, UDA.

95. *Colorado River Basin Project*, Hearings (1967), 146–147.

96. *Colorado River Basin Project*, Hearings (1967), 251, 258–266; Stewart L. Udall, "Report to the President," March 14, 1967, Box 138, fd: "Reports to the President," Stewart L. Udall Papers, SCUAL.

97. *Colorado River Basin Project*, Hearings (1967), 418, 420, 423.

98. Ibid., 525–526.

99. Ibid.; Pearson, "Plan to Dam Grand Canyon," 98, quoting the *Arizona Republic*, March 14, 1967. Also see the *New York Times*, March 14, 1967.

100. Ingram, *Water Politics*, 60.

101. Ibid.; Johnson, *Central Arizona Project*, 205–206.

102. Stewart L. Udall to Clinton Anderson, May 22, 1967, Box 169, fd: "April–September 1967," Stewart L. Udall Papers, SCUAL.

103. Irv Sprague to Jim Jones, June 6, 1967, Box 67, fd: "Appointment File Diary Backup, June 7, 1967," President's Appointment File, Diary Backup, Lyndon B. Johnson Presidential Papers, LBJPL.

104. *Denver Post*, June 25, 1967; Felix L. Sparks to Members, Colorado Water Conservation Board, Colorado River Advisory Committee, and Colorado Congressional Delegation, June 6, 1967, Box 83, fd: "CAP–mark-up work file," Series VI, Gordon Allott Papers, UCAUCB.

105. Stewart L. Udall to President Lyndon B. Johnson, June 17, 1967, Box 205, fd: "FG 145 6-1-67–7-31-67," Papers of Lyndon B. Johnson, White House Central Files, LBJPL; Stewart L. Udall Journal, June 25, 1967, Box 136, fd: "June–August 1967," Stewart L. Udall Papers, SCUAL.

106. Stewart L. Udall, "Report to the President," July 25, 1967, Box 133, fd: "Reports to the President," Stewart L. Udall Papers, SCUAL; Pearson, "Plan to Dam Grand Canyon," 121; Johnson, *Central Arizona Project*, 205.

107. Rice, *Carl Hayden*, 150.

108. John Rhodes interview with Ross R. Rice, fd: 96, Ross R. Rice Papers, SCASUL, December 6, 1973; Johnson, *Central Arizona Project*, 205; Pearson, "People Above Scenery," passim.

109. Ingram, *Water Politics*, 61.

110. *Daily Sentinel*, August 5 and 8, 1967.

111. Johnson, *Central Arizona Project*, 205; Tucson *Arizona Daily Star*, August 9, 1967; John Rhodes interview with Ross R. Rice, December 6, 1973.

112. John Rhodes interview with Ross R. Rice, December 6, 1973; Ingram, *Water Politics*, 61.

113. Morris Udall to John McCormack, August 11, 1967, Box 90, fd: 1/3, John Rhodes Papers, SCASUL; Ingram, *Water Politics*, 61; Carl Hayden to Michael J. Kirwan,

August 10, 1967, Box 5, fd: 12, Carl Hayden Papers, SCASUL; Wayne N. Aspinall to Michael J. Kirwan, August 18, 1967, Box 274, fd: "Legislation, Interior and Insular Affairs, Colorado River Basin Project," Wayne Aspinall Papers, UDA.

114. Carl Hayden, "Statement to Appropriations Committee," Box 4, fd: 2, Carl Hayden Papers, SCASUL; memorandum (no author indicated) to Stewart L. Udall, September 14, 1967, Box 134, fd: 2, Stewart L. Udall Papers, SCUAL; Gordon Allott to Carl Hayden, September 25, 1967, Box 275, fd: "1967 Legislation, Interior and Insular Affairs Committee, Colorado River Basin Project," Wayne Aspinall Papers, UDA; *Daily Sentinel*, September 28, 1967.

115. John Rhodes interview with Ross R. Rice, December 6, 1973; Roy Elson interview, April 27–August 21, 1990; Wallace Duncan, confidential letter to Roy Elson, September 27, 1967, Box 15, fd: 5, Carl Hayden Papers, SCASUL. Duncan, presumably, worked for the Legislative Reference Service of the Library of Congress.

116. Rhodes interview with Ross R. Rice, December 6, 1973; Roy Elson interview, April 27–August 21, 1990; *Time*, October 20, 1967; *Daily Sentinel*, September 29, 1967; *Congressional Record*, October 10, 1967, S14540; *Daily Sentinel*, October 4, 1967. Before Aspinall's return, Dirksen had recommended Aspinall's censure, to which the Coloradan responded, "He [Dirksen] is a grand old man but he isn't running me and he isn't running my Committee." Bear in mind that Aspinall was a young man of seventy-one at this time. Dirksen also opposed Hayden's unusual maneuver. See *Los Angeles Times*, October 12, 1967.

117. Wayne N. Aspinall interview with Ross R. Rice, October 23, 1973, Ross R. Rice Collection, SCASUL.

118. Wayne N. Aspinall to Governor John Love, October 11, 1967, Box 274, fd: "1967 Legislative Interior and Insular Affairs, Committee, Colorado River Basin Project," Wayne Aspinall Papers, UDA; *Los Angeles Times*, October 12, 1967.

119. Ival V. Goslin, December 28, 1967, Box 308, fd: "L-11-b-1," Wayne Aspinall Papers, UDA; Morris Udall, memorandum on conference between Morris Udall and Chairman Aspinall, January 2, 1968, Box 169, fd: "1968," Stewart L. Udall Papers, SCUAL; Central Arizona Project Association, "Situation Report," January 6, 1968, Box 4, fd: 1, Carl Hayden Papers, SCASUL.

120. *Colorado River Basin Project, Pt. II*, Hearings, Subcommittee on Irrigation and Reclamation, House Committee on Interior and Insular Affairs, 90th Cong., 2d Sess., on H.R. 3300 and S. 1004, January 30–February 2, 1968, passim.

121. Ibid., 695–696, 708, 710.

122. Johnson, *Central Arizona Project*, 216–217. On Black Mesa, see Richard O. Clemmer, "Black Mesa and the Hopi," in *Native Americans and Energy Development*, ed. Joseph G. Jorgenson (Cambridge, MA: Anthropology Resource Center, 1978), 17–34; Jerry Kammer, *The Second Long Walk: The Navajo-Hopi Land Dispute* (Albuquerque: University of New Mexico Press, 1980), 87, wrote that in approving the Black Mesa coal lease, Interior Secretary Udall hailed it as a "boon for an economically depressed area."

123. Wayne Aspinall, "Statement on Aspinall Substitute," February 8, 1968, Box 15, fd: 5, Carl Hayden Papers, SCASUL; Central Arizona Project Association, "Situation Report," March 8, 1968, Box 15, fd: 3, Carl Hayden Papers, SCASUL.

124. Wayne N. Aspinall to Stewart L. Udall, March 8, 1968, Box 169, fd: "1968," Stewart L. Udall Papers, SCUAL.

125. Aspinall to Udall, March 8, 1968; and Stewart L. Udall to Wayne N. Aspinall, March 12, 1968, Box 169, fd: "1968," Stewart L. Udall Papers, SCUAL.

126. Johnson, *Central Arizona Project*, 219.

127. Central Arizona Project Task Force, memorandum for the files, March 29, 1968, Box 15, fd: 5, Carl Hayden Papers, SCASUL.

128. Irv Sprague to Barefoot Sanders, May 8, 1968, Box 1, fd: "Colorado River Basin," Office Files of Irvine H. Sprague, LBJPL; Johnson, *Central Arizona Project*, 220–221; *Congressional Record*, May 15, 1968, S13404.

129. Morris Udall to Wayne N. Aspinall, May 22, 1968, Box 15, fd: 3, Carl Hayden Papers, SCASUL; John Rhodes to Wayne N. Aspinall, May 17, 1968, Box 308, fd: "L-11-b-1," Wayne Aspinall Papers, UDA.

130. Morris K. Udall to Wayne N. Aspinall, July 14, 1968, and Morris K. Udall to Wayne N. Aspinall, n.d., ca. July 16–17, 1968, Box 308, fd: "L-11-b-1," Wayne Aspinall Papers, UDA; Johnson, *Central Arizona Project*, 224, lists conference committee members. For the Senate, members were Jackson (Washington), Hayden (Arizona), Anderson (New Mexico), Gruening (Alaska), Kuchel (California), Church (Idaho), Jordan (Idaho), and Allott (Colorado). The House conferees included Aspinall, Johnson (California), Edmundson (Oklahoma), Saylor (Pennsylvania), Hosmer (California), Burton (Utah), and Udall (Arizona).

131. Ira Whitlock, memorandum to the secretary (Stewart Udall), August 1, 1968, Box 138, fd: "SLU and Staff (Ira Whitlock)," Stewart L. Udall Papers, SCUAL; Ingram, *Water Politics*, 63; Wayne N. Aspinall to Ralph and Anna [Aspinall], July 26, 1968, Box 29, fd: "1968 Family, Personal Correspondence, P–Z," Wayne Aspinall Papers, UDA.

132. "Remarks of the President at the Signing of S. 1004, the Colorado River Project Bill," September 30, 1968, Box 308, fd: "L-11-b-1," Wayne Aspinall Papers, UDA; August, *Vision in the Desert*, 201–203.

133. Morris Udall interview with Ross R. Rice, fd: 110, Ross R. Rice Papers, SCASUL, November 30 and December 9 and 30, 1972.

134. Rhodes interview with Ross R. Rice, December 6, 1973.

CHAPTER SIX

THE ENVIRONMENTAL MOVEMENT'S "MOST DURABLE FOE"

Wayne Aspinall always considered himself a strong conservationist in the tradition of Theodore Roosevelt or Gifford Pinchot. Near the end of his life, Aspinall argued that he had been a conservationist "before most of today's citizens were born." There is little doubt that promoting western reclamation was Aspinall's chief interest throughout his twenty-four-year congressional career, but the chairman's shaping hand was evident in a wide range of land-use issues. Not only was he a principal architect and gatekeeper of the Wilderness Act, he also helped formulate many of the nation's park and recreation policies, public-land regulations, and mining laws from the 1950s through the 1970s. Of course, his efforts and their outcomes were not always appreciated. To environmentalists, Aspinall was their "most durable foe." In 1972, David Brower said of him that the environmental movement had seen "dream after dream dashed on the stony continents of Wayne Aspinall."[1]

THE JOHNSON CONSERVATION LEGACY

In 1965, Denver's *Rocky Mountain News* reported that Aspinall, the West's most powerful member of Congress, had set "a new standard" for balking President Johnson's plans on several conservation issues. The cause of Aspinall's instant animosity was easy to discern—disappointment over LBJ's presidential appointments to the Public Land Law Review Commission. In response, the Coloradan planned to drag his feet on several bills considered important to Interior Secretary Udall and the Johnson administration.[2] In contrast to his predecessor John F. Kennedy, Lyndon Johnson and his wife, Lady Bird, had a strong affection for the land. Though the Vietnam War would command Johnson's attention in the years ahead, the president had a comfortable regard for the judgments of Interior Secretary Stewart Udall and in general gave him free rein to forge a Johnson administration conservation legacy.[3] Needless to say, Wayne Aspinall would have a say in how that record was shaped.

On balance, Wayne Aspinall had a deep regard for Lyndon B. Johnson, both as a president and as a legislator. Johnson and Aspinall dealt with one another openly; if Johnson needed Aspinall's cooperation, he would call the chairman and simply ask for it.[4] Udall, given a free hand by Johnson, evolved into more of a zealot (at least as far as Aspinall was concerned), moving the nation's conservation agenda toward the environmental fringe by emphasizing single-use recreation instead of multiple use of the land.[5] At the same time, Udall believed Aspinall was becoming increasingly rigid and undemocratic in his exercise of Interior Committee power. But the record shows that even given their deteriorating relationship, Udall and Aspinall, along with such Senate stalwarts as Clinton Anderson and Henry Jackson, created more national parks, monuments, and conservation legislation than had other legislators at any other period in U.S. history.[6] In retrospect, however, Udall found it strange that in this era of progress, no new national parks or monuments were created amid the magnificent scenery of Aspinall's Fourth Congressional District. Aspinall's strict adherence to multiple-use doctrines mitigated against his enthusiasm for parks and monuments, which the Coloradan equated with locking up multiple-use resources.[7]

One bill, more than others, illustrates both the Udall-Johnson desire to create a conservation legacy and Aspinall's reluctance to support it: the creation of Redwood National Park in northern California in 1968. Aspinall felt the same way about the Wild and Scenic Rivers legislation that passed Congress in 1968—it simply seemed unnecessary to him. Left to himself, Aspinall would not have established this new national park, believing that enough of the spectacular trees were protected by California's state-park system. The Colorado congressman sought to safeguard the interests of the larger West's resource users—in this case, the timber industry—from what he might have characterized as the capricious, unnecessary, and idealistic plans of environmental zealots. In 1963, the Sierra Club inaugurated a campaign to establish a Redwood National Park. Seeking to capitalize on the momentum gathered in 1964's "Conservation Congress," the Sierra Club, congressional supporters, and the Johnson administration all began pushing hard for a national-park bill in 1965. In his 1965 "Conservation Message," President Johnson had requested that Congress establish a Redwood National Park. Interior Secretary Udall had told the president that this was truly a "last chance opportunity, for unless we act in the sixties it will be too late." After months of study, planning, and negotiation with the State of California and private industry, a bill proposing 54,000-acre Redwood National Park was ready for congressional consideration in 1966.[8]

As was by now the custom with legislation bearing strong conservation overtones, the Senate was the first to hold hearings. Aspinall earned the enmity of park advocates by announcing on March 1 that the Interior Committee would not take action on the Redwood Bill during the Eighty-ninth Congress. Aspinall's decision in effect delayed congressional consideration of the measure until the start of the Ninetieth Congress in 1967. Redwood Park supporters felt a special urgency to complete a bill because of reports that timber companies were busy cutting groves scheduled for inclusion within the national park's boundaries. Park supporters scorned Aspinall's delay, castigating him as a tool of the timber interests.[9]

Heading into 1967, Secretary Udall labeled the Redwood Bill a "must." Though Aspinall's National Parks Subcommittee began considering the Redwood Bill in 1967, Chairman Aspinall refused to promise fast action. In a letter to future Colorado governor Richard Lamm (then a young Democratic Party activist), Aspinall indicated that even dire predictions of doom for threatened redwood stands would not influence him to move the bill quickly. He added that environmentalists like Lamm "did not seem to realize or will not accept the fact that the Treasury just doesn't have unlimited funds for these purposes." The issue, according to Aspinall, would be decided by "logic" not "emotionalism." In an effort to inspire Aspinall to act, in July 1967, bill supporters asked President Johnson to pressure the crusty Coloradan. Johnson's deft touch and persuasive powers were on display in a July 10 letter to Aspinall. The president stated that he considered the Redwoods Bill to be "of first and highest priority" but added that he also understood the Interior Committee's "substantial workload and your proper insistence that the work be done in a thorough and orderly manner." Aspinall responded immediately, indicating that his committee had discovered that the Redwood Park issues were more complex than he had first thought and that the National Parks Subcommittee would need to schedule hearings and tour the site of the proposed park.[10]

A 65 million–acre Redwood National Park Bill passed the Senate in late 1967. One important feature was a compromise empowering the interior secretary to trade National Forest Service lands for redwood stands owned by private companies. Though this provision had its critics, it made the bill less costly and more appealing to politicians like California governor Ronald Reagan, who had insisted upon economic compensation for damages to the local logging economy.[11]

As 1968 began, the Redwood Park proposal competed for House Interior Committee attention with many other major pieces of legislation, including the Wild and Scenic Rivers Bill and the Central Arizona Project. At National Parks Subcommittee hearings in Eureka, California, near the proposed park, Chairman Aspinall seemed receptive to the complaints of local citizens who feared a devastating economic impact to the timber industry if a Redwood National Park were created.[12]

Wayne Aspinall on the phone in his Washington, D.C., office. Courtesy, UCAUCB.

Preservationists in California and around the nation expressed outrage when Aspinall's Interior Committee proposed a disappointingly small 25,000-acre park. In a letter to conservation leader Horace M. Albright, Aspinall had intimated that his House bill would be smaller than the Senate's; however, Aspinall made it clear to Albright that he would not stand in the way of a larger bill during conference committee sessions with the Senate. His main concern, it seems, was to build some protection into the bill to offset the economic devastation that the local logging economy would suffer.[13] More than ever, the House Interior Committee chair saw himself as the voice of the increasingly beleaguered western resource user.

Aspinall's small Redwood Bill elicited a massive outpouring of letters to House committee members. Aspinall received more "hate" mail for his Redwood proposal than for any other initiative in his congressional career. Aspinall asked an employee of the Interior Committee to analyze the mail in terms of content, origin, and intent. More than 22,000 letters favored a Redwood National Park, with only 800 opposed. Predictably, the letters boiled down to a battle between conservation organizations and the timber industry. The Sierra Club and Georgia-Pacific had inspired much of the mail, both for and against. Once the impact of the two interest groups was factored in, it became clear that most of the remaining letters favored a Redwood Park of "reasonable size," one that would consolidate existing state parks and not "overly impair lumber operations or the local economy."[14] One letter to Aspinall declaring the House bill "unreasonable" came from Alan Merson, a young assistant professor of law at the University of Denver who four years later would challenge for Aspinall's congressional seat. Aspinall replied to Merson after the House, under suspension of rules, passed a bill for a 28,000-acre Redwood National Park. To Merson and others who attacked the park's meager size in the House bill, Aspinall pledged to work for a "reasonable increase" during conference-committee sessions with the Senate. Aspinall defended the unusual procedure by which the bill was passed (it did not allow amendments), citing the interests of time: the Ninetieth Congress was fast approaching its conclusion. To many national observers, passing the bill under rules suspension only heightened their suspicion of Aspinall's intent toward a Redwood National Park.[15]

Aspinall chaired the conference committee, which began meeting in August. Working with Republican John Saylor, three other House members, and five senators, Aspinall knew well before the last bargain had been struck that the final bill would be "a good bit larger than the House bill." After several sessions, the conference committee agreed on a 58,000-acre park. About half of the acreage came from existing state parks; the remainder came from new land acquisitions. President Lyndon B. Johnson signed the bill on October 2, 1968.[16]

Aspinall endured massive national criticism throughout the Redwood episode. Chided for its snail's pace, Aspinall's system did not allow room for special bills that needed fast treatment. The chairman took bills in their order. Each bill—and the constituency supporting it—had to wait its turn. Investigative journalist Drew Pearson dubbed the chairman "molasses-moving Aspinall" during this ordeal. What Pearson and other critics did not fully understand was the imposing number of environmentally significant bills Aspinall was dealing with in 1968, including the Wild and Scenic Rivers Bill, National Trails legislation, the Colorado River Basin Project, and a North Cascades National Park bill, among others. Though he adhered strictly to procedure, Aspinall was acting in good faith. Early in the Redwood struggle, he personally wrote to timber companies, urging them to voluntarily cease operations in areas projected for inclusion within the park's borders. Later, a formal moratorium on cutting replaced the voluntary compliance until legislation could be authorized. With a 58,000-acre park in the offing—closer to the size of the Senate's proposal—Aspinall appeared vindicated. In reference to the many angry and critical letters he had received from preservationists, Aspinall said he "would rather be an individual's target at the beginning of the game and his darling at the end, rather than vice versa."[17]

By the end of the Johnson years, in December 1968 and January 1969, Aspinall's and Interior Secretary Udall's relationship had deteriorated precipitously. With little more than a month left in the administration, Udall began taking steps to ensure Lyndon Johnson's—and his own—place in U.S. conservation history. Aware that at the end of their terms, several twentieth-century presidents had used their executive powers and the Antiquities Act of 1906 to set aside federal lands as national monuments and wildlife refuges and to add to existing monuments and refuges, Udall submitted plans to significantly enhance the nation's protected public lands. He was given the green light and asked by close presidential advisors to carefully touch base with key congressional leaders, including Aspinall.[18]

Udall hoped his proposals, which designated a number of new national monuments, including several large ones in Alaska and two in his native Arizona, would dwarf all previous "midnight" presidential conservation initiatives. With the administration slated to leave office on January 20, 1969, Udall indicated to Johnson and the presidential staff that he had received generally positive reaction from congressional leaders, though one presidential advisor, DeVier Pierson, told the president that he did not think Udall had carefully discussed the national monuments with all of them. Perhaps to test this assertion, President Johnson called Aspinall several weeks before the end of his administration to see whether Udall had checked with the House Interior Committee chair. Aspinall indicated that Udall had not. This angered Aspinall because he and Udall had made an agreement in the early days of the Kennedy administration that if Udall wanted to take any executive action that might involve legislative responsibility, he would discuss it with Aspinall first. Aspinall had learned about

Udall's proposal from secondhand sources before LBJ's phone call, but not through the interior secretary himself.[19]

Aspinall later maintained that Udall almost lost his job in the final weeks of the Johnson administration over his failure to consult with *all* congressional leaders before proceeding with the executive orders. Belatedly, Udall reported on congressional opinion, noting that most congressional leaders—with the exception of Aspinall and some members of Alaska's delegation—supported the massive plan to bolster the nation's conservation heritage. Undersecretary of the Interior John Carver recalled that Udall's last-minute proclamation proposal severely damaged what had been a generally constructive working relationship between Udall and Aspinall. And the fact that Udall had also suggested withdrawing substantial acreage from public use several weeks before—again without talking to Aspinall—could not have helped.[20]

With the last day of the administration looming and Johnson's press conference to announce the monuments already scheduled, Udall closed his office door and dictated his final letter as interior secretary. Appropriately, it was sent to Wayne Aspinall, who had dominated, frustrated, and ultimately shaped so much of the Udall-Kennedy-Johnson conservation legacy. "It is fitting that it should be directed to you, because more than any other member of the Congress[,] you have been the master carpenter of the legislative achievements of the past eight years." Udall expressed his hope that the president would sign the national-monument proclamations and denied any partisan political purpose in encouraging the president's action. Later that day, Lyndon Johnson indeed signed the proclamations, but not for the 7 million acres that Udall recommended. Instead, at the insistence of his advisors, Aspinall, and his own good political sense, Johnson signed an executive order for only 300,000 acres—including only one new national monument (Marble Canyon, in Udall's Arizona) and enlarging only a few other monuments and wildlife refuges.[21]

Aspinall and President Johnson had maintained a cordial relationship on other matters. In 1967, when Aspinall was being pushed to act on the Redwood proposal, LBJ announced the appointment of Aspinall's son, Owen, as governor of American Samoa. Owen, married to a native Samoan, had briefly served as attorney general and then secretary general of the territory. The choice of Owen Aspinall, as Stewart Udall told Lyndon Johnson, would undoubtedly help propel the president's conservation program along with the powerful chairman. "We could get real mileage out of this one," Udall predicted. LBJ summoned Aspinall to a late-afternoon Oval Office meeting in early June 1967. The president offered the pleased chairman, who had suspected Johnson was going to engage in some arm-twisting on the stalled Redwood Bill, the chance to call Owen with the good news. Not wanting to appear to have arranged the appointment, Aspinall demurred, suggesting the president do it himself. Still, Wayne Aspinall was a proud father. After the announcement was made public, the

In the Oval Office, Wayne Aspinall and President Johnson discuss many of the difficult legislative issues facing the American West during the summer of 1967. Courtesy, LBJPL.

president and Lady Bird entertained Wayne, Julia, Owen, and Tafa, Owen's wife, on the Truman Balcony at the White House.[22]

In 1968, Aspinall repaid Johnson's favor by telling anyone who asked that the beleagured Johnson was his presidential choice for 1968. But the March 12 New Hampshire primary proved disastrous for the president. Antiwar Minnesota Democrat Eugene McCarthy nearly staged an upset. In the primary's wake, Johnson asked his congressional liaisons to find out who congressional Democrats were supporting for president in 1968. Johnson was becoming increasingly unpopular by late March. Not only was Eugene McCarthy attracting huge crowds, Robert Kennedy entered the race four days after the New Hampshire vote. On March 31, Johnson stunned the nation by dropping out of the presidential race. Aspinall, who had remained loyal to Johnson up to this point, would later transfer his support to Hubert H. Humphrey.[23]

PUBLIC LAND LAW REVIEW COMMISSION

Throughout the Johnson years, Aspinall remained deeply involved in studying the nation's public lands. By 1963, he had become convinced that only a thorough review of the multitude of U.S. land laws could save Congress and the nation future aggravation in dealing with public land–use, wilderness, and min-

President Lyndon Johnson and Lady Bird (in the background) host Aspinall, his son Owen, and Owen's wife, Tafa, to celebrate Owen's appointment as governor of American Samoa in 1967. Courtesy, LBJPL.

eral policy–planning issues in the event of national emergencies. There is also little doubt that the Colorado congressman parlayed his desire for a Public Land Law Review Commission (PLLRC) into a condition for final action on Wilderness legislation.

The PLLRC had been Aspinall's pet project for years. Since the Northwest Ordinance of 1787, Congress had passed more than 5,000 laws to guide the administration and disposal of the public domain. Many of the laws were obsolete, contradictory, and no longer rooted in the reality of twentieth-century political culture. As Aspinall frequently said, the body of land law was all the more important to consider because one-third of the nation's land belonged to the public. Thirty-six percent of Colorado—and well over half of Aspinall's congressional district—was in the public domain. Aspinall's interest in a PLLRC emerged during discussions with the Kennedy administration on how to proceed toward a Wilderness Act. On January 17, 1963, in a lengthy reply to Aspinall, President Kennedy agreed that the system of public-land law "warrants a comprehensive review."[24] The Kennedy administration favored Aspinall's project yet internally feared that the Coloradan would use the commission, like the ORRRC, as a means to delay meaningful action on the Wilderness Bill until the PLLRC study had been completed.[25] With Aspinall's assurances on this point, discussions began among the White House, the Bureau of the Budget, the attorney general's office, and the Agriculture and Interior Departments. With the go-ahead, Aspinall happily introduced legislation for a PLLRC on August 14, 1963.[26]

The PLLRC became entangled with the movement for a Wilderness Bill in both 1963 and 1964. As noted, Wilderness advocates both in and out of Congress understood that Aspinall's ardent desire for a PLLRC could be used to loosen his grip on the Wilderness Bill. Undoubtedly, this consideration played a role in the Interior Committee's 1964 reporting of a Wilderness Act after it had floundered for more than half a decade.[27] There is speculation that during Aspinall's final conversation with President Kennedy on November 20, 1963, Aspinall agreed to move the Wilderness Bill forward and the president encouraged him to proceed with a Public Land Law Review Commission.[28] Not surprisingly, legislation to establish a PLLRC had little difficulty before Aspinall's committee or on the floor of Congress, where it passed 339–29 in March 1964. After the Senate passed the bill, President Johnson signed it into law on September 19, making the PLLRC part of what even Aspinall was calling "one of the brightest pages in the history of conservation law."[29]

In its conception, the Public Land Law Review Commission, Aspinall's brainchild, contradicts Stewart Udall's assessment that Aspinall had only a restrictive view of the Interior Committee's role and jurisdiction.[30] The PLLRC's vision was broad, sweeping, and potentially revolutionary. Although there had been several previous federal land commissions in 1879, 1903, and 1930, the recommendations of each body were for the most part ignored and had little long-term impact. The PLLRC of 1964 differed markedly from its predecessors in two important respects: its broad charge and its membership composition.[31] Its charge included studying all laws, policies, and practices governing public lands to determine present and future demands on these lands, and recommending changes in laws and administration to enable the American people to realize maximum benefit from these lands.[32] Consisting of nineteen members, the PLLRC was the first U.S. land-study commission to include members of Congress. Each house appointed six members from its Committee on Interior and Insular Affairs, three from the majority and three from the minority party. Six members of the public would be appointed by the president. Finally, the eighteen members would elect a commission chair.[33]

Well before Congress had authorized a PLLRC, Aspinall was freely speculating on how it would exceed the drab legacy of previous land commissions. Most of all, the PLLRC would require a strong and energetic chair. In October 1963, almost a year ahead of the bill's passage, Aspinall predicted to a correspondent that the PLLRC's leader would be "the one that makes or breaks the commission." Two months later, Aspinall told influential western Colorado judge and cattleman Dan Hughes that there is "no question that the Chairman is the key man in the operation." Aspinall assured Hughes that western land users would "have an understanding friend at this post." Aspinall apparently believed that he might well be that "understanding friend," as he easily engineered his appointment to the commission in October 1964. Aspinall went on to ensure that the commission's director, who had a large research staff often exceeding fifty people, would be Milton A. Pearl. Pearl, a skilled public land–law technician and unquestioned Aspinall loyalist, drafted most of the original PLLRC legislation.[34]

The commission's organizational meeting was delayed for several months because of yet another rift between Aspinall and New Mexico senator Clinton P. Anderson. Anderson, also a commission member, objected to the appointment of Pearl, a House Interior Committee staff member, as director. The New Mexican also would have to be persuaded not to obstruct Aspinall's election as PLLRC chair.[35]

Though he controlled the chairship and the day-to-day operations of the commission through Pearl, Aspinall still delayed in organizing the PLLRC. The *Rocky Mountain News* reported that Aspinall was deeply disappointed with either the quality or the political orientation of President Johnson's appointees. The president had apparently ignored Aspinall's recommendations. Aspinall could ascribe this slight to poor White House congressional liaison work or conflict between "left-over Kennedy people" and Johnson appointees, but he still found this slight "embarrassing." As a western Colorado newspaper aptly phrased it, Aspinall would continue stalling until he was satisfied that the PLLRC, his pride and joy, comprised people he knew and trusted, those he was certain were not slanted toward Wilderness advocacy and outdoor recreation.[36]

In a revealing exchange of letters, Aspinall told the chair of the Civil Service Commission, John W. Macy, Jr., that if the appointments were any indication, the White House had lost sight of the commission's goals. Rather than being absorbed in the intricacies of public-land law, four of the president's appointees were "interested, generally, in conservation questions as such." President Johnson's choices included the philanthropic Wilderness advocate Laurence S. Rockefeller; land-use planner Philip Hoff; Bureau of Land Management administrator H. Byron Mock; Forestry professor Maurice Goddard; Mrs. Percy Maxim Lee, described by Macy as a "spokesman for the conservation-minded women of America"; and Professor Robert Emmet Clark of the University of New Mexico, founder of the *Journal of Natural Resources* and a leading expert on land law.[37]

Aspinall eventually was satisfied with both the commission's makeup and his ability to direct its deliberations. In conjunction with Senator Anderson, he issued a call for the PLLRC's organizational meeting in July 1965. At the July 14 meeting, Aspinall was elected commission chair, and Pearl was tapped as its staff director. Senator Henry "Scoop" Jackson (D-WA) took the lead in nominating

Wayne Aspinall addressing a meeting of the Public Land Law Review Commission. The PLLRC was one of Aspinall's most cherished congressional endeavors. Courtesy, UCAUCB.

both men, a move that short-circuited any potential Senate criticism from those who feared House domination of the PLLRC. After accepting the chairship, Aspinall denied that he had sought it. "My reluctant acceptance . . . was at the specific unanimous request of the other Commissioners." To those charging that Aspinall now had double responsibilities as chair of both the PLLRC and the House Interior Committee, positions that flirted with conflict of interest, Aspinall seemed unfazed, pointing out that if he had been a regular commissioner, the same allegations could have been leveled against him. It never occurred to Wayne Aspinall to play only a supporting role in the PLLRC.[38]

The PLLRC began hearings in the spring of 1966. Over the next five years, it met intermittently in Washington and in the field, spending countless hours and more than $7 million to conduct its assessment of the nation's public-land laws. An advisory council of thirty-four members also offered input. Twenty-five advisors were selected by the original commissioners; nine others were appointed by federal agencies with a stake in federal land and resource management. Most members of the advisory council represented public land–user industries. The PLLRC's daily operations were overseen by Milton Pearl, who also supervised the work of numerous contractors, usually experts in specialized fields of land law who wrote monographs and consulted for the commission.[39]

The PLLRC would be tackling an immense subject that, when viewed in the social context of the late 1960s, with its rising tide of environmental concern, opened the commission's work to unexpectedly close public scrutiny. As the commission's chair, Aspinall took many opportunities to speak out on the commission's purpose and goals. As he envisioned it, the PLLRC might counteract the dangerous trend wherein Congress had been shunning its constitutional obligation to make laws and policies for federal land management. Congress, Aspinall believed, had been allowing the executive branch free control to exert its capricious political will upon federal land management. To Aspinall, the Constitution was clear on this point—Congress was to write the laws. Hopefully, the PLLRC would offer clear guidelines for interpretation and implementation of public-land law. Unfortunately, to Aspinall, members of the executive branch had "taken their own counsel" and allowed public-land administrators too much flexibility and discretion in the application of the public-land laws. Aspinall did not see any need for redefining conservation to fit late 1960s broadened ecological concepts. The "basic precepts" of conservation first articulated by Theodore Roosevelt and Gifford Pinchot at the turn of the century and reaffirmed by Franklin Roosevelt were "sound." Aspinall hoped to clarify the law and its application to avoid executive-branch policy making undertaken to satisfy the vocal demands of an increasingly radical environmental agenda. Aspinall used the PLLRC to affirm his leanings as a conservationist in the Pinchotian sense of the word.[40]

The Public Land Law Review Commission, known to be Aspinall's pet, was exposed, from time to time, to dangerous political cross-currents. In December 1966, PLLRC staff director Milton Pearl informed Aspinall that he had "grave doubts" that the commission could accomplish its task within the $4 million budget and the time frame allotted (the study was due by December 31, 1967). The following year, Aspinall introduced a bill calling for more time and more money. The question of a PLLRC extension came to a head in September 1967, at the height of the CAP struggle between Carl Hayden and Wayne Aspinall. There is little doubt that Hayden, as chair of the Senate Appropriations Committee, considered holding up funding for Aspinall's PLLRC. Arizona's representative to the PLLRC, F. N. Smith, reported that most commission members who knew Hayden trusted the senator's integrity. Though desperate to see the CAP's enactment, Hayden had "never gone that far, and it is not expected that he would do so at this time." Hayden and Aspinall amicably resolved their CAP impasse by October 1967 (see Chapter 5), and Hayden, as evidence of his goodwill, wrote a strong letter to President Johnson's budget director, Charles L.

Schultze, endorsing the extension and recommending the funding increase for the PLLRC. PL 90-213, signed by President Johnson on September 18, 1967, extended the study deadline to June 30, 1970, and increased its appropriations by more than $3 million.[41]

In 1969, Aspinall indicated that the PLLRC's report would be ready both on time and within budget. By then, Aspinall had already started the crucial political tactic of lowering public expectations for the report. Noting that it would be up to Congress to act on the commission's many recommendations, Aspinall said that whenever an executive-branch official like Secretary Udall made policy without the guidance of Congress, he "made our job more difficult." Aspinall was referring to Udall's attempt, in the final days of the Johnson administration, to create more national monuments, add acreage to others, and increase grazing fees by administrative fiat. Aspinall viewed Udall's actions as an attempt at prejudging the PLLRC's conclusions and circumventing its labors. Of course, it was also the type of administrative behavior Aspinall disliked the most: public-land policy by administrative caprice.[42]

By late spring 1969, the Public Land Law Review Commission was embroiled in a public-relations debacle that would taint the study's ultimate reception. Helene Monberg, a freelance journalist and a regular contributor to several western newspapers, accused Aspinall and the PLLRC of withholding important commission information from the public. Using the Freedom of Information Act of 1966, Monberg challenged the PLLRC's policy of not allowing its contractor manuscripts to be made public. Monberg was interested in examining PLLRC contractor studies of the massive executive-action federal land withdrawals relating to the West's oil-shale industry. PLLRC policy had been not to disclose contractor study findings until its final report had been filed with the president and Congress. Under pressure from both Monberg and Samuel J. Archibald of the University of Missouri's Freedom of Information Center, Aspinall agreed to consider allowing access to contractor studies before they reached the president or Congress. On May 10, 1969, the PLLRC agreed to publish the reports. Monberg, still angered by the cloak of secrecy that had shrouded the PLLRC since its inception, accused Aspinall and the commission of having a "complete bankruptcy" in its press relations. Monberg had originally complained when Aspinall had tried to limit her access to only Director Pearl, a PLLRC press officer, and himself. Monberg had hoped to have access to PLLRC staff researchers and project contractors as well.[43]

Monberg's anger with Aspinall and the PLLRC foreshadowed public reaction to the final report. In her view, the few PLLRC reports she had glanced at were error-prone, poorly written, and generally lacking in broad public interest. Monberg found nothing in them to warrant the secrecy surrounding PLLRC deliberations, which had included closed meetings. Monberg warned that unless the reports improved and the PLLRC upgraded its press relations, "its work will be still-born." Monberg had strongly supported the PLLRC's mission from the start (it was "vital to the future of the West," she had once thought), but she could not envision, from the perspective of 1969, how the commission's recommendations would ever be implemented with its pervasive "anti-press, anti-information" attitude. The "whole matter is a tragedy," she concluded.[44]

Yet Aspinall, who refused to brook criticism of any project he felt deeply about, believed the study was on the right track. Throughout the investigation, he remained in close contact with the American West's basic land-user constituencies, reassuring them that they had nothing to fear from the PLLRC's findings. Speaking before the National Western Mining Congress on February 14, 1970, Aspinall emphasized that a "near hysteria" had overtaken the nation's consideration of environmental issues, but he went on to assure the mining executives that although the PLLRC would pay attention to environmental factors, they would "keep them in perspective" and make "practical, down to earth recommendations." Aspinall concluded that the final report of the PLLRC would not be "unduly influenced by the emotional environmental binge" sweeping the nation in 1970.[45]

On June 23, 1970, in a White House Rose Garden ceremony, Wayne Aspinall presented to President Nixon One Third of a Nation: A Report to the President and to the Congress, the findings of the Public Land Law Review Commission. The 342-page study contained 137 specific major recommendations, 18 basic recommendations, and 250 more recommendations described as "supplementary." Reflecting Aspinall's respect for the multiple-use concept, One Third of a Nation recommended that all public-land issues be concentrated under a new Department of Natural Resources with standing committees in each house of Congress. Such an arrangement would enhance congressional oversight of public-land issues, long an Aspinall goal. The report paid close but gentle attention to the mining industry, urging the federal government to help stimulate the oil-shale industry, which had a major potential presence in Aspinall's congressional district. Mineral exploration, the report recommended, should receive preference over most, if not all, other public-land uses. The range-management section delighted the cattle industry. Recommendation 37 stated, "Public land forage policies should be flexible, designed to attain maximum economic efficiency in the production and use of forage from the public lands, and to support regional economic growth." The forest-management section noted the primacy of economic factors in decisions involving timber resources. The report recommended that federal timber policy should consider the economic health of local communities dependent on timber production, that timber sale procedures should be simplified, and that an "accelerated program of timber access roads" should be implemented. One Third of a Nation did take note of outdoor recreation as a growing national interest but suggested following the guideline of dominant use to reconcile competing interests for the same land parcel. Use priorities would be established for each section of land. The concept of dominant use, it was hoped, would help clarify the somewhat hazy and overworked idea of multiple use.[46]

Within days of its release, few people who cared about the nation's public lands were neutral about *One Third of a Nation*. The environmental community and many leading U.S. newspapers rushed to condemn the study. The *Idaho Statesman* did not mince words: the PLLRC "seemed to be guarded by the dollar sign." The *Christian Science Monitor* saw *One Third of a Nation* as only a "useful explication of the status quo," not a guide to the nation's resource future, and the *New York Times* believed that the report would call forth "alarm signals from every conservation group in the land."[47]

As predicted by the *New York Times*, the Sierra Club roundly criticized the report. Owing its entire existence to Wayne Aspinall, *One Third of a Nation* only delineated the "traditional view of the rural West." Thus, the commission's study was "oriented toward maximum immediate commercial exploitation." According to the Sierra Club's Phil Berry, *One Third of a Nation* was predicated upon an America and a world with an "ever-expanding economy and unlimited resources." Former interior secretary Stewart Udall called the PLLRC report a "disappointing performance," a "goodies for all report that apparently pleases nobody." Udall saw Aspinall's "stamp on nearly every line." Filled with trade-offs, the report "worked against long-term environmental values." Not surprisingly, a Ralph Nader task force condemned the PLLRC's recommendation that timbering be the "dominant use *wherever* the loggers want to cut." The Nader study noted that *One Third of a Nation* made only "general" and "unspecific" references to environmental-protection issues. Even the popular magazine *Sports Illustrated* attacked the PLLRC for recommending the "accelerated exploitation and disposal" of the nation's public land, "some of the purest . . . and least ransacked on earth."[48]

A number of Public Land Law Review Commission members attempted to distance themselves from *One Third of a Nation*. Harold Peterson's critical writing in *Sports Illustrated* observed that both Senator Henry Jackson (D-WA) and Representative John Saylor (R-PA) were less than enthusiastic about the report. An aide to commission member Laurence Rockefeller noted that the philanthropist was "very outspoken" about the PLLRC's findings but felt "outnumbered and outmaneuvered" by Aspinall's forces.[49]

Wayne Aspinall believed that many PLLRC critics had not only failed to carefully read the report, they had made up their minds on its content well in advance of its publication. Despite the tide of public criticism, Aspinall embraced *One Third of a Nation* as one of his most worthwhile public-service efforts, believing the report offered a blueprint for future legislation. Aspinall hoped to implement as many of the report's recommendations as possible as quickly as possible, and to this end, he proposed H.R. 9211, which he based on

PLLRC findings. To his disappointment, the Ninety-second Congress, Aspinall's last, failed to enact the legislation. Aspinall had pinned great hopes on H.R. 9211, which, in the Nader report's estimate, would have "allowed the maximum possible development" of public lands. This bill would also have curbed the secretary of the interior's power to withdraw public lands without congressional approval—a perennial Aspinall bugaboo. In addition, H.R. 9211 would have given Congress a stronger veto over proposed Wilderness tracts and planning for potential Wilderness areas in national forests.[50]

Aspinall's inability to translate the PLLRC's recommendations into legislation became one of the great frustrations of his House career. The congressman did, however, later take pride in several important bills that were passed by subsequent Congresses and owed their genesis to *One Third of a Nation* findings. The Federal Land Policy and Management Act of 1976 (FLPMA) provides the most notable example. Also known as the Bureau of Land Management's Organic Act, FLPMA was first introduced in Congress in 1971, incorporating provisions recommended by the PLLRC, the Interior Department, and individual members of Congress. After five years of legislative give and take, the bill passed Congress in 1976. Aspinall later recalled that during the PLLRC study, it became apparent that many of the laws governing the BLM had little to do with that agency's modern mission. In short, the laws needed "overhauling . . . to take care of the needs of the changing times." Aspinall proudly asserted that more than forty—"in some form or another"—of the PLLRC's recommendations became part of FLPMA. Aspinall was proud to be considered a founder of this "far-reaching legislation," though its five-year incubation period no doubt taxed his legendary "patience, . . . so important to a successful public servant." FLPMA gave some coherence to the BLM's extraordinary mission as custodian of vast tracts of public land in the American West by defining its planning operations and determining its system of land classification and inventory. Its most controversial feature, as far as the West's public-land users were concerned, was the requirement that the BLM inventory all of its lands for possible inclusion in the national wilderness protection system.[51]

Wayne Aspinall's role in creating, defining, and implementing the Public Land Law Review Commission ranked among his most significant tasks as a U.S. Representative. It was also one of his least appreciated efforts. The task of sifting through hundreds—even thousands—of old and often conflicting federal land laws would not have excited many people. However, Wayne Aspinall, who loved the minutiae of legislation more than most Washington politicians, found this exercise both stimulating and vital to the West's future. At a reunion of PLLRC members and staffers held at the University of Denver in 1977, Aspinall called that panel one of the "greatest Commissions to ever serve our country." Though most of its recommendations had not yet been enacted, Aspinall took heart that the study had been "kept continuously alive since its release."[52]

One Third of a Nation may have met or exceeded Aspinall's standards, but it failed to meet the expectations of the growing number of Americans who had started to challenge the dominant values in U.S. society, especially those who had begun questioning, in historian Hal Rothman's words, "the status, meaning, and condition of the environment."[53] Between the PLLRC's authorization in 1964 and the release of its final report in 1970, a new set of environmental assumptions had crept into the national consciousness. Many Americans now viewed old ideas of economic progress "in a different light."[54] To these citizens, *One Third of a Nation* seemed to confirm the existing emphasis on maximum use of public lands, a trend many believed had brought the nation to the brink of environmental Armageddon by 1970. To this increasingly influential group of critics, Wayne Aspinall's mere affiliation with the PLLRC provided yet another reason why he might be considered the nation's most dangerous environmental foe.

THE MINERS' FRIEND

Aspinall's relations with the mining industry reveal his faith in the traditional uses of public land and demonstrate how the events of the late 1960s and early 1970s left him, in the words of a popular song from the era, somewhat "dazed and confused." Wayne Aspinall had always felt comfortable in the presence of people who worked with their hands, shaping the earth toward some useful end. Cattle ranchers, irrigation farmers, and miners were held by Aspinall in almost reverential awe. As a congressman, inspired by a political worldview of constant scientific and economic progress, Aspinall worked to see that these people, an influential sector of his Western Slope constituency, would always be able to wrest a good living from the region's public lands.

Aspinall equated a healthy mining industry with the national interest. In a 1966 address—"Public Land Policies for Progress"—delivered to the Climax Molybdenum Company, Aspinall invited the mining industry to "make known your interest for the public land policies of the future." Aspinall loved to scold delegates to state and national mining-association meetings about their need to devote more attention to public relations: "one of the greatest shortcomings of the mining industry," Aspinall told the 1967 meeting of the American Mining Congress, "is its failure to tell its story to the general public."[55] Aspinall never saw a dark side to the West's mining industry, and in his defense, few people of his generation gave deep thought to its often sorrowful environmental legacy.

If the mining industry proved reluctant to promote itself, Aspinall never hesitated to act as its chief public-relations officer. He made it a career-long task to sing its praises. In particular, Congressman Aspinall had a strong affiliation with the uranium and oil-shale industries; both had a considerable presence in the Fourth Congressional District. Both were characterized by an entrepreneurial spirit that Aspinall admired. In addition, both industries based their hopes for the future on the advances of science and technology. A member of the

Congressional Joint Committee on Atomic Energy since 1961, Aspinall became a tireless promoter of uranium mining and the nation's nuclear future. His interest in uranium was not accidental; his congressional district was home to the largest concentrations of uranium ore in the United States. A regional office of the Atomic Energy Commission opened its doors in Grand Junction, and uranium refineries were located in the Western Slope communities of Grand Junction, Rifle, Maybell, Gunnison, Uravan, Naturita, Slick Rock, and Durango. Several major mining companies participated in the uranium business in western Colorado, including Climax, Karmac, Union Carbide, U.S. Vanadium, and others.[56] Always an advocate of high guaranteed prices for uranium, Aspinall all too often overlooked or downplayed the hazards and serious environmental and personal tolls inflicted by the uranium and nuclear-energy industry.

In 1967, the Joint Committee on Atomic Energy held hearings on the issue of radiation exposure among uranium miners. This in itself was something of a miracle. The Joint Committee usually functioned as a mouthpiece for the uranium and nuclear-energy industry. The committee's sudden interest in this health question was inspired by public awareness and outrage over health conditions in the uranium-mining field. In March 1967 the *Washington Post* published an article detailing the high incidence of lung cancer among Colorado uranium miners. Until this point, the American public had rarely thought about uranium mining. If it did, it was considered in the Cold War context of bomb shelters, and the magnificent promise of nuclear energy as the nation's future fuel of choice.

The hearings, lasting from May to August 1967, focused on the need to establish radiation exposure standards for uranium miners. Though a high incidence of cancer among miners was confirmed, a parade of state, federal, and corporate officials tried to downplay the health threat. Aspinall, who remained unconvinced that strict standards were needed, argued that the uranium companies should not be singled out for condemnation. After all, they were merely serving their country, mining and preparing a critical substance for the nation's Cold War efforts. Even though the mining companies, not surprisingly, objected to health standards, they had been cooperative during the hearings. "If you represented these people as I do, you would expect this [high level of cooperation] because this has been their history for all time. When they were given the call to serve their country by furnishing uranium, they did what was expected of them." Although Aspinall undoubtedly admired the entrepreneurial spirit that characterized the uranium industry, he neglected to mention that the mining companies may also have been motivated by generous federal subsidies and great corporate profits.[57]

With the scientific community and general public becoming aware of serious health hazards derived from exposure to uranium, radon, and sister elements, Aspinall remained an unabashed promoter of nuclear energy. As he told the

National Western Mining Conference in 1968, the recent hearings "succeeded in setting straight some of the misleading statements . . . on projections of excessive mortality and the assumed effects of radiation at very low levels." Confident that science and technology could conquer any occupational hazards, Aspinall remained wildly optimistic that nuclear power would hold a central place in the nation's energy future. His layman's faith in technology led him to the conclusion that the uranium industry was worth what he saw as "minor" health risks to individual miners; the mining companies would move to correct these problems without undue government intervention, he believed. "I stand ready to help," he told the National Western Mining Conference.[58]

Aspinall was always ready to help the industry, especially in his capacity as chair of the Raw Materials Subcommittee of the Joint Committee on Atomic Energy. The committee recommended continuation of government programs to guarantee a healthy market for uranium production. In addition, he was in a perfect position to see how the nation's atomic energy program might benefit the Fourth Congressional District. In the early 1960s, the AEC purchased uranium mainly for the production of nuclear weapons. During Aspinall's tenure on the Joint Committee on Atomic Energy, the emphasis shifted to nonmilitary applications such as power production, medicine, agriculture, and, to Aspinall's delight, mining. This AEC shift thrilled Aspinall, who envisioned a healthy uranium market for the many large and small uranium producers in his district. The federal government's uranium purchase program was due to expire on December 31, 1966. Aspinall worked diligently to discover new markets for the nation's uranium supply, hoping that the federal government would extend its purchase program. To Aspinall's pleasure, in November 1962, the AEC ensured the domestic uranium market through 1970.[59]

Two things worked to undermine Aspinall's credibility as a spokesperson for the nation's nuclear future. The first was the 1969 detonation of a 40-kiloton underground explosive device at Rulison, Colorado, in an attempt to stimulate the production of natural gas. The second was Aspinall's difficulty in reacting to rising public concern over health hazards created by the Western Slope's warm embrace of the uranium industry. Both exposed Aspinall's almost naive faith in scientific progress. By the early 1970s, when the United States began questioning its earlier infatuation with atomic energy, many Coloradans were perplexed by their congressman's continued optimism about the uranium industry and nuclear power.

Aspinall had particular faith in the Project Plowshare Program, which had the potential to integrate some of his strongest political interests, applying the power of nuclear energy to the mining industry. The origins of Project Plowshare are embedded in the 1954 Atomic Energy Act, which states that "the development, use, and control of atomic energy shall be directed so as to make the maximum contribution to the general welfare" with a "program of conducting, assisting, and fostering research and development in order to encourage maximum scientific and industrial progress."[60] Project Plowshare was authorized by the AEC to investigate and develop peaceful applications for nuclear explosives. The program, inaugurated in 1957, envisioned three categories of peaceful applications for nuclear explosives: excavation, natural-resource development (also known as "underground engineering"), and scientific research. Aspinall envisioned the immediate benefits for underground engineering in his part of the West. A 1966 AEC study discussed the possibility of using explosives to fracture oil-shale formations to stimulate the permeability of low-productivity natural-gas fields. Aspinall found this type of peaceful nuclear application fascinating, especially since it could benefit the Fourth Congressional District's mining industry. He supported the project enthusiastically, finding the collaboration between the private sector and the federal government—in this case the AEC—on atomic-energy exploration and research exciting.[61] A willing mouthpiece for the atomic industry, Aspinall routinely gave speeches to organizations interested in AEC activities, including the American Nuclear Society. The evidence suggests that many of these talks were written by the staff of the Joint Committee on Atomic Energy.[62]

The Rulison experiment had its origins in Project Plowshare's plan to use nuclear explosives to stimulate gas production from deep and low-productivity gas reservoirs. By 1966, Aspinall was publicly intimating that the AEC, in concert with the private sector, was contemplating several experiments to demonstrate the feasibility of using nuclear blasts for gas production. In a June 1966 address, Aspinall revealed that the powerful Joint Committee had overruled the objections of the Bureau of the Budget to schedule the first such nuclear experiment: Project Gasbuggy in northern New Mexico's San Juan Basin.[63]

With the 26-kiloton Gasbuggy explosion on December 10, 1967, western Colorado became suspicious of risks associated with underground nuclear blasts. At the moment of detonation, a shower of rocks fell from the ceiling of the Anvil Points oil-shale mine near Rifle, Colorado. Was this a coincidence or not? Immediately, rumors began circulating, alleging that "seismic waves from the Gasbuggy event caused a fall of rock from the roof" of the Anvil Points mine. The connection could not be proven, but scientists and government officials did not discount the possibility. Another popular explanation blamed passing Denver and Rio Grande trains for loosening the rocks. The conclusions of official investigations into the Anvil Points incident centered on the need to "concern ourselves with mining properties out to a considerably greater distance than we have previously thought" when conducting underground nuclear detonations. Gasbuggy, a small blast when compared with what was on the AEC's drawing board, took place 195 miles south of Anvil Points.[64]

Though clear evidence of the merits of the Gasbuggy blast were still lacking, AEC scientists and private-sector financiers moved confidently forward to the next experiment, at Rulison, Colorado. Located seventy miles from Grand Junction, the Rulison "shot," as it locally became known, would be a 40-kiloton blast—more than twice the power of the Hiroshima bomb. By 1969, however, the American public had awakened to the dangers of radiation, nuclear power, and unchecked political authority. This experiment seemed to play to the deepest concerns of many Coloradans. No longer blindly trusting of political authority, many Western Slope citizens resented having their home region turned into a nuclear playground, voicing fears of possible "lingering effects of low level radiation . . . present in the Rulison gas."[65]

The scientific and engineering side of Project Rulison developed fast, and last-minute safety concerns were all but overlooked, necessitating a three-month-plus delay. In addition, the secretary of the interior, Walter Hickel, was, in the words of one AEC official, "gun shy" over the reactions of environmental groups to the scheduled detonation. One AEC official, exasperated over the holdup, recommended proceeding with future blasts without the support of the Interior Department. At a series of local public meetings, citizens voiced concerns over possible radiation contamination and other health hazards. Two significant worries that surfaced concerned the detonation's potential impact on local dams and reservoirs, including the nearby Collbran Project and Harvey Gap Reservoir, not far from Rifle. Aspinall, too, grew impatient with the delay and pointed his finger, out of public view, at Rulison planners who should have known about these local safety issues "months and years ago" rather than at the last minute.[66]

As the Rulison Project's early September detonation, which had been rescheduled several times, grew closer, public fears over its immediate and long-range health hazards grew. The Aspen, Colorado, city council passed a resolution against the explosion, expressing concern over "possible immediate and long-range dangers of the blast." Local newspapers carried opinions for and against the explosion. After several more short delays due to less-than-optimal weather, the Rulison blast took place at 3:00 P.M. on September 10, 1969. The shot was witnessed by 300 invited observers, an estimated twenty to thirty media representatives, and several groups of demonstrators. According to the AEC's official report, the surrounding communities of Grand Valley, Collbran, Rulison, Rifle, DeBeque, and Glenwood Springs "all felt distinct ground motion," which "observers likened to that of a minor earthquake." Damage reports were minor: a few rocks dislodged, reports of cracked plaster, windows, and house foundations. About $60,000 in claims were eventually filed.[67]

Several issues related to the Rulison Project hurt Aspinall's political reputation. Anti-nuclear protests both before and after the blast linked his name to AEC use of western Colorado as an experimental site. Controversy surrounding Project Plowshare on the Western Slope inspired another round of protests when the next blast occurred in 1973 at Rio Blanco, seventy miles northeast of

Grand Junction. In 1974, the high-tide mark of modern liberalism in Colorado, the state's voters passed a law ending further nuclear explosions unless they were first approved by statewide vote.[68]

Some Colorado politicians began distancing themselves from Project Plowshare after Rulison, but Wayne Aspinall was not among them. He remained as upbeat as ever about the nation's nuclear future. Placing full trust in scientific and technical experts who built the nation's bombs or dams was a habit adopted early in his congressional career. Aspinall seemed pleased by the Rulison shot, observing that local damage had not been "as serious as what was projected." When Senator Daniel K. Inouye (D-HI) called Aspinall's attention to potential tsunamis following another scheduled Plowshare blast in the Aleutian Islands, Aspinall indicated that he was not "too concerned over what apparently alarms you." To constituents' worries over the Rulison shot, Aspinall expressed confidence that all scientific safety projections had been met. In his view, innovative experiments like Rulison were necessary to keep abreast of the nation's future energy needs. "Americans," he told a concerned constituent, were "demanding so many of the good things of life today," and those good things had to come from somewhere; all the nation's luxuries—indeed, its very economy—he told her, came from the earth and the substances within it. For better or worse, Aspinall continued to trust the nation's atomic energy experts.[69]

While Aspinall remained true to his intellectual moorings by supporting the nuclear experiments of the Plowshare program, the discontent emerging from Grand Junction and other Western Slope towns that had so willingly embraced the atom during and after World War II only grew stronger. Uranium contamination became a major public issue in Colorado and the West after 1966, when the U.S. Public Health Service and the AEC publicly disagreed over the danger posed by uranium tailings dotting the Western Slope. As the story unfolded, the Colorado congressman was genuinely puzzled over how to react. Aspinall, the most prominent federal figure on the Western Slope, was the person local citizens and town officials looked to for leadership when demanding compensation and remediation for uranium hazards. But it was on this issue that loyalty to his constituents clashed with his faith in science. Aspinall would only reluctantly provide a measure of help on this crucial public-health issue.

Uranium tailings—refuse materials resulting from the processing of uranium ores—have a long radioactive half-life and pose a real public threat if they leach into local river systems or blow into surrounding population areas. Public concern skyrocketed following a report by the U.S. Public Health Service (dated October 1965 but revealed to the public in March 1966) that recommended taking "immediate, interim steps" to stabilize tailings piles. The Public Health Service warned particularly of the dangers radium contamination posed to the West's rivers and reservoirs. In an analysis of the Public Health Service study, *The New Republic* reported that the AEC opposed the report's release, a point explicitly denied by AEC officials.[70] The AEC and the Department of Health, Education, and Welfare continued to deny that the tailings piles posed a threat to human health. The AEC concluded that "from a radiological safety stand-point," licensing control of the piles was unnecessary. The State of Colorado began monitoring the issue in 1966, urging the AEC not to allow private com-panies to cease mill operations until the tailings piles had been stabilized for safety.[71]

The issue of public health pitted the AEC and Joint Committee on Atomic Energy against a growing public perception that western Colorado's health was being compromised by official inaction. Wayne Aspinall was placed in the un-comfortable position of representing both the "official" viewpoint of the AEC and the interests of his western Colorado constituents. He instinctively trusted the technical experts of the AEC, believing the public's health could not be in serious danger. In a revealing exchange with a constituent from Durango who feared public-health problems from local mill tailings, Aspinall assured the man that the AEC and the Joint Committee on Atomic Energy were not "trying to whitewash" any health issues. He then defended his refusal to criticize the companies that provided the United States with nuclear fuel. Companies like Vanadium Company of America came to the nation's aid during times of emer-gency. His less-than-critical perspective stemmed in part from his admiration of the uranium industry's patriotic role during World War II and the Cold War.[72]

From the time the public began worrying about mill tailings, the AEC and the Joint Committee on Atomic Energy maintained a consistent position until late 1971: "the uranium piles in the Colorado River Basin present no radiologi-cal health hazards at the present." Significantly, John T. Conway, executive director of the Joint Committee on Atomic Energy, advised Aspinall that the AEC's uranium-procurement contracts did not require mill operators to take "any specific action with respect to tailings management." Wayne Aspinall would publicly uphold these positions until the AEC later revised its official position. The Joint Committee's staff carefully monitored media coverage of developing public concern over the tailings and combated negative news with rejoinders, letters to the editor, and campaigns to correct the record. Officials of the AEC trailed a CBS news crew across the Western Slope in 1966 as it filmed stories of possible tailings hazards.[73]

Public concern over uranium-related hazards in western Colorado seemed to ebb and flow with the changing tenor of news reports on the issue, but by the end of the decade, the "cultural revolution" had permanently altered the nation's attitudes toward uranium and radiation. Historian Hal Rothman has noted that the nation's "growing distrust of government" linked with an expanding inter-est in environmentalism to make anti-nuclear sentiment a major part of the environmental agenda.[74] In Grand Junction, a town once proudly known as "America's Atomic Capital," the mill-tailing concern took a new and deadly twist in the late 1960s with the revelation that since the early 1950s, thousands of Grand Junction homes, businesses, and schools had been built with tailings material as construction fill. In some cases tailings had been mixed with concrete and used to stabilize buildings. Modern Grand Junction had been literally built upon a radioactive foundation.

The tailings problem exploded in 1970 when both national and regional news media began assessing the magnitude of Grand Junction's problem. A *McCall's* magazine story from late 1970 labeled Grand Junction "America's Most Radioactive City," noting with irony that it had once called itself the "All-American City with Foresight." Between 1952 and 1966, at least 3,000 buildings were constructed utilizing tailings material from the Climax Uranium mill located along the Colorado River near downtown Grand Junction. The article, written by Nancy Wood, indicted the AEC for failing to take a stand against the health risks posed by the tailings piles, which were so high that local residents referred to them as "the dunes." Children routinely played among and climbed the radioactive hills. Most Grand Junction residents had no idea that their new homes were built, in many cases, atop layers of radioactive sand. Wood found one local AEC official who admitted to knowing that local builders were using the tailings in their construction efforts, but he insisted that the AEC had no legal authority to halt the tailings removals.[75]

The commission's official mantra for years had been that residents had nothing to fear from tailings-related health hazards. By the late 1960s, however, both the U.S. Public Health Service and Colorado state health officials had begun questioning the AEC's position. In 1970, the Colorado Health Department began surveying homes built with mill tailings and concluded, after only preliminary studies, that the radiation levels often exceeded safe levels, with some readings "dangerously high for human occupancy."[76]

During the 1960s, the AEC's official legal position, apparent in memorandum upon memorandum, stressed that once uranium had been processed by AEC contractors, the byproducts were not the commission's legal responsibility. Since the days of the Manhattan Project, the federal government's emphasis in Grand Junction had been to find the necessary raw materials and bring them to the mills for processing. Grand Junction had grown accustomed to living with the nuclear industry, which had provided a good living for many Western Slope citizens. Most nuclear facilities, ranging from those emphasizing nuclear weaponry, such as suburban Denver's Rocky Flats, to the standard rural Western Slope uranium mill, had engaged in de facto programs of waste storage and management.[77] But the emphasis on fast production, rooted in Cold War perceptions of imminent danger, tended to overlook long-term storage and disposal questions that a more environmentally sensitive American public was now concerning itself with. Amidst the accusations and finger pointing of the late 1960s and early 1970s, the AEC continued to claim immunity from responsibility while arguing that the State of Colorado needed to manage the tailings. The State argued that it had been left out of the atomic-energy decisions. Why, then, was it suddenly the State's responsibility to clean up the mess that had been made on Colorado's federal lands?[78]

The political toll mounted with every month of inaction. Still, Aspinall's faith in AEC scientists remained strong, despite calls for the Joint Committee on Atomic Energy to "control its unruly child," the AEC. "I do not believe there is any cause for alarm" over the Grand Junction situation, Aspinall maintained in August 1970. The AEC, he argued, parroting the official party line, had "discharged its legal responsibility as far as off-site uses of mill tailings from uranium piles were concerned." The only problem Aspinall saw involved public relations: the AEC needed to be more "vigorous in providing information and leadership to state and local health authorities." The Colorado congressman continued to discount the health risks from Grand Junction's tailings.[79]

With a public-relations and possible public-health nightmare on its hands, the City of Grand Junction demanded action. In writing the *McCall's* article, author Nancy Wood had interviewed a radiological health expert who predicted that within two years, "Grand Junction could be declared a disaster area." In November 1970, the Grand Junction Chamber of Commerce formed a committee to inspire state and federal officials to act on the city's behalf. Grand Junction officials believed that the mere semblance of remedial action would go a long way toward restoring public confidence in the city's health environment. Still, pressing questions remained: who would take responsibility for the situation, what needed to be done, and who would pay for any remedial action?[80] Dale Hollingsworth, director of the Grand Junction Chamber of Commerce during this nightmare era, remembered that it was perceived danger, more than actual danger, that devastated the city's image.[81]

By 1971, pressure for the AEC and Congress to take action became intense. In testimony presented in Denver before Aspinall's Raw Materials Subcommittee in late October, several scientists claimed that exposure to the tailings in homes, businesses, and public buildings could lead to genetic problems, cancer, and lower birthrates. The Colorado Health Department was also openly calling for the removal of the tailings from buildings by this time. The major breakthrough that sparked official remediation efforts occurred on December 7, 1971, when James Schlesinger, chair of the AEC, admitted its mistake in allowing the tailings to be used in construction. Schlesinger further indicated that the federal government might be willing to defray a portion of the tailings-removal costs. Admitting only partial AEC wrongdoing, Schlesinger was careful not to shoulder all the blame. There was plenty to spread around—the State of Colorado, the private companies who milled the uranium, and the construction companies who used the tailings all deserved a share of the condemnation. Schlesinger reminded the press that the agency "had no legal responsibility for the situation" but felt a "moral" need to admit that a health risk might exist. Grand Junction, Schlesinger asserted, was in "no immediate danger," but the radiation levels in many buildings were "higher than we would prefer." Remedial action would therefore be taken. Aspinall, who had discussed with Schlesinger at length the possible shape of remediation legislation, suggested to Ken Johnson, editor of the *Daily Sentinel*, that securing money from Congress for the project would be no easy chore.[82]

Before Schlesinger's admission of "moral responsibility," the *Daily Sentinel* believed that both Aspinall and the AEC were now regarded in a "bad light" by some Western Slope residents. After a constituent accused Aspinall of being a tool of the AEC, the congressman was forced to deny "advancing the cause of the Atomic Energy Commission against the needs of the people whom I have the honor to represent." After the fall 1971 hearings and the AEC's admission of partial responsibility, Aspinall could begin drafting federal legislation to provide cleanup money. Still, several questions remained. How much responsibility should the federal government take? What share of the funds should the State of Colorado contribute, if any? What radiation levels should be considered safe?[83]

Grand Junction officials were encouraged by the news that the AEC and the federal government had accepted "some responsibility," calling it a "breakthrough" but not the "final answer." On February 9, 1972, Aspinall introduced H.R. 13068, which authorized funds for the AEC to arrange with the State of Colorado to share tailings-removal costs. Colorado senators Gordon Allott and Peter Dominick introduced Senate bills identical to Aspinall's. H.R. 13068 authorized the AEC to provide up to 75 percent of the costs of a state remedial-action program. Aspinall made it clear that his bill reflected neither "legal liability nor responsibility" on the part of the AEC or the State of Colorado. At the same time, appropriate legislation was introduced in the Colorado General Assembly to provide the remainder of the necessary funding.[84]

The bill passed Congress in 1972, and Grand Junction officials hoped that remediation efforts might begin by the end of the year. The federal government planned to contribute $5 million; the State of Colorado was committed to contributing an additional $1.66 million. The scope of this first remediation program was actually quite small, with only about 1,500 structures targeted for varying levels of cleanup. In 1978, a much more ambitious and effective remediation program, the Uranium Mill Tailings Remedial Action (UMTRA) Project, passed Congress. Larger in scope, UMTRA addressed more than the use of tailings in construction, focusing on the stabilization, disposal, and control of tailings piles in nine western states plus Pennsylvania and only requiring the states to foot 10 percent of the bill. UMTRA's original cost estimate was $300–$500 million in fiscal 1981 dollars.[85]

The tailings disaster would dominate Grand Junction's modern history long after Wayne Aspinall had left Congress, retired to Colorado, and died. UMTRA maintained a presence in the Grand Valley and throughout the Western Slope until the 1990s. Both the Rulison shot and the uranium public-health debacle damaged Aspinall's credibility at a time when he was under attack on many fronts from environmental groups. His relentless promotion of the uranium industry and the perception that his dealings with the PLLRC favored corporate activities on the West's public lands led to allegations that he was insensitive to the environment and to public-health worries. Collectively, these events opened Aspinall to charges that he had lost his perspective and had fallen out of touch with the concerns of average constituents. Aspinall would be forced to battle these allegations throughout 1972, another election year.

ENDNOTES

1. Grand Junction (CO) *Daily Sentinel*, October 10, 1983.

2. *Rocky Mountain News*, May 2, 1965. Another key environmentalist bill that Aspinall was criticized for delaying was the Wild and Scenic Rivers Bill. It passed Congress in 1968.

3. Irving Bernstein, *Guns or Butter: The Presidency of Lyndon Johnson* (New York: Oxford University Press, 1996), 266–267.

4. Wayne N. Aspinall interview with Al Look, Mesa County Oral History Project (OH-120, Part 1), Research Center and Special Library, Museum of Western Colorado, Grand Junction, CO (hereafter cited as MWC), January 10, 1978.

5. Wayne N. Aspinall interview with Joe B. Frantz, Lyndon B. Johnson Presidential Library (hereafter cited as LBJPL), June 14, 1974.

6. The record is truly remarkable for the Johnson years, 1963–1968. The Johnson record shows sixteen new national historic sites, six new national recreation areas, four national monuments, four national parks, three national memorials, five national seashores and lakeshores, one farm park, one international park, one national scenic riverway, and one national scenic trail. See Bernstein, *Guns or Butter*, 272–273.

7. Stewart L. Udall interview with author, Grand Junction, CO, March 31 and April 1, 1998.

8. Carol Edmunds, *Wayne Aspinall: Mr. Chairman* (Lakewood, CO: Crown Point, 1980), 184; Gary E. Elliott, *Senator Alan Bible and the Politics of the New West* (Reno: University of Nevada Press, 1994), 142–143; Stewart L. Udall, "Report to the President," May 18, 1965, Box 121, fd: 7, Stewart L. Udall Papers, Special Collections, University of Arizona Library, Tucson, AZ (hereafter cited as SCUAL).

9. Susan R. Schrepfer, *The Fight to Save the Redwoods: A History of Environmental Reform, 1917–1978* (Madison: University of Wisconsin Press, 1983), 143–144; Stewart L. Udall, memorandum to the president, August 31, 1966, Box 226, fd: "Aspinall, Wayne, Cong.," Name Files, Lyndon B. Johnson Presidential Papers, LBJPL.

10. Wayne N. Aspinall to Richard D. Lamm, February 3, 1967, Box 276, fd: "L-11-d," Wayne Aspinall Papers, University of Denver Archives, Denver, CO (hereafter cited as UDA); Lyndon Johnson to Wayne Aspinall, July 10, 1967, and Wayne N. Aspinall to Lyndon Johnson July 12, 1967, Box 226, fd: "Aspinall, Wayne, Cong.," Name Files, Lyndon B. Johnson Presidential Papers, LBJPL.

11. Stewart L. Udall, "Report to the President," October 10, 1967, Box 133, fd: "Reports to the President," Stewart L. Udall Papers, SCUAL; Schrepfer, *Fight to Save the Redwoods*, 150.

12. Schrepfer, *Fight to Save the Redwoods*, 151–152.

13. Ibid., 154; Wayne N. Aspinall to Horace Marden Albright, June 11, 1968, Box 310, fd: "L-11-d," Wayne Aspinall Papers, UDA.

14. Ernest J. Easton to Wayne N. Aspinall, June 17, 1968, Box 326, fd: "L-11-d," Wayne Aspinall Papers, UDA.

15. Alan Merson to Wayne N. Aspinall, July 11, 1968, and Wayne N. Aspinall to Alan Merson, July 17, 1968, Box 326, fd: "L-11-d," Wayne Aspinall Papers, UDA; Schrepfer, *Fight to Save the Redwoods*, 155–156.

16. Larry Brown, *Aspinall* (Gunnison, CO: Western State College Foundation, 1996), 34; Ira Whitlock, memorandum to Secretary Udall, September 9, 1968, Box 138, fd: "SLU and Staff (Ira Whitlock)," Stewart L. Udall Papers, SCUAL.

17. Edmunds, *Wayne Aspinall*, 187–188; Wayne N. Aspinall to C. E. Moritz, August 5, 1968, Box 310, fd: "L-11-d," Wayne Aspinall Papers, UDA.

18. See the correspondence (list follows) in Box 12, fd: "Udall National Monuments," Office of the President, Lyndon B. Johnson Presidential Papers, LBJPL. Udall to President Johnson, July 7, 1968; DeVier Pierson to President Johnson, December 6, 1968; DeVier Pierson to President Johnson, December 12, 1968; Stewart Udall to President Johnson, December 19, 1968; DeVier Pierson to President Johnson, January 9, 1969; Stewart Udall to President Johnson, January 10, 1969; DeVier Pierson, memorandum for the file, January 19, 1969; Office of the White House Press Secretary, news release, January 20, 1969. Hal Rothman, *America's National Monuments: The Politics of Preservation* (Lawrence: University of Kansas Press, 1989), details this episode and discusses Aspinall's earlier anger at President Eisenhower for circumventing Congress in creating the C & O Canal National Monument during the final days of his administration in 1961, 224–227.

19. See the correspondence in Box 12, fd: "Udall National Monuments," Office of the President, Lyndon B. Johnson Presidential Papers, LBJPL; Wayne N. Aspinall interview with Nancy Whistler, Association of Former Members of Congress Project, Manuscript Division, Library of Congress, Washington, DC, February 15, 1979.

20. John Carver interview with William Moss, John F. Kennedy Presidential Library, November 18, 1969.

21. Stewart L. Udall to Wayne N. Aspinall, January 20, 1969, Box 181, fd: "Department of the Interior. Misc. Correspondence, January 1969," Wayne Aspinall Papers, UDA; David R. Brower, "Environmental Activist, Publicist, and Prophet," oral history conducted by Susan R. Schrepfer, Regional Oral History Office, the Bancroft Library, University of California at Berkeley, 1974–1978, 171; see correspondence in Box 12, fd: "Udall National Monuments," Office of the President, Lyndon B. Johnson Presidential Papers, LBJPL.

22. Memorandum to the president, June 5, 1967, Box 226, fd: "Aspinall, Wayne, Cong.," Name Files, Lyndon B. Johnson Presidential Papers, LBJPL; Wayne Aspinall interview, June 14, 1974.

23. Barefoot Saunders to President Johnson, March 25, 1968, Box 226, fd: "Aspinall, Wayne, Cong.," Name Files, Lyndon B. Johnson Presidential Papers, LBJPL; Robert Dallek, *Flawed Giant: Lyndon Johnson and His Times, 1961–1973* (New York: Oxford University Press, 1998), 528–530.

24. Wayne N. Aspinall, *Capitol Comments*, March 14, 1964, Box 166, fd: "L-113-2-c," Wayne Aspinall Papers, UDA; John F. Kennnedy to Wayne N. Aspinall, January 17, 1963, Box 489, fd: "LE/NR-1–LE/NR-6-1, White House Central Files, John F. Kennedy Presidential Papers, John F. Kennedy Presidential Library, Boston, MA (hereafter cited as JFKPL).

25. Phillip S. Hughes to Lee White, n.d., ca. January 1963, Box 7, fd: "Public Land Laws Study, 8/1/62–6/25/63," White House Staff Files, Lee White General Files, John F. Kennedy Presidential Papers, JFKPL.

26. "Draft Plan, Land Laws Review," Box 7, fd: "Public Land Laws Study, 8/1/62–6/25/63," White House Staff Files, Lee White General Files, John F. Kennedy Presidential Papers, JFKPL.

27. *Albuquerque Journal*, August 25, 1963. Paul R. Wieck of the *Journal's* Washington Bureau speculated that Anderson might "play rough" with Aspinall's PLLRC legislation to help pry the Wilderness Bill from Aspinall's clutches. Wieck recalled that Anderson had used the same tactic in 1962 to move New Mexico's Navajo–San Juan Project out of committee.

28. See p. 15 of Ralph Nader Task Force, "Citizens Look at Congress: Wayne Aspinall," Box 1, fd: 13, Wayne N. Aspinall Papers, University of Colorado Archives, University of Colorado at Boulder, Boulder, CO.

29. Wayne N. Aspinall, *Capital Comments*, March 14, 1964.

30. Robert G. Kaufman, *Henry M. Jackson: A Life in Politics* (Seattle: University of Washington Press, 2000), 167, cites an interview with Stewart L. Udall as the source for this statement.

31. See PLLRC director Milton A. Pearl's article "Public Land Commissions," *Our Public Lands* 17, No. 2 (Summer 1967), 14–17. *Our Public Lands* was the official magazine of the Bureau of Land Management. Pearl summarizes previous land commissions and what distinguishes the PLLRC from the others.

32. Pearl, "Public Land Commissions," 17.

33. See PL 88-606, 78 Stat. 982; Pearl, "Public Land Commissions," 14.

34. Wayne Aspinall interview, June 14, 1974.

35. Ibid.

36. Wayne N. Aspinall to Ed Johnson, January 8, 1965, and Aspinall to J. Fred Schneider, January 26, 1965, Box 186, fd: 48, Wayne Aspinall Papers, UDA; *County Mail*, February 3, 1965.

37. John W. Macy, Jr., to Wayne N. Aspinall, January 11, 1965, and Wayne N. Aspinall to John W. Macy, Jr., January 13, 1965, Box 186, fd: 48, Wayne Aspinall Papers, UDA.

38. Elmer Staats to Lee White, n.d., ca. July 1965, Box 405, fd: "PLLRC," White House Central Files, Lyndon B. Johnson Presidential Papers, LBJPL; Wayne N. Aspinall to James G. Patton, August 12, 1965, Box 186, fd: 48, Wayne Aspinall Papers, UDA.

39. See Library of Congress, Legislative Research Service, *The Public Land Law Review Commission* (Washington, DC: Legislative Reference Service, 1970), in Box 406, fd: 48, Wayne Aspinall Papers, UDA; J. Brooks Flippen, *Nixon and the Environment* (Albuquerque: University of New Mexico Press, 2000), 95.

40. Wayne N. Aspinall, "The Public Land Law Review Commission: Origins and Goals," *Natural Resources Journal* 7, no. 2 (1967): 149-152.

41. Memorandum for the CAP files, September 13, 1967, Box 4, fd: 2, Carl Hayden Papers, Special Collections, Arizona State University Library, Tempe, AZ (hereafter cited as SCASUL); Carl Hayden to Charles L. Schultze, December 6, 1967, Box 4, fd: 2, Carl Hayden Papers, SCASUL.

42. "Remarks of Honorable Wayne N. Aspinall, Chairman, Public Land Law Review Commission, at the Western Mining Conference, Denver, Colorado, February 1, 1969," Box 355, fd: "Pub 6," Wayne Aspinall Papers, UDA.

43. Helene C. Monberg to Wayne N. Aspinall and Milton Pearl, May 25, 1969; Samuel J. Archibald to Wayne N. Aspinall, February 21, 1969; and Milton A. Pearl to Members of the Public Land Law Review Commission, March 14, 1969, all in Box 333, fd: "48a," Wayne Aspinall Papers, UDA.

44. Monberg to Aspinall and Pearl, May 25, 1969.

45. "Remarks of Honorable Wayne N. Aspinall Before the National Western Mining Conference, Denver, CO, February 14, 1970," Box 369, fd: 48, Wayne Aspinall Papers, UDA; *Rocky Mountain News*, February 15, 1970.

46. Legislative Reference Service, *The Public Land Law Review Commission* (August 1970), Box 369, fd: 48, Wayne Aspinall Papers, UDA, contains a digest of the larger report and lists the recommendations. See pages 9, 21-22; Roy M. Robbins, *Our Landed Heritage: The Public Domain, 1776-1970*, 2d ed. (Lincoln: University of Nebraska Press, 1976), 476; Elliott, *Senator Alan Bible*, 179; Edmunds, *Wayne Aspinall*, 229-230.

47. Newspaper reactions quoted in Robbins, *Our Landed Heritage*, 470-471.

48. Michael P. Cohen, *The History of the Sierra Club, 1892-1970* (San Francisco: Sierra Club Books, 1988), 448; Stewart L. Udall, "On Environment," *Chicago News*, July 13, 1970, in Box 369, fd: 48, Wayne Aspinall Papers, UDA; Ralph Nader Task Force, "Citizens Look at Congress," 16; Harold Peterson, "Moving in for a Land Grab," *Sports Illustrated* 33, no. 2 (July 13, 1970): 27; Flippen, *Nixon and the Environment*, 95-96.

49. Peterson, "Moving in for a Land Grab," 27.

50. Nader Task Force, "Citizens Look at Congress," 17; Edmunds, *Wayne Aspinall*, 238.

51. Edmunds, *Wayne Aspinall*, 238; James Muhn and Hanson R. Stuart, *Opportunity and Challenge: The Story of BLM* (Washington, DC: U.S. Department of the Interior, 1988), 166-172; Wayne N. Aspinall, "Speech to the Bureau of Land Management," Reno, NV, January 24 and 31, 1978, Vivian Passer Collection, Grand Junction, CO.

52. "Statement of Wayne N. Aspinall to the PLLRC Reunion, Denver, April 1-2, 1977," Box 36, fd: 14, Wayne Aspinall Papers, UCAUCB; Wayne N. Aspinall, "Prologue: Public Land Law Review Commission Revisited," *Denver Law Journal* 54, nos. 3-4 (1977): 383-384.

53. Rothman, *The Greening of a Nation?*, 84.

54. Ibid.

55. Wayne N. Aspinall, "Public Land Policies for Progress," November 19, 1966, Box 246, no file, Wayne Aspinall Papers, UDA; Wayne Aspinall comments to American Mining Congress, 1967, Vivian Passer Collection, Grand Junction, CO.

56. Robert Sullenberger, "100 Years of Uranium Activity in the Four Corners Region," *Journal of the Western Slope* 7, no. 4 (1992): 1–82.

57. Peter H. Eichstaedt, *If You Poison Us: Uranium and Native Americans* (Santa Fe, NM: Red Crane Books, 1994), 93–94; *Washington Post,* March 9, 1967; *Radiation Exposure of Uranium Miners,* Hearings, Subcommittee on Research, Development, and Radiation, Joint Committee on Atomic Energy, 90th Cong., 1st Sess., May 9–August 10, 1967.

58. Wayne N. Aspinall, address to the National Western Mining Conference, "Nuclear Energy Fits in the Energy Fuels Program," February 9, 1968, Box 317, fd: "1968 Publicity," Wayne Aspinall Papers, UDA.

59. Wayne N. Aspinall interview, June 14, 1974; Wayne N. Aspinall, "Statement at Panel Discussion, American Mining Congress, September 13, 1961," Box 94, fd: "L-22-b," Wayne Aspinall Papers, UDA; Atomic Industrial Forum, "The Domestic Uranium Raw Materials Industry" (May 1962), Box 106, fd: "103-b," Wayne Aspinall Papers, UDA; Grand Junction *Daily Sentinel,* November 17, 1962.

60. "Plowshare, Filing Memo," October 1, 1966, Box 235, fd: "L-22," Wayne Aspinall Papers, UDA.

61. John T. Conway to Wayne N. Aspinall, June 20, 1966, Box 235, fd: "L-22-a," Wayne Aspinall Papers, UDA.

62. "Plowshare, Filing Memo"; Wayne N. Aspinall, statement, May 9, 1966, Box 235, fd: "L-22-a," Wayne Aspinall Papers, UDA.

63. Wayne N. Aspinall, "Remarks to 12th Annual Meeting of the American Nuclear Society, June 21, 1966," Box 235, fd: "L-22-a," Wayne Aspinall Papers, UDA.

64. Robert S. Brundage, memorandum to file, March 19, 1968, Box 305, fd: 100, Wayne Aspinall Papers, UDA.

65. See Christian J. Buys, "Isaiah's Prophecy: Project Plowshare in Colorado," *Colorado Heritage* 1 (1989): 33.

66. AEC news release, n.d., Box 342, fd: "100-b," Wayne Aspinall Papers, UDA; *Daily Sentinel,* March 30, 1969; Wayne N. Aspinall to Everett Collins, June 11, 1969, Box 340, fd: "100-a," Wayne Aspinall Papers, UDA.

67. Aspen (CO) City Council, Resolution No. 13, 1969, Box 351, fd: "L-22-a," Wayne Aspinall Papers, UDA; Atomic Energy Commission, "Project Rulison," September 12, 1969, Box 340, fd: "100-a," Wayne Aspinall Papers, UDA; Buys, "Isaiah's Prophecy," 36.

68. Buys, "Isaiah's Prophecy," 37.

69. Daniel K. Inouye to Wayne N. Aspinall, September 18, 1969, and Wayne N. Aspinall to Daniel K. Inouye, September 23, 1969, Box 340, fd: "100-a," Wayne Aspinall Papers, UDA; Wayne N. Aspinall to Mrs. Claude Graham, October 6, 1969, Box 340, fd: "100-a," Wayne Aspinall Papers, UDA.

70. Philippe G. Jacques to Gilbert A. Harrison, March 17, 1966, Box 235, fd: "L-22-a," Wayne Aspinall Papers, UDA; "Uranium Mystery in the Colorado Basin," *The New Republic* 154, no. 10 (March 5, 1966): 9.

71. U.S. Department of Health, Education, and Welfare, Federal Water Pollution Control Administration, news release, March 22, 1966, Box 235, fd: "L-22-a," Wayne Aspinall Papers, UDA; R. L. Cleare to Glenn T. Seaborg, April 23, 1966, Box 235, fd: "L-22-a," Wayne Aspinall Papers, UDA.

72. Wayne N. Aspinall to H. W. Hawk, April 25, 1966, Box 235, fd: "L-22-a," Wayne Aspinall Papers, UDA.

73. John T. Conway to All [Joint Committee] Members, May 5, 1966; John T. Conway to Wayne N. Aspinall, April 15, 1966; and John T. Conway to Wayne N. Aspinall, March 20, 1966, all in Box 235, fd: "L-22-a," Wayne Aspinall Papers, UDA.

74. Rothman, *Greening of a Nation?*, 143.

75. Nancy Wood, "America's Most Radioactive City," *McCall's* 97, no. 12 (September 1970): 46–122.

76. Script, *ABC Evening News*, January 26, 1970, Box 335, fd: "100-a," Wayne Aspinall Papers, UDA.

77. Bruce Hevly and John M. Findlay, "The Atomic West: Region and Nation," in *The Atomic West*, ed. Bruce Hevly and John M. Findlay (Seattle: University of Washington Press, 1998), 7.

78. Script, *ABC Evening News*, January 26, 1970.

79. Wayne N. Aspinall press release, August 14, 1970, which quotes Aspinall's remarks on the floor of Congress for August 12, 1970.

80. Wood, "America's Most Radioactive City," 46–122; Dale J. Hollingsworth to William Cleary, November 24, 1970, Box 376, fd: "100-d," Wayne Aspinall Papers, UDA.

81. Dale J. Hollingsworth interview with author, Grand Junction, CO, December 18, 1996.

82. *New York Times*, December 7, 1971; Wayne N. Aspinall to Ken Johnson, December 9, 1971, Box 426, fd: "L-22," Wayne Aspinall Papers, UDA.

83. *Daily Sentinel*, December 2, 1971; Wayne N. Aspinall to Kirk W. Whiteley, December 6, 1971, Box 426, fd: "L-22," Wayne Aspinall Papers, UDA.

84. *Daily Sentinel*, January 21, 1972; Wayne N. Aspinall to Gladys Wilson, January 25, 1972, Box 461, fd: "1972 Legis, JCAE, GJ Mill Tailings," Wayne Aspinall Papers, UDA; H.R. 13068 in *Use of Uranium Mill Tailings for Construction Purposes*, Hearings, Subcommittee on Raw Materials of the Joint Committee on Atomic Energy, 92d Cong., 1st Sess., 1971, 28–29; *Congressional Record*, February 9, 1972, H1013.

85. *DOE News*, April 18, 1985, in Uranium Mill Tailings Vertical File, John Tomlinson Library, Mesa State College, Grand Junction, CO.

CHAPTER SEVEN

THE JOURNEY HOME: ASPINALL RETURNS TO COLORADO, 1970–1983

FORESHADOWINGS: THE 1970 PRIMARY

Wayne Aspinall's congressional career is a magnificent study in western American political power: how to achieve it, how to hold it, and, ultimately, how to lose it. William Deverill wrote that "people who have had power in western American life have been reluctant to give it up."[1] Aspinall was no exception. All around him the signs were evident that he had overstayed his welcome in Washington. His foot-dragging on Wilderness, his obstructionist attitude toward new national parks, his continued enthusiasm for large-scale reclamation projects, and his inability to see the sinister side of nuclear power were only the most obvious indications that it was time to retire. Aspinall, however, remained oblivious, secure in his status as a living legend. Those closest to him, including irrigation district officials, state and regional water bureaucrats, cattle ranchers, and mining-industry representatives, all had a strong stake in Aspinall's continued presence in office. It was his role on the House Interior Committee—so important to western politics—that allowed these industries their special access to public lands and federal support.

The world was changing all around Wayne Aspinall. His wife's health, which had been delicate for years, began deteriorating in 1969. A stroke, followed by a bout with pneumonia, weakened her condition. On July 2, Julia had a pacemaker installed, but she died a week later, after forty-nine years of marriage. Less than two months after that, Wayne's brother, Ralph, died as well. In the fall of 1969, Aspinall seemed sad and somewhat confused but kept up his routine of hard work and his usual public demeanor. "I am back in the harness," he wrote sister Mary at the end of July, "trying to carry on enough work so that I don't have too much time on my hands." He had always enjoyed football, especially the Washington Redskins, and the fall of 1969 found him attending football games with House doorkeeper "Fishbait" Miller, to whom Aspinall had grown close over the years. By December 1969, Aspinall could report in the weekly newsletters he sent to his family that during the Christmas holidays, he had begun enjoying the company of Essie Best, recently widowed from Frank Best, an old Mount Lincoln School friend. Wayne had always considered Essie his first girlfriend; they had had a few dates when Aspinall, a year older than Essie, was in ninth grade.[2]

Now that Wayne and Essie were on their own, they began seeing more of each other. They married in Grand Junction on July 12, 1970, about a year after Julia's death. The union made Aspinall extremely happy. As he told an Ohio relative, "what a wonderful thing it is to be relieved of loneliness." To another friend, Aspinall bragged that he and Essie should have a good marriage because between the two of them, they had "99.5 years of married life experience." Essie made Wayne's last years in Congress and his retirement pleasant. Essie, "a good companion," seemed to enjoy, as Julia had, the quiet times with Wayne and was not interested in the social whirl that attracted many people to the nation's capital. Wayne and Essie did a fair amount of traveling, especially in their first years together. In late 1970, the congressman took his new bride on a trip around the world—"I think this is pretty good for people of our age," he told a correspondent.[3]

That year, 1970, had been transitional for yet another reason. For the first time in his long congressional career, Wayne Aspinall faced a primary-election challenge. Since 1964's reapportionment, Aspinall's campaigns had become increasingly difficult and considerably more expensive to conduct. Car caravans, his preferred method of campaign travel, did not work as well over a district stretching from Utah to the Nebraska border; more attention had to be paid to nonprint media. In 1968, the Aspinall campaign produced a film for the growing number of Fourth Congressional District television stations, though his longtime campaign manager, Grand Junction attorney Charles Traylor, tried to keep Aspinall off the airwaves because "he was terrible on TV."[4]

Although he never ran what modern politicians would consider an expensive campaign, Aspinall's campaign style and conduct were better suited to an earlier era. Mass-media blitzes and campaign-finance reform that required full donor disclosure did not suit Aspinall's disposition. Before campaign finance–reform laws such as the 1971 Federal Election Campaign Act, money would simply appear in Aspinall's campaign coffers (though the congressman did insist upon keeping lists of donors). Much of it came from individuals and companies associated with the West's extractive industries. Money would often be funneled to Aspinall from, for example, a mining company through the auspices of its corporate attorney. As Aspinall's former campaign treasurer remarked, it was not unusual in the days before campaign finance reform for $1,000 checks to "appear as if by magic."[5]

By 1971, the new Federal Election Campaign Act had hamstrung such freewheeling contributors.[6] Furthermore, the new law required disclosure of campaign contributors and the size of their donations. In 1970, even before the new law took effect, Aspinall suffered from allegations that he was a tool of the West's extractive industries. Indeed, an examination of his donor records reveals that an inordinate number of people with connections to the mining and cattle industries helped fill Aspinall's campaign war chest. Validly or not, increasing numbers of constituents were concerned that Aspinall was beholden to such special-interest groups.[7] This belief wreaked particular havoc on Aspinall's efforts in the primary campaign of 1972.

Wayne Aspinall faced his first primary-election challenge as a congressman in 1970. His victory margins had been solid, though unspectacular, since Colorado's General Assembly redrew the district in 1964. Aspinall still represented the Western Slope, but his district now also included the large Front Range cities of Greeley and Fort Collins, plus some conservative, Republican-dominated counties on the eastern plains. His mammoth district stretched from Utah to Nebraska, and Wyoming to New Mexico. Aspinall's election strategy was to appeal to moderate and conservative Democrats, independent voters, and moderate Republicans. In this manner, he could overcome the liberal pockets of resistance: the college towns, especially Fort Collins, and that traditional locus of Western Slope anti-Aspinall sentiment, Pitkin County.

So successful had he become at garnering Republican support that he received a peculiar sort of backhanded endorsement at the 1968 Republican National Convention. Congressman Rogers Morton (R-MD), a member of Aspinall's Interior Committee and Richard M. Nixon's convention floor manager, paid a visit to Colorado's delegation and infuriated them by singing the praises of Democrat Wayne Aspinall. All Coloradans "should be proud" to have a man like Aspinall in Congress, Morton told the incredulous group. In his enthusiasm for Aspinall, Morton failed even to mention Aspinall's 1968 Republican opponent, state senator Fred Anderson. This story underscores a challenge Aspinall would face over the next two years: he could gather the votes of many Republicans and independent voters in a general election, but could he attract enough support from rank-and-file Democrats, especially when the Colorado Democratic Party, like much of the nation, was in the throes of a liberal revolution? Increasing numbers of Colorado Democrats opposed the Vietnam War and had started to embrace an aggressive environmental agenda. In 1970, Aspinall, in the minds of many Front Range Democrats, no longer understood or accurately represented his constituency.[8]

On June 10, 1970, the *Denver Post*'s headline announced, "Heavens May Fall in Fourth District." *Post* columnist Tom Gavin revealed that a last-minute challenge to "Wayne Aspinall, giver of dams," had emerged for the first time in Aspinall's congressional career. Aspinall, Gavin wrote, "who IS the 4th District," would face forty-two-year-old Richard Perchlik, mayor of Greeley and a professor of political science at the University of Northern Colorado. As Gavin told the story, liberal Democrats from the Front Range were dismayed that they had no general-election choice between the conservative candidates of the Republican Party and Aspinall, who essentially voted Republican. Aspinall was targeted by elements in his party because of his advanced age, lengthy tenure, anti-environment record, and support of the Vietnam War.[9]

Aspinall's office had anticipated that the congressman would be attacked on these issues, but in the general election, not in a primary race. In March 1970, Aspinall's staff had engaged consultant Watt Pye to update the candidate's image, assuming that one "possible area of weakness would be the younger voters." Pye suggested marketing Aspinall's legacy in more personal ways to grab the attention of the youthful voter. Aspinall had spent his entire career "changing things to benefit people," giving them more opportunity to "do [their] own thing," Pye wrote, borrowing an overworked cliché of the era.[10]

Aspinall seemed unconcerned about Perchlik's primary challenge. "If he can get on the ballot, more power to him," Aspinall remarked to longtime campaign manager Charles J. Traylor. Officially announcing his candidacy in mid-June, Perchlik managed to gather enough Democratic support to be listed on the ballot, but Aspinall earned top-line designation. With the primary slated for early September, Aspinall supporters decided to run a low-visibility campaign against the challenger. Perchlik, however, ran an aggressive race, citing Aspinall's age (seventy-four), his record on "human issues," and his "rejection of Democratic ideals." Perchlik also sounded two themes that would resonate increasingly well with Colorado voters: the immorality of the war in Vietnam and the many threats to the West's environment, Colorado's in particular. The environment, Perchlik argued in a strong attack against Aspinall's influential position as chair of the House Interior Committee, continued "to be exploited by the powerful mining, lumbering, and industrial interests," who in turn were "protected by influential friends in the U.S. Congress." The West, Perchlik asserted, recalling the Rulison shot, had become the "playground of the Atomic Energy Commission." As for Aspinall, Perchlik asserted that the chairman's positions and legacy had become "irrelevant" to the concerns of most Fourth Congressional District voters.[11]

Perchlik was correct on at least one assertion: Aspinall did not appear to be in sync with Colorado's Democratic Party. The 1970 Colorado state Democratic convention debated and passed an idealistic and progressive set of resolutions at which Aspinall could only "shake his head." The delegates recommended creating a state atomic energy commission to implement safety standards for facilities such as Rocky Flats and actions such as the Rulison blast. The Democrats also passed an abortion-rights statement and a strong resolution that condemned the Vietnam War and asked for the immediate withdrawal of U.S. troops.[12]

Though Aspinall's enthusiasm for the Vietnam War was not what it once was, this veteran of two world wars felt duty-bound to accept the decisions of the president as commander-in-chief, be he Lyndon Johnson or Richard Nixon. As late as 1972, the *Daily Sentinel* characterized Aspinall's attitude toward the Vietnam War as "rally 'round the flag; your country right or wrong." By 1970, Aspinall found himself more in agreement with Republicans than with Democrats on issues like Vietnam and the environmental crisis. As Aspinall told a constituent, "I generally subscribe to President Kennedy's version of the domino theory of communist expansion . . . we are probably as well [off] fighting back communist expansion in Southeast Asia than we would be if we waited until it reached our own doorstep." Evidence was mounting that the revitalized Colorado Democratic Party had the strength to assert some power by 1970. Aspinall's old law-school friend and longtime political associate Congressman Byron Rogers lost top-line ballot designation at his district assembly gathering in June 1970 to Craig Barnes, a young Denver attorney and Vietnam War "peace now" advocate.[13]

Aspinall conducted what could only be termed a low-key primary campaign.[14] As the challenger, Perchlik tried to show that the incumbent had failed to protect Colorado's environment and was beholden to special interests who profited wildly from the state's natural resources. With endorsements from Front Range environmental groups such as the local chapters of Friends of the Earth, Perchlik characterized Aspinall as an "indiscriminate" dam builder with a campaign coffer filled by timber, mining, and livestock interests. Perchlik also drew attention to Aspinall's advanced age and the corrupt congressional seniority system, which rewarded longevity, not ability. In his advertisements, the Greeley professor depicted himself flanked by his young family (including four children), striding energetically down the street. He was the candidate "with a stake in the future." Perchlik never failed to question Aspinall's Democratic Party loyalty, noting that the congressman voted more like an independent or a Republican, a difficult charge for Aspinall to refute. Aspinall voted blindly for economic growth without considering the consequences. Perchlik summarized the results of Aspinall's "chamber of commerce outlook" as "growth for growth's sake . . . the philosophy of a cancer cell," anticipating Colorado's even stronger embrace of environmental thinking two years later.[15]

Despite Perchlik's energetic campaign, Aspinall cruised to a comfortable primary-election triumph on September 8 by a 12,000-vote margin, more than doubling his challenger's totals. The *Daily Sentinel* had endorsed Aspinall despite "the mutters of liberal conservationists." But several strong pockets of resistance did not augur well for the chairman's future. As always, Aspinall swept the Western Slope, with the exception of Pitkin County. Larimer County, with populous

Fort Collins and Colorado State University, also went to Perchlik. The Greeley mayor, however, failed to carry his own Weld County.[16]

The experience of Aspinall's old friend Byron Rogers in many ways foreshadowed Aspinall's fate two years later. Peace activist Craig Barnes edged the veteran congressman by a twenty-seven-vote margin to gain the Democratic nomination for Denver's congressional district. In November's general election, Aspinall faced a more traditional opponent in conservative Republican Bill Gossard. Aspinall had little trouble dispatching Gossard by a 15,000-vote margin. The 1970 primary race may not have seemed overly threatening to Aspinall, but in raising issues such as the congressman's age, seniority, environmental record, and links to special interests, Perchlik was a "stalking horse" for a stronger primary-election candidate two years later.[17]

As Aspinall began his twelfth term in office in 1971, he faced further uncomfortable evidence that his world was rapidly changing when his committee rose in rebellion against his strict authority.

THE COMMITTEE REVOLUTION

For the first eight to ten years of Aspinall's reign over the House Interior Committee, most members took pride in the chairman and the reputation that the Interior Committee had earned for fairness and order. Beginning about 1966, however, signs of unrest began appearing as some Interior Committee members complained privately about Aspinall's dictatorial behavior. The movement to liberalize Interior Committee rules took shape in the Democratic Study Group (DSG). Formed in 1957 to better inform party members on civil rights and other progressive issues, the DSG had become the bastion of congressional liberals and reformers by the late 1960s. A powerful bloc, this group realized that the nation's interest in a healthier environment could be a useful political tool. Wayne Aspinall, both as a committee chair and a legislator, only stood in the way.[18]

Few congressional committee chairs had the reputation for efficiency and thoroughness that Aspinall enjoyed. The chairman's strict adherence to rules and procedure allowed the Interior Committee to process a tremendous amount of legislation. However, the Aspinall system came with a high price: by the middle of the 1960s, some members of the Committee on Interior and Insular Affairs were ready for change. "Wayne Aspinall commanded the respect of everyone," Stewart Udall remembered, "but at the same time he kept such tight control of the Committee" that he alienated some of its more youthful members. "Wayne played the game" like the old southern committee chairmen, who often commanded "more power than thirty Congressmen." Courteous unless directly challenged, Aspinall treated Interior Committee members with respect, but not to the point of sharing power with them. "He was a dictator with a velvet glove."[19]

Other observers, especially those serving under Aspinall in the 1960s, were not as kind in their assessments. To some, Aspinall was a "tyrant" or "dictator" who "ran the Committee like it was his personal fiefdom." "He completely dominated the Committee," according to California Democrat Phil Burton, who took an instant dislike to Aspinall, an antipathy that seemed mutual. Elected to the Eighty-eighth Congress, Burton despised the seniority system from the start. Aspinall's insistence on strict rules and procedures made Burton feel at times "as if we were in kindergarten." In 1968, Lloyd Meeds (D-WA) exploded at Aspinall after the chairman cut Meeds off during a committee session, moving on to another member. Meeds quickly shouted that he was not finished and deserved more consideration from the chairman. Furthermore, "he felt he had received little consideration from him this entire year." According to an eyewitness, this challenge to Aspinall's authority brought cold silence to the committee room. After allowing the next member to speak, the chairman simply went back to Meeds and allowed him to make his point. Aspinall retained control over the situation, but Meeds became another Interior Committee member who felt stifled by Aspinall's insistence upon established procedures.[20]

By 1968, the United States was undergoing reform and revolution on many levels, and the halls of Congress were no exception. Some of Aspinall's committee members saw little that was democratic about the way he ran the committee, and targeted the situation for change. Old committee chairs like Aspinall just wanted members "to sit there and vote," Stewart Udall recalled, "and we ought to have more say about things." After the 1970 election, a successful revolution against Aspinall's authority took place. Led by Phil Burton and supported by Lloyd Meeds, Morris Udall, Patsy Mink, and others, the group legally reformed the rules of the House Interior Committee, limiting Aspinall's power in both symbolic and real ways.[21]

The revolution occurred in January 1971. Many newcomers to the House Interior Committee had desired membership because that committee handled most of the environmental legislation of the late 1960s; some of the younger and more idealistic members hoped to influence the adoption of more preservation-oriented natural-resource policies. They had grown frustrated with Aspinall's insistence upon rules and method; some even saw this as the chairman's way of stifling their legislative agendas.[22]

Aspinall had always dominated use of the Interior Committee's professional staff. In addition, he had traditionally scheduled subcommittee meetings at his discretion so that they would not conflict and he could attend all of them in his capacity as chair of the full committee. The new rules that the committee adopted in January 1971 increased the ability of subcommittee chairs to schedule their own hearings, request a budget, and utilize professional committee staff. Though they now could hire a staff member, only one subcommittee chair, Burton, chose to do so that year. Under the new rules, the members could also vote to ratify choices for subcommittee chairs. Aspinall viewed all this as "having the sergeants making decisions for the captain." To an old Grand Junction friend, Aspinall sounded like a man nearing the end of the trail, confessing that "this drive toward liberalism, organization of committees, etc., is causing me to wonder if I haven't reached the place where I should let some younger and more militant person take over." Friends close to the chairman believed the revolution had caught him by surprise and wounded him deeply. The "mutiny" of 1971 provided indisputable evidence that Aspinall's political world was crumbling.[23]

In a postscript to the revolution, Philip Burton, who became chair of the House Democratic Caucus in the 1970s, credited Aspinall with inspiring him to push for a more thoroughgoing reform of the House Committee structure in the mid-1970s. "Aspinall ran the House Interior Committee like a martinet." Though honest and hardworking, Aspinall "treated the Committee members like children—we were not able to participate in the committee policy in any way."[24]

COLORADO'S 1972 REDISTRICTING

Despite the committee revolution, Aspinall began 1972 with most of his power intact. The revolution's results were more symbolic than real, but they heralded general congressional disenchantment with the congressional committee and seniority system. A January 1972 *Wall Street Journal* article described the Coloradan as "The Ruler of the Land." This phrase aptly conveys Aspinall's by-now-legendary ability to shape the politics of the American West. But as the 1970 primary-election challenge demonstrated, Aspinall's growing estrangement from his own party revealed weaknesses that an astute candidate might exploit. In 1972, another major event exposed Aspinall to the political challenge of his lifetime. The Colorado General Assembly began redrawing legislative boundaries. As early as 1971, when preliminary discussions began, astute observers predicted that with Colorado's state government under Republican control, Aspinall might face a hostile redistricting, making him vulnerable to defeat in 1972. The chairman's lengthy tenure was viewed as particularly fragile that year because his election victory margins had been diminishing since 1964's reapportionment.[25]

As early as 1971, Aspinall sensed the shift in the political winds and hoped to prevent the division of Colorado's Western Slope into two districts. In a letter to Western Slope Republican state senator Dan Noble, Aspinall emphasized that a district was much easier to represent "where there is a community of interest." The Western Slope, with its abundant public lands, mining industry, and livestock-based economy, shared such an interest. It is little wonder that Aspinall urged Noble to fight against rumored plans to divvy up the Western Slope.[26]

Colorado's lawmakers faced a difficult task in redistricting in 1971–1972. The state's growing population qualified it for a fifth House seat. Colorado's Republican majority hoped to redraw, or gerrymander, the districts to maximize the party's chances of winning several strong seats. With 1972's primary-election season fast approaching, the Colorado Assembly still had not accepted a redistricting plan. By early April, the plan with the most support proposed separating the Western Slope counties and reassigning them to larger congressional districts, anathema to Wayne Aspinall and most politically astute Western Slope citizens. Under this scenario, Aspinall's new Fourth District would contain Western Slope counties from Delta County north to the Wyoming border, but a significant urban population north of Denver in Adams County would now be incorporated, adding to the northeastern Colorado areas he already represented. All Western Slope members of the state legislature but one opposed the reapportionment plan; still the bill managed to pass the House by a slim margin (33–30). With the Senate vote looming, Aspinall broke his policy of public silence on the measure. "The Republicans will be the losers if the state is divided," the *Daily Sentinel*'s headline proclaimed, paraphrasing Aspinall on the State House's action. If the Republicans were "damned fools enough to sacrifice western Colorado by dividing it," they would only gain a short-term advantage, Aspinall warned.[27]

The Senate reapportionment vote a week later was also close. In the days leading up to it, Western Slope political leaders tried to gather support to defeat the measure. The only alternative plan with any chance of success would have placed Aspinall and fellow Democrat Frank Evans in the same district—not a pleasant scenario for either Democrat. Many Colorado Republicans feared this plan because Evans had intimated that if this alternative passed, he would quit the House and challenge Republican senator Gordon Allott. On April 10, the Senate voted 18–17 against a proposal to keep the Western Slope congressional district intact. It then voted 18–15 to adopt the plan to split the Western Slope into two districts.[28]

Only one Western Slope senator voted to reject the plan to retain a unified Western Slope—Grand Junction Republican C. K. "Chet" Enstrom. Enstrom, who had already announced he would not run for re-election in 1974, felt safe to vote his conscience. "It may be a mistake and it won't be my first one," Enstrom said. In the eyes of many Western Slope residents, Enstrom, a noted Grand Junction ice cream and candy manufacturer, may have carried out the ultimate act of treason by voting to diminish the Western Slope's collective influence. James Golden, chair of the Mesa County Democratic Party, vigorously condemned Enstrom for selling out the Western Slope's political future. "Enstrom felt a stronger allegiance and greater responsibility towards the Republicans of Eastern Colorado than toward the constituents of the area he represents," Golden asserted. Several feverish last-minute attempts to force reconsideration of the reapportionment failed.[29]

After the reapportionment debacle, Wayne Aspinall faced a major choice: to retire or to run for a thirteenth term in a new and strange Fourth Congressional District. Time was running out, but Aspinall, as always, would not be hurried into a decision. He had followed the redistricting proceedings carefully and understood how drastically the dynamics of his district had changed with the addition of a large Denver suburban population. Most of all, as he told a constituent, he felt sickened that the Colorado General Assembly had taken "the worst possible action . . . in the interest of western Colorado and the relationship between western Colorado and eastern Colorado."[30] While the twelve-term congressman pondered his future, the calendar advanced. By early June, the state's political brokers were openly wondering whether the seventy-six-year-old Aspinall had decided to retire to his new home overlooking the Colorado River.

THE FINAL CAMPAIGN: THE 1972 PRIMARY

The portents for Aspinall's political future did not seem auspicious by the summer of 1972. Earlier that year, Charles J. Traylor, Aspinall's trusted campaign manager for twenty years, had resigned his post. Traylor claimed this had nothing to do with Aspinall or his politics—the Grand Junction lawyer simply needed to devote more time to his increasing caseload. This may have been true, but Traylor, in retrospect, admitted to seeing the writing on the wall. His candidate had overstayed his welcome in Washington, and it was in Aspinall's best interest to go home. Traylor's organizational skill would be missed in 1972, but with or without the Grand Junction attorney, Aspinall was in deep political trouble.[31]

Even though Traylor had decided to not participate in 1972, Aspinall had yet to make up his mind about seeking another term. During the reapportionment debate, Aspinall made few public comments on the process. But by May 1972, with the plan in place, the congressman was ready to speak his mind. In many respects, Aspinall already sounded both hurt and beaten. Splitting the Western Slope into two districts, each with large Front Range population components, would "plow under" the labors of his fifty-year political career, which had always emphasized the protection of western Colorado's interests. The Republican-controlled legislature awarded nineteen of Aspinall's former counties to Democratic Representative Frank Evans. Not wishing to insult Evans, Aspinall simply stated that Evans, a liberal maintaining a strong urban-issue orientation but lacking in seniority, would not be able "to give the help to the traditional interests that I have been able to give to them." Evans, most Colorado politician pundits believed, stood a stronger chance of being re-elected in his newly configured district than Aspinall. An Aspinall aide went on record in May 1972, stating he believed that Aspinall had gotten the toughest new district to run in. "I don't know what he will do now," the aide said of Aspinall's plans.[32]

Sources close to the General Assembly's Republican leadership indicated that they were pleased with the results of the reapportionment. Placing Evans and Aspinall in the same district might have endangered Allott's Senate seat. Instead, they had opted to carve several safe Republican House districts and give Evans a territory he should win. Republican leaders had downgraded Aspinall's chances for holding his congressional seat, predicting that he would face "rising opposition" from "some of the younger elements on the Western Slope."[33] If Aspinall lost, the Republicans would gain a seat in the House.

By late spring, Aspinall had begun receiving encouragement from influential Democrats to seek another term. In May, Greeley attorney James H. Shelton expressed concern that Aspinall had yet to announce his candidacy but conceded that the road ahead might be a difficult one. The problem, as Shelton diagnosed it, was that everyone who supported Aspinall assumed he would remain in Congress regardless of what they did on the candidate's behalf. "Not everyone gets worked up over supporting those who carry the load for us. It seems so popular at the moment to tear things down," Shelton observed, sounding an accurate but ominous note. Shelton offered his assistance if Aspinall chose to run: "the hope that you will stay [in Congress] forever sums up the way we feel about you." The Greeley lawyer did confirm that Alan Merson, a Summit County attorney, might be a potential primary opponent. Shelton had heard Merson speak and doubted he would pose a significant challenge. "He was not an impressive speaker" and failed to arouse much interest. Discounting Merson would prove a costly Aspinall mistake.[34]

Shelton's speculation about a possible Merson candidacy was accurate. On May 20, Alan Merson traveled to Mesa County, the seat of Aspinall's power, and announced his candidacy for the chairman's congressional seat. A Colorado resident for four years, Merson was an attorney, land-use consultant, and University of Denver law professor. Though crediting the incumbent with "twelve distinguished terms in office," Merson remarked that changes throughout Colorado and the nation "demanded new and vigorous action" from a member of Congress. Merson attacked Aspinall for being slow to recognize the nation's developing energy crisis, for promoting policies that fed constant growth, for reflexively building needless water projects, and for being the tool of special interests. For several years, Aspinall had taken a considerable beating on the latter charge, even earning the wrath of investigative reporter Jack Anderson, who ran a nationally syndicated column. In one exposé, Anderson charged Aspinall with hosting a party at Harper's Ferry, West Virginia, for energy-company lobbyists, or as Anderson called them, "golden-tongued persuaders from Mobil Oil, Humble Oil, and Standard Oil of Indiana." Aspinall, one of the House of Representatives' legislative lords, resented it when an Anderson associate asked who was footing the bill. "We'd better not go into that. This is my business," Aspinall snapped. "I'm not about to betray my friends."[35] During the campaign, Merson would point out Aspinall's strong relationship with special interests who profited from the Fourth District's public lands at every opportunity.

It is evident that Aspinall and his forces underestimated the strength and appeal of Merson's candidacy. A May 26 letter from Gordon Ibbotson, chair of the Weld County Democratic Central Committee, barely mentioned the Merson threat, focusing instead on discussing possible Republican candidates for November's general election. Ibbotson predicted that Merson and Douglas Phelps of Fort Collins, another announced candidate, would split the youthful anti-Aspinall vote but would fail to garner the 20 percent delegate support needed to gain primary-ballot designation at the Fourth Congressional District assembly scheduled for mid-July.[36]

In early June, Aspinall's credibility as a candidate concerned with the environment suffered a severe blow when the political organization Environmental Action (EA) placed him at the top of its "Dirty Dozen" list of legislators targeted for defeat in 1972. Seven of the twelve politicians who made the list that year would be defeated. In according Aspinall this dubious distinction, Environmental Action cited his foot-dragging on the Redwood National Park Bill; his "devoted support" of oil shale, timber, ranching, dam building, and atomic testing; and his efforts to cripple the National Environmental Policy Act of 1970. Aspinall branded Environmental Action's charges as "obviously politically motivated," and, indeed, Jim Moynihan, Alan Merson's campaign manager, admitted to providing the group with information. Environmental Action also announced it would support Merson's efforts to unseat Aspinall.[37]

By the middle of June, Aspinall still had not announced his candidacy, though he continued to receive supplications all but begging him to run. When he decided to seek re-election, he would cite these letters and personal contacts as influential in his decision. Aspinall had sensed by this time that the youth vote and the presidential candidacy of George McGovern were transforming Colorado's electorate into something he did not totally understand. As Aspinall confided to Lawrence F. O'Brien, chair of the Democratic National Committee, the "intense drive" carried on by the McGovern campaign had begun taking control of some of the Fourth District's precincts and counties and stood a good chance of dominating the district assembly and state convention. Aspinall, who had been a delegate to the Democratic state convention since 1922, did not believe he would be tapped this time. "If I am correctly informed, I have not been chosen to be a delegate to either one of the assemblies."[38]

After months of vacillation, on June 15 Wayne Aspinall informed Amos W. Allard, chair of the Fourth Congressional District's Democratic Central Committee, that he intended to seek his party's nomination for Congress at the July 21 district assembly in Denver. Aspinall's late announcement came with an uncharacteristically long and detailed justification of his candidacy. He believed that he remained the best person to represent the Fourth District and the only Western Slope politician who might still win election in the new district.

The letter to Allard reveals a different side of Aspinall. Here was a candidate who seemed to have lingering doubts not only about his decision to run, but also about his chances of winning. Three times in the letter, Aspinall describes his candidacy as being influenced by the "will of the people." He had decided to run because he did not want to turn his back "if my fellow citizens wish for me to continue to serve them." These people, Aspinall believed, could not be adequately represented by anyone else. If, however, his new district opted for another candidate, "I shall understand."[39]

Although Aspinall had publicly hesitated in making his decision to seek another term, part of him seemed to have been preparing for the run all along. In the spring and summer of 1972, Aspinall had accepted several speaking engagements that offered him a chance to position himself as an environmentalist—or at least to qualify his support of the ecological revolution sweeping the nation. Aspinall had anticipated that environmental concerns would be a major issue in the 1972 campaign.

In an address he provocatively titled "The Credo of a Twentieth Century Conservationist," Aspinall staked his claim to the conservationist mantle. Moving beyond that, he called himself an "environmentalist," which he quickly amended to "constructive environmentalist." Admitting that the "conservationist-preservationist-environmentalist" movement of the middle to late 1960s had had a "healthy effect on the thinking of most of the people of the world," Aspinall proceeded to qualify what constituted good environmentalist behavior. Most environmentalists, he maintained, were not "constructive"; instead, unable to envision any politically realistic means of implementing their ideas, they remained happy simply to utter their "happy phrases." Thus, their contribution to a badly needed national environmental dialogue was a negative one. If the environmental extremists could somehow blow up the 690 dams built under the Reclamation Act of 1902, the nation's agricultural economy would collapse, electric power "would be drastically curtailed," and major metropolitan centers would suddenly lack both water and power. Seasonal floods would occur, and—Aspinall's greatest nightmare—"most of the 207.5 million acre-feet of water" would flow underutilized to the sea. Wise use of natural resources was needed to keep the United States free and strong; the nation's already high dependence on energy imports represented a dangerous trend, Aspinall remarked, with more prescience than he knew at the time. But his attempt to reinvent himself as an environmental prophet failed utterly in 1972, a year when America seemed bent on rebelling against traditional authorities and experimenting with new ideas. Aspinall, the leading member of the "Dirty Dozen," symbolized what needed to be overthrown in order for the environmental movement to achieve success.[40]

Remarkably, even during his efforts to brand himself as a voice for conservation, Aspinall was openly acting as a legislative brake on several bills crucial to the environmental community. Even President Nixon tried to jolt the congressman into action. In a revealing exchange of letters, Nixon urged Aspinall to release several key environmental bills from the grip of the Interior Committee. The National Land Use Policy Act (H.R. 4332), the Mined Area Protection Act (H.R. 5689), and the National Resource Lands Management Act (H.R. 10049) all remained stalled under Aspinall's care. Nixon pointed out that public backing for the bills was strong. Aspinall's response was anything but reassuring. After noting his qualified support, Aspinall indicated that each bill represented a radical departure from past practices; therefore his committee would need more time than usual to deal with them. It was not until late in his letter that the real reason for Aspinall's reluctance to act emerged. In submitting suggested revisions to Aspinall's committee, the Interior Department had blatantly ignored the "many basic provisions of the Public Land Law Review Commission." This had been the "biggest factor in prolonging our consideration of that legislation."[41]

The most obvious sticking point between Aspinall and the Nixon administration concerned, not surprisingly, "differences in Executive Branch and Legislative Branch responsibilities." In addition, both Aspinall and Senator Henry Jackson had introduced bills that over the next four years would evolve into the Federal Land Policy Management Act of 1976 (FLPMA), also known as the BLM Organic Act. Aspinall's version (H.R. 7211) differed starkly from Jackson's (S. 921), and from the bill that actually passed Congress four years later. Aspinall's bill, written from the PLLRC blueprint, called for dominant use as the basic land-management criterion. With little mention of wilderness, the bill assigned states strong roles in the land-use planning process. Aspinall's system anticipated the demands of the Sagebrush Rebels of the late 1970s. It is little wonder that many environmentalists opposed Aspinall's H.R. 7211. Even while seeking re-election, Aspinall remained busy attempting to shape the nation's land policies well into 1972, his last full year in office.[42]

Meanwhile, the primary campaign moved into a crucial phase when the Fourth Congressional District Assembly convened in Denver on July 21, 1972. While Aspinall was back in Washington attempting to sell his land-use philosophy, Merson's forces had been busy garnering delegate support at the precinct, county, and district levels. Merson was benefiting from the youthful "McGovern for President" euphoria and the fact that this would be the first national election in which eighteen-year-olds had the right to vote.[43] Merson sent letters to all delegates to Democratic county meetings, asking for their support. "Times are changing," his message began. "Problems are accelerating. And new representation is needed in the Fourth District." Apparently, the Fourth District Assembly thought so, too, awarding Merson top-line ballot designation over Aspinall by a vote of 312–277.[44]

Aspinall feigned unconcern in a letter to his family shortly after the Fourth District Assembly. Merson's triumph did not surprise him. Most of the younger man's support came from the urban Front Range corridor and the "young people who had been on McGovern's train."[45] With elements in his party turning against him, Aspinall knew it was time to fight. From this point on, he planned a hard-hitting campaign looking not just to the September 12 primary, but all the way to the November 5 election. Aspinall believed that once he started to campaign, he could quickly regain the advantage.[46]

Aspinall's "hard-hitting" campaign actually bore a much closer resemblance to his "noncampaign" against primary opponent Richard Perchlik in 1970. In Washington most of the summer, Aspinall did not return home to begin campaigning until about August 20. By his own estimate, he had lost 150,000 of his old constituents to Frank Evans and gained 115,000 new ones from urban Adams County, which included the Denver suburbs of Westminster, Brighton, and Northglenn. Meanwhile, Merson had sustained a high-energy campaign all summer, receiving crucial support from Environmental Action and the League of Conservation Voters. The League of Conservation voters, founded in 1970 largely through the personal financial resources of Marion Edey, raised money, established an advisory board that included David Brower, and, like Environmental Action, targeted anti-environmental incumbent politicians to unseat. The League of Conservation Voters (LCV) had raised approximately $20,000 for Merson—about half his campaign war chest—and also supplied sorely needed staff expertise and volunteer help. In one publication, the LCV noted that Aspinall was "in serious trouble back home." "Drastically redistricted," he faced a skilled and vigorous campaign waged by "sincere conservationist" Alan Merson. The League's plea for funds made it clear that a little money could nudge Merson over the top in a close race. Aspinall, the LCV observed, was "well financed by the interests he represents." The LCV asserted that Aspinall maintained a "nineteenth century attitude toward natural resources" and continued to champion legislation that would give Congress—not federal land administrators—the power to make land-use decisions.[47]

Merson made an energetic attempt to capture the student vote, which, after the 26th Amendment, loomed large in the Fourth District, home to two major colleges, Colorado State University in Fort Collins and the University of Northern Colorado in Greeley. A letter from Merson, who described himself as "young, progressive and vigorous," awaited each returning student, appealing for "a dollar or two" to help defeat Aspinall, "a member of the Deadly Dozen, a group of hawkish Congressmen who support our presence in Vietnam" and the man "identified by a national environmental group as *the* worst environmental Congressman in Washington, . . . responsible, more than any other lawmaker for the rape of Colorado."[48]

By contrast, Aspinall's campaign hoped to win the Western Slope by the "largest possible" margin while holding its own in the new areas. Most of the criticism of the incumbent's environmental record originated outside of the state, a point Aspinall made over and over in his abbreviated campaign. He tried to characterize himself as a "good hand for Colorado," someone who could safely map the road to the future. America, he told a campaign crowd, could not afford to lock up its natural resources when its people were becoming increasingly dependent on foreign sources of oil that were "not always friendly to the United States." Instead, he argued, the nation needed to "produce energy wisely while protecting other values," including recreation and scenery.[49]

Fourth District voters could never confuse Aspinall's and Merson's personalities or positions; the contrasts could not have been starker. The election pitted the seventy-six-year-old veteran of twelve terms in Congress and two world wars, the "shaper of the modern American West," against a young environmental lawyer who lacked practical political experience. Both Colorado and the Fourth Congressional District had reached a crossroads in 1972. Colorado had been accorded the honor of hosting the 1976 Winter Olympics. Sensing the state's mood against environmental threats, unchecked growth, and the cost of the event, Democratic state representative Richard Lamm led a drive to place the question of whether the state should host this huge international event on November's general-election ballot. Citizen resistance to the Olympics had set in, animated by some of the same cultural forces that drove both the McGovern and Merson campaigns. Aspinall, viewed as a conduit for badly needed federal funds to defray some of the exorbitant costs of the games, was cast as one of the establishment "villains" scheming to force the event upon an unaware Colorado public. Lamm, hoping that a budgetary argument might turn Aspinall against the Olympics, remarked in a letter to the congressman that his opposition was motivated more by fears of high projected costs to Colorado than by forebodings of environmental disaster.[50]

Aspinall did not allow himself to be drawn deeply into the public debate over the Olympics, though the rumor had spread in April that he would use his position on the Interior Committee to stifle the flow of federal funds to Colorado in revenge for the General Assembly's redistricting. It is unlikely, however, that he would have done so. Aspinall's main interest by late summer 1972 was not the Olympics, it was political survival.

When it became apparent that Aspinall's political career was at stake, campaign money began flowing like pipeline oil into Aspinall's treasury. The candidate's 1972 financial ledger reads like a directory of the American West's major extractive companies. Money came from Humble Oil, Western Crude Oil, the Alaska Loggers Association, Sun Oil Company, Signal Drilling Company, the Utah Mining Association, the Union 76 Oil Political Awareness Fund, Chevron Oil Company, The Oil Shale Company (TOSCO), Kimberly-Clark Corporation, National Forest Products Association, American Metals Climax Company, Marathon Oil Company, Amoco Production Company, and the

Federal Timber Purchasers Association, to name but a sampling. The pace of the contributions increased markedly in mid-August, when Aspinall's political troubles became apparent. Many companies gave several times, often in the names of various executive officers, typically in $100–$500 increments. The American West's extractive industries had an old trusted friend in Wayne Aspinall, who shared their vision for the region. They appreciated his many past favors and did not want to lose him.[51]

The conservationist assault on Aspinall, coupled with the McGovern campaign's antiwar orientation and the powerful new youth vote, upset the balance of Colorado's Democratic Party in 1972. It was a year of revolutionary change, a time to discard old ideas. Aspinall's managers gamely attempted to plug their candidate into the new atmosphere, but advertising strategies that emphasized the need to continue mineral and oil exploration on the nation's public lands did not endear the elderly candidate to Colorado's young and energized electorate. Increasingly desperate, Aspinall's advisors considered bringing in Arizona's Morris Udall to speak on behalf of the chairman's conservation credentials. Testimonials for Aspinall were obtained from other moderate conservationists, but such desperate last-ditch remedies accomplished little. Targeted by national environmental organizations, Aspinall was attacked without mercy. *Field and Stream* labeled him "in a class by himself," one who "absolutely must go." Even *Reader's Digest* thrashed Aspinall. The *New York Times* weighed in on Colorado's election by endorsing Merson, a move that undoubtedly helped fill Merson's campaign treasury with out-of-state environmentalist money. Grand Junction's *Daily Sentinel* rallied to Aspinall's defense, noting that the national environmental movement seemed to be "ganging up" on the Coloradan.[52]

Aspinall's public-relations firm used the *New York Times* endorsement as a chance to help Aspinall with Colorado voters, many of whom resented eastern attempts to dominate the West. An Aspinall news release issued on the eve of the election remarked that apparently "the *New York Times* has decided that the people of Colorado are incapable of making their own political decisions. This is an insult reflecting on the intelligence of the voters of the Fourth Congressional District."[53]

On the campaign trail since late August, Aspinall had sensed that he might not win. On the day of the primary, he wrote to his family that a loss was indeed possible. After telling his son Owen that Colorado's early fall weather was beautiful, Aspinall remarked, "and we may get to enjoy it more than we perhaps feel at the moment, but that won't be too bad, either."[54]

The prediction proved correct. Despite the *Daily Sentinel's* editorial plea that "we need Aspinall," the majority of the new Fourth Congressional District did not think so. Alan Merson, who had only lived in Colorado for four years, defeated the man who personified the Western Slope, winning by 1,600 votes. For the first time since before the legendary Edward T. Taylor, the Fourth Congressional

District would be represented by someone other than a Western Slope resident. Merson would square off with Republican James P. Johnson of Fort Collins in the general election. Nearly all of Merson's margin of victory came from the new area of Adams County. Merson also polled impressively in the college towns of Greeley (Weld County) and Fort Collins (Larimer County). Of course, nobody was surprised when Merson also trounced Aspinall in Pitkin County.[55]

In the election's immediate aftermath, Aspinall, not openly bitter, blamed redistricting as the main cause of defeat.[56] Looking forward to a "well-deserved retirement," he also expressed fears that his defeat would "undoubtedly delay," or perhaps even prevent, implementing the recommendations of the PLLRC, Aspinall's final public-service dream. Admitting that his advanced age and stance toward the environment had influenced the election's outcome, Aspinall nevertheless denied that these issues had affected the votes of people who knew him. Aspinall, after twenty-four years in Congress, still believed in personal politics.[57]

While the environmental community celebrated Aspinall's political demise, a shocked Fourth Congressional District began to assess his legacy. What would life be like without Wayne Aspinall? More than a few voters immediately left the Democratic Party in the wake of his defeat. The congressman's former secretary, Alta Noland, telephoned him after the election to say, "Wayne, I am no longer a conservative Democrat." Aspinall's response was characteristically succinct: "I have always said the Republicans are the ones that elected me." Amos W. Allard, who headed the Fourth Congressional District Democratic Central Committee, immediately "resigned and became a Republican" after Aspinall's loss to Merson. A young, environmentally minded Mesa College professor who was delighted with Merson's triumph recalled that some older faculty members at the Grand Junction college who were Republicans blamed themselves for the chairman's loss. Many Fourth District Republicans believed they should have temporarily changed their voter registrations to help Aspinall in the primary.[58]

In an election wrap-up entitled "They're Sorry Aspinall Lost," *Denver Post* columnist Tom Gavin listed several dozen people and the amount of money they had contributed to Aspinall's campaign. Starting with Denver oilman Marvin Davis's $1,000, Gavin went on to list a virtual who's who of the West's energy industry. Gavin pointed out that the $2,000 donation from the Democratic Congressional Campaign Committee should not have been made to Aspinall because normally "official party committees stay out of primary battles." Gavin's article also discussed Merson's donor list; most of his financial support came from the East Coast.[59]

Although Gavin did not regret Aspinall's defeat, many other Coloradans and members of the political establishment did. Soon, condolences and thank-you letters for past favors began flooding Aspinall's mailbox. On October 18, the House of Representatives stopped regular business to hear more than three dozen tributes to Aspinall from its members. One member from Illinois likened

Aspinall to Lincoln. California Republican Craig Hosmer, a longtime Interior Committee member, said working with Aspinall was like earning a Ph.D. in political expertise. Arizona's Sam Steiger chose to verbally assault the environmentalists who had engineered Aspinall's defeat. After listing Aspinall's conservation achievements, Steiger accused the environmentalists who placed Aspinall on the "Dirty Dozen" list of circulating a "blatant, ludicrous, and vicious lie." Among the letters of condolence were notes from Marion Clawson, former director of the Bureau of Land Management; Congressman Gerald Ford; and friends in industry (among them Weyerhauser Corporation, Kennecott Copper, and Boise Cascade, to name but a few), as well as expressions of regret from the boards of almost every reclamation district in the West. But it was probably Morris Udall who best summarized the impact of Aspinall's defeat, calling it "the end of an era."[60]

Perhaps the most astute election postmortem was offered by retired *Denver Post* political reporter and longtime Aspinall acquaintance Bert Hanna. In "A Salute to an Old Pol Who Ran One Time Too Many," Hanna revealed that he had been "saddened" in June to learn that Aspinall was running again. Why had Aspinall felt compelled to stay in office? Hanna wondered. Why had he remained in the public storm, the subject of merciless attacks from the environmental movement? Hanna's answer: "self-justification." Aspinall was desperate to protect his many accomplishments from new values that threatened to destroy his life's work.[61]

Hanna's analysis was perceptive and on the mark. Aspinall wanted to harmonize his love of natural-resource development with the age of environmental protection. For Aspinall, this meant overseeing implementation of the Public Land Law Review Commission's report, which Aspinall believed had been misunderstood and turned into a tempting target for ecological extremists. Aspinall also committed the fatal sin of many who remain in authority for too long—he believed he had become indispensable.[62]

ASPINALL IN RETIREMENT

Wayne Aspinall did not take retirement—or anything else in his life—lightly. Though he joked about spending his time fishing and playing poker, he tackled retirement with the same focus, intensity, and organization he had brought to his twelve terms in Congress. By late fall, Aspinall had rationalized his defeat to Merson as the result of redistricting.[63] A measure of vindication awaited Aspinall in the November election, when Republican Jim Johnson defeated Merson.

Colorado's electorate was clearly in the mood for radical change. The anti-Olympic ballot measure won, demonstrating that Coloradans were deeply concerned about the costs of growth. Liberal Democrat Floyd Haskell beat three-term incumbent conservative Republican Gordon Allott for a U.S. Senate seat. In Denver, liberal Democrat Pat Schroeder won election to the first of her many

House terms. Aspinall looked at these changes and simply shook his head. He could not bring himself to support McGovern because the forces that sustained the peace candidate had helped defeat Aspinall. But he did not want to vote for Nixon, either. As a result, Aspinall simply did not cast a vote for president in 1972. His estrangement from the "new" Colorado Democratic Party would continue until the end of his life.[64]

In his final months in Congress, Aspinall welcomed Congressman-elect Johnson to Washington and introduced him as "my Congressman." In several interviews, Aspinall expressed both pride and bitterness. Aspinall predicted that the age of ecology "fanatics" was nearing an end. This group of people, he maintained, "seem to believe they can see beautiful landscapes and smell pine forests better than anyone else." In another interview before leaving Washington, Aspinall asserted that "no person has been a leader like I have" on western resource issues. He admitted that his biggest disappointment in the final months of his tenure had been the House's failure to pass H.R. 7211, which would have made much of his PLLRC vision a reality. The measure had been strenuously opposed by environmental groups.[65]

Aspinall returned to the Grand Valley and moved with Essie into a comfortable but not ostentatious home in Palisade, keeping up a vigorous pace as long as his health allowed. He continued trying to influence the nation's natural-resource policies, working as a consultant to mining companies and organizations promoting western resource development. The theme of his final decade was starkly revealed in a letter to President Nixon written several weeks after the 1972 general election. Aspinall predicted a national energy crisis unless the United States began developing its own substantial natural resources. Aspinall's prophecy would come true with the Arab oil embargo of 1973–1974. "Today," he lectured Nixon, "we are in a total energy deficit that is growing every day," to the detriment of the nation's economy and world prestige. The United States had to mobilize immediately to meet the dimensions of the crisis. For the next ten years, Aspinall worked to position the companies and people of the West to be the nation's chief energy suppliers. In the process, he crusaded against the environmental community for placing developmental roadblocks in the path of his dreams for America's energy future.[66]

Aspinall's interests in retirement paralleled his favored congressional activities. When not busy in his basement study (patterned after his Washington, D.C., congressional office) overlooking the Colorado River, Aspinall worked for Club-20, the western Colorado lobbying organization, and as a consultant for AMAX (American Metals Climax). He also was active on the boards of many organizations, including the Mountain States Legal Foundation and his own educational foundation at Mesa College in Grand Junction. Any political dignitaries passing through Grand Junction usually stopped to pay their respects to the former chairman, including Gerald Ford, Senator Bob Dole, and Senator Gary Hart.

Aspinall in his home office on Aspinall Drive, Palisade, Colorado, during his retirement. The Colorado River, so integral to his life and career, meandered directly beneath his office window. Courtesy, Daily Sentinel *Collection, MWC.*

Aspinall closely followed a set daily agenda. Without a routine, he "would not have a reason to get up," he told his last secretary, Vivian Passer. Still obsessed with not wasting time, Aspinall would spend any spare moments reading. He particularly loved Louis L'Amour's novels of the Old West, but he also enjoyed Gore Vidal's historical fiction, as well as biographical studies of notable political figures such as the Roman emperor Augustus and Alexander the Great. His love of teaching and learning brought him to the University of Wyoming in 1975, where he occupied the Milward Simpson Distinguished Chair of Political Science. When his sense of order and decorum confronted the relaxed study habits and appearance of 1970s college students, Aspinall nevertheless came away "pleasantly surprised" and energized by his students. But to no one's astonishment, Aspinall called his class roll every day. "I guess I'm old-fashioned," the eighty-year-old college professor admitted.[67]

His consulting work kept the former congressman busy. He maintained a relationship with AMAX until the end of his life. A typical Aspinall report might suggest to AMAX how and when to try to influence Congress in the controversy surrounding attempts to change the Mining Law of 1872, a law many environmentalists considered outmoded and a roadblock to western environmental health. In Congress, Aspinall had always protected the 1872 law, which gave the mining industry great freedom to search for vital minerals and to profit from the West's public domain. As a consultant, he indicated at what point in the hearings AMAX should ask to present its position to maximize its political advantage. In 1977, Aspinall advised AMAX to allow Morris Udall, now chair of the Interior Committee, to spend the early part of the hearings sounding off about the law to relieve "some of the heat" he had been feeling from environmentalists. Later, when the atmosphere had calmed, would be the best time for the mining industry to rationally present its case against revision of the law.[68]

In 1976, Aspinall's work for AMAX became the focus of a national investigation sparked by journalist Jack Anderson. Anderson alleged that in 1974, during House debate on the Coal Surface Mining Bill (which would have made strip-mining reclamation more costly for the industry), Aspinall returned to Washington, D.C., used his House privileges as a former member of Congress, and was present on the floor, influencing his former colleagues to vote against the bill. Aspinall's recollections of the event differed markedly. Aspinall admitted to being on the House floor, which was his privilege at that time under House rules. But, he asserted, "I have never asked any Congressman to vote for or against any bill." However, "when asked by former colleagues my thinking on legislation, I am always glad to give my personal opinion." After Jack Anderson's story broke in 1976, Congressman John Anderson (R-IL) introduced a resolution, which passed 371–1, denying floor access to former members of Congress who now served as professional lobbyists. The old House rules had allowed former Representatives floor access except when the matter under debate was one the former member was personally interested in or trying to influence. This rule, however, was only informally enforced, if at all.[69]

Aspinall's profession of innocence was supported by his Fourth District successor, Jim Johnson. Johnson had accompanied Aspinall to the House floor in 1974, where, by Johnson's account, Aspinall shook hands with "thirty to fifty people but did not say one word to anybody about the strip mining bill." After Anderson's resolution was introduced, Aspinall wrote a vigorous defense of his actions to the Illinois congressman and future presidential candidate, asking for the names of the Representatives who had witnessed the illegal lobbying. John Anderson denied that his bill was aimed at Aspinall, though he righteously pointed out that Aspinall had been in violation even of the old House rules because of his affiliation with a mining company. In 1980, Aspinall was criticized for his AMAX lobbying activities against the Colorado Wilderness bill then under debate. The *Daily Sentinel* noted that the former congressman

President Gerald Ford and Wayne Aspinall near the end of Aspinall's long life. Ford and Aspinall both came to Congress after the 1948 election and remained good friends. Courtesy, Daily Sentinel *Collection, MWC.*

regularly contacted members of Colorado's congressional delegation to make his opposition to the bill known.[70]

In 1976, Aspinall demonstrated his penchant for political independence by endorsing Republican presidential candidate Gerald Ford, eschewing his own party's candidate, Georgia governor Jimmy Carter. Ford was a natural choice for Aspinall, who had been increasingly uncomfortable with the liberal tilt of the Democratic Party since the late 1960s. Ford, Aspinall believed, understood the needs of the West better than Jimmy Carter. Aspinall feared that the Georgia governor would became a captive of the environmental movement's radical fringe.[71]

The events following Carter's election justified Aspinall's fears. In the first weeks of his new administration, Jimmy Carter submitted a list of water projects earmarked for funding suspension. Carter's "hit list," as it became known in the West, included nineteen water projects, eight of them located in the West, including the half-built Central Arizona Project and Colorado's Dolores, Fruitland Mesa, and Savery–Pot Hook Projects. Carter based his decisions on economic, environmental, and safety considerations. The immediate reaction in the West, which was experiencing a severe drought, was that the president of the United States had essentially declared war on the region. After a storm of protest and delicate face-to-face negotiations between the Carter administration and congressional leaders, the president announced what were to be his final decisions on April 18, 1977. The three Colorado projects remained on the list, though the Central Arizona Project was restored. Meanwhile, the tug-of-war between Carter and western political leaders continued until most of the projects achieved some degree of funding. Marc Reisner's assessment of the episode is that the Carter administration's "dam saboteurs" discovered that victories over the congressional "pork-barrel system tend to be short-lived."[72]

After Carter announced his reclamation cuts, Wayne Aspinall took immediate action, speaking out against the Georgian's decision. How could Jimmy Carter understand an area like the West? Aspinall asked rhetorically. The president's chief natural-resource advisors had been Aspinall's enemies in Congress. "They don't understand what it is to live in a country where there is no water to amount to anything in the latter part of June, July, August, and September unless you have it stored." In a letter to Carter, Aspinall argued that the West would lose confidence in government if water-project opponents reneged on project authorizations enacted by former Congresses. "Such a law or laws should not be broken unilaterally." As with Congress's failure to act upon most of his PLLRC recommendations, Aspinall was pained to see some of his life's best work—western reclamation projects—undermined by executive caprice.[73] As he told a member of Garfield County's Soil Conservation District, "It doesn't sit well with me to have an individual, even a President of the United States, come in and undo a great deal of the work I had helped to accomplish over a period of years . . . I think it is fair to say that a 'flat land cracker' [Jimmy Carter] has no idea of what the West needs in the way of development."[74]

Aspinall continued his journey toward the political right wing after the 1976 election. Outspoken as ever, he argued for the need to roll back environmental regulations that stifled the nation's search for domestic energy sources. Other moves by the Carter administration angered Aspinall. In 1978, Carter used the Antiquities Act of 1906 to set aside 56 million acres as seventeen new national monuments in Alaska. By the end of the decade, many western land users had become convinced that most executive-branch public-land decisions were being based on an environmentalist agenda. Finally, state politicians, public-land users, and energy companies began a movement to protest the growing political influence of environmentalists in land-use decision making. The Sagebrush Rebellion, rooted in "reoccurring [sic] themes of ignorance about the West's concerns, heavy-handed federal bureaucrats, and violations of states' rights," had arrived.[75]

For many years, Wayne Aspinall had insisted that states should determine which water projects they wanted to build. He had also complained about federal bureaucratic decision making and asserted the right of Congress to determine land-use priorities. Through these positions, Aspinall became a major intellectual influence on the Sagebrush Rebellion, which sought to return extensive federal landholdings to the states on the principle that the states were better positioned to manage the land more efficiently. In the late 1970s, Aspinall worked closely with both James G. Watt and Joseph Coors of the Mountain States Legal Foundation, whose members borrowed freely from language Aspinall had been using for fifteen years to describe the environmental movement. In one of his speeches, Watt, the foundation's director, called environmentalists "a group of extremists who don't concern themselves with balanced perspective or improvement in the quality of life for mankind." Watt, like Aspinall, had, over the years, contrasted the "selfishness" of environmentalists with true conservationists who sought a balance between humanity's needs and nature's limits. In 1978, at Aspinall's invitation, Watt delivered an address to the Club-20 meeting in Grand Junction. He came away with one vivid impression: the "Western Slope would be much better off if Wayne Aspinall were still representing that region. It was clear to me that Wayne was still the hero of that group and they all long for the powerful leadership that he provided them for so many years."[76]

Aspinall helped the Mountain States Legal Foundation solicit funds and members. In a letter sent out under his signature, Aspinall declared that "if one person from our state loses his liberties in an opportunity for proper and sound development of his economic rights, we all lose." Aspinall joined the Mountain States Legal Foundation board at the recommendation of brewer and businessman Joseph Coors. He proudly sported the title "Director Emeritus."[77]

Aspinall's main base of political operations during his retirement was Club-20. Aspinall enjoyed traveling across the Western Slope, holding public meetings, reporting to Club-20's president, and representing the group at meetings. As head of its Natural Resources Committee, Aspinall easily slipped back into his chairmanlike demeanor, holding hearings on such topics as the Roadless Area Review Study, Wilderness proposals, and Carter's hit list. Former Club-20 president John Vanderhoof, a Republican who served as Colorado's governor from 1973 to 1975, recalled that Aspinall viewed his connection with Club-20 as the "crowning enjoyment" of his long political career. Aspinall ran the Natural Resources Committee "the same damned way" he ran the House Interior Committee, complete with official stenographic record.[78]

Aspinall's active engagement with Club-20 uncovered in western Colorado the presence of many of the same attitudes that brought the Sagebrush Rebellion to prominence in the West as a whole. At one 1978 Grand Junction meeting Aspinall presided over, public discussion revealed a consensus for opposing additions to Colorado's wilderness acreage and reaffirming the management of public lands through multiple use. Under Aspinall and Vanderhoof, Club-20 made the transition from tourism-promotion group to a powerful lobby for the region's water interests and energy economy. Aspinall's influence cannot be overestimated. In 1996, Club-20's president pointed out that Aspinall's involvement enhanced the group's effectiveness and viability. "We're still trading on the reputation and credibility he helped build for this organization."[79]

The Sagebrush Rebellion reached its zenith in the late 1970s and early 1980s. Through his work for Club-20, the Mountain States Legal Foundation, and AMAX, Aspinall gave the rebellion strong support. Westerners resented the growing web of environmental regulations, bureaucratic red tape, and unilateral political decisions such as Carter's water-project hit list. The rebels demanded more say in land-use decisions and a return of some—or all—federal lands to the states. In the words of one of its founders, Congressman Jim Santini (D-NV), the Sagebrush Rebellion demanded "home rule for the West." At the national level, Santini and Senator Orrin Hatch (R-UT) introduced bills for the return of National Forest Service and BLM lands to the western states.[80]

The fires of the Sagebrush Rebellion cooled rapidly following the election of self-described "Sagebrush rebel" Ronald Reagan to the presidency in 1980. Reagan appointed Mountain States Legal Foundation chief James G. Watt as secretary of the interior, a move warmly endorsed by Wayne Aspinall, who continued his estrangement from the Democratic Party by supporting westerner Reagan. After Watt's nomination, Aspinall congratulated his young protégé but cautioned him not to "try and move too fast." It had taken decades for public-land management to become influenced by environmental organizations and it would "take considerable time to get us back on track," Aspinall predicted. Watt's appointment and actions to ease federal environmental controls fanned the flames of liberal counterrevolution in the early 1980s, eventually claiming Watt as a victim. But with a friend in office, Aspinall backed off from his position as an ardent rebel, noting to Vernon Ravenscroft, the president of Sagebrush Rebellion, Incorporated, that the movement now had "friends in the high places of authority." Aspinall hoped to help promote the government's "divestiture of the federal estate," but "far along in 85 [years of age,] I cannot promise too much."[81]

Youthful Colorado politicians like Democratic senator Gary Hart continued to seek Aspinall's advice. Hoping to locate federal funding for energy impact aid to towns in western Colorado rocked by the late 1970s oil-shale boom, Hart asked Aspinall how best to proceed. Later, Hart sought Aspinall's advice on and endorsement in the 1980 Senate race. Aspinall told Hart that in conservative western Colorado, he would have a difficult time reconciling his appealing public pronouncements with his liberal voting record. At one point, Aspinall advised the ambitious Hart ("as one old enough to be your grandfather") to discourage his friends from publicizing his presidential ambitions, urging the young man instead to focus on being a "good Senator from the West." If Hart followed this advice, other opportunities might eventually present themselves. "Just a few thoughts from an old politician who also had some opportunities for other positions," Aspinall concluded, perhaps thinking back to the elusive Colorado governorship and Interior Department secretaryship.[82]

In the early 1980s, Aspinall's health visibly deteriorated, the inevitable result of age and a lifetime of public service. Diagnosed with prostate cancer in 1977, Aspinall had been in questionable health for some time. His illness caused problems on occasion, but he maintained a busy routine until well into 1982. After several stints in the hospital for cancer treatment, Aspinall decided to return to his Palisade home in June 1983 to be attended by visiting nurses. His wife, Essie, died of Parkinson's disease the following month. Wayne's cancer had progressed to the point that he was unable to leave home to attend her memorial service. According to Owen Aspinall, Wayne, fittingly enough, was on the phone to Washington discussing an environmental matter just one week before his death. The end came for Mr. Chairman at 11:45 on the morning of October 9, 1983.[83]

ASPINALL'S LEGACY AND WESTERN POLITICS

What should history make of Wayne Aspinall's career? If even his successors in Congress cannot agree on the meaning of his life and career, how can historians? On rising to the chairship of the House Natural Resources Committee (the successor to the Interior Committee), California Democrat George Miller removed the portrait of Aspinall that had adorned the Interior Committee hearing room since 1960, replacing it with the likeness of Morris Udall, another longtime Interior Committee chair and someone known to be more sensitive to environmentalist positions. When the Republicans regained control of the House following the 1994 election, Congressman Ben Nighthorse Campbell, in a direct shot at environmentalist Miller, rescued Aspinall's portrait from storage and restored it to its traditional place of prominence in the committee room.[84] As this episode demonstrates, in death, Aspinall had become a polarizing symbol for two camps competing to shape the future of the American West. One group believed Aspinall represented the hollow vision of those whose desire to command the West and its environmental riches had inflicted untold and likely irreparable damage on the region. The other lauded him as the politician who did the most to develop the West's parsimonious lands and make them a hospitable place for people to live.

In truth, Aspinall's significance cannot be broken down so simply. He viewed himself first and foremost as a westerner—a member of a conscious minority. Like his political mentor Edward T. Taylor, Aspinall recognized that the strongest contribution he could make to Colorado and the West would be to rise through and dominate a key committee. As chair of the House Interior and Insular Affairs Committee, he truly was the ruler of the land, serving under four presidents and handling virtually every important piece of legislation from

1959 to 1973 that affected the American West. It is worth noting that during Aspinall's era, the congressional committee structure reserved tremendous power to the chair. Aspinall was one of the lords of Congress in a heyday of strong congressional leaders. A former Aspinall aide who went on to work for Aspinall's successor, Jim Johnson, starkly highlighted the difference between working for Aspinall and working for Johnson. "When I worked for Mr. Aspinall, I would hear a click on the other end of the line and it would be the heels snapping together . . . when I worked for Mr. Johnson and heard the click . . . it was them hanging up."[85]

Aspinall helped create what Donald Worster termed "the greatest hydraulic society ever built in history." Though environmentally sensitive scholars often write Aspinall off as a fanatic who "never saw a dam he didn't like," his work on the CRSP, Fryingpan-Arkansas Project, and Colorado River Basin Project made post–World War II reclamation in the West a reality. Aspinall authorized more than $1 billion in reclamation projects for his district and more than $5 billion overall. In many parts of Colorado, Aspinall is fondly recalled as the politician who made the state viable. Outside the door of Aspinall's memorial service in 1983, Colorado governor Richard Lamm, a frequent critic of Aspinall, told a reporter, "You can't take a drink of water in Colorado without remembering Wayne Aspinall."[86]

Aspinall shaped the land of the modern West in numerous ways. The Wilderness Act of 1964, the cornerstone of U.S. environmentalism, became law because of Aspinall's ability to reshape the bill into something that did not overtly threaten the traditional West's public-land users. Some critics have accused the Wilderness Act of being watered down, but the bill blends the idealism of Howard Zahniser with Wayne Aspinall's western political pragmatism. Aspinall did not want to make it easy for land to pass into the Wilderness system; his insistence on the affirmative action of Congress ensured that any additional parcels of Wilderness would have a broad base of support. The bill works. Today, more than 100 million acres are protected by the Wilderness Act.[87] Even some of his old enemies from the Sierra Club were in awe of Aspinall's ability to balance divergent interests in his legislation.[88]

Aspinall's values, formed during the post-frontier era in the American West, dictated that the land remain a source of continued economic growth. By the late 1960s, however, opinion in both the nation as a whole and the American West had started to change. The environmental movement did not subscribe to Aspinall's philosophy of balancing the many interests seeking access to public lands in the West; for too long, compromise had only spelled ecological disaster. Aspinall, in turn, viewed extreme environmentalists as selfish and unrealistic. By the end of his congressional career, Aspinall seemed to believe that the United States, as evidenced by the youth rebellion, a disastrous war in Southeast Asia, an extreme environmental movement, and a looming energy

Receiving honors. Eddie Box of the Southern Ute tribe honors Aspinall with a blanket during this 1980 ceremony, in which three western Colorado dams were collectively named the Wayne N. Aspinall Storage Unit of the Colorado River Storage Project. Courtesy, Daily Sentinel Collection, MWC.

crisis, had lost its moorings. How could society be foolish enough to deny the need to use nature's bounty?

During his final years in Congress, Aspinall's creative role diminished as he found himself sponsoring legislation that few really wanted. His failure to translate PLLRC recommendations into concrete legislation is one example. Far more often, he interposed himself between the political agenda of environmental groups and the economic freedoms of the land users he had always protected. His role became increasingly negative. Aspinall viewed legislation such as the National Environmental Policy Act as unnecessary; NEPA and its ilk would only create additional procedures and layers of bureaucracy, and public-land projects would suffer needless delays.[89] Aspinall protected the mining industry by refusing to hold hearings on the question of revising the Mining Law of 1872.

The new politics of environmental preservation clouded Aspinall's reclamation vision. As early as 1971, he saw the reclamation community running scared from an increasingly imposing body of laws and regulations designed to protected the environment. With projects already delayed through stingy appropriations, Aspinall knew just where to place the blame. "The most acute problem" facing water-resource development in the 1970s remained the "ecology-binge" as practiced by the lunatic fringe of the environmental movement. The new body of environmental laws such as NEPA and the enforcement mechanisms of the Environmental Protection Agency (EPA) had begun stifling and delaying reclamation projects, making them more costly and enabling environmental groups to challenge projects in court. Aspinall's last great reclamation triumph, the Colorado River Basin Project (1968), provides a prime example. The flurry of environmental legislation mandated CRBP compliance, affecting both its timetable and construction costs through delays and inflation. Wesley E. Steiner of the Arizona Water Commission reported in 1972 that no portion of the CAP had yet been built. Four years after its authorization, Steiner's primary concern was bringing the Central Arizona Project into compliance with the dictates of NEPA—even though NEPA was enacted a year after the Central Arizona Project was authorized. Environmental impact statements had to be written, reviewed, and approved before construction could commence. Most reclamation projects in the 1970s and beyond faced a comparable barrage of environmental legal challenges.[90]

Aspinall's five CRBP water projects were similarly plagued. After he left Congress, not only were no new water projects for Colorado authorized, but the state lost the political clout to secure needed reclamation funding. Even before Aspinall's departure, Colorado's water planners could sense that the five projects were low on the list of federal priorities. In 1969, Felix L. Sparks charged Secretary Udall, who had just left office, with double-crossing Colorado. In that year's budget, both the CAP and Utah's Dixie Project received considerable money for planning, but Colorado failed to receive "a dime." The CRBP Act mandated that both the CAP and the Colorado projects proceed concurrently. This, however, did not occur, due in part to strong environmentalist challenges to some of the authorized projects, like Animas–La Plata and the state's loss of political strength after Aspinall left office. By 2000, only two of the five projects that Aspinall and Sparks had fought so hard for had been built: Dallas Creek and Dolores.[91]

The age of large-scale reclamation coincided, fittingly, with the end of Wayne Aspinall's congressional career. According to Donald Worster, big reclamation died in the early 1970s for several reasons. No more cheap water was available. The projects that had not been built, like Animas–La Plata, had horrible cost-benefit ratios. In addition, it became clear to many observers that small-scale yeoman farmers had not been the major beneficiaries of western irrigation water. Instead, "large growers and ranchers . . . had accumulated substantial wealth at public expense." Still other critics raised questions about the adverse ecological impacts of reclamation, including salinization, siltation, groundwater degradation, and destruction of ecosystems.[92]

It is thus little wonder that in his old age, Wayne Aspinall looked back on the 1950s and 1960s as the glory days. In a letter to Stewart Udall, Aspinall celebrated that era because it "gave leadership a chance to operate." Later, in the 1970s, the nation became too liberal, "went too far to the extreme." By 1981, Aspinall saw the potential under the Reagan revolution for the pendulum to swing too far in the other direction. Balancing the interests of the many remained the cornerstone of Aspinall's public-land philosophy to the end of his life.[93]

Stewart Udall, despite his differences with Aspinall, did not deny the importance of Aspinall's political contribution. Though the chairman could be a "brakeman" on vital conservation legislation as well as an autocrat, Udall admitted in a 1998 interview that Aspinall's voice, as much as anyone's, "spoke for the West." In 1996, on the hundredth anniversary of Aspinall's birth, Colorado senator Ben Nighthorse Campbell reflected upon Aspinall's legacy and called him the "bridge between the old West and the modern West."[94]

ENDNOTES

1. William Deverill, "Fighting Words: The Significance of the American West in the History of the United States," in *A New Significance: Re-envisioning the History of the American West*, ed. Clyde Milner II (New York: Oxford University Press, 1996), 63–64.

2. Wayne N. Aspinall to Ercile Stewart, January 12, 1971; Wayne N. Aspinall to Mary Rait, June 10, 1969; Wayne Aspinall to Children, July 7, 1969; and Wayne Aspinall to Tafa and Robert Aspinall, July 9, 1969, all in Box 34, fd: "P-2," Wayne Aspinall Papers, University of Denver Archives, Denver, CO (hereafter cited as UDA); Wayne Aspinall to Mr. and Mrs. Leonard White, July 25, 1969, and Wayne Aspinall to Children, November 17, 1969, and December 1, 1969, Box 31, fd: "P-2," Wayne Aspinall Papers, UDA.

3. Wayne N. Aspinall to Isabelle and John Manchine, July 22, 1970, Box 32, fd: "Marriage," Wayne Aspinall Papers, UDA; "Solon to Wed," *Washington Evening Star*, June 17, 1970; Wayne Aspinall to Ercile Stewart, January 12, 1971.

4. "How to Organize an Aspinall Campaign Caravan," ca. 1964, Box 7, fd: "Advertising Caravans," Wayne N. Aspinall Papers, University of Colorado Archives, University of Colorado at Boulder, Boulder, CO (hereafter cited as UCAUCB); Charles Traylor speaking on Wayne Aspinall 100th Birthday Anniversary Videocassette, April 3, 1996, Archives and Special Collections, Mesa State College, Grand Junction, CO (hereafter cited as MSC). See list of radio stations in the Fourth Congressional District for 1966 in Box 9, fd: 4, Wayne N. Aspinall Papers, UCAUCB.

5. Pat Gormley interview with author, Grand Junction, CO, August 23, 1994. The Wayne N. Aspinall Papers at UCAUCB contain rich documentation on Aspinall's campaigns, campaign costs, and campaign donors through the years.

6. For a good summary of campaign finance laws, see "The FEC and the Federal Campaign Finance Law," August 1996, <http://www.fec.gov/pages/fecfeca.htm> (November 27, 2000). This digest of campaign law asserts that the 1971 legislation brought the loose body of campaign law together under a more uniform statute, "instituting more stringent disclosure requirements for federal candidates, political parties, and political action committees (PACs)." Abuses were still common, however, because no central administrative authority existed to enforce the law. The public, however, was more sensitized to the importance of this issue.

7. *Durango* (CO) *Herald*, August 16, 1970.

8. Joseph McCaffrey, "Meet the Member: Wayne Aspinall," WMAL Radio broadcast script, Box 10, fd: 12, Wayne N. Aspinall Papers, UCAUCB; Carl Ubbelohde, Maxine Benson, and Duane Smith, *A Colorado History*, 7th ed. (Boulder, CO: Pruett Publishing, 1995), 341; Carl Abbott, Stephen J. Leonard, and David McComb, *Colorado: A History of the Centennial State*, 3d ed. (Niwot: University Press of Colorado, 1994), 338–339.

9. *Denver Post*, June 10, 1970.

10. Watt Pye to Bill Cleary, April 13, 1970, Box 10, fd: 11, Wayne N. Aspinall Papers, UCAUCB.

11. Wayne N. Aspinall to Charles J. Traylor, June 11, 1970, Box 390, fd: "Pol-4," Wayne Aspinall Papers, UDA; *Denver Post*, June 16, 1970.

12. *Denver Post*, June 28, 1970.

13. Grand Junction (CO) *Daily Sentinel*, April 27, 1972; Wayne N. Aspinall to Tom Quammen, March 7, 1968, Box 325, fd: "11d," Wayne Aspinall Papers, UDA; *Denver Post*, June 16, 1970.

14. *Daily Sentinel*, September 6, 1970; *Denver Post*, September 3, 1970.

15. Steven T. Powers to Fellow Conservationists, n.d., ca. August 1970, Box 390, fd: "Pol-4," Wayne Aspinall Papers, UDA; "Richard A. Perchlik Speaks Out on Conservation," Box 390, fd: "Pol-4," Wayne Aspinall Papers, UDA; *Denver Post*, September 3, 1970; *Daily Sentinel*, September 5, 1970.

16. *Daily Sentinel*, September 6 and 9, 1970. Aspinall defeated Gossard 77,260–61,994. See "Fourth Congressional District Results, 1970," Box 10, fd: 17, Wayne N. Aspinall Papers, UCAUCB.

17. Peace candidate Craig Barnes, also a strong advocate of busing to achieve public-school racial integration, lost the general election to Republican Craig McKevitt, breaking the Democrats' twenty-five-year stranglehold on that district. Two years later, Democrat Pat Schroeder would reunite the Democrats and unseat McKevitt. See Stephen J. Leonard and Thomas J. Noel, *Denver: From Mining Camp to Metropolis* (Niwot: University Press of Colorado, 1990), 378, 380.

18. Lee McIlvain interview with author, Grand Junction, CO, February 11 and 18, 1998; James L. Sundquist, *Politics and Policy: The Eisenhower, Kennedy, and Johnson Years* (Washington, DC: Brookings Institution, 1968), 403–405; Donald W. Carson and James W. Johnson, *Mo: The Life and Times of Morris K. Udall* (Tucson: University of Arizona Press, 2001), 94–103.

19. Stewart L. Udall interview with author, Grand Junction, CO, March 31 and April 1, 1998; Carson and Johnson, *Mo*, 95.

20. Lee McIlvain interview, February 11 and 18, 1998; Stewart L. Udall interview, March 31 and April 1, 1998; *Daily Sentinel*, February 4, 1975; Ira Whitlock to Stewart L. Udall, August 2, 1968, Box 138, fd: "SLU and Staff (Ira Whitlock)," Stewart L. Udall Papers, Special Collections, University of Arizona Library, Tucson, AZ (hereafter cited as SCUAL).

21. Lee McIlvain interview, February 11 and 18, 1998; Stewart L. Udall interview, March 31 and April 1, 1998.

22. Richard F. Fenno, Jr., *Congressmen in Committees* (Boston: Little, Brown, 1973), 285–286; *Denver Post*, February 14, 1971; Wayne N. Aspinall to James P. Rigg, Jr., February 11, 1971, Box 33, fd: "P-16," Wayne Aspinall Papers, UDA; Lee McIlvain interview, February 11 and 18, 1998.

23. Ibid.

24. *Daily Sentinel*, February 4, 1975. Lee McIlvain said the "revolution" may have made the committee function in a more democratic fashion, but it did so at the expense of efficiency. In the aftermath, Aspinall and his successors had trouble seeing the "big picture" because of the growing autonomy of the subcommittee chairs. See Lee McIlvain interview, February 11 and 18, 1998.

25. *Wall Street Journal*, January 21, 1972; Milton C. Cummings, Jr., "Reapportionment in the 1970s: Its Effects on Congress," in *Reapportionment in the 1970s*, ed. Nelson Polsby (Berkeley: University of California Press, 1971), 33.

26. Wayne N. Aspinall to Dan Noble, March 9, 1971, Box 463, fd: "Pol-1a," Wayne Aspinall Papers, UDA.

27. *Daily Sentinel*, April 3, 1972; Wayne Aspinall interview with Nancy Whistler, Association of Former Members of Congress Project, Manuscript Division, Library of Congress, Washington, D.C., February 15, 1979.

28. *Daily Sentinel*, April 8 and 11, 1972. The *Daily Sentinel* covered this matter thoroughly through early May. Though Governor Love signed the bill, he professed to not be enamored with it.

29. Ibid.

30. Wayne N. Aspinall to A. Hills, May 25, 1972, Box 463, fd: "Pol-1a," Wayne Aspinall Papers, UDA.

31. Charles J. Traylor to Wayne N. Aspinall, February 9, 1972, Steven C. Schulte Collection, Grand Junction, CO; Charles J. Traylor interview with author, Grand Junction, CO, November 18, 1994.

32. *Daily Sentinel*, May 1, 1972.

33. *Daily Sentinel*, April 3, 1972.

34. James H. Shelton to Wayne N. Aspinall, May 19, 1972, Box 465, fd: "1972," and Wayne N. Aspinall to James H. Shelton, May 22, 1972, Box 465, fd: "1972," Wayne Aspinall Papers, UDA. Aspinall received letters from many people encouraging him to try for another term. Several influential cattle ranchers asked him to run again, as did a group of notable Democrats from Larimer County (Fort Collins). See examples of these types of letters in Box 465, fd: "Pol-4," Wayne Aspinall Papers, UDA.

35. "Announcement Remarks, Alan Merson," May 20, 1972, Box 465, fd: "1972," Wayne Aspinall Papers, UDA; Jack Anderson, "Washington Merry-Go-Round: Aspinall Host at a Lobby Party," December 15, 1969.

36. Gordon Ibbotson to Wayne N. Aspinall, May 26, 1972, Box 465, fd: "Pol-4," Wayne Aspinall Papers, UDA.

37. Environmental Action, press statement, June 7, 1972, Box 465, no file name, Wayne Aspinall Papers, UDA; *Rocky Mountain News*, June 8, 1972.

38. Wayne N. Aspinall to Lawrence F. O'Brien, June 14, 1971, Box 64, fd: "Wayne N. Aspinall Personal Correspondence," Wayne Aspinall Papers, UDA.

39. Wayne N. Aspinall to Amos W. Allard, June 15, 1972, Box 465, no file name, Wayne Aspinall Papers, UDA.

40. Wayne N. Aspinall, "Credo of a Twentieth Century Conservationist," address to the Society of American Foresters, May 5, 1972, Box 11, fd: 16, Wayne N. Aspinall Papers, UCAUCB. Aspinall gave similar talks to other groups, among them "The Ecological Ingredient of Political Decision Making," delivered to the Thorne Ecological Institute in Aspen, Colorado, on July 6, 1972, and "The Anatomy of a Land Use Planning Policy," delivered three days earlier to a conference in Fort Collins, Colorado. See Box 462, fd: "Publicity 5," Wayne Aspinall Papers, UDA, for the latter two speeches.

41. Richard Nixon to Wayne N. Aspinall, April 24, 1972, and Wayne N. Aspinall to Richard Nixon, May 9, 1972, Box 64, fd: "WNA Leadership Correspondence," Wayne Aspinall Papers, UDA.

42. R. McGreggor Cawley, *Federal Land, Western Anger: The Sagebrush Rebellion and Environmental Politics* (Lawrence: University of Kansas Press, 1993), 36–38; Wayne Aspinall to Richard Nixon, May 9, 1972.

43. By virtue of the Twenty-sixth Amendment, adopted in 1971.

44. Alan Merson to "Mesa County Democrat," July 4, 1972, Box 465, fd: "Pol-4," Wayne Aspinall Papers, UDA.

45. Wayne Aspinall to Family, July 24, 1972, Box 36, fd: "P-2," Wayne Aspinall Papers, UDA.

46. Wayne N. Aspinall to Family, August 7, 1972, Box 36, fd: "P-2," Wayne Aspinall Papers, UDA; League of Conservation Voters to "Conservationist," August 1972, Box 11, fd: 7, Wayne N. Aspinall Papers, UCAUCB; Robert Gottlieb, *Forcing*

the Spring: The Transformation of the American Environmental Movement (Washington, DC: Island Press, 1993), 146.

47. League of Conservation Voters to Conservationists, August 1972, Box 11, fd: 7, Wayne N. Aspinall Papers, UCAUCB.

48. Merson for Congress to "Student," August 9, 1972, Box 11, fd: 18, Wayne N. Aspinall Papers, UCAUCB.

49. *Daily Sentinel*, August 22, 1972; *Denver Post*, August 20, 1972; "Aspinall—A Good Hand for Colorado," Box 11, fd: "1972 Primary—General File," Wayne N. Aspinall Papers, UCAUCB.

50. Abbott, Leonard, and McComb, *Colorado*, 338–339; Richard Lamm to Wayne N. Aspinall, May 8, 1972, Box 454, fd: "L-11-d-2," Wayne Aspinall Papers, UDA. The Denver Olympics Committee (DOC) was questioned and condemned throughout 1972 for underestimating the costs of the event. For a sampling of this concern, see *Rocky Mountain News*, March 23 and April 12, 1972. The organization Citizens for Colorado's Future coordinated the anti-Olympics referendum campaign.

51. See Aspinall's campaign finance files in Box 11, fd: 2, Wayne N. Aspinall Papers, UCAUCB. This folder contains numerous official 1972 campaign reports and donor lists. Also see Box 464, fd: "Campaign Spending 1972," Wayne N. Aspinall Papers, UCAUCB. Both sets of records demonstrate that the majority of Aspinall's campaign monies in 1972 came from the West's extractive industries.

52. *Daily Sentinel*, September 3, 1972.

53. Aspinall Campaign news release, September 8, 1972, Box 11, fd: "1972 Primary—General File," Wayne N. Aspinall Papers, UCAUCB.

54. Wayne Aspinall to Owen et al., September 12, 1972, Box 36, fd: "P-2," Wayne Aspinall Papers, UDA.

55. *Daily Sentinel*, September 8, 12, and 13, 1972; *Denver Post*, September 13, 1972.

56. *Daily Sentinel*, September 13, 1972.

57. *Daily Sentinel*, September 14, 1972. In a letter to a constituent several days after the election, Aspinall succinctly summarized why he had lost: "redistricting, . . . environmental issues, and age." See Wayne N. Aspinall to Leo A. Bouret, September 21, 1972, Box 463, fd: "Pol-1a," Wayne Aspinall Papers, UDA.

58. Alta Noland, Mesa County Oral History Project (OH-1098), Research and Special Collections, Museum of Western Colorado, Grand Junction, CO (hereafter cited as MWC), March 1, 1989; Wayne Allard to Shane Henry, October 1, 1999, author's collection; Bruce Bauerle interview with author, Grand Junction, CO, December 4, 1997.

59. *Denver Post*, September 18, 1972.

60. *Congressional Record*, October 18, 1972, 10423, 10417; letters of condolence and thank-you notes are in Box 466, fd: "1972 Condolences," Wayne Aspinall Papers, UDA.

61. *Denver Post*, September 24, 1972.

62. Charles J. Traylor interview, November 18, 1994; Tommy Neal interview with author, Grand Junction, CO, January 4, 1997.

63. Wayne N. Aspinall to Mr. and Mrs. Sam French, September 26, 1972, Box 36,

fd: "P-2," Wayne Aspinall Papers, UDA. In one letter, Aspinall blamed much of the loss on Adams County, "the bedroom of Denver, and they just did not take kindly to me in my endeavor to see that there was wise and multiple use of our natural resources." Also see Wayne N. Aspinall to David J. Miller, October 6, 1972, Box 463, fd: "Pol-1c," Wayne Aspinall Papers, UDA; Wayne N. Aspinall to Mrs. M. C. Brewer, December 5, 1972, Box 36, fd: "P-1-a," Wayne Aspinall Papers, UDA.

64. Robert Tweedell, "Wayne Aspinall: A Man to Remember," in "Empire" (Sunday magazine supplement), *Denver Post*, May 4, 1980, passim.

65. Wayne N. Aspinall to James P. Johnson, November 13, 1972, Box 36, fd: "P-3," Wayne Aspinall Papers, UDA; *Rocky Mountain News*, December 21 and October 20, 1972.

66. Wayne N. Aspinall to Richard Nixon, November 20, 1972, Box 376, fd: "L-22," Wayne Aspinall Papers, UDA.

67. Vivian Passer interview with author, Grand Junction, CO, January 25, 1996; *Denver Post*, October 3, 1973, and December 7, 1975.

68. Wayne N. Aspinall to Stanley Dempsey, n.d., ca. September 1977, Box 32, fd: 21, Wayne N. Aspinall Papers, UCAUCB.

69. *Daily Sentinel*, September 10, 1976.

70. Ibid.; *Washington Post*, September 10, 1976, and other newspaper clippings in Box 35, fd: 11, Wayne N. Aspinall Papers, UCAUCB; John B. Anderson to Wayne N. Aspinall, September 21, 1976, Box 35, fd: 11, Wayne N. Aspinall Papers, UCAUCB; *Daily Sentinel*, December 4, 1980.

71. Wayne N. Aspinall to Gerald Ford, April 13, 1976, and Wayne N. Aspinall to Gerald Ford, August 22, 1975, Box 30, fd: 21, Wayne N. Aspinall Papers, UCAUCB; *Daily Sentinel*, October 25, 1976.

72. Peter Wiley and Robert Gottlieb, *Empires in the Sun: The Rise of the New American West* (New York: Putnam, 1982), 56–57; Cawley, *Federal Land, Western Anger*, 82; (Denver) *Rocky Mountain News*, February 27, 1977; Marc Reisner, *Cadillac Desert: The American West and Its Disappearing Water*, rev. ed. (New York: Penguin Books, 1993), 323.

73. Wayne N. Aspinall interview, February 15, 1979; Wayne N. Aspinall to Jimmy Carter, April 28, 1977, Box 37, fd: 48, Wayne N. Aspinall Papers, UCAUCB.

74. Wayne N. Aspinall to F. N. Starbuck, March 9, 1977, Box 37, fd: 48, Wayne N. Aspinall Papers, UCAUCB.

75. Cawley, *Federal Land, Western Anger*, 85, 90.

76. James G. Watt, speech to Conservation Foundation, May 8, 1978, Box 34, fd: 48, Wayne N. Aspinall Papers, UCAUCB; Wayne N. Aspinall to Joseph Coors, July 10, 1979, Box 34, fd: 48, Wayne N. Aspinall Papers, UCAUCB; James G. Watt to Joseph Coors, October 5, 1972, Box 34, fd: 45, Wayne N. Aspinall Papers, UCAUCB.

77. Wayne N. Aspinall to "Gentlemen," n.d., ca. 1977, Box 34, fd: 43, Wayne N. Aspinall Papers, UCAUCB.

78. John Vanderhoof interview with author, Grand Junction, CO, March 29, 1995.

79. Club-20, Natural Resources Committee Meeting summary, September 29, 1978, Box 27, fd: 29, Wayne N. Aspinall Papers, UCAUCB; Wiley and Gottlieb,

Empires in the Sun, 128–129; Larry Brown, *Aspinall* (Gunnison, CO: Western State College Foundation, 1996), 42–43.

80. *Rocky Mountain News*, November 23, 1980; "West Senses Victory in Sagebrush Rebellion," *U.S. News and World Report* 89, no. 22 (December 1, 1980): 29–30.

81. Wayne N. Aspinall to James G. Watt, December 29, 1980, Vivian Passer Collection, Grand Junction, CO; Wayne N. Aspinall to James G. Watt, January 27, 1981, Box 39, fd: 30, Wayne N. Aspinall Papers, UCAUCB; Wayne N. Aspinall to Vernon F. Ravenscroft, July 6, 1981, Box 31, fd: 47, Wayne N. Aspinall Papers, UCAUCB.

82. Gary Hart to Wayne N. Aspinall, July 25, 1979; Wayne N. Aspinall to Gary Hart, August 1, 1979; Wayne N. Aspinall to Gary Hart, April 28, 1980; and Wayne N. Aspinall to Gary Hart, July 6, 1978, all in Box 30, fd: 55, Wayne N. Aspinall Papers, UCAUCB.

83. *Palisade Tribune*, October 13, 1983; Wayne Aspinall to Children, September 27, 1982, Vivian Passer Collection, Grand Junction, CO; Vivian Passer interview, January 25, 1996; Owen Aspinall interview with author, Grand Junction, CO, December 20, 1994; *Daily Sentinel*, October 10, 1983. Interestingly enough, Interior Secretary Watt resigned on October 10, 1983, one day after Aspinall's death, a victim of moving too fast to loosen environmental restrictions on public lands and making many offensive comments about the groups, such as the Native Americans, he was charged to protect. See Cawley, *Federal Land, Western Anger*, 134.

84. Wayne Allard to Shane Henry, October 1, 1999.

85. Quoted in the *Fort Collins Coloradoan*, February 8, 1981, Box 26, fd: 27, Wayne N. Aspinall Papers, UCAUCB.

86. Donald Worster, *Rivers of Empire: Water, Aridity, and the Growth of the American West* (New York: Pantheon Books, 1985), 276; *Craig (CO) Daily Press*, n.d., Box 1, fd: 25, Wayne N. Aspinall Papers, UCAUCB.

87. *Daily Sentinel*, March 31, 1996.

88. Jeffrey Ingram to Wayne N. Aspinall, May 22, 1968, Box 308, fd: "L-11-b-1," Wayne Aspinall Papers, UDA.

89. Brown, *Aspinall*, 28.

90. Wesley E. Steiner, "Second Down, Six and One Half Years to Go," speech to Water Resources Conference, April 12, 1972, Box 1, fd: "Arizona," William Nelson Papers, MSC.

91. See the series of undated reports from the *Daily Sentinel's* Washington Bureau ca. 1970s in Box 3, fd: 20, William Nelson Papers, MSC. As of this writing, it appears as if a considerably stripped-down version of the controversial Animas–La Plata Project might finally be constructed. However, even this version, known by friends and foes alike as "Animas–La Plata light," has inspired strong and determined opposition.

92. Donald Worster, "The Dream of Water," *Montana: The Magazine of Western History* 36, no. 4 (Autumn 1986): 73–74.

93. Wayne N. Aspinall to Stewart L. Udall, May 11, 1981, Box 37, fd: 20, Wayne N. Aspinall Papers, UCAUCB.

94. Stewart L. Udall interview, March 31 and April 1, 1998; *Daily Sentinel*, March 31, 1996.

SOURCES CONSULTED

MANUSCRIPT COLLECTIONS

Arizona State University, Special Collections Department, Tempe, Arizona
  Carl Hayden Papers
  John Rhodes Papers
  Ross R. Rice Papers
Colorado Historical Society, Denver, Colorado
  Edward Taylor Papers
Denver Public Library, Denver, Colorado
  Howard Zahniser Collection
  Papers of The Wilderness Society
John F. Kennedy Presidential Library, Boston, Massachusetts
  John F. Kennedy Pre-presidential Papers
  John F. Kennedy Presidential Papers
  White House Central Files
  White House Staff Files
Library of Congress, Manuscript Division, Washington, D.C.
  Clinton P. Anderson Papers
Lyndon B. Johnson Presidential Library, Austin, Texas
  Administrative History of the Department of the Interior
  Bill Moyers Office Files
  Lyndon B. Johnson Presidential Papers
  Name Files
  White House Central Files
Mesa State College, Archives and Special Collections, Grand Junction, Colorado
  Walter Walker Papers

Wayne Aspinall 100th Birthday Anniversary Videocassette, April 3, 1996
William Nelson Papers
Museum of Western Colorado, Research Center and Special Library, Grand Junction, Colorado
Al Look Collection
Biographical Files
Dan Roberts Family Collection
Marian Fletcher Collection
R. L. Polk, *Grand Junction City and Mesa County Directory*, 1909 and 1912–1925
Research Files: Dalton Trumbo
National Archives, Washington, D.C.
U.S. House Interior and Insular Affairs Committee Papers, Center for Legislative Archives
Steven C. Schulte (Author's) Collection, Grand Junction, CO
Alta Noland to Larry Brown, May 4, 1996
Alta Noland to Steven C. Schulte, January 24, 1996
Alta Noland, Untitled Memoir
Charles J. Traylor to Wayne N. Aspinall, February 9, 1972
Wayne Allard to Shane Henry, October 1, 1991
University of Arizona, Southwest Collection, Tucson, Arizona
Morris K. Udall Papers
Stewart L. Udall Papers
University of Colorado Archives, University of Colorado at Boulder, Boulder, Colorado
Frank Delaney Papers
Gordon Allott Papers
J. Edgar Chenoweth Papers
Robert Fay Rockwell Papers
Wayne N. Aspinall Papers
University of Denver Archives, Denver, Colorado
Kynewisbok (1918, 1920)
University of Denver Catalogue (1925)
Wayne Aspinall Papers
Vivian Passer Collection, Grand Junction, Colorado
Wayne Aspinall, A Family Message to My Family, Mss.
Wayne N. Aspinall Autobiographical Mss.

NEWSPAPERS

Albuquerque Journal
Albuquerque Tribune
Arizona (Tucson) Daily Star
Arizona (Phoenix) Republic
Aspen (CO) Times
Delta (CO) Independent
Denver Post

(Denver) *Rocky Mountain News*
Durango (CO) Herald
Grand Junction (CO) *Daily Sentinel*
Los Angeles Times
Montrose (CO) Daily Press
New York Times
Palisade (CO) Tribune
Pueblo (CO) *Star-Chieftain*
Pueblo (CO) *Star-Journal*
Wall Street Journal
Washington (DC) Daily News
Washington (DC) Evening Star
Washington Post

ORAL INTERVIEWS

Aspinall, Owen. Interview with author. Grand Junction, CO. December 20, 1994.

Aspinall, Wayne. Interview with Al Look. Mesa County Oral History Project (OH-120, Part 1). Research Center and Special Library, Museum of Western Colorado. January 10, 1978.

Aspinall, Wayne. Interview with Al Look. Mesa County Oral History Project (OH-120, Part 2). Research Center and Special Library, Museum of Western Colorado. January 1978.

Aspinall, Wayne N. Interview with Charles T. Morrisey. John F. Kennedy Presidential Library. November 10, 1965.

Aspinall, Wayne N. Interview with Helen Hansen. Mesa County Oral History Project (OH-473). Research Center and Special Library, Museum of Western Colorado. August 10, 1981.

Aspinall, Wayne N. Interview with Joe B. Frantz. Lyndon B. Johnson Presidential Library. June 14, 1974.

Aspinall, Wayne N. Interview with Ross R. Rice. Ross R. Rice Collection, Special Collections, Arizona State University Library. October 23, 1973.

Association of Former Members of Congress Project, Manuscript Division, Library of Congress, Washington, D.C.

INTERVIEWS WITH:

Allott, Gordon
Aspinall, Wayne
Chenoweth, J. Edgar
Fannin, Paul
Hosmer, Craig
Udall, Stewart

Bauerle, Bruce. Interview with author. Grand Junction, CO. December 4, 1997.

Brower, David R. "Environmental Activist, Publicist, and Prophet." Oral history conducted by Susan R. Schrepfer. Regional Oral History Office, Bancroft Library,

University of California at Berkeley. 1974–1978.

Carver, John. Interview with William Moss. John F. Kennedy Presidential Library. November 18, 1969.

DeSautels, Claude. Interview with Louis Oberdorfer. John F. Kennedy Presidential Library. May 16, 1964.

Dolan, Joseph F. Interview with Charles T. Morrisey. John F. Kennedy Presidential Library. December 1, 1964.

Elson, Roy. Interview by U.S. Senate Historical Office. Special Collections, Arizona State University Library. April 27–August 21, 1990.

Gormley, Pat. Interview with author. Grand Junction, CO. August 23, 1994.

Hollingsworth, Dale. Interview with author. Grand Junction, CO. December 18, 1996.

McIlvain, Lee. Interview with author. Grand Junction, CO. February 11 and 18, 1998.

Neal, Tommy. Interview with author. Grand Junction, CO. January 4, 1997.

Noland, Alta. Interview with author. Grand Junction, CO. January 24, 1996.

Noland, Alta. Mesa County Oral History Project (OH-1050). Research Center and Special Library, Museum of Western Colorado. March 31, 1989.

Noland, Alta. Mesa County Oral History Project (OH-1098). Research Center and Special Library, Museum of Western Colorado. March 1, 1989.

Passer, Vivian. Interview with author. Grand Junction, CO. January 25, 1996.

Rhodes, John. Interview with Ross R. Rice. Ross R. Rice Papers, Special Collections, Arizona State University Library. December 6, 1973.

Sundal, David. Interview with Al Look. Mesa County Oral History Project (OH-444). Research Center and Special Library, Museum of Western Colorado. May 14, 1981.

Sundal, David. Interview with Evelyn Kyle and Alberta Francis. Mesa County Oral History Project (OH-493). Research Center and Special Library, Museum of Western Colorado. March 1, 1982.

Sundal, David. Mesa County Historical Society Program, (OH-158) Research Center and Special Library, Museum of Western Colorado. January 23, 1978.

Traylor, Charles J. Interview with author. Grand Junction, CO. November 18, 1994.

Udall, Morris. Interview with Ross. R. Rice, Ross R. Rice Papers, Special Collections, Arizona State University Library. November 30 and December 9 and 30, 1972.

Udall, Stewart L. Interview with author. Grand Junction, CO. March 31 and April 1, 1998.

Udall, Stewart L. Phone interview with author. November 10, 1997.

Udall, Stewart L. Interview with William Moss. John F. Kennedy Presidential Library. February 16, 1970.

Vanderhoof, John. Interview with author. Grand Junction, CO. March 29, 1995.

White, Lee C. Interview with William Moss. John F. Kennedy Presidential Library. March 17, 1970.

White, Mary. Interview with author. Grand Junction, CO. February 14, 1996.

GOVERNMENT DOCUMENTS

Central Arizona Project. Hearings. Subcommittee on Irrigation and Reclamation, House Committee on Interior and Insular Affairs, 88th Cong., 2d Sess., on H.R. 6796 et al. 1964.

Colorado River Basin Project. Hearings. Subcommittee on Irrigation and Reclamation, House Committee on Interior and Insular Affairs, 90th Cong., 1st Sess., on H.R. 3300 et al. 1967.

Colorado River Basin Project, Pt. II. Hearings. Subcommittee on Irrigation and Reclamation, House Committee on Interior and Insular Affairs, 90th Cong., 2d Sess., on H.R. 3300 and S. 1004. 1968.

Colorado River Storage Project. Hearings. Subcommittee on Irrigation and Reclamation, House Committee on Interior and Insular Affairs, 83d Cong., 2d Sess., on H.R. 4449 et al. 1954.

Conference Report to Accompany S. 4. U.S. House of Representatives, 88th Cong., 2d Sess., Report No. 1829. 1964.

Congressional Record

Lower Colorado River Basin Project. Hearings. Subcommittee on Irrigation and Reclamation, House Interior and Insular Affairs Committee, 89th Cong., 1st Sess., on H.R. 4671 et al. 1965.

Lower Colorado River Basin Project. Hearings. Subcommittee on Irrigation and Reclamation, House Interior and Insular Affairs Committee, 89th Cong., 2d Sess., on H.R. 4671 et al. 1966.

Outdoor Recreation Resources Review Commission. *Outdoor Recreation for America* (Washington, DC: GPO, 1962).

Radiation Exposure of Uranium Miners. Hearings. Subcommittee on Research, Development, and Radiation. Joint Committee on Atomic Energy, 90th Cong., 1st Sess. May 9–August 10, 1967.

To Establish a National Wilderness Preservation System. Hearings. Subcommittee on Public Lands, House Interior and Insular Affairs Committee, 87th Cong., 1st Sess., on S. 174 et al. 1961.

To Establish a National Wilderness Preservation System. Hearings. Subcommittee on Public Lands, House Interior and Insular Affairs Committee, 87th Cong., 2d Sess., on S. 174 et al. 1962.

Upper Colorado River Basin Compact. Hearings. Subcommittee on Irrigation and Reclamation, House Interior and Insular Affairs Committee, 81st Cong., 1st Sess., on H.R. 2325 et al. 1949.

Use of Uranium Mill Tailings for Construction Purposes. Hearings. Subcommittee on Raw Materials of the Joint Committee on Atomic Energy, Congress of the United States, 92d Cong., 1st Sess. 1971.

Wilderness Preservation System. Hearings. Subcommittee on Public Lands, House Interior and Insular Affairs Committee, 88th Cong., 2d Sess., on H.R. 9070 et al. 1964.

BOOKS

Abbott, Carl. "The Federal Presence." In *The Oxford History of the American West*, ed. Clyde A. Milner II, Carol A. O'Connor, and Martha A. Sandweiss. New York: Oxford University Press, 1994: 469–500.

———. *The Metropolitan Frontier: Cities in the Modern American West*. Tucson: University of Arizona Press, 1993.

Abbott, Carl, Stephen J. Leonard, and David McComb. *Colorado: A History of the Centennial State*. 3d ed. Niwot: University Press of Colorado, 1994.

Almond, Gabriel A., and Sidney Verba. *The Civic Culture: Political Attitudes and Democracy in Five Nations*. Boston: Little, Brown, 1965.

Ashby, LeRoy, and Rod Gramer. *Fighting the Odds: The Life of Senator Frank Church*. Pullman: Washington State University Press, 1994.

Athearn, Robert G. *The Mythic West in Twentieth-Century America*. Lawrence: University of Kansas Press, 1986.

August, Jack. L., Jr. *Vision in the Desert: Carl Hayden and Hydropolitics in the American Southwest*. Fort Worth: Texas Christian University Press, 1999.

Baker, Richard Allan. *Conservation Politics: The Senate Career of Clinton P. Anderson*. Albuquerque: University of New Mexico Press, 1985.

Bernstein, Irving. *Guns or Butter: The Presidency of Lyndon Johnson*. New York: Oxford University Press, 1996.

Brauer, Carl M. *John F. Kennedy and the Second Reconstruction*. New York: Columbia University Press, 1977.

Brown, Larry. *Aspinall*. Gunnison, CO: Western State College Foundation, 1996.

Burner, David. *John F. Kennedy and a New Generation*. Glenview, IL: Scott Foresman/ Little, Brown College Division, 1988.

Campbell, Angus, Philip E. Converse et al. *The American Voter*. New York: John Wiley and Sons, 1960.

Carson, Donald W., and James W. Johnson. *Mo: The Life and Times of Morris K. Udall*. Tucson: University of Arizona Press, 2001.

Cawley, R. McGreggor. *Federal Land, Western Anger: The Sagebrush Rebellion and Environmental Politics*. Lawrence: University of Kansas Press, 1993.

Clemmer, Richard O. "Black Mesa and the Hopi." In *Native Americans and Energy Development*, ed. Joseph G. Jorgenson. Cambridge, MA: Anthropology Resource Center, 1978: 17–34.

Cohen, Michael P. *The History of the Sierra Club, 1892–1970*. San Francisco: Sierra Club Books, 1988.

Conkin, Paul K. *Big Daddy from the Pedernales: Lyndon Baines Johnson*. Boston: Twayne, 1986.

Cook, Bruce. *Dalton Trumbo*. New York: Charles Scribner, 1977.

Cosco, Jon M. *Echo Park: Struggle for Preservation*. Boulder, CO: Johnson Books, 1995.

Cummings, Milton C., Jr. "Reapportionment in the 1970s." In *Reapportionment in the 1970s*, ed. Nelson Polsby. Berkeley: University of California Press, 1971.

Dallek, Robert M. *Flawed Giant: Lyndon Johnson and His Times, 1961–1973*. New York: Oxford University Press, 1998.

——. *Lone Star Rising: Lyndon Johnson and His Times, 1908–1960*. New York: Oxford University Press, 1991.

Davidson, James West, Mark H. Lytle et al. *Nation of Nations: A Narrative History of the American Republic*. 3d ed. Boston: McGraw Hill, 1998.

Davis, Sandra K. "Water Politics in Colorado: Change, or Business as Usual?" In *Politics in the Postwar American West*, ed. Richard Lowitt. Norman: University of Oklahoma Press, 1995.

Deverill, William. "Fighting Words: The Significance of the American West in the History of the United States." In *A New Significance: Re-envisioning the History of the American West*, ed. Clyde Milner II. New York: Oxford University Press, 1996.

Echstaedt, Peter H. *If You Poison Us: Uranium and Native Americans*. Santa Fe, NM: Red Crane Books, 1994.

Edmunds, Carol. *Wayne Aspinall: Mr. Chairman*. Lakewood, CO: Crown Point, 1980.

Elliott, Gary E. *Senator Alan Bible and the Politics of the New West*. Reno: University of Nevada Press, 1994.

Farmer, Jared. *Glen Canyon Dammed: Inventing Lake Powell*. Tucson: University of Arizona Press, 1999.

Fenno, Richard F., Jr. *Congressmen in Committees*. Boston: Little, Brown, 1973.

Ferrell, Robert H. *Harry S. Truman and the Modern Presidency*. Boston: Little, Brown, 1983.

Flader, Susan L. *Thinking Like a Mountain: Aldo Leopold and the Evolution of an Ecological Attitude Toward Deer, Wolves, and Forests*. Madison: University of Wisconsin Press, 1974.

Flippen, J. Brooks. *Nixon and the Environment*. Albuquerque: University of New Mexico Press, 2000.

Fox, Stephen. *The American Conservation Movement: John Muir and His Legacy*. Madison: University of Wisconsin Press, 1981.

Fradkin, Philip L. *A River No More: The Colorado River and the West*. Berkeley: University of California Press, 1996.

Goldberg, Robert Alan. *Hooded Empire: The Ku Klux Klan in Colorado*. Urbana: University of Illinois Press, 1981.

Gottlieb, Robert. *Forcing the Spring: The Transformation of the American Environmental Movement*. Washington, DC: Island Press, 1993.

Gullan, Harold I. *The Upset That Wasn't: Harry S. Truman and the Crucial Election of 1948*. Chicago: Ivan R. Dee, 1998.

Gulliford, Andrew. *Boomtown Blues: Colorado Oil Shale, 1885–1985*. Niwot: University Press of Colorado, 1989.

Harvey, Mark W.T. *A Symbol of Wilderness: Echo Park and the American Conservation Movement*. Albuquerque: University of New Mexico Press, 1994.

Heath, Jim F. *Decade of Disillusionment: The Kennedy-Johnson Years.* Bloomington: Indiana University Press, 1975.

Hevly, Bruce, and John M. Findlay, eds. *The Atomic West.* Seattle: University of Washington Press, 1998.

High Country News. *Western Water Made Simple.* Washington, DC: Island Press, 1987.

Hirt, Paul W. *A Conspiracy of Optimism: Management of the National Forests Since World War Two.* Lincoln: University of Nebraska Press, 1994.

History of Palisade, Colorado. Vol. 1. Palisade, CO: *Palisade Tribune,* 1963.

Hundley, Norris, Jr. *Water and the West: The Colorado River Compact and the Politics of Water in the American West.* Berkeley: University of California Press, 1975.

——. "The West Against Itself: The Colorado River—An Institutional History." In *New Courses for the Colorado River: Major Issues for the Next Century,* ed. Gary D. Weatherford and F. Lee Brown. Albuquerque: University of New Mexico Press, 1986.

Ingram, Helen. *Water Politics: Continuity and Change.* Albuquerque: University of New Mexico Press, 1990.

Iverson, Peter. *Barry Goldwater: Native Arizonan.* Norman: University of Oklahoma Press, 1997.

——. *The Navajo Nation.* Westport, CT: Greenwood Press, 1981.

Johnson, Rich. *The Central Arizona Project: 1918–1968.* Tucson: University of Arizona Press, 1977.

Kammer, Jerry. *The Second Long Walk: The Navajo-Hopi Land Dispute.* Albuquerque: University of New Mexico Press, 1980.

Kaufman, Robert G. *Henry M. Jackson: A Life in Politics.* Seattle: University of Washington Press, 2000.

Kearns, Doris. *Lyndon Johnson and the American Dream.* New York: Harper and Row, 1976.

Leonard, Stephen J. *Trials and Triumphs: A Colorado Portrait of the Great Depression, with FSA Photographs.* Niwot: University Press of Colorado, 1993.

Leonard, Stephen J., and Thomas J. Noel. *Denver: From Mining Camp to Metropolis.* Niwot: University Press of Colorado, 1990.

Leuchtenburg, William. *Franklin D. Roosevelt and the New Deal.* New York: Harper and Row, 1963.

——. *The Perils of Prosperity: 1914–1932.* Chicago: University of Chicago Press, 1958.

Lowitt, Richard. *The New Deal and the West.* Norman: University of Oklahoma Press, 1984.

Lowitt, Richard, and Maurine Beasley, eds. *One Third of a Nation: Lorena Hickok Reports on the Great Depression.* Urbana: University of Illinois Press, 1981.

Malone, Michael P., and Richard W. Etulain. *The American West: A Twentieth-Century History.* Lincoln: University of Nebraska Press, 1989.

Manchester, William. *Death of a President: November 1963*. New York: Harper and Row, 1967.

Martin, John Bartlow. *Adlai Stevenson and the World: The Life of Adlai Stevenson*. Garden City, NY: Anchor Books, 1978.

Martin, Russell. *A Story That Stands Like a Dam: Glen Canyon and the Struggle for the Soul of the West*. New York: Henry Holt, 1989.

Masters, Nicholas A. "Committee Assignments." In *Congressional Behavior*, ed. Nelson W. Polsby. New York: Random House, 1971.

McCool, Daniel. *Command of the Waters: Iron Triangles, Federal Water Development, and Indian Water*. Tucson: University of Arizona Press, 1994.

McCreanor, Emma. *Mesa County, Colorado: A 100 Year History, 1883–1983*. Grand Junction: Museum of Western Colorado Press, 1983.

McCulloch, David. *Truman*. New York: Simon and Schuster, 1992.

Meine, Curt. *Aldo Leopold: His Life and Work*. Madison: University of Wisconsin Press, 1988.

Morgan, Neil. *Westward Tilt: The American West Today*. New York: Random House, 1963.

Morrow, William. *Congressional Committees*. New York: Charles Scribner's Sons, 1969.

Muhn, James, and Hanson R. Stuart. *Opportunity and Challenge: The Story of BLM*. Washington, DC: U.S. Department of the Interior, 1988.

Nash, Gerald. *The American West Transformed: The Impact of the Second World War*. Lincoln: University of Nebraska Press, 1985.

Nash, Roderick. *Wilderness and the American Mind*. 3d ed. New Haven, CT: Yale University Press, 1982.

Nash, Roderick, and Gregory Graves. *From These Beginnings: A Biographical Approach to American History*. 5th ed. New York: HarperCollins, 1995.

Norland, Jim. *The Summit of a Century: A Pictorial History of the University of Denver*. Denver: University of Denver, 1963.

Opie, John. *Nature's Nation: An Environmental History of the United States*. Fort Worth, TX: Harcourt Brace College Publishers, 1998.

Pach, Chester J., Jr., and Elmo R. Richardson. *The Presidency of Dwight D. Eisenhower*. Lawrence: University of Kansas Press, 1991.

Palisade, Colorado: Its Advantages, Resources, Possibilities. Palisade, CO: *Palisade Tribune*, 1904.

Parmet, Herbert S. *Jack: The Struggles of John F. Kennedy*. New York: Dial Press, 1980.

Reichard, Gary W. *Politics as Usual: The Age of Truman and Eisenhower*. Arlington Heights, Il: Harlan Davidson, 1988.

Reisner, Marc. *Cadillac Desert: The American West and Its Disappearing Water*. Rev. ed. New York: Penguin Books, 1993.

Rice, Ross. R. *Carl Hayden: Builder of the American West*. Lanham, MD: University Press of America, 1994.

Richardson, Elmo R. *Dams, Parks, and Politics: Resource Development and Preservation in the Truman-Eisenhower Era.* Lexington: University Press of Kentucky, 1973.

Ringholz, Raye C. *Uranium Frenzy: Boom and Bust on the Colorado Plateau.* New York: W. W. Norton, 1989.

Robbins, Roy M. *Our Landed Heritage: The Public Domain, 1776–1970.* 2d ed. Lincoln: University of Nebraska Press, 1976.

Rothman, Hal. *America's National Monuments: The Politics of Preservation.* Lawrence: University of Kansas Press, 1989.

——. *The Greening of a Nation? Environmentalism in the United States Since 1945.* Fort Worth, TX: Harcourt Brace, 1998.

Salvatore, Nick. *Eugene V. Debs: Citizen and Socialist.* Urbana: University of Illinois Press, 1982.

Schlesinger, Arthur, Jr. *Robert Kennedy and His Times.* Boston: Houghton Mifflin, 1978.

——. *A Thousand Days: John F. Kennedy in the White House.* Boston: Houghton Mifflin, 1965.

Schrepter, Susan R. *The Fight to Save the Redwoods: A History of Environmental Reform, 1917–1978.* Madison: University of Wisconsin Press, 1983.

Steinberg, Alfred. *Sam Rayburn: A Biography.* New York: Hawthorn Books, 1975.

Stouffler, Samuel. *Communism, Conformity, and Civil Liberties.* Garden City, NY: Doubleday, 1955.

Sundquist, James L. *Politics and Policy: The Eisenhower, Kennedy, and Johnson Years.* Washington, DC: Brookings Institution, 1968.

Trumbo, Dalton. *Eclipse.* London: Lovat Dickson and Thompson, 1935.

Tyler, Daniel. *The Last Water Hole in the West: The Colorado–Big Thompson Project and the Northern Colorado Water Conservancy District.* Niwot: University Press of Colorado, 1992.

Ubbelohde, Carl, Maxine Benson, and Duane Smith. *A Colorado History.* 7th ed. Boulder, CO: Pruett Publishing, 1995.

Udall, Morris K. *Too Funny to Be President.* New York: Henry Holt, 1988.

Udall, Stewart L. *The Quiet Crisis.* New York: Holt, Rinehart and Winston, 1963.

Vandenbusche, Duane, and Duane A. Smith. *A Land Alone: Colorado's Western Slope.* Boulder, CO: Pruett Publishing, 1981.

White, Richard. *It's Your Misfortune and None of My Own: A New History of the American West.* Norman: University of Oklahoma Press, 1991.

Wickens, James F. *Colorado in the Great Depression.* New York: Garland Publishing, 1979.

Wiley, Peter, and Robert Gottlieb. *Empires in the Sun: The Rise of the New American West.* New York: Putnam, 1982.

Worster, Donald. *Rivers of Empire: Water, Aridity, and the Growth of the American West.* New York: Pantheon Books, 1985.

Worster, Donald, ed. *An Unsettled Country: Changing Landscapes of the American West.* Albuquerque: University of New Mexico Press, 1994.

PERIODICALS

Aspinall, Wayne N. "The Public Land Law Review Commission: Origins and Goals." *Natural Resources Journal* 7, no. 2 (1967): 149–152.

Baird, Kenneth. "The Ku Klux Klan in Grand Junction." *Journal of the Western Slope* 4, no. 1 (1989): 6–55.

Brooks, Paul. "Congressman Aspinall vs. The People of the United States." *Harper's Magazine* 226 (March 1963): 60–63.

Buys, Christian J. "Isaiah's Prophecy: Project Plowshare in Colorado." *Colorado Heritage* 1 (1989): 28–39.

Chenoweth, William L. "Raw Materials Activities of the Manhattan Project on the Colorado Plateau." *Nonrenewable Resources* 6, no. 1 (1997): 33–41.

Congressional Quarterly Fact Sheet (January 23, 1959): 109.

DeVoto, Bernard. "Sacred Cows and Public Lands." *Harper's Magazine* 197 (July 1948): 44–45.

———. "The West: A Plundered Province." *Harper's Magazine* 169 (August 1934): 355–364.

Edmunds, Carol. "Young Wayne Aspinall Had a Good Head for Wrangling, a Good Hand for Gavels." In *Westworld* (Sunday magazine supplement), Grand Junction *Daily Sentinel*, April 30, 1978.

Golden, David. "William J. Moyer: The Rise and Fall of a Small-Town Progressive in Western Colorado." *Journal of the Western Slope* 10, no. 3 (1995): 1–17.

Hundley, Norris, Jr. "Water and the West in Historical Imagination." *Western Historical Quarterly* 27 (Spring 1996): 5–31.

McCarthy, Michael. "He Fought for His West." *Colorado Heritage* 1 (1988): 33–44.

Mease, Kristi. "The Labor Shortage and Its Solution During World War II in the Grand Valley in Western Colorado." *Journal of the Western Slope* 7, no. 3 (1992): 1–5.

Moley, Raymond. "Rube Goldberg of the Rockies." *Newsweek* 43, no. 21 (May 24, 1954): 100.

No author. "Aspinall, Wayne (Norviel)." *Current Biography Yearbook* (1968): 32–33.

No author. "If Kennedy Wins White House—Look for the 'Young Deal.'" *U.S. News and World Report* 49, no. 4 (July 25, 1960): 54–58.

No author. "Uranium Mystery in the Colorado Basin." *The New Republic* 154, no. 10 (March 5, 1966): 9.

No author. "West Senses Victory in Sagebrush Rebellion." *U.S. News and World Report* 89, no. 22 (December 1, 1980): 29–30.

Pearl, Milton A. "Public Land Commissions." *Our Public Lands* 17 No. 2 (Summer 1967): 14–17.

Peterson, Harold. "Moving in for a Land Grab." *Sports Illustrated* 33, no. 2 (July 13, 1970): 22–27.

Smith, Thomas G. "John F. Kennedy, Stewart Udall, and New Frontier Conservation." *Pacific Historical Review* 64 (August 1995): 329–362.

Stegner, Wallace. "Battle for the Wilderness." *The New Republic* 130 (February 15, 1954): 13–15.

Sullenberger, Robert. "100 Years of Uranium Activity in the Four Corners Region." *Journal of the Western Slope* 7, no. 4 (1992): 1–82.

Tope, Richard E. "Objective History of Grand Junction, Colorado, Part Two." *Journal of the Western Slope* 10, no. 2 (1995): 1–80.

Tweedell, Robert. "Wayne Aspinall: A Man to Remember." In *Empire* (Sunday magazine supplement), *Denver Post*, May 4, 1980.

Wood, Nancy. "America's Most Radioactive City." *McCall's* 97, no. 12 (September 1970): 46–122.

Worster, Donald. "The Dream of Water." *Montana: The Magazine of Western History* 36, no. 4 (Autumn 1986): 73–74.

THESES, DISSERTATIONS, AND PAPERS

McCarty, Patrick Fargo. "Big Ed Johnson of Colorado: A Political Portrait." M.A. thesis, University of Colorado at Boulder, 1958.

Mehls, Carol Jean Drake. "Into the Frying Pan: J. Edgar Chenoweth and the Fryingpan-Arkansas Reclamation Project." Ph.D. diss., University of Colorado at Boulder, 1986.

Pearson, Byron E. "People Above Scenery: The Struggle over the Grand Canyon Dams, 1963–1968." Ph.D. diss., University of Arizona, 1998.

———. "The Plan to Dam Grand Canyon: A Study in Utilitarianism." M.A. thesis, Northern Arizona University, 1992.

Peterson, F. Ross. "The Creation of an Environmental Agenda: Stewart L. Udall Takes Charge, 1961–64." Paper presented at the meeting of the Western History Association, St. Paul, MN, October 17, 1997.

Raley, Bradley F. "The Collbran Project and the Bureau of Reclamation, 1937–1963: A Case Study in Western Resource Development." M.A. thesis, University of Houston, 1992.

———. "Irrigation, Land Speculation, and the History of Grand Junction, Colorado." Paper presented at the meeting of the Western History Association, October 1996.

Sayles, Stephen Paul. "Clair Engle and the Politics of California Reclamation, 1943–1960." Ph.D. diss., University of New Mexico, 1978.

ELECTRONIC SOURCES

No Author. "The FEC and the Federal Campaign Finance Law." August 1996. <http://www.fec.gov/pages/fecfeca.htm> (November 27, 2000).

INDEX